The
NEW
DIABETIC
COOKBOOK

More than 200 Delicious Recipes for a
Low-Fat, Low-Sugar, Low-Cholesterol,
Low-Salt, High-Fiber Diet

FOURTH EDITION

MABEL CAVAIANI

CB

CONTEMPORARY BOOKS

A TRIBUNE COMPANY

Library of Congress Cataloging-in-Publication Data

Cavaiani, Mabel.
    The new diabetic cookbook : more than 200 delicious recipes
for a low-fat, low-sugar, low-cholesterol, low-salt, high-fiber diet /
Mabel Cavaiani. — 4th ed.
       p.   cm.
    Previously published: 1994.
    Includes bibliographical references and index.
    ISBN 0-8092-3164-6
    1. Diabetes—Diet therapy—Recipes.   I. Title.
RC662.C38   1996
641.5′6314—dc20   96-9413
                                            CIP

Featured on the cover: Grecian Shrimp and Baby Artichoke Brochette,
page 140

Front cover photograph by Tony Berardi

Published by Contemporary Books
An imprint of NTC/Contemporary Publishing Company
Two Prudential Plaza, Chicago, Illinois 60601-6790
Manufactured in the United States of America
International Standard Book Number: 0-8092-3164-6
10   9   8   7   6   5   4   3   2   1

For my godchild, Vicki Riley Glastetter,
who has always been a joy to me

Contents

Foreword by Dr. Joseph Turner Crockett . . . . *vii*
Acknowledgments . . . . *ix*
Introduction to the Fourth Edition . . . . *xi*
1 Diabetes *1*
2 Food Exchanges *5*
3 Calculating Food Exchanges *29*
4 Planning for Special Menus *59*
5 Cholesterol *77*
6 Equipment and Ingredients *85*
7 Understanding the New Food Labels *103*
8 Soups *108*
9 Fish *130*
10 Poultry *147*
11 Meats *169*
12 Vegetables, Etc. *194*
13 Salads and Salad Dressings *227*
14 Breads *269*
15 Pies *314*
16 Cakes *329*
17 Cookies *348*
18 Beverages *376*
19 Canning and Freezing Foods *385*
20 Glossary *401*
Index *405*

Foreword

There are estimated to be approximately 13 million persons in America with diabetes—and about 6.5 million of these people are unaware of having the disease.

The most usual form of diabetes is diabetes mellitus, which has both metabolic and vascular components that are interrelated. The metabolic component is related to a deficiency of insulin activity and is associated with hyperglycemia and altered fat and protein metabolism. Vascular components consist of a speed-up of fatty deposits in the blood vessels and changes in the kidney and eye blood vessels. Treatment of diabetics aims to keep the blood sugar as close to normal as possible. This requires maintaining a balance between diet, insulin, and exercise.

Most people are aware of the importance of diet in the treatment of diabetes. In fact it is possible to completely control the milder forms of diabetes with diet alone without added insulin. The usual diet for diabetics is a balance of carbohydrates, fats, and proteins specifically computed for each individual. It is extremely important that an individual adhere closely to the given diet in addition to eating at regular intervals. It is also important that the individual exercise and maintain a normal weight for his or her sex, type, and build.

There has been much research done in the last few years on the components of diabetic diets. These researchers recommend that the old diabetic diets be changed to include more carbohydrates of the polysaccharides type and less fat of the saturated type. The American Diabetes Association also suggests that high-fiber, unrefined carbohydrates be substituted for highly refined carbohydrates with low fiber content. The addition of dietary fiber reduces blood sugar levels after meals. The British Diabetes Association basically agrees and also discourages high salt intake to help control cardiovascular complications.

Recommendations on diet alone will be useless if the person does not comply. The diets must be acceptable to individuals in terms of both palatability and the availability of the foods. Diets should interfere as little as possible with the dietary habits of the individual.

This new book by Mabel Cavaiani is a compilation of recipes for use by diabetics. She has taken many commonly known recipes and adapted them to comply with the latest recommendations of the American Diabetes Association and the American Dietetic Association. Her recipes replace much of the monosaccharides and disaccharides with polysaccharides, increase the amount of dietary fiber, decrease the amount of salt, and replace the cholesterol and saturated fats with unsaturated fats. In the process she has brought much more interesting variety into the restrictive diet of diabetics. She is a diabetic, a member of the American Diabetes Association, and a retired member of the American Dietetic Association, who recognizes the need for a book such as this. We both hope you will enjoy this book and use it to add interest and variety to your own diet.

—Joseph Turner Crockett, M.D., L.F.A.P.A.
San Diego, California

Acknowledgments

I would like to thank the following persons for their encouragement and professional help in developing and writing this book. Without their support I could never have written it.

Dr. Susan Urbatsch, Mary Agnes Jones, R.D., Muriel Urbashich, R.D., Nancy Johnson, R.D., Dorothy Berzy, R.D., Mabel Frances Gunsallus, R.D., M.S., Edith Robinson, R.D., M.S., Eva Burrack, F.S.S., Mary Klicka, R.D., M.S., Frances Lee, R.D., M.S., Patti Dillon, M.S., Julie M. Cull, R.D., Mindy Greufe, R.D., "Chef Dave" Hutchins, Frances Nielsen, Vera and Aulden Wilson, Hazel and Ed Gernand, and finally my husband, Charles Cavaiani, and my sister, Shirley Sniffin. Their patience and support while I was writing this book helped make it all possible.

I would also like to thank the following organizations for background information and resource material used in this book.

The American Diabetes Association, Inc.
The American Dietetic Association
The American Heart Association
Iowa State University Extension Service
U.S. Department of Agriculture
U.S. Food and Drug Administration
HCF Nutrition Research Foundation, Inc.
Hill Nutrition Associates, Inc.

Introduction to the Fourth Edition

We decided to do this third revision of *The New Diabetic Cookbook* in order to include the *1995 Exchange Lists for Meal Planning* established and published by the American Diabetes Association, Inc. and the American Dietetic Association.

The new exchange lists aren't all that different from the previous exchange lists. They were and are based on the fat, protein, and carbohydrate (starch) content of foods. The new exchange lists are based on previous exchange lists with some important additions. There are additional listings in the meat and meat substitute groups and the fats group. Carbohydrate foods are now included in a new listing titled "Other Carbohydrates List," which includes foods that are high in carbohydrate from all groups so they can be more easily and correctly interchanged in your diabetic diet. All of these changes will give more flexibility to the diet and will make it easier to follow.

The second revision included information regarding the sugar content of each recipe as well as new recipes. Those changes are retained in this revision and also included is additional nutritive information for each recipe.

The American Diabetes Association, Inc. gave us the following guidelines regarding sugar: recipes containing more than 1 teaspoon but less than 1 tablespoon (5–15 gm) of caloric sweetener per serving are for occasional use only; try to limit the number of servings of these foods to one a day. Recipes containing more than 1 tablespoon (15 gm) of caloric sweetener per serving are generally not recommended for people with diabetes.

I am pleased to be able to tell you that I haven't used one or more tablespoons of sugar in any of these recipes, but we thought it might be helpful to list the amount of sugar per serving along with other nutritive values whenever I have included sugar as one of the ingredients in a recipe. I have considered honey, corn syrup, and molasses the equivalent of sugar (sucrose). I have not used any fructose, maltose, lactose, dextrose, or fruit juice concentrate in the recipes, but they should also be considered the equivalent of sugar if you use them or see them listed as an ingredient.

A great deal of study on the advantages of fiber in the diabetic and low-cholesterol diets has shown that we should take the use of an increased amount of fiber very seriously. I have tried to use fiber-rich recipes as often as possible, and I hope you will take advantage of them to increase the fiber in your diet. Remember also that fiber needs liquid to expand, and the indiscriminate addition of fiber without enough water can cause complications.

Once again, I say, as I do in all my modified-diet cookbooks: This is a cookbook, not a diet manual. Many books that are written to help people on a special diet are filled with "you can't do this" or "you must do that." I feel that no matter what your special diet may be, there are many familiar foods that you can and should have in your diet. Both Dr. Crockett and I feel that unless a diet includes familiar foods, it will not be followed, and that it is better to talk about the foods you are allowed rather than the ones that are no longer allowed on your diet.

I must admit that when I first became diabetic I felt as though the world had dropped out from under me. I remember telling my mother, "I'm such a good cook—and now I can't ever cook anything good again." That was a ridiculous statement, but it expressed my feelings at the time. It was a shock to me to discover that I was diabetic. We had always worried that my husband Chuck might become diabetic sometime because his mother, brother, sister, and nephew were all diagnosed as diabetic at different times—but we had never worried about me because no one in my family had diabetes.

I am a dietitian and should have recognized the symptoms, but I didn't. I only knew I felt terrible and didn't seem to get any better. I consulted Dr. Susan Urbatsch, my family doctor, who ordered a blood profile, and when the results were returned it was evident that I was diabetic. Of course, she investigated further but there wasn't much doubt about it after that first test.

I don't know if it is easier or harder for a diabetic who is also a dietitian. In one way it is easier because you don't need any diet counseling, you don't have questions regarding the suitability of different foods for your diet, and you don't have much trouble deciding if you can or can't have a certain food. However, I think it may actually be more difficult to be a dietitian because you are never free to relax and forget about your diet— you know what will happen to you if you do. I've seen too many people in the hospital or nursing home who were minus a foot or a leg or blind because they didn't think it made any difference whether they followed their diet and exercised regularly. It is so easy to say that you will put it off until tomorrow—but for a diabetic that tomorrow is right now and you'd better get with it or you will pay dearly for it later.

The low-cholesterol part of my diet didn't bother me because I had been keeping a low-cholesterol kitchen for many years. The doctor put my husband Chuck on a low-cholesterol diet when we were first married, and because I liked the diet and thought the food was good, I had always followed it right along with him. Dr. Urbatsch didn't tell me that I had a high cholesterol count or put me on a low-cholesterol diet, but the fact that 75 percent of all diabetics die of atherosclerosis or related diseases convinced me that I should follow a low-cholesterol diet even more carefully when I knew I was a diabetic.

All of the recipes in this book are suitable for a low-cholesterol diabetic diet. I might even suggest that if you are on a low-cholesterol diet and want to lose weight (even if you aren't a diabetic), you might find it useful to use these recipes to help take off those extra pounds. Fiber is included in many of these recipes because research has shown that fiber helps keep blood sugar lower for a diabetic and helps bring down the cholesterol count. Low-sodium variations are given for recipes whenever it is possible—I have found that so many people who need the low-cholesterol diabetic diet also have some sodium restrictions.

Our local diabetes association branch has been a big help to me. The support of others who have your problems seems to be particularly helpful, and this association is very active in providing information that is most useful to diabetics. I hope you will contact your own local association and let them help you as much as they have helped me.

I hope you will find these recipes beneficial. I have tried to use foods that are nationally available and foods that most people stock regularly—I do dislike cookbooks that use recipes with strange-sounding names and even more unusual ingredients. These are recipes that my family and I use regularly, and I hope they will become standards in your home also.

—Mabel Cavaiani
Wadena, Iowa

1

Diabetes

Diabetes is a very common disease, and there seem to be more people diagnosed as diabetics every day. According to the American Diabetes Association, there are 13 million people with diabetes in the United States, half of whom don't know they have diabetes. Six hundred and fifty thousand people will join the ranks of known diabetics this year, and 160,000 people will die from diabetes or related diseases.

Diabetes is not something that happens to other people. One out of 20 people in the United States has some form of diabetes, and one out of four families is affected in some way by it. Although there is no cure for diabetes at this time, a great deal of research is being done, and it is hoped that sometime in the near future diabetes can be prevented or cured.

There are several different types of diabetes:

1. *Type I*, insulin-dependent diabetes, is generally found in children and young adults. Patients with Type I diabetes must take insulin because their bodies produce little or no insulin, which is needed for utilization of glucose in the body.

2. *Type II*, non-insulin-dependent diabetes, usually occurs in overweight adults 40 years or older. It can generally be controlled by weight loss, diet, and sometimes oral medication. In this type of diabetes, some insulin is produced, but it isn't used effectively. It can often be prevented or cured if the patient returns to a normal weight and performs regular exercise.

3. *Gestational diabetes* occurs in some pregnant women and can be controlled by diet. Most of these women return to nor-

mal after their babies are born, but they need to watch their weight and get regular exercise because a large percentage of them will develop diabetes as they get older.

4. *Impaired glucose tolerance* is diagnosed when a patient's blood sugar levels are between normal and diabetic. This condition is generally treated with diet and weight loss to prevent the development of diabetes later in life.

5. *Secondary diabetes* can be caused by drugs or chemicals as well as pancreatic or endocrine disease.

The warning signs of diabetes are:

> *Type I*
> Frequent urination
> Abnormal thirst
> Unusual hunger
> Weight loss
> Irritability
> Weakness or fatigue
> Nausea and vomiting
>
> *Type II*
> Excess weight
> Drowsiness
> Blurred vision
> Tingling and numbness in hands and feet
> Skin infections
> Slow healing of cuts, especially on the feet
> Itching, particularly in the vaginal area

When your doctor tells you that you have diabetes, the doctor will probably discuss your diet with you or send you to a registered dietitian, nutritionist, or a certified diabetes educator who can discuss your diet with you. Don't let your doctor send you off with just a sheet of paper with instructions to follow that diet. You need more than that. Each patient's diet should be written especially for him or her, considering his or her age, weight, physical condition, lifestyle, and eating habits, and it can only be written on an individual basis. A diabetic diet is not all that easy to follow at first, and you need all the help you can get . . . and remember, once you get your diet, you must follow it. You can probably make some modifications after you are familiar with the diet, but it is important to follow it faithfully at first.

Many doctors don't have the time to spend with you discussing your diet, but they can and should recommend someone who can help you. If your doctor doesn't recommend someone to help you, ask your local hospital for help. They may have a diabetes support group, or they can recommend someone to help you.

Once you find someone to help you, be perfectly frank. Discuss your lifestyle, likes and dislikes, budgetary problems, and whether you would be willing to cook special foods or if you want very simple foods. Tell them if you carry a lunch to work or if you depend on restaurants at noon. (I recommend carrying your lunch if possible.) Help them help you plan a diet that fits your lifestyle, budget, and capabilities.

Diabetes can be overwhelming at first. It can make you feel as though you are alone in the world. Trying to cope with a new diet, insulin shots, if necessary, establishing an exercise program, and losing weight, if necessary, can be overwhelming. It was hard on me and doubly hard on my husband, whose mother had died of complications from diabetes. Life can be pretty grim around your house for a while, but you'll learn to cope with it before long and discover there is life after diabetes.

Now that I have had diabetes for fourteen years and have learned to live with it, I always tell new diabetics that one of the biggest helps, next to a supportive family, is a group of people who also have diabetes and know what you are experiencing. The best way to find this supportive group is to join your local chapter of the American Diabetes Association. If you don't have a local association, you may be able to find one in a neighboring community. If you aren't able to find a local group, write to: The American Diabetes Association, National Service Center, 1660 Duke Street, Alexandria, VA 22314. They can give you the address of your state association, which can help you find the nearest local chapter. After you find the nearest chapter, attend the meetings. Some people refuse to attend meetings because they don't want to admit they are diabetic. This is ridiculous and harms only them. When you attend these meetings you can meet other diabetics and discover you aren't alone; there are others out there who care and are trying to help each other. Don't feel bewildered—get out and get some information and use it to make your life happier and more comfortable.

2
Food Exchanges

Exchange lists are the backbone of the diabetic diet. The number and kind of exchanges you can have for each meal will be determined by your doctor and/or dietitian, depending upon your age, sex, amount of activity, and whether or not you need to lose weight. Each exchange has an established nutritional value. The total of your exchanges during the day is the total amount of carbohydrate, protein, and fat that your doctor decides you need to feel your best. Each of the items in an exchange list has approximately the same nutritional value.

The following exchange lists (copyright © 1995 American Diabetes Association, Inc., American Dietetic Association) have been reprinted with permission. The exchange lists are the basis of a meal planning system designed by a committee of the American Diabetes Association and the American Dietetic Association. While designed primarily for people with diabetes and others who must follow special diets, the exchange lists are based on principles of good nutrition that apply to everyone. There are seven basic exchanges with variations in some of the lists. They are starches, fruit, milk, other carbohydrates, vegetables, meats, and fats.

Foods are listed with their serving sizes, which are usually measured after cooking. When you begin, you should measure the size of each serving. This may help you learn to "eyeball" correct serving sizes.

The following chart shows the amount of nutrients in one serving from each list.

Groups/list	Carbohydrate (grams)	Protein (grams)	Fat (grams)	Calories
Carbohydrate				
Starch	15	3	1 or less	80
Fruit	15	–	–	60
Milk				
Skim	12	8	0–3	90
Low-fat	12	8	5	120
Whole	12	8	8	150
Other				
Carbohydrate	15	varies	varies	varies
Vegetable	5	2	–	25
Meat and Meat Substitute				
Very lean	–	7	0–1	35
Lean	–	7	3	55
Medium-fat	–	7	5	75
High-Fat	–	7	8	100
Fat	–	–	5	45

The new exchange lists emphasize that *Healthy Eating* is the first step in taking care of your diabetes. You can make a difference in your blood glucose control through your food choices. You do not need special foods. In fact, the foods that are good for you are good for everyone.

If you have diabetes, it is important to eat about the same amount of food at the same time each day. Regardless of what your blood glucose level is, try not to skip meals or snacks. Skipping meals and snacks may lead to large swings in blood glucose levels.

To keep your blood glucose levels near normal, you need to balance the food you eat with the insulin your body makes or gets by injection and with your physical activities. Blood glucose monitoring gives you information to help you with this balancing act. Near-normal blood glucose levels help you feel better and they may reduce or prevent complications from diabetes.

The number of calories you need depends on your size, age, and activity level. Children and adolescents must eat enough calories so they grow and develop normally. Don't limit their calories to try to control blood glucose levels. Instead, adjust their insulin to cover the calories they need.

Of course, everyone needs to eat nutritious foods. Our good health depends on eating a variety of foods that contain the right amount of carbohydrate, protein, fat, vitamins, minerals, fiber, and water.

Carbohydrate, protein, and fat are found in the food you eat. They supply your body with energy, or calories. Your body needs insulin to use this energy. Insulin is made in the pancreas. If you have diabetes, either your pancreas is no longer making insulin or your body can't use the insulin it is making. In either case, your blood glucose levels are not normal.

Carbohydrate: Starch and sugar in foods are carbohydrates. Starch is in breads, pasta, cereals, potatoes, peas, beans, and lentils. Naturally present sugars are in fruits, milk, and vegetables. Added sugars are in desserts, candy, jams, and syrups. All these carbohydrates provide 4 calories per gram and can affect your blood glucose levels.

When you eat carbohydrates, they turn into glucose and travel in your bloodstream. Insulin helps the glucose enter the cells, where it can be used for energy or stored. Eating the same amounts of carbohydrate daily at meals and snacks can help you control your blood glucose levels.

Protein: Protein is in meats, poultry, fish, milk and other dairy products, eggs, dried beans, and peas. Starches and vegetables also have small amounts of protein.

The body uses protein for growth, maintenance, and energy. Protein has 4 calories of energy per gram. Again, your body needs insulin to use the protein you eat.

Fat: Fat is in margarine, butter, oils, salad dressings, nuts, seeds, milk, cheese, meat, fish, poultry, snack foods, ice cream, and desserts.

There are different types of fat. Monounsaturated fats are found in canola oil, olive oil, nuts, and avocados. The polyunsaturated fats found in corn oil, soybean oil, or sunflower oil are also good choices. (See Chapter 5 for saturated fats.)

After you eat fat, it travels in your bloodstream. You need insulin to store fat in the cells of your body. Fats are used for energy. In fact, fats have 9 calories per gram, more than two times the calories you get from carbohydrates and protein.

Vitamins and minerals: Most foods in this book are good sources of vitamins and minerals. If you eat a variety of these foods, you probably do not need a vitamin or mineral supplement.

Salt or Sodium: High blood pressure may be made worse by eating too much sodium (salt and salty foods). Try to use less salt in cooking and at the table. In the exchange lists, foods which are high in sodium (400 milligrams or more sodium per exchange) have an asterisk by them.

Alcohol: You may have an alcoholic drink occasionally. If you take insulin or a diabetic pill, be sure to eat food with your drink. Ask your dietitian about a safe amount of alcohol for you and how to work it into your meal plan.

What to eat and when: You and your dietitian will work out a meal plan to get the right balance between your food, medication, and exercise. The list of food choices (exchange lists) in this book can help you make interesting and healthy food choices. Exchange lists and a meal plan help you know what to eat, how much to eat, and when to eat.

Exchange lists: These foods are listed together because they are alike. Each serving of food has about the same amount of carbohydrate, protein, fat, and calories as the other foods on that list. That is why any food on the list can be "exchanged" or traded for any other food on the same list. For example, you can trade the slice of bread you might eat for breakfast for ½ cup of cooked cereal. Each of these foods equals one starch choice.

Exchange information is based on foods found in grocery stores. However, food companies often change ingredients in their products. That is why you need to check the Nutrition Facts panel of the food label.

See your dietitian regularly when you are first learning how to use your meal plan and exchange lists. Your meal plan can be adjusted to fit changes in your lifestyle, such as work, school, vacation, or travel. Regular nutrition counseling can help you make positive changes in your eating habits.

Starch list: Cereals, grains, pasta, bread, crackers, snacks, starchy vegetables, and cooked dried beans, peas, and lentils are starches. In general one starch is: ½ cup cereal, grain, pasta, or starchy vegetable; 1 ounce of bread products such as 1 slice of bread; or ¾ ounce to 1 ounce of most snack foods. (Some snack foods may also have added fat.)

Bread exchanges with 15 grams carbohydrate, 3 grams protein, 0–1 grams fat, and 80 calories include the following:

Bagel, ½ (1 ounce)
Reduced calorie bread, 2 slices (1½ ounces)
Bread, white, whole wheat, pumpernickel, rye,
    1 slice (1 ounce)
Bread sticks, crisp, 4 inches long × ½ inch,
    2 (⅔ ounce)
English muffin, ½
Hot dog or hamburger bun, ½ (1 ounce)
Pita, ½, 6 inches across
Roll, plain, small, 1 (1 ounce)
Raisin bread, unfrosted, 1 slice (1 ounce)
Tortilla, corn, 6 inches across, 1
Tortilla, flour, 7–8 inches across, 1
Waffle, 4½ inches square, 1

Cereals and grain exchanges with 15 grams carbohydrate, 3 grams protein, 0–1 grams fat, and 80 calories include the following:

Bran cereals, ½ cup
Bulgur, cooked, ½ cup
Cereals, uncooked, ½ cup
Cereals, unsweetened, ready to eat, ¾ cup
Cornmeal, dry, 3 tablespoons
Couscous, dry, ⅓ cup
Flour, dry, 3 tablespoons
Granola, low-fat, ¼ cup
Grapenuts, ¼ cup
Grits, cooked, ½ cup
Kasha, cooked, ½ cup
Millet, cooked, ¼ cup
Muesli, ¼ cup
Oats, cooked, ½ cup
Pasta, cooked, ½ cup
Puffed cereal, 1½ cups

Rice milk, ½ cup
Rice, white or brown, cooked, ⅓ cup
Shredded wheat, ½ cup
Sugar-frosted cereal, ½ cup
Wheat germ, 3 tablespoons

Starchy vegetable exchanges with 15 grams carbohydrate, 3 grams protein, 0–1 grams fat, and 80 calories include the following:

Baked beans, ⅓ cup
Corn, ½ cup
Corn on the cob, medium, 1 (5 ounces)
Mixed vegetables with corn, peas, or pasta, 1 cup
Peas, green, ½ cup
Plantain, ½ cup
Potato, baked or boiled, 1 small (3 ounces)
Potato, mashed, ½ cup
Squash, winter (acorn, butternut), 1 cup
Yam, sweet potato, plain, ½ cup

Crackers and snack exchanges with 15 grams carbohydrate, 3 grams protein, 0–1 grams fat, and 80 calories include the following:

Animal crackers, 8
Graham crackers, 2½ inches square, 3
Matzoh, ¾ ounce
Melba toast, 4 slices
Oyster crackers, 24
Popcorn (popped, no fat added, or low-fat microwave), 3 cups
Pretzels, ¾ ounce
Rice cakes, 4 inches across, 2
Saltine type crackers, 6
Snack chips, fat-free (tortilla, potato), 15–20 (¾ ounce)
Whole wheat crackers, no fat added, 2–5 (¾ ounce)

Dried beans, peas, and lentils (cooked) which count as 1 starch exchange plus 1 very lean meat exchange include the following:

Beans and peas (garbanzo, pinto, kidney, white,
  split, black-eyed), ½ cup
Lima beans, ⅔ cup
Lentils, ½ cup
Miso, 3 tablespoons

Starchy foods prepared with fat which count as 1 starch exchange plus 1 fat exchange include the following:

Biscuit, 2½ inches across, 1
Chow mein noodles, ½ cup
Cornbread, 2-inch cube, 1 (2 ounces)
Crackers, round, butter type, 6
Croutons, 1 cup
French-fried potatoes, 16–25 (3 ounces)
Granola, ¼ cup
Muffin, small, 1 (1½ ounces)
Pancake, 4 inches across, 2
Popcorn, microwave, popped, 3 cups
Sandwich crackers, cheese or peanut butter
  filling, 3
Stuffing, bread (prepared), ⅓ cup
Taco shell, 6 inches across, 2
Waffle, 4½ inches square, 1
Whole wheat crackers, fat added, 4–6 (1 ounce)

Fruit list with 15 grams carbohydrate and 60 calories includes fresh and canned fruits and fruit juices, all prepared without added sugar. Food labels for fruits may contain the words "no sugar added" or "unsweetened." This means that no sucrose (table sugar) has been added. Generally, fruit canned in light syrup has the same amount of carbohydrate per serving as the "no sugar added" or the juice pack. All canned fruits on the fruit list are based on one of these three types of pack. Portion sizes for canned fruits are for the fruit and a small amount of juice. Count ½ cup cranberries or rhubarb sweetened with sugar substitute as free foods.

Fruit exchanges with 15 grams carbohydrate and 60 calories include the following:

Apple, unpeeled, small, 1 (4 ounces)
Applesauce, unsweetened, ½ cup

Apples, dried, 4 rings
Apricots, fresh, 4 whole (5½ ounces)
Apricots, dried, 8 halves
Apricots, canned, ½ cup
Banana, small, 1 (4 ounces)
Blackberries, ¾ cup
Blueberries, ¾ cup
Cantaloupe, small, ⅓ melon (11 ounces) or
    1 cup cubes
Cherries, sweet, fresh, 12 (3 ounces)
Cherries, sweet, canned, ½ cup
Dates, 3
Figs, fresh, 1½ large or 2 medium (3½ ounces)
Figs, dried, 1½
Fruit cocktail, ½ cup
Grapefruit, large, ½ (11 ounces)
Grapefruit sections, canned, ¾ cup
Grapes, small, 17 (3 ounces)
Honeydew melon, 1 slice (10 ounces) or
    1 cup cubes
Kiwi, 1 (3½ ounces)
Mandarin oranges, canned, ¾ cup
Mango, small, ½ fruit (5½ ounces) or ½ cup
Nectarine, small, 1 (5 ounces)
Orange, small, 1 (6½ ounces)
Papaya, ½ fruit (8 ounces) or 1 cup cubes
Peach, medium, fresh, 1 (6 ounces)
Peaches, canned, ½ cup
Pear, large, fresh, ½ (4 ounces)
Pears, canned, ½ cup
Pineapple, fresh, ¾ cup
Pineapple, canned, ½ cup
Plums, small, 2 (5 ounces)
Plums, canned, ½ cup
Prunes, dried, 3
Raisins, 2 tablespoons
Raspberries, 1 cup
Strawberries, 1¼ cups whole berries
Tangerines, small, 2

Watermelon, 1 slice (13½ ounces) or
    1¼ cups cubes

Fruit juices

Apple juice/cider, ½ cup
Cranberry juice cocktail, ⅓ cup
Cranberry juice cocktail, reduced calorie,
    1 cup
Fruit juice blends, 100 percent juice, ⅓ cup
Grape juice, ⅓ cup
Grapefruit juice, ½ cup
Orange juice, ½ cup
Pineapple juice, ½ cup
Prune juice, ⅓ cup

Milk list includes different types of milk and milk products. Cheeses are on the meat list and cream and other dairy fats are on the fat list. Based on the amount of fat they contain, milks are divided into skim/very low-fat milk, low-fat milk, and whole milk. Chocolate milk, frozen yogurt, and ice cream are on the other carbohydrates list. Non-dairy creamers are on the free foods list. Rice milk is on the starch list and soy milk is on the medium-fat meat list. Milk and yogurt are good sources of calcium and protein. Check the food label. The higher the fat content of milk and yogurt, the greater the amount of saturated fat and cholesterol. Choose lower-fat varieties. For those who are lactose intolerant, look for lactose-free varieties of milk. One cup equals 8 fluid ounces or ½ pint.

Skim and very low-fat milk exchanges with 12 grams carbohydrate and 0–3 grams fat per serving include the following:

Skim milk, 1 cup
½ percent milk, 1 cup
1 percent milk, 1 cup
Nonfat or low-fat buttermilk, 1 cup
Evaporated skim milk, ½ cup
Nonfat, dry milk, ⅓ cup dry
Plain nonfat yogurt, ¾ cup
Nonfat or low-fat fruit flavored yogurt sweetened
    with aspartame or with a nonnutritive
    sweetener, 1 cup

Low-fat milk exchanges with 12 grams carbohydrate and 5 grams fat include the following:

> 2 percent milk, 1 cup
> Plain low-fat yogurt, ¾ cup
> Sweet acidophilus milk, 1 cup

Whole milk exchanges with 12 grams carbohydrate and 8 grams fat include the following:

> Whole milk, 1 cup
> Evaporated whole milk, ½ cup
> Goat's milk, 1 cup
> Kefir, 1 cup

Other carbohydrates list with 15 grams carbohydrate or 1 starch, or 1 fruit, or 1 milk. Items on this list can be substituted for a starch, fruit, or milk choice in your meal plan. Some choices will also count as 1 fat exchange. They can be substituted in the meal plan even though they contain added sugars or fat. However, they do not contain as many important vitamins and minerals as the choices on the starch, fruit, or milk list. When you plan to use these foods in your meal plan, be sure to include foods from all of the lists to eat a balanced meal. Always check the nutritive information on the food label. It will be your most accurate source of information. Because many of these foods are concentrated sources of carbohydrate and fat, the portion sizes are often very small. Look for salad dressings in smaller amounts on the Free Foods List. Many fat-free or reduced-fat products made with fat replacers contain carbohydrate. When eaten in large amounts, they may need to be counted. Talk with your dietitian to determine how to count these in your meal plan.

Other carbohydrates that count as one exchange with 15 grams of carbohydrate or 1 starch or 1 fruit or 1 milk include the following:

> Angel food cake, unfrosted, ¹⁄₁₂ cake,
> > 2 carbohydrates
> Brownie, small, unfrosted, 2-inch square,
> > 1 carbohydrate, 1 fat
> Cake, unfrosted, 2-inch square, 1 carbohydrate,
> > 1 fat

Cake, frosted, 2-inch square, 2 carbohydrates,
    1 fat
Cookie, fat-free, 2 small, 1 carbohydrate
Cookie or sandwich cookie with creme filling,
    2 small, 1 carbohydrate, 1 fat
Cupcake, frosted, 1 small, 2 carbohydrates, 1 fat
Cranberry sauce, jellied, ¼ cup, 2 carbohydrates
Doughnut, plain, cake, 1 medium (1½ ounces),
    1½ carbohydrates, 2 fat
Doughnut, glazed, 3¾ inches across (2 ounces),
    2 carbohydrates, 2 fats
Fruit juice bars, frozen, 100 percent juice, 1 bar
    (3 ounces), 1 carbohydrate
Fruit snacks, chewy (puréed fruit concentrate),
    1 roll (¾ ounce), 1 carbohydrate
Fruit spread, 100 percent fruit, 1 tablespoon,
    1 carbohydrate
Gelatin, regular, ½ cup, 1 carbohydrate
Gingersnaps, 3, 1 carbohydrate
Granola bar, 1 bar, 1 carbohydrate, 1 fat
Granola bar, fat-free, 1 bar, 2 carbohydrates
Hummus, ⅓ cup, 1 carbohydrate, 1 fat
Ice cream, ½ cup, 1 carbohydrate, 2 fats
Ice cream, light, ½ cup, 1 carbohydrate, 1 fat
Ice cream, fat-free, no sugar added, ½ cup,
    1 carbohydrate
Jam or jelly, regular, 1 tablespoon, 1 carbohydrate
Milk, chocolate, whole, 1 cup, 2 carbohydrates,
    1 fat
Pie, fruit, 2 crusts, ⅙ pie, 3 carbohydrates, 2 fats
Pie, pumpkin or custard, ⅛ pie, 1 carbohydrate,
    2 fats
Potato chips, 12 to 18 (1 ounce), 1 carbohydrate,
    2 fats
Pudding, regular, made with low-fat milk, ½ cup,
    2 carbohydrates
Pudding, sugar-free, made with low-fat milk,
    ½ cup, 1 carbohydrate

Salad dressing, fat-free, ¼ cup, 1 carbohydrate

Sherbet, sorbet, ½ cup, 2 carbohydrates

Spaghetti or pasta sauce, canned, ½ cup,
1 carbohydrate, 1 fat

Sweet roll or Danish, 1 (2½ ounces),
2½ carbohydrates, 2 fats

Syrup, light, 2 tablespoons, 1 carbohydrate

Syrup, regular, 1 tablespoon, 1 carbohydrate

Syrup, regular, ¼ cup, 4 carbohydrates

Tortilla chips, 6–12 (1 ounce), 1 carbohydrate,
2 fats

Yogurt, frozen, low-fat, fat-free, ⅓ cup,
1 carbohydrate, 0–1 fat

Yogurt, frozen, fat-free, no sugar added, ½ cup,
1 carbohydrate

Yogurt, low-fat, with fruit, 1 cup, 3 carbohydrates,
0–1 fat

Vanilla wafers, 5, 1 carbohydrate, 1 fat

Vegetable list includes vegetables with small amounts of carbohydrate and calories. You should try to eat at least 2 or 3 vegetable choices each day. In general, one vegetable exchange is ½ cup cooked vegetables or vegetable juice or 1 cup raw vegetables. If you eat 1 or 2 vegetable choices at a meal, you do not have to count the calories or carbohydrates because they contain small amounts of these nutrients. Fresh and frozen vegetables contain less salt than canned vegetables. Drain and rinse canned vegetables if you want to reduce the salt. Choose more dark green and dark yellow vegetables, such as spinach, broccoli, romaine, carrots, chilies, and peppers. Brussels sprouts, cauliflower, greens, peppers, spinach, and tomatoes are good sources of Vitamin C. If you eat more than 4 cups of raw vegetables or 2 cups of cooked vegetables at 1 meal, count them as 1 carbohydrate choice. Starch vegetables such as corn, peas, winter squash, and potatoes that contain larger amounts of calories and carbohydrates are on the Starch list.

Vegetable exchange: one exchange, which is 1 cup raw vegetables or ½ cup cooked vegetables with 5 grams carbohydrate, 2 grams protein, 0 grams fat, and 25 calories, includes the following:

Artichoke or artichoke hearts
Asparagus
Beans (green, wax, or Italian)
Bean sprouts
Beets
Broccoli
Brussels sprouts
Cabbage
Carrots
Cauliflower
Celery
Cucumber
Eggplant
Green onions or scallions
Greens (collars, kale, mustard, turnip)
Kohlrabi
Leeks
Mixed vegetables (without corn, peas, or
    pasta)
Mushrooms
Okra
Onions
Pea pods
Peppers (all varieties)
Radishes
Salad greens (endive, escarole, lettuce, romaine,
    spinach)
Sauerkraut*
Spinach
Summer squash
Tomato
Tomatoes, canned
Tomato sauce*
Tomato/vegetable juice*
Turnips
Water chestnuts
Watercress
Zucchini

---

* = 400 mg or more sodium per exchange

Meat and meat substitutes list contains both protein and fat. In general, one meat exchange is: 1 ounce meat, fish, poultry, or cheese or ½ cup cooked, dried beans. Based on the amount of fat they contain, meats are divided into very lean, lean, medium-fat, and high-fat. This is done so you can see which ones contain the least amount of fat. One ounce (one exchange) of each of these includes:

> *Very lean* with 0 grams carbohydrate, 7 grams protein, 0–1 grams fat, and 35 calories.
>
> *Lean* with 0 grams carbohydrate, 7 grams protein, 3 grams fat, and 55 calories.
>
> *Medium-fat* with 0 grams carbohydrate, 7 grams protein, 5 grams fat, and 75 calories.
>
> *High-fat* with 0 grams carbohydrate, 7 grams protein, 8 grams fat, and 100 calories.

- Choose very lean and lean meat choices whenever possible. Items from the high-fat group are high in saturated fat, cholesterol, and calories and can raise blood cholesterol levels. Meats do not have any fiber but dried beans, peas, and lentils are good sources of fiber. Some processed meats, seafood, and soy products may contain carbohydrate when consumed in large quantities. Check the Nutrition Facts on the label to see if the amount is close to 15 grams. If so, count it as a carbohydrate choice as well as a meat choice.

- Weigh meat after cooking and removing bones and fat. Four ounces of raw meat is equal to 3 ounces of cooked meat. Some examples of meat portions are:

> 1 ounce cheese = 1 meat choice and is about the size of a 1-inch cube.
>
> 2 ounces meat = 2 meat choices, such as 1 small chicken leg or thigh or ½ cup cottage cheese or tuna.
>
> 3 ounces meat = 3 meat choices and is about the size of a deck of cards, such as 1 medium pork chop, 1 small hamburger, ½ of a whole chicken breast, or 1 unbreaded fish fillet.

- Limit your choices from the high-fat group to 3 times per week or less.

- Most grocery stores stock Select and Choice grades of meat. Select grades of meat are the leanest meats. Choice grades contain a moderate amount of fat, and Prime cuts of meat have the highest amount of fat. Restaurants usually serve Prime cuts of meat.

- "Hamburger" may contain added seasoning and fat, but ground beef does not.

- Read labels to find products that are low in fat and cholesterol (5 grams or less of fat per serving).

- Dried beans, peas, and lentils are also found on the Starch list.

- Peanut butter, in smaller amounts, is also found on the Fats list.

- Bacon, in smaller amounts, is also found on the Fats list.

Meal planning tips: Bake, roast, broil, poach, steam, or boil these foods rather than frying. Place meat on a rack so the fat will drain off during cooking. Use a nonstick spray and a nonstick pan to brown or fry foods. Trim off visible fat before and after cooking. If you add flour, bread crumbs, coating mixes, fat, or marinades when cooking, ask your dietitian how to count it in your meal plan.

Very lean meat and substitutes exchanges with 0 grams carbohydrate, 7 grams protein, 0–1 grams fat, and 35 calories include the following:

> Poultry: Chicken or turkey (white meat, no skin), Cornish hen (no skin), 1 ounce
>
> Fish: Fresh or frozen cod, flounder, haddock, halibut, trout, tuna (fresh or canned in water), 1 ounce
>
> Shellfish: Clams, crab, lobster, scallops, shrimp, imitation shellfish, 1 ounce
>
> Game: Duck or pheasant (no skin), venison, buffalo, ostrich, 1 ounce

Cheese with 1 gram or less fat per ounce: Non-fat
or low-fat cottage cheese, fat-free cheese,
1 ounce

Other: Processed sandwich meats with 1 gram or
less fat per ounce, such as deli thin, shaved
meats, chipped beef*, turkey ham, 1 ounce

Egg whites, 2

Egg substitute, plain, ¼ cup

Hot dogs with 1 gram or less fat per ounce*,
1 ounce

Kidney (high in cholesterol), 1 ounce

Sausage with 1 gram or less fat per ounce,
1 ounce

Count as 1 very lean meat and 1 starch exchange: Dried
beans, peas, lentils (cooked), ½ cup.

Lean meat and substitutes exchanges with 0 grams
carbohydrate, 7 grams protein, 3 grams fat, and 55 calories
include the following:

Beef: USDA Select or Choice grades of lean beef
trimmed of fat, such as round, sirloin, and
flank steak, tenderloin, roast (rib, chuck,
rump), steak (porterhouse, cubed), ground
round, 1 ounce

Pork: Lean pork, such as fresh ham; canned,
cured, or boiled ham; Canadian bacon*;
tenderloin; center cup chop, 1 ounce

Lamb: Roast, chop, leg, 1 ounce

Veal: Lean chop, roast, 1 ounce

Poultry: Chicken or turkey (dark meat, no skin),
chicken (white meat with skin), domestic duck
or goose (well drained of fat, no skin),
1 ounce

Fish:
Herring, (uncreamed or smoked), 1 ounce
Oysters, 6 medium
Salmon (fresh or canned), catfish, 1 ounce
Sardines (canned), 2 medium

* = 400 mg or more sodium per exchange

Tuna (canned in oil, drained), 1 ounce
Game: Goose (no skin), rabbit, 1 ounce
Cheese
4.5 percent fat cottage cheese, ¼ cup
Parmesan, grated, 2 tablespoons
Cheese with 3 grams or less fat per ounce,
1 ounce
Other:
Hot dogs with 3 grams or less fat per ounce*,
1½ ounces
Processed sandwich meat with 3 grams or less
fat per ounce, such as turkey pastrami or
kielbasa, 1 ounce
Liver, heart (high in cholesterol), 1 ounce

Medium-fat meat and substitutes exchanges with 0 grams carbohydrate, 7 grams protein, 5 grams fat and 75 calories include the following:

Beef: Most beef products fall into this category
(ground beef, meatloaf, corned beef, short
ribs, Prime grades of meat trimmed of fat,
such as prime rib), 1 ounce
Pork: Top loin, chop, Boston butt, cutlet, 1 ounce
Lamb: Rib roast, ground, 1 ounce
Veal: Cutlet (ground or cubed, unbreaded),
1 ounce
Poultry: Chicken, dark meat (with skin), ground
turkey or ground chicken, fried chicken (with
skin), 1 ounce
Fish: Any fried fish product, 1 ounce
Cheese with 5 grams or less fat per ounce:
Feta, or mozzarella, 1 ounce
Ricotta, ¼ cup (2 ounces)
Other:
Egg (high in cholesterol, limit to 3 per week), 1
Sausage with 5 grams or less fat per ounce,
1 ounce
Soy milk, 1 cup

---

* = 400 mg or more sodium per exchange

Tempeh, ¼ cup

Tofu, 4 ounces or ½ cup

High-fat meat and substitutes exchanges with 0 grams carbohydrate, 8 grams fat, and 100 calories include the following:

Pork: Spareribs, ground pork, pork sausage, 1 ounce

Cheese: All regular cheeses such as American*, cheddar, Monterey Jack, Swiss, 1 ounce

Other:

Processed sandwich meats with 8 grams or less fat per ounce such as bologna, pimiento loaf, salami, 1 ounce

Sausage, such as bratwurst, Italian, knockwurst, Polish, smoked, 1 ounce

Hot dog (turkey or chicken)*, 1 (10 per pound)

Bacon, 3 slices (20 slices per pound)

Count as one high-fat meat plus one fat exchange:

Hot dog (beef, pork, or combination)*, 1 (10 per pound)

Peanut butter (contains unsaturated fat), 2 tablespoons

Fat List fats are divided into three groups based on the main type of fat they contain: monounsaturated, polyunsaturated, and saturated. Small amounts of monounsaturated and polyunsaturated fats in the foods we eat are linked with good health benefits. Saturated fats are linked with heart disease and cancer. In general, one fat exchange is: 1 teaspoon of regular margarine or vegetable oil or 1 tablespoon of regular salad dressing. All fats are high in calories. Limit serving sizes for good nutrition and health. If blood pressure is a concern, choose fats in the unsalted form to help lower sodium intake, such as unsalted peanuts. Check the Nutrition Facts on food labels for serving sizes. One fat exchange is based on a serving size containing 5 grams of fat. When selecting regular margarines, choose those with liquid vegetable oil as the first ingredient. Soft margarines are not as saturated as stick margarines. Soft mar-

---

* = 400 mg or more sodium per exchange

garines are healthier choices. Avoid those listing hydrogenated or partially hydrogenated fat as the first ingredient. When selecting low-fat margarines, look for liquid vegetable oil as the second ingredient. Water is usually the first ingredient. When used in smaller amounts, bacon and peanut butter are counted as fat choices. When used in larger amounts, they are counted as high-fat meat choices. See the Free Foods List for nondairy coffee creamers, whipped topping, and fat-free products, such as margarines, salad dressings, mayonnaise, sour cream, cream cheese, and nonstick cooking spray.

Monounsaturated fat exchanges with 5 grams fat and 45 calories include the following:

> Avocado, medium, ⅛ (1 ounce)
> Oil (canola, olive, peanut), 1 teaspoon
> Olives: ripe, (black), 8 large
>   green (stuffed)*, 10 large
> Nuts
>   almonds, cashews, 6 nuts
>   mixed (50 percent peanuts), 6 nuts
>   peanuts, 10 nuts
>   pecans, 4 halves
> Peanut butter, smooth or crunchy, 2 teaspoons
> Sesame seeds, 1 tablespoon
> Tahini paste, 2 teaspoons

Polyunsaturated fat exchanges with 5 grams fat and 45 calories include the following:

> Margarine, stick, tub, or squeeze, 1 teaspoon
>   lower fat (30 percent to 50 percent vegetable oil), 1 tablespoon
> Mayonnaise: regular, 1 teaspoon
>   reduced fat, 1 tablespoon
> Nuts, walnuts, English, 4 halves
> Oil (corn, safflower, soybean), 1 teaspoon
> Salad dressing, regular*, 1 tablespoon
>   reduced fat, 2 tablespoons
> Miracle Whip Salad Dressing*, regular,
>   2 teaspoons

---

* = 400 mg or more sodium per exchange

reduced fat, 1 tablespoon
Seeds, pumpkin, sunflower, 1 tablespoon

Saturated fats exchanges with 5 grams of fat and 45 calories include the following:

Bacon, cooked, 1 slice (20 slices per pound)
Bacon grease, 1 teaspoon
Butter, stick, 1 teaspoon
   whipped, 2 teaspoons
   reduced-fat, 1 tablespoon
Chitterlings, boiled, 2 tablespoons (½ ounce)
Coconut, sweetened, shredded, 2 tablespoons
Cream, half and half, 2 tablespoons
Cream cheese, regular, 1 tablespoon (½ ounce)
   reduced-fat, 2 tablespoons (1 ounce)
Fatback or salt pork. Use a piece 1″ × 1″ × ¼″ if you plan to eat the fatback cooked with vegetables. Use a piece 2″ × 1″ × ½″ when eating only the vegetables with the fatback removed.
Shortening or lard, 1 teaspoon
Sour cream, regular, 2 tablespoons
   reduced-fat, 3 tablespoons

Free foods list. A free food is any food or drink that contains less than 20 calories or less than 5 grams carbohydrate per serving. Foods with a serving size listed should be limited to three servings per day. Be sure to spread them out throughout the day. If you eat all three servings at one time it could affect your blood glucose. Foods listed without a serving size can be eaten as often as you like.

Fat-free or reduced-fat foods include the following:

Cream cheese, fat-free, 1 tablespoon
Creamers, nondairy, liquid, 1 tablespoon
Creamers, nondairy, powdered, 2 teaspoons
Mayonnaise, fat-free, 1 tablespoon
Mayonnaise, reduced-fat, 1 teaspoon
Margarine, fat-free, 4 tablespoons
Margarine, reduced-fat, 1 teaspoon

---

* = 400 mg or more sodium per exchange

Miracle Whip, non-fat, 1 tablespoon
Miracle Whip, reduced-fat, 1 teaspoon
Nonstick cooking spray
Salad dressing, fat-free, 1 tablespoon
Salad dressing, fat-free, Italian, 2 tablespoons
Salsa, ¼ cup
Sour cream, fat-free or reduced-fat, 1 tablespoon
Whipped topping, regular or light, 2 tablespoons

Sugar-free or low-sugar foods include the following:

Candy, hard, sugar-free, 1 candy
Gelatin dessert, sugar-free
Gelatin, unflavored
Gum, sugar-free
Jam or jelly, low sugar or light, 2 teaspoons
Syrup, sugar-free, 2 tablespoons
Sugar substitutes, alternatives, or replacements
that are approved by the Food and Drug
Administration (FDA) are safe to use. Common
brand names include:
Equal (aspartame)
Sprinkle Sweet (saccharin)
Sweet One (acesulfame)
Sweet-10 (saccharin)
Sugar Twin (saccharin)
Sweet'n Low (saccharin)
Weight Watchers Smart Options (saccharin)

Drinks include the following:

Bouillon, broth, consomme*
Bouillon or broth, low sodium
Carbonated or mineral water
Cocoa powder, unsweetened, 1 tablespoon
Coffee or tea
Club soda
Diet soft drinks, sugar-free
Drink mixes, sugar-free
Tonic water, sugar-free

Condiments include the following:

* = 400 mg or more sodium per exchange

> Catsup, 1 tablespoon
> Horseradish
> Lemon juice
> Lime juice
> Mustard
> Pickles, dill*, 1½ large
> Soy sauce, regular or light*
> Taco sauce, 1 tablespoon
> Vinegar

Seasonings. Be careful with seasonings that contain sodium or salts, such as garlic or celery salt and lemon pepper. Free seasonings include the following:

> Flavoring extracts
> Garlic
> Herbs, fresh or dried
> Pimiento
> Spices
> Tabasco* or hot pepper sauce
> Wine, used in cooking
> Worcestershire sauce

Combination foods list. Many of the foods we eat are mixed together in various combinations. These combination foods do not fit into any one exchange list. Often it is hard to tell what is in a casserole dish or prepared food item. This is a list of exchanges for some typical combination foods. The list will help you fit these foods into your meal plan. Ask your dietitian for information about any other combination foods you would like to eat. (If you like, you can calculate the food exchanges in your own recipes, using the information in Chapter 3 "Calculating Food Exchanges.")

Entrées include the following:

> Tuna noodle casserole, lasagna, spaghetti with meatballs, chili with beans, macaroni and cheese*, 1 cup (8 ounces), 2 carbohydrates, 2 medium-fat meats
> Chow mein (without noodles or rice), 2 cups (16 ounces), 1 carbohydrate, 2 lean meats

* = 400 mg or more sodium per exchange

Pizza, cheese, thin crust*, ¼ of 10-inch round
(5 ounces), 2 carbohydrates, 2 medium-fat
meats, 1 fat

Pizza, meat topping, thin crust*, ¼ of 10-inch
round (5 ounces), 2 carbohydrates, 2 medium-
fat meats, 2 fats

Pot pie*, 1 (7 ounces), 2 carbohydrates,
1 medium-fat meat, 4 fats

Frozen Entrées include the following:

Salisbury steak with gravy, mashed potato*,
1 (11 ounces), 2 carbohydrates, 3 medium-fat
meats, 3–4 fats

Turkey with gravy, mashed potato, dressing*,
1 (11 ounces), 2 carbohydrates, 2 medium-fat
meats, 2 fats

Entrée with less than 300 calories*, 1 (8 ounces),
2 carbohydrates, 3 lean meats

Soups include the following:

Bean*, 1 cup, 1 carbohydrate, 1 very lean meat

Cream (made with water)*, 1 cup (8 ounces),
1 carbohydrate, 1 fat

Split pea (made with water)*, ½ cup (4 ounces),
1 carbohydrate

Tomato (made with water)*, 1 cup (8 ounces),
1 carbohydrate

Vegetable beef, chicken noodle, or other broth
types*, 1 cup (8 ounces), 1 carbohydrate

Fast foods include the following (ask at your favorite fast
food restaurant for nutrition information about your favorite
fast food):

Burritos with beef*, 2, 4 carbohydrates,
2 medium-fat meats, 2 fats

Chicken nuggets*, 6, 1 carbohydrate, 2 medium-
fat meats, 1 fat

Chicken breast and wing, breaded and fried*,
1 each, 1 carbohydrate, 4 medium-fat meats,
2 fats

---

* = 400 mg or more sodium per exchange

Fish sandwich/tartar sauce*, 1, 3 carbohydrates,
   1 medium-fat meat, 3 fats
French fries, thin, 20–25, 2 carbohydrates, 2 fats
Hamburger, regular, 1, 2 carbohydrates, 2
   medium-fat meats
Hamburger, large*, 1, 2 carbohydrates, 3 medium-
   fat meats, 1 fat
Hog dog with bun*, 1, 1 carbohydrate, 1 high-fat
   meat, 1 fat
Individual pan pizza*, 1, 5 carbohydrates,
   3 medium-fat meats, 3 fats
Soft-serve cone, 1 medium, 2 carbohydrates, 1 fat
Submarine sandwich*, 1 sub (6 inches),
   3 carbohydrates, 1 vegetable, 2 medium-fat
   meats, 1 fat
Taco, hard shell*, 1 (6 ounces), 2 carbohydrates,
   2 medium-fat meats, 2 fats
Taco, soft shell*, 1 (3 ounces), 1 carbohydrate,
   1 medium-fat meat, 1 fat

You will notice that many of the exchanges listed with the recipes are different from the ones you are accustomed to using. This is because the new exchange system is more precise and descriptive so we can be more accurate. We frequently use the term "starch exchange" when you might be expecting "bread exchange." If there is a doubt in your mind regarding the values of a certain recipe or exchange, consult the listings in this chapter. I'm sure that after you get accustomed to the new exchange listings, you will appreciate them as much as I do.

---

* = 400 mg or more sodium per exchange

3

Calculating
Food Exchanges

Information about food exchanges is basic to good management of your diabetic diet. You need to learn as much about them as possible—what they are and how to use them.

Food exchanges are a method of measuring food values so that a diabetic can control the amount of carbohydrate and other nutrients consumed. The nutritional value of the exchanges has been determined by the American Dietetic Association. You can't change their values, but you can work with them better when you understand more about them. They have been standardized as follows.

The exchanges are established in grams—which are more familiar to other nationalities than to Americans since we are still using the British system of pounds and ounces. Grams are a measure of weight used in most laboratories and research centers here in our country as well as abroad. One ounce equals 28.35 grams, so that a 1-ounce slice of bread that contains 15 grams of carbohydrate is about half carbohydrate and the rest water, fiber, fat, and other ingredients. A vegetable exchange that weighs 3½ to 4 ounces contains only 5 grams of carbohydrate and therefore has a much smaller percentage of carbohydrate and a larger percentage of fiber, water, and other nutrients. A fruit exchange has about 15 grams of carbohydrate, and a milk exchange has 12 grams of carbohydrate in 8 ounces of milk. Since the percentage of carbohydrate in a food is important to us, it is helpful to realize that most vegetables have a much smaller percentage of carbohydrate than bread and some of the starchier vegetables.

COMPOSITION OF FOOD GROUPS OR EXCHANGES PER SERVING

Food Exchanges	Carbohydrate (grams)	Protein (grams)	Fat (grams)	Calories
Carbohydrate Group				
Starch	15	3	1 or less	80
Fruit	15	–	–	60
Milk				
Skim	12	8	0–3	90
Low-fat	12	8	5	120
Whole	12	8	8	150
Other				
Carbohydrates	15	varies	varies	varies
Vegetables	5	2	–	25
Meat and Meat Substitute Group				
Very lean	–	7	0–1	35
Lean	–	7	3	55
Medium-fat	–	7	5	75
High-Fat	–	7	8	100
Fat Group	–	–	5	45

At first most diabetics tend to use recipes that have been calculated by someone else—it's hard enough to get used to thinking in terms of exchanges without worrying about how they were determined. After a while, though, you begin to wonder why you can't use some of your own recipes. The next step generally is comparing a recipe that has been calculated with one of your own recipes and accepting the exchanges determined for the other recipe for your own recipe. This isn't too bad an idea, but it can cause trouble sometimes because the recipes aren't exactly alike. Some little ingredient in your recipe can throw the whole calculation off and your recipe may be less accurate than you realize.

The final and best step is learning to calculate your own recipes. Sometimes you may have to juggle your own around a bit—cutting out some of the flour, cutting down on the sugar, or substituting a low-carbohydrate vegetable for a high-starch one—but eventually you'll learn how to manage your own recipes after you learn to calculate them.

In order to establish the nutritive values of each portion in a recipe, you must calculate the total nutritive values of the complete recipe, divide by the number of servings the recipe yields, and then compare the nutritive values of each portion with the chart showing the carbohydrate, protein, and fat values of each of the exchanges.

Calculating your own recipes would be very difficult if it weren't for all of the excellent information available to us—thanks to so many dedicated people who have worked hard establishing the nutritive values of foods.

It is helpful to collect information about the nutritive values of foods you use every day. There is an increasing amount of help available from many sources. Now that most cans and packages include nutritive information on the labels, you can collect that information and use it to establish a file of your own. Many of the cereal companies have very complete information available regarding their products, and most companies will send it to you if you are unable to find it on the package. The following books contain information that is invaluable when calculating recipes:

Nutritive Value of American Foods in Common Units, Agricultural Handbook 456, U.S. Department of Agriculture. Washington, D.C.: Superintendent of Documents, U.S. Printing Office, 1975.

Nutritive Value of Foods, Home and Garden Bulletin 72, U.S. Department of Agriculture. Washington, D.C.: Superintendent of Documents, U.S. Printing Office, 1977.

Composition of Foods, Raw, Processed, and Prepared, Agriculture Handbook No. 8, U.S. Department of Agriculture. Washington, D.C.: Superintendent of Documents, U.S. Printing Office, 1963, and all current revisions.

Food Values of Portions Commonly Used, Bowes and Church, J. B. Lippincott Company.

The first three books are available in many large cities from the U.S. Government printing office stores, or may be ordered at your local county extension agent office or purchased from the Superintendent of Documents, U.S. Government Printing Office, Washington, D.C. 20402.

RECIPE ANALYSIS

The nutritive values that concern us most are calories (CAL), carbohydrate (CHO), protein (PRO), fat, and for some of us, sodium (NA). To calculate a recipe, the simplest procedure is to make a chart showing the list of ingredients and the nutritive values of each. When I started this book, I worked out the following form and took it to the printer so that I wouldn't have to draw it up every time I wanted to calculate a recipe. If you'd like, you can copy it for your own use, or you can draw up your own form to include whatever information you would like to have on the recipe. I didn't include cholesterol on the form; however, there is a table of cholesterol in Chapter 6, "Equipment and Ingredients," if you would like to check your cholesterol intake. Personally, I feel that you should avoid anything that contains cholesterol. Some dietitians and doctors tell you that you can have 2 or 3 eggs weekly; however, I feel that you should avoid egg yolks and other cholesterol-rich foods completely—at least when you are first starting your low-cholesterol diet and trying hard to bring down that cholesterol count.

When I use this form, I list the ingredients for each recipe and then look for the appropriate values for each ingredient in one of my references—for instance, as I did for the Yankee Cornbread recipe (see Index).

After you have calculated the total nutritive values of the recipe, divide the total of each of the elements (CAL, CHO, PRO, FAT, and NA) by the total number of portions to get the nutritive values per serving. Then compare it with the table at the beginning of this chapter to decide how many food exchanges you will get from each serving—as I did at the bottom of the recipe analysis.

ADJUSTING YOUR RECIPE

Your recipe probably won't turn out exactly the way you want it to the first time. I have tested most of the recipes in this book several times. The first time I test a recipe, I use the ingredients listed in the basic recipe, cutting down on the sugar or fat or

RECIPE ANALYSIS

Name of recipe _____ Date tested _____

Source of recipe _____

Type and number of pans used _____

_____

Temperature _____ Number of servings _____

Baking or cooking time _____

Comments on recipe _____

Ingredient	Amt.	Cal.	CHO (gm)	PRO (gm)	Fat (gm)	NA (mg)
Total nutritive values						
Divided by the total number of portions						
Rounded to the nearest number						
Number of food exchanges equal to nutritive value:						

whatever else I think I need to reduce. While some recipes need a little sugar for color and texture, you will be surprised at the amount of sugar you can take out of a recipe and still get a pretty good product. On the first test of a recipe with the sugar reduced, I add sugar substitute equal to the amount of sugar that I removed. I probably will cut down on the sugar substitute on the next testing because I don't like the taste of an excessive amount of it, but I need to determine how much I want to use in the final recipe. Remember when you are adding sugar substitute that Equal (NutraSweet) breaks down if it is baked or heated too long; if you are using prolonged heat, use some other kind of sugar substitute. I try to add Equal after I have taken whatever I'm cooking off the heat, which seems to work very well; or else I use it in things that don't need to be cooked, such as gelatin or fruit.

You can also reduce the fat in a recipe quite a bit, although you do need some fat in baked goods for texture and tenderness.

After the first time you test a recipe and calculate its nutritive values, you can decide how much more you need to cut ingredients in order to have a product suitable for your use. Sometimes the calories or fat or carbohydrate are too high and you need to try it again, cutting down on the offending ingredient. It is possible to repeatedly try a recipe and never get it right, but generally, you can work with it and find a variation of the original recipe that you can use. One important thing to remember is to write down exactly what you use when you are testing a recipe. It is so frustrating to get just what you want in a recipe and then forget exactly how much of each ingredient you used.

Another way to control the food exchanges is by dividing a recipe into the size portions that conform to what you can have. In the bread chapter, you will notice that the number of slices per loaf varies according to the recipe. That is because I need to cut a certain size slice to arrive at a bread exchange for each slice. To find this, I divide the total grams of carbohydrate in the recipe by 15, which is the amount allowed for a bread exchange; that tells me how many slices I need from each loaf in order to have each slice equal one bread exchange.

RECIPE ANALYSIS

Name of recipe <u>Yankee Cornbread</u> Date tested <u>July 25</u>
Source of recipe <u>My favorite recipe</u>
Type and number of pans used <u>mixer bowl and 9-inch</u>
<u>square baking pan</u>
Temperature <u>400 degrees</u> Number of servings <u>16</u>
Baking or cooking time <u>25 minutes</u>
Comments on recipe <u>Chuck's favorite, good texture + color</u>

Ingredient	Amt.	Cal.	CHO (gm)	PRO (gm)	Fat (gm)	NA (mg)
Corn meal	1 cup	502	108.2	10.9	1.7	1
all-purpose flour	1 cup	455	95.1	13.1	1.3	3
baking powder	4 tsp	20	4	trace	0	1,316
sugar	1/4 cup	193	49.8	—	—	trace
instant dry milk	1/4 cup	61	9	6	trace	93
salt	1/4 tsp	—	—	—	—	533
liquid egg sub.	1/4 cup	25	1	5	0	80
vegetable oil	1/4 cup	482	—	—	54.5	—
Total nutritive values		1,738	267.1	35	57.5	2,026
Divided by the total number of portions	16	108.6	16.7	2.19	3.59	126.6
Rounded to the nearest number		109	17	2	4	127
Number of food exchanges equal to nutritive value:						
1 Starch		80	15	3	4	
1 Fat		45			5	
		125	15	3	9	

I find a calculator a big help when calculating recipes. It is much faster and gives me more confidence that my totals are correct.

When I became diabetic and had to calculate all my recipes, I realized how lucky I had been to work for Miriam H. Thomas back when I first started working for the government. Then a research chemist in Chicago, she introduced me to the world of food analysis and calculations. I remember telling her that I was a dietitian used to working in restaurants, and that I'd never get all of those calculations straight. She told me I was perfect for the job because a dietitian would realize the importance of calculating the nutritive values of the Army rations very carefully. So I persevered and eventually it all made sense.

After Miriam's office moved to Natick, Massachusetts, I worked for a few months for Mary Klicka, a dietitian/nutritionist at the same center. Among other things, Mary was developing foods for the space program, and I learned something new and interesting every day. She used to fascinate me with her knowledge of the nutritive content of almost anything, and has given me the nutritive analysis of several foods that I couldn't find in any of my other references.

After Mary Klicka moved to Natick, I transferred to the Menu Planning Division of the Army Food Service Center in Chicago, where I worked for several years under the direction of Marion Bollman. While there, I worked on Army menus and also learned how to write recipes. When the Armed Forces decided to set up a joint recipe file, Marion appointed me as the Army representative on the Armed Forces Recipe Service File Committee. We spent a lot of time working on that file, which was a real learning experience and gave me the background necessary to start writing my own cookbooks.

As an aid in developing recipes for my cookbooks, I keep a chart of nutritive values of many ingredients that I use a lot so I don't have to look them up every time. This is very helpful to me, and since it is likely to be helpful for you also, I'm including it in this chapter. I have only included foods which may be used on a low-cholesterol diet. I have not included egg yolks, cream, or other high-fat foods. However, I did relent and include chocolate chips because you might like to use them occasionally—and you should have their nutritive value so you will know how many you can use.

When calculating meat recipes, I subtract the values for any fat that cooks out of the meat, using the values for fat in the chart. I chill the fat and then measure it very carefully after it is hardened in the refrigerator.

Although you can't use much of them, I have included sugars because research now shows a little can be used as long as it is calculated in the total exchanges for that food. You might discuss this with your doctor; however, most doctors and dietitians concur that a small amount will not upset your sugar count. (See Introduction, page xi.)

The following measures may also help you in your own calculations:

3 teaspoons = 1 tablespoon
4 tablespoons = ¼ cup
5⅓ tablespoons = ⅓ cup
8 tablespoons = ½ cup
10⅔ tablespoons = ⅔ cup
12 tablespoons = ¾ cup
16 tablespoons = 1 cup
2 cups = 1 pint
4 cups = 1 quart
4 quarts = 1 gallon
16 ounces = 1 pound

I have used pound and cup measures for many items in this table so that from them you can calculate your own recipes.

Remember as you are using this information that it is specifically aimed at the person on a low-cholesterol diabetic diet. All values for fruits and fruit juices are without any added sweetener, and meats that are high in fat are not included—nor are any other products that are not approved on a low-cholesterol diet.

I hope you will be encouraged to use this information in calculating your own favorite recipes and to devise variations of other recipes that will help to add some spice and variety to your diet.

NUTRIENT ANALYSIS OF ACCEPTABLE FOODS

Food Item	Amount	Kcal	Cho (gm)	Pro (gm)	Fat (gm)	Sat Fat (gm)	Chol (mg)	Fiber (gm)	Na (mg)
VEGETABLES									
Artichoke	1 med	60	13	4	Trace	Trace	0	6.7	120
Asparagus, cooked	½ cup	22	4	2	Trace	Trace	0	3.1	4
Beans, lima, dry, cooked	1 cup	216	39	15	1	Trace	0	13.5	4
Beans, green lima, cooked	1 cup	209	40	12	1	Trace	0	7.1	29
Beans, great northern, cooked	1 cup	209	37	15	1	Trace	0	6	4
Beans, navy, dry, cooked	1 cup	258	48	15	1	Trace	0	6.6	2
Beans, pinto, dry, cooked	1 cup	234	44	14	1	Trace	0	6.8	3
Beans, green, cooked	½ cup	22	5	1	Trace	Trace	0	1.1	2
Beans, green, raw	½ cup	17	4	1	Trace	Trace	0	1	3
Bean sprouts, mung, cooked	1 cup	26	5	3	Trace	Trace	0	na	12
Bean sprouts, mung, raw	½ cup	16	3	2	Trace	Trace	0	0.6	3
Bamboo shoots, canned	1 cup	25	4	2	1	Trace	0	3.9	9
Beets, cooked	1 cup	26	6	1	Trace	Trace	0	2.2	42
Broccoli, raw	½ cup	12	2	1	Trace	Trace	0	1.2	12
Broccoli, cooked	½ cup	22	4	2	Trace	Trace	0	2	20
Brussels sprouts, raw	½ cup	19	4	1	Trace	Trace	0	2.6	11
Brussels sprouts, cooked	½ cup	30	7	2	Trace	Trace	0	3.4	16
Cabbage, raw	½ cup	8	2	Trace	Trace	Trace	0	0.8	6
Cabbage, cooked	½ cup	16	4	1	Trace	Trace	0	2.1	14
Cabbage, red, raw	½ cup	9	2	Trace	Trace	Trace	0	0.7	4
Cabbage, red, cooked	½ cup	16	3	1	Trace	Trace	0	1.8	4
Carrots, raw	½ cup	24	6	1	Trace	Trace	0	1.8	19

Food	Serving								
Carrots, cooked	½ cup	35	8	1	Trace	Trace	0	1.5	51
Cauliflower, raw	½ cup	12	2	1	Trace	Trace	0	1.2	8
Cauliflower, cooked	½ cup	15	3	1	Trace	Trace	0	1.4	4
Celeriac, raw	½ cup	30	7	1	Trace	Trace	0	na	78
Celery, raw	½ cup	10	2	Trace	Trace	Trace	0	1	52
Celery, cooked	½ cup	14	3	1	Trace	Trace	0	1.4	68
Chard, Swiss, raw	½ cup	3	1	Trace	Trace	Trace	0	0.3	38
Chard, Swiss, cooked	½ cup	18	4	2	Trace	Trace	0	na	158
Chicory leaves, raw	½ cup	21	4	2	Trace	Trace	0	1.4	41
Chives, raw	1 tbsp	1	Trace	Trace	Trace	Trace	0	0.1	Trace
Collards, cooked	½ cup	17	4	1	Trace	Trace	0	na	10
Corn, sweet, raw	½ cup	66	15	2	1	Trace	0	2.5	12
Corn, sweet, cooked	½ cup	89	21	3	1	Trace	0	3	14
Corn, sweet, canned	½ cup	83	20	3	1	Trace	0	1.5	286
Corn, canned, cream-style	½ cup	92	23	2	1	Trace	0	1.5	365
Cowpeas, raw	½ cup	65	14	2	Trace	Trace	0	na	3
Cowpeas, cooked	½ cup	79	17	3	Trace	Trace	0	na	3
Cress, garden, raw	½ cup	8	1	1	Trace	Trace	0	na	4
Cucumber, raw	½ cup	7	2	Trace	Trace	Trace	0	0.5	1
Eggplant, raw	½ cup	11	3	Trace	Trace	Trace	0	0.5	2
Eggplant, cooked	½ cup	13	3	Trace	Trace	Trace	0	1	1
Endive, raw	½ cup	4	1	Trace	Trace	Trace	0	0.6	6
Garlic, raw	1 clove	4	1	Trace	Trace	Trace	0	0.1	1
Gingerroot, raw	¼ cup	17	4	1	Trace	Trace	0	na	3
Kale, raw	½ cup	17	3	1	Trace	Trace	0	2.2	15
Kale, cooked	½ cup	21	4	1	Trace	Trace	0	3.3	15

Food Item	Amount	Kcal	Cho (gm)	Pro (gm)	Fat (gm)	Sat Fat (gm)	Chol (mg)	Fiber (gm)	Na (mg)
Kohlrabi, raw	½ cup	19	4	1	Trace	Trace	0	0.8	14
Kohlrabi, cooked	½ cup	24	5	1	Trace	Trace	0	na	17
Leeks, raw	½ cup	32	7	1	Trace	Trace	0	0.6	10
Leeks, cooked	½ cup	16	4	Trace	Trace	Trace	0	na	5
Lettuce, butterhead	½ cup	4	1	Trace	Trace	Trace	0	0.3	1
Lettuce, romaine	½ cup	4	1	Trace	Trace	Trace	0	0.5	2
Lettuce, iceberg	½ cup	5	1	Trace	Trace	Trace	0	0.3	3
Mushrooms, raw	½ cup	9	2	1	Trace	Trace	0	0.5	1
Mushrooms, cooked	½ cup	21	4	2	Trace	Trace	0	1.7	2
Mustard greens, raw	½ cup	7	1	1	Trace	Trace	0	0.2	7
Mustard greens, cooked	½ cup	11	1	2	Trace	Trace	0	1.6	11
Okra, raw	½ cup	19	4	1	Trace	Trace	0	1.6	4
Okra, cooked	½ cup	25	6	1	Trace	Trace	0	na	4
Onion, raw	½ cup	30	7	1	Trace	Trace	0	1.3	2
Onion, cooked	½ cup	46	11	1	Trace	Trace	0	2.2	3
Onion, green, raw	½ cup	16	4	1	Trace	Trace	0	1.2	8
Parsley, raw	¼ cup	5	1	Trace	Trace	Trace	0	0.7	6
Parsnips, raw	½ cup	50	12	1	Trace	Trace	0	3	7
Parsnips, cooked	½ cup	63	15	1	Trace	Trace	0	2.1	8
Peas, green, raw	½ cup	58	10	4	Trace	Trace	0	2.9	4
Peas, green, cooked	½ cup	67	13	4	Trace	Trace	0	3.3	2
Peppers, sweet green, raw	½ cup	14	3	Trace	Trace	Trace	0	0.8	1
Peppers, sweet green, cooked	½ cup	19	5	1	Trace	Trace	0	1.2	1
Peppers, sweet yellow, raw	1 large	na	na	na	na	na	na	na	na

Peppers, chili, raw	½ cup	30	7	2	Trace	2	0	1.1	5
Pickle, cux, dill	1 med	12	3	Trace	Trace	Trace	0	0.8	833
Pickle, sweet	1 large	41	11	Trace	Trace	Trace	0	0.4	329
Pickle, relish, sweet	¼ cup	80	21	Trace	Trace	Trace	0	na	495
Pimiento, canned	1 tbsp	3	1	Trace	Trace	Trace	0	na	2
Potatoes, white, raw	½ cup	59	13	2	Trace	2	0	1.2	5
Potatoes, white, baked, no skin	½ cup	57	13	1	Trace	1	0	0.9	3
Potatoes, white, boiled	½ cup	67	16	1	Trace	1	0	1.2	4
Potatoes, white, mashed	½ cup	111	18	2	1	4	2	1.7	310
Pumpkin, cooked	½ cup	24	6	1	Trace	1	0	na	1
Radicchio, raw	½ cup	5	1	Trace	Trace	Trace	0	na	4
Radishes, red, raw	½ cup	10	2	Trace	Trace	Trace	0	1.3	14
Radishes, white, raw	½ cup	7	1	1	Trace	Trace	0	na	8
Rutabaga, raw	½ cup	25	6	1	Trace	Trace	0	1.7	14
Rutabaga, cooked	½ cup	29	7	1	Trace	Trace	0	1.7	15
Shallots, raw	1 tbsp	7	2	Trace	Trace	Trace	0	0.1	1
Spinach, raw	½ cup	6	1	1	Trace	Trace	0	0.7	22
Spinach, cooked	½ cup	21	3	3	Trace	Trace	0	2	63
Squash, summer, raw	½ cup	13	3	1	Trace	Trace	0	0.8	1
Squash, summer, cooked	½ cup	18	4	1	Trace	Trace	0	1.3	1
Squash, winter, raw	½ cup	21	5	1	Trace	Trace	0	1	2
Squash, winter, cooked	½ cup	40	9	1	1	Trace	0	2.9	1
Sweet potatoes, raw	½ cup	70	16	1	Trace	Trace	0	2	9
Sweet potatoes, cooked	½ cup	172	40	3	Trace	Trace	0	4.9	21
Tomatillos, raw	1 med	11	2	Trace	Trace	Trace	0	na	Trace
Tomatoes, red, raw	1 med	26	6	1	Trace	Trace	0	1.6	11

Food Item	Amount	Kcal	Cho (gm)	Pro (gm)	Fat (gm)	Sat Fat (gm)	Chol (mg)	Fiber (gm)	Na (mg)
Tomatoes, red, cooked	½ cup	32	7	1	Trace	Trace	0	1	13
Tomato, paste, canned	½ cup	110	25	5	1	Trace	0	5.6	1035
Tomato, puréed, canned	½ cup	51	13	2	Trace	Trace	0	2.9	499
Tomato, sauce, canned	½ cup	37	9	2	Trace	Trace	0	1.8	738
Turnips, raw	½ cup	18	4	1	Trace	Trace	0	1.2	44
Turnips, cooked	½ cup	14	4	1	Trace	Trace	0	1.6	39
Turnip greens, raw	½ cup	15	3	1	Trace	Trace	0	1.3	22
Turnip greens, cooked	½ cup	14	3	1	Trace	Trace	0	2.2	21
Water chestnuts, canned	½ cup	35	9	1	Trace	Trace	0	3.2	6
Watercress, raw	½ cup	2	Trace	Trace	Trace	Trace	0	0.4	7

LEGUMES

Food Item	Amount	Kcal	Cho (gm)	Pro (gm)	Fat (gm)	Sat Fat (gm)	Chol (mg)	Fiber (gm)	Na (mg)
Beans, dry, black	1 cup	662	121	42	3	1	0	25.6	10
Beans, dry, cranberry	1 cup	653	117	45	2	1	0	18.1	12
Beans, dry, great northern	1 cup	621	114	40	2	1	0	73.2	26
Beans, dry, kidney	1 cup	613	110	43	2	Trace	0	19.1	44
Beans, dry, lima	1 cup	602	113	38	1	Trace	0	33.8	32
Beans, dry, navy	1 cup	697	126	46	3	1	0	20.2	29
Beans, dry, pink	1 cup	720	135	44	2	1	0	18.7	17
Beans, dry, pinto	1 cup	656	122	40	2	Trace	0	23.2	19
Carob flour	1 cup	394	92	5	1	Trace	0	41	36
Chickpeas, dry	1 cup	728	121	39	12	1	0	12.8	48
Lentils, dry	1 cup	649	110	54	2	Trace	0	21.9	19

Food	Amount								
Lentils, cooked	1 cup	230	40	18	1	1	0	7.9	4
Peas, split	1 cup	672	119	48	2	Trace	0	11	30
Tofu, raw firm	½ cup	183	5	20	11	2	0	na	18
Tofu, raw regular	½ cup	94	2	10	6	1	0	1.5	9

FRUIT (JUICE PACK)

Food	Amount								
Avocado, puréed	1 cup	370	17	5	35	6	0	4.6	23
Avocado, whole	1	324	15	4	31	5	0	4	20
Apricots, raw	3	51	12	1	Trace	Trace	0	1.4	1
Apricots, canned	½ cup	60	15	1	Trace	0	0	0.6	5
Applesauce, canned, unsweetened	½ cup	52	14	Trace	Trace	Trace	0	1.8	2
Apple, raw	1 med	81	21	Trace	1	Trace	0	3	0
Banana, raw	1 med	105	27	1	1	Trace	0	1.8	1
Blackberries, raw	1 cup	75	18	1	1	Trace	0	6.5	0
Blueberries, raw	1 cup	81	20	1	1	Trace	0	3.3	9
Cherries, sour, red, raw, pitted	1 cup	52	13	1	1	Trace	0	1.2	3
Cherries, sour, red, canned, unsw	1 cup	87	22	2	Trace	Trace	0	na	17
Cherries, sweet, raw	1 cup	104	24	2	1	Trace	0	2.2	0
Cherries, sweet, canned	1 cup	135	35	2	Trace	0	0	0.6	8
Cranberries, raw	1 cup	54	14	Trace	Trace	Trace	0	4	1
Currant, red, fresh	1 cup	63	15	2	Trace	Trace	0	4.8	1
Dates, dry	1 cup	490	131	4	1	Trace	0	9.1	5
Elderberries, raw	1 cup	105	27	1	1	Trace	0	na	na
Figs, raw	1 med	37	10	Trace	Trace	Trace	0	1.4	1
Figs, canned, unsweetened	1 cup	131	35	1	Trace	Trace	0	na	2

Food Item	Amount	Kcal	Cho (gm)	Pro (gm)	Fat (gm)	Sat Fat (gm)	Chol (mg)	Fiber (gm)	Na (mg)
Figs, dried	1 cup	508	130	6	2	Trace	0	18.5	22
Gooseberries, raw	1 cup	66	15	1	1	Trace	0	na	2
Grapefruit, fresh	½	38	10	1	Trace	Trace	0	0.7	0
Grapes, concord	1 cup	58	16	1	Trace	Trace	0	1.5	2
Grapes, European	1 cup	114	1	28	1	Trace	0	2.6	3
Groundcherries, raw	1 cup	74	16	3	1	Trace	0	na	na
Guava, raw	1 cup	84	20	1	1	Trace	0	8.9	5
Kiwifruit, raw	1 med	46	11	1	Trace	Trace	0	2.6	4
Lemon, raw	1 med	22	12	1	Trace	Trace	0	na	3
Lime, raw	1 med	20	7	Trace	Trace	Trace	0	na	1
Mango, raw	1 med	135	35	1	1	Trace	0	2.2	4
Melon, cantaloupe	1 cup	56	13	1	Trace	Trace	0	1.3	14
Melon, casaba	1 cup	44	11	2	Trace	Trace	0	1.4	20
Melon, honeydew	1 cup	60	16	1	Trace	Trace	0	1.5	17
Melon, watermelon	1 cup	51	11	1	1	Trace	0	0.6	3
Nectarines	1 med	67	16	1	1	Trace	0	2.2	0
Orange, fresh, peeled	1 med	62	15	1	Trace	Trace	0	3.1	0
Papaya, fresh	1 med	119	30	2	Trace	Trace	0	2.8	9
Peaches, raw	1 med	55	14	1	Trace	Trace	0	2.1	0
Pears, raw	1 med	98	25	1	1	Trace	0	4.3	0
Persimmon, raw	1 med	32	8	Trace	Trace	Trace	0	na	Trace
Pineapple, raw	1 cup	76	19	1	1	Trace	0	1.9	2
Pineapple, canned	1 cup	150	39	1	Trace	Trace	0	1.9	3
Plantain, raw	1 med	218	57	2	1	Trace	0	4.1	7

Plantain, cooked	1 cup	179	48	1	Trace	Trace	0	3.5	6
Plums, raw	1 cup	91	21	1	1	Trace	0	3.5	0
Plums, purple, canned, unsweet	1 cup	102	27	1	Trace	0	0	na	2
Pomegranate, raw	1	105	26	1	Trace	Trace	0	0.9	5
Prunes, dry	1 cup	385	102	4	1	Trace	0	11.6	6
Prunes, cooked	1 cup	227	60	2	Trace	Trace	0	14	4
Quince, raw	1 med	52	14	Trace	Trace	Trace	0	1.8	4
Raisins, seedless	1 cup	435	115	5	1	Trace	0	7.7	17
Raspberries, raw	1 cup	60	14	1	1	Trace	0	5.8	0
Rhubarb, raw	1 cup	26	6	1	Trace	Trace	0	2.2	5
Strawberries, raw	1 cup	46	11	1	1	Trace	0	4	2
Tangerine, raw	1 med	37	9	1	Trace	Trace	0	1.7	1

JUICES

Apple	1 cup	116	29	Trace	Trace	Trace	0	0.3	7
Apricot nectar	1 cup	141	36	1	Trace	Trace	0	1.5	8
Grapefruit, canned, unsweetened	1 cup	94	22	1	Trace	Trace	0	Trace	2
Grape	1 cup	155	38	1	Trace	Trace	0	0	8
Lemon, bottled	1 tbsp	3	1	Trace	Trace	0	0	Trace	3
Lime, bottled	1 tbsp	3	1	Trace	Trace	Trace	0	Trace	2
Orange	1 cup	112	27	2	Trace	Trace	0	0.5	2
Pineapple	1 cup	140	35	1	Trace	0	0	Trace	3
Prune	1 cup	182	45	2	Trace	Trace	0	2.6	10
Tomato	1 cup	41	10	2	Trace	Trace	0	Trace	881

Food Item	Amount	Kcal	Cho (gm)	Pro (gm)	Fat (gm)	Sat Fat (gm)	Chol (mg)	Fiber (gm)	Na (mg)
MEATS									
Composite of lean beef without fat, cooked	100 gm	216	0	30	10	4	86	0	67
Composite of lean beef without fat, raw	100 gm	144	0	21	6	2	59	0	63
Beef brisket, without fat, braised	100 gm	242	0	30	13	5	93	0	70
Beef chuck, arm, without fat, braised	100 gm	216	0	33	8	3	101	0	66
Beef round, without fat, broiled	100 gm	191	0	29	7	3	78	0	64
Beef, tenderloin, without fat, broiled	100 gm	211	0	28	10	4	84	0	63
Beef, top sirloin, without fat, broiled	100 gm	195	0	30	7	3	89	0	66
Beef, ground, ex lean, raw, 17% fat	100 gm	234	0	19	17	7	69	0	66
Beef, ground, regular, raw, 27% fat	100 gm	310	0	17	27	11	85	0	68
Lamb, composite of lean only, without fat, raw	100 gm	134	0	20	5	2	65	0	66
Lamb, composite of lean only, without fat, cooked	100 gm	206	0	28	10	3	92	0	76
Lamb, leg without fat, raw	100 gm	128	0	21	5	2	64	0	62
Lamb, leg, without fat, roasted	100 gm	191	0	28	8	3	89	0	68

Lamb, loin without fat, raw	100 gm	143	0	21	6	2	66	0	68
Lamb, loin, without fat, broiled	100 gm	216	0	30	10	3	95	0	84
Lamb, shoulder without fat, raw	100 gm	144	0	20	7	2	66	0	70
Lamb, shoulder, without fat, braised	100 gm	283	0	33	16	6	117	0	79
Lamb, cubed for stew without fat, raw	100 gm	134	0	20	5	2	65	0	65
Lamb, cubed for stew without fat, braised	100 gm	223	0	34	9	3	108	0	70
Lamb, ground, raw, 23% fat	100 gm	282	0	17	23	10	73	0	59
Lamb, ground, broiled	100 gm	283	0	25	20	8	97	0	81
Veal, composite of lean only, without fat, raw	100 gm	112	0	20	3	1	83	0	86
Veal, composite of lean only, without fat, cooked	100 gm	196	0	32	7	2	118	0	89
Veal, leg without fat, raw	100 gm	107	0	21	2	1	78	0	64
Veal, leg, without fat, braised	100 gm	203	0	37	5	2	135	0	67
Veal, cubed for stew without fat, raw	100 gm	109	0	20	3	1	84	0	83
Veal, cubed for stew without fat, braised	100 gm	188	0	35	4	1	145	0	93
Veal, ground, raw, 7% fat	100 gm	144	0	19	7	3	82	0	82
Veal, ground, broiled	100 gm	172	0	24	8	3	103	0	83
Rabbit, tame, composite, raw	100 gm	136	0	20	6	2	57	0	41

Food Item	Amount	Kcal	Cho (gm)	Pro (gm)	Fat (gm)	Sat Fat (gm)	Chol (mg)	Fiber (gm)	Na (mg)
Rabbit, tame, composite, stewed	100 gm	206	0	30	8	3	86	0	37
Pork, fresh, composite of lean only, raw	100 gm	147	0	20	7	2	65	0	64
Pork, fresh, composite of lean only, cooked	100 gm	212	0	29	10	3	86	0	59
Pork, fresh, ham, lean only without fat, raw	100 gm	136	0	20	5	2	68	0	55
Pork, fresh, ham, lean only without fat, cooked	100 gm	211	0	29	9	3	94	0	64
Pork, fresh, loin, lean only without fat, raw	100 gm	143	0	21	6	2	59	0	52
Pork, fresh, loin, lean only without fat, roasted	100 gm	209	0	29	10	4	81	0	52
Pork, Canadian bacon, unheated	100 gm	157	2	21	7	2	50	0	1409
Pork, Canadian bacon, heated	100 gm	185	1	24	8	3	58	0	1546
Ham, boneless, cooked, unheated	100 gm	182	3	18	11	3	57	0	1317
Ham, boneless, cooked, heated	100 gm	178	Trace	23	9	3	59	0	1500
Ham, boneless, ex lean, cooked unheated	100 gm	131	1	19	5	2	47	0	1429
Ham, boneless, ex lean, cooked heated	100 gm	145	2	21	6	2	53	0	1203
Ham, country-style, lean only, raw	100 gm	195	Trace	28	8	3	71	0	2660

POULTRY

Chicken, broiler, fryer, meat only, raw	100 gm	0	119	21	3	1	70	0	77
Chicken, broiler, fryer, meat only, stewed	100 gm	0	177	27	7	2	83	0	70
Chicken, roaster, meat only, raw	100 gm	0	111	20	3	1	65	0	75
Chicken, roaster, meat only, roasted	100 gm	0	167	25	7	2	75	0	75
Chicken, breast, meat only, raw	100 gm	0	110	23	1	Trace	58	0	65
Chicken, breast, meat only, ckd	100 gm	0	165	31	4	1	85	0	74
Chicken, thigh, meat only, raw	100 gm	0	119	20	4	1	83	0	86
Chicken, thigh, meat only, ckd	100 gm	0	209	26	11	3	95	0	88
Turkey, composite, meat only, raw	100 gm	0	117	22	3	1	68	0	73
Turkey, composite, meat only, cooked	100 gm	0	168	29	5	2	77	0	74
Turkey, light meat only, without skin, raw	100 gm	0	114	23	2	1	62	0	67
Turkey, light meat only, without skin, cooked	100 gm	0	154	30	3	1	69	0	68
Turkey, dark meat only, without skin, raw	100 gm	0	123	20	4	1	75	0	80
Turkey, dark meat only, without skin, cooked	100 gm	0	185	29	7	2	88	0	82
Turkey, ground, raw, 7% fat	100 gm	0	142	17	7	2	73	0	94

Food Item	Amount	Kcal	Cho (gm)	Pro (gm)	Fat (gm)	Sat Fat (gm)	Chol (mg)	Fiber (gm)	Na (mg)
Turkey, ground, cooked	100 gm	229	0	24	14	4	69	0	83
Turkey ham, dark meat	100 gm	128	Trace	19	5	2	62	0	996
Turkey roll	100 gm	149	2	18	7	2	55	0	586
Turkey frankfurter	2 oz	128	1	8	10	3	60	0	808

FISH

Food Item	Amount	Kcal	Cho (gm)	Pro (gm)	Fat (gm)	Sat Fat (gm)	Chol (mg)	Fiber (gm)	Na (mg)
Catfish, fillets, raw	100 gm	135	0	16	26	2	47	0	53
Bass, raw	100 gm	114	0	19	4	1	68	0	70
Carp, raw	100 gm	127	0	18	6	1	66	0	49
Codfish, raw	100 gm	82	0	18	1	Trace	43	0	54
Eel, raw	100 gm	184	0	18	12	2	126	0	51
Haddock, raw	100 gm	87	0	19	1	Trace	57	0	68
Halibut, raw	100 gm	110	0	21	2	Trace	32	0	54
Mackerel, Atlantic, raw	100 gm	205	0	19	14	3	70	0	90
Mackerel, Pacific, raw	100 gm	157	0	20	8	2	47	0	86
Monkfish, raw	100 gm	76	0	14	2	Trace	25	0	18
Mullet, striped, raw	100 gm	117	0	19	4	1	49	0	65
Ocean perch, raw	100 gm	94	0	19	2	Trace	42	0	75
Perch, composite, raw	100 gm	91	0	19	1	Trace	90	0	62
Pike, Northern, raw	100 gm	88	0	19	1	Trace	39	0	39
Pike, walleye, raw	100 gm	93	0	19	1	Trace	86	0	51
Pollock, Atlantic, raw	100 gm	92	0	19	1	Trace	71	0	86

Pompano, raw	100 gm	164	0	18	9	4	50	0	65
Rockfish, composite, raw	100 gm	94	0	19	2	Trace	35	0	60
Roughy, orange, raw	100 gm	126	0	15	7	Trace	20	0	63
Salmon, Atlantic, raw	100 gm	142	0	20	6	1	55	0	44
Salmon, chinook, raw	100 gm	180	0	20	10	3	66	0	47
Salmon, chum, raw	100 gm	120	0	20	4	1	74	0	50
Salmon, coho, raw	100 gm	146	0	22	6	1	39	0	46
Salmon, pink, raw	100 gm	116	0	20	3	1	52	0	67
Salmon, pink, canned, undrained	100 gm	139	0	20	6	2	55	0	554
Salmon, sockeye, raw	100 gm	168	0	21	9	1	62	0	47
Salmon, sockeye, canned, drained	100 gm	153	0	20	7	2	44	0	538
Surimi	100 gm	99	7	15	1	Trace	30	0	143
Tuna, canned in oil, drained	100 gm	198	0	29	8	2	18	0	354
Tuna, canned in water, drained	100 gm	131	0	30	1	Trace	42	0	356

SHELLFISH

Crab, Alaska king, raw	100 gm	84	0	18	1	Trace	42	0	836
Crayfish, cooked, meat only	100 gm	114	0	24	1	Trace	178	0	68
Shrimp, composite, raw	100 gm	106	1	20	2	Trace	152	0	148
Clam, canned, drained	100 gm	148	5	26	2	Trace	67	0	112
Mussels, blue, raw	100 gm	86	4	12	2	Trace	28	0	286
Oysters, eastern, raw	100 gm	69	4	7	2	1	55	0	112
Scallops, composite, mixed species, raw	100 gm	88	2	17	1	Trace	33	0	161

DAIRY PRODUCTS

Food Item	Amount	Kcal	Cho (gm)	Pro (gm)	Fat (gm)	Sat Fat (gm)	Chol (mg)	Fiber (gm)	Na (mg)
Skim milk, fresh	1 cup	86	12	8	Trace	Trace	5	0	127
Skim milk, evaporated	1 cup	199	29	19	1	Trace	10	0	293
Ice milk, hard	½ cup	92	15	3	3	2	9	0	56
Ice milk, soft serve	½ cup	111	19	4	2	1	10	0	62
Sherbet, orange	½ cup	132	29	1	2	1	5	0	44
Milk, instant, dry nonfat	1 cup	243	35	24	Trace	Trace	12	0	373
Milk, instant, dry nonfat	½ cup	122	18	12	Trace	Trace	6	0	187
Milk, instant, dry nonfat	⅓ cup	80	12	8	Trace	Trace	4	0	123
Milk, instant, dry nonfat	¼ cup	61	9	6	Trace	Trace	3	0	93
Milk, instant, dry nonfat	1 tbsp	15	2	1	Trace	Trace	1	0	23
Buttermilk, dry	1 cup	464	59	41	7	4	83	0	620
Buttermilk, dry	½ cup	232	29	21	3	2	41	0	310
Buttermilk, dry	¼ cup	116	15	10	2	1	21	0	155
Buttermilk, dry	1 tbsp	29	4	3	Trace	Trace	5	0	39
Yogurt, plain, low-fat	½ cup	71	8	6	2	1	7	0	79
Yogurt, plain, fat-free	½ cup	64	9	7	Trace	Trace	2	0	86
Yogurt, frozen, composite of fruit flavors	½ cup	Varies greatly with brand							
Egg substitute, liquid	1 cup	100	4	5	0	0	0	0	320
Egg substitute, liquid	⅓ cup	33	1	1	0	0	0	0	106
Egg substitute, liquid	¼ cup	25	1	4	0	0	0	0	80
Egg substitute, liquid	1 tbsp	6	Trace	Trace	0	0	0	0	20

Egg white, large	1	17	Trace	4	0	0	0	0	55
Egg, large	1	75	1	6	5	2	213	0	63

CHEESE

Cottage with 2% milk	1 cup	203	8	31	4	3	18	0	918
Cottage with 1% milk	1 cup	163	6	28	2	1	9	0	918
Mozzarella, with part skim milk	1 oz	72	1	7	5	3	16	0	132
Neufchâtel	1 oz	9	1	3	7	4	22	0	113
Parmesan, grated	1 oz	111	1	10	7	5	19	0	454
Ricotta with part skim milk	1 cup	339	13	28	19	12	76	0	308
Cheddar, low-fat	1 oz	50	1	6	2	na	na	0	na
Cheese food	1 oz	93	2	6	7	4	18	0	337

NUTS AND SEEDS (unsalted)

Almonds, dry roasted	1 oz	167	7	5	15	1	0	3.2	3
Brazil nuts	1 oz	186	4	4	19	5	0	5.7	1
Cashews, dry roasted	1 oz	163	9	4	13	3	0	0.9	5
Chestnuts, European, raw, peel	1 oz	64	14	1	Trace	Trace	0	na	Trace
Filberts, dry roasted	1 oz	188	5	3	19	1	0	1.7	1
Macadamia nuts, dried	1 oz	199	4	2	21	3	0	2.6	1
Peanuts, oil roasted	1 oz	165	5	7	14	2	0	2.5	2
Peanuts, dry roasted	1 oz	166	6	7	14	2	0	2.3	2
Peanut butter, chunky, salted	2 tbsp	190	7	8	16	3	0	2.1	157

Food Item	Amount	Kcal	Cho (gm)	Pro (gm)	Fat (gm)	Sat Fat (gm)	Chol (mg)	Fiber (gm)	Na (mg)
Peanut butter, smooth, salted	2 tbsp	191	5	9	16	2.8	0	1.9	151
Pecan, dry roasted	1 oz	187	6	2	18	1	0	na	Trace
Pine nuts, dry, pignolia	1 oz	146	4	7	14	2	0	3	1
Pine nuts, piñon	1 oz	161	5	3	17	3	0	3	20
Pistachio nuts, dry roasted	1 oz	172	8	4	15	2	0	3.1	2
Walnuts, black, dry	1 oz	172	3	7	16	1	0	1.4	Trace
Walnuts, English, dry	1 oz	182	5	4	18	2	0	1.4	3
Pumpkin and squash seeds, shelled, roasted	1 oz	148	4	9	12	2	0	1.9	5
Sesame seeds, whole, roasted	1 oz	161	7	5	14	2	0	3.3	3
Sunflower seed kernels, dried	1 oz	162	5	6	14	1	0	3	1
FATS									
Margarine—corn oil, stick	½ cup	815	1	1	91	15	0	0	1070
	1 tbsp	102	Trace	Trace	11	2	0	0	134
Corn Oil	1 cup	1927	0	0	218	28	0	0	0
	1 tbsp	120	0	0	14	2	0	0	0
SUGARS									
Chocolate chips, semisweet	1 cup	811	108	7	50	30	0	na	19
	1 tbsp	51	7	Trace	3	2	0	na	1
Cocoa	1 tbsp	12	3	1	1	Trace	0	1.6	1

Food	Measure								
Honey	1 cup	1031	279	1	0	0	0	0	14
Marshmallows	1 oz	90	23	1	Trace	0	0	0	13
Sugar, brown, packed	1 cup	827	214	0	0	0	0	0	86
Sugar, granulated	1 cup	48	12	0	0	0	0	0	Trace
Sugar, powdered	1 cup	467	119	0	Trace	0	0	0	1
Syrup, corn, light	1 cup	925	251	0	0	0	0	0	397
Syrup, maple	1 cup	825	212	0	1	Trace	0	0	28
Syrup, sorghum	1 cup	957	247	0	0	0	0	0	26
Syrup, molasses, light	1 cup	872	226	0	Trace	Trace	0	0	121

CEREAL AND STARCHES

Food	Measure								
Barley, pearl, light	1 cup	704	155	20	2	Trace	0	31.2	18
Bran, wheat	1 cup	130	39	9	3	Trace	0	25.4	1
Breads, commercial									
French or Vienna	1 oz	78	15	2	1	Trace	0	0.8	173
rye	1 oz	73	14	2	1	Trace	0	1.8	187
white	1 oz	76	14	2	1	Trace	Trace	0.7	153
whole wheat	1 oz	70	13	3	1	Trace	Trace	2	149
Bread crumbs, dry	1 cup	427	78	14	6	1	Trace	4.5	931
Bulgur, dry, cracked wheat	1 cup	479	106	17	2	Trace	0	25.6	24
Cornmeal	1 cup	505	107	12	2	Trace	0	7.2	4
Flour									
all purpose	1 cup	455	95	13	1	Trace	0	3.4	3
bread	1 cup	495	99	16	2	Trace	0	2.3	3
cake	1 cup	395	85	9	1	Trace	0	na	2

Food Item	Amount	Kcal	Cho (gm)	Pro (gm)	Fat (gm)	Sat Fat (gm)	Chol (mg)	Fiber (gm)	Na (mg)
rye, light	1 cup	374	82	9	1	Trace	0	14.9	2
soybean, low-fat	1 cup	286	33	41	6	1	0	9	16
whole wheat or graham	1 cup	407	87	16	2	Trace	0	15.1	6
Graham crackers	1 dble	59	11	1	1	Trace	0	0.4	85
crumb	1 cup	480	88	8	8	na	na	3.6	720
Macaroni, dry	1 lb	1684	339	58	7	1	0	10.9	32
cooked	1 cup	197	40	7	1	Trace	0	2.2	1
Noodles, dry, commercial	1 lb	1730	323	64	19	4	431	12.3	95
cooked	1 cup	213	40	8	2	1	53	3.5	11
chow mein, canned	1 cup	237	26	4	14	2	0	1.8	197
Oat bran	1 cup	231	62	16	7	1	0	15	4
Oatmeal, dry	1 cup	311	54	13	5	1	0	8.4	3
Rice									
brown, raw	1 cup	685	143	15	5	1	0	6.5	13
brown, cooked	1 cup	216	45	5	2	Trace	0	3.3	10
white, instant, dry	1 cup	360	79	7	Trace	Trace	0	1.5	6
white, long-grain, raw	1 cup	675	148	13	1	Trace	0	1.9	9
white, long-grain, cooked	1 cup	265	57	6	1	Trace	0	0.7	4
wild, raw	1 cup	571	120	24	2	Trace	0	8.3	11
Rolled oats, dry	1 cup	311	54	13	5	1	0	8.4	3
Tapioca, dry, pearl	1 tbsp	35	9	Trace	Trace	Trace	0	na	45

CONDIMENTS

Food Item	Amount	Kcal	Cho (gm)	Pro (gm)	Fat (gm)	Sat Fat (gm)	Chol (mg)	Fiber (gm)	Na (mg)
Baking powder	1 tsp	2	1	0	0	0	0	0	489

Baking soda	1 tsp	0	0	0	0	0	0	1261
Cream of tartar	1 tsp	8	2	0	0	0	na	2
Chicken bouillon concentrate	1 cube	6	1	1	Trace	0	0	960
Catsup	1 tbsp	16	4	Trace	Trace	0	0.2	178
Mustard, prepared	1 tsp	4	Trace	Trace	Trace	0	na	65
Olives, green	1 oz	33	Trace	4	Trace	0	0.7	680
Olives, ripe	1 oz	33	2	3	Trace	0	0.9	247
Salt	1 tsp	0	0	0	0	0	0	2200
Sesame butter (tahini)	1 tbsp	89	3	8	1	0	1.4	17
Soy sauce	1 tbsp	10	2	Trace	0	0	0	1029
Vinegar	1 tbsp	2	1	0	0	0	0	Trace
Worcestershire sauce	1 tbsp	15	3	0	0	0	0	165
Yeast, active dry	1 pkt	21	3	3	Trace	0	1.9	4

Notes

1. Na means the information was not available.
2. Trace means a very small amount.
3. 100 grams is approximately 3½ ounces.
4. 100 grams of cooked chopped meat, fish, or poultry is generally ⅞ cup of the meat, fish, or poultry.

This information is an average of many samples of the item. If a can or package you want to use has a different nutritive analysis, substitute that information for this, but check the portion sizes carefully for the product you want to use.

4

Planning for Special Menus

Menus can be very helpful when you plan your diabetic diet. Actually, writing it down often helps clarify the relationship of menu items and makes it easier to see the whole thing in perspective.

It is important to eat everything listed in a diabetic daily meal plan. Changes should not be made without first checking with your doctor. You can sometimes save something from a meal for a snack or eat a little earlier or later than scheduled, but even that must be planned in advance.

When I am planning menus I always try to include the following:

Two or three servings of meat, poultry, or fish daily
Five or more servings of fruits and vegetables daily
Three or four servings of whole grain cereals daily
The appropriate amount of milk or other dairy products

Desserts and other less necessary extras are included only after all other nutritional needs have been met. Because fiber is helpful to most people, I also try to include as many foods rich in fiber as possible.

All of the necessary ingredients for a well-balanced menu are included in the diabetic daily food plan, so if you are following your food plan you needn't worry about having a balanced diet. I often hear people tell diabetics how well they look, and I think to myself that they would also look that good if they consumed as good a diet as most diabetics do.

When I'm helping diabetics plan their menus, we generally

start out with the following guidelines. However, your own doctor, dietitian, or nutritionist may develop a different plan for you depending on your age, sex, and physical activity.

BASIC DAILY FOOD EXCHANGE ALLOWANCE AT DIFFERENT CALORIC LEVELS

Exchanges	1200	1400	1600	1800	2000
Breakfast					
Carbohydrate group					
Starch	2	2	2	2	2
Fruit	1	1	2	2	2
Skim milk	1	1	1	1	1
Meat group	–	–	–	–	–
Fat group	1	1	1	1	1
Lunch or dinner at noon					
Carbohydrate group					
Starch	2	2	2	2	3
Fruit	1	1	1	1	1
Skim milk	–	–	–	½	½
Meat group (lean)	3	3	3	3	3
Vegetables	1	1	1	1	1
Fat group	1	1	1	2	2
Dinner or supper in the evening					
Carbohydrate group					
Starch	1	2	2	3	3
Fruit	1	1	1	1	1
Skim milk	–	–	–	½	½
Meat group (lean)	2	2	3	3	3
Vegetables	1	2	2	2	2
Fat group	–	1	1	1	1
Evening snack					
Carbohydrate group					
Starch	–	–	1	1	1
Fruit	1	1	1	1	2
Skim milk	1	1	1	1	1
Fat group	–	–	–	–	1

This menu plan is based on the groups in the new exchange lists. Please remember that not all of your starch exchanges should be used for bread. Starch exchanges should also be used for starchy vegetables and items from the other food groups such as the Other Carbohydrates group or high-fiber bran muffins; of course, you can use part of them for some simple desserts such as ice milk, frozen yogurt, or angel food cake.

The number of exchanges for each diet is based on the following table, which lists the number of exchanges for different caloric levels and the percentages of carbohydrate (CHO), protein (PRO), and fat (FAT) included at the different levels. As you see, the table follows the high-carbohydrate, low-fat, and moderate-protein diet recommended by the American Diabetic Association, Inc., and the American Dietetic Association.

After the basic menu is planned, it must be extended to provide a diet modification at each level of the diabetic diet. I have extended the following menus as I would have extended them at work, with a column for each of the levels of the diet. To read the menu, find the diet heading that you need and then plan to use everything in that column for your diet for that meal. Some foods are free and you can use as much of them as you like— that is indicated, as well as the portion size for each item.

I hope you will find the following menus useful and that they will help you find ways to include new items—especially the recipes in this book—in your own diet plans.

MENU PLAN FOR DIABETIC DIETS

Exchanges	1200	1400	1600	1800	2000
Carbohydrate group					
Starch	5	6	7	8	9
Fruit	4	4	5	5	6
Skim milk	2	2	2	3	3
Meat group (lean)	5	5	6	6	6
Fat group	2	3	3	4	5
Vegetables	2	3	3	3	3
Total calories	1,235	1,385	1,580	1,795	1,980
Percentages					
CHO	57	57	55	58	58
PRO	24	23	23	22	21
FAT	19	20	22	20	21
Total percent	100	100	100	100	100

New Year's Day

Dinner at noon

Fruit Soup * *with melba toast rounds*
Baked ham
Escalloped potatoes
Creole Green Beans *
Tossed vegetable salad with Vinaigrette Dressing *
Stewed Cranberries *
Relish tray (dill pickles, celery, and carrot sticks)
Skim milk, coffee, or tea
Lemon Pie *

Food Item	1200	1400	1600	1800	2000
Fruit Soup	½ cup at all levels of the diet				
Melba toast rounds					5
Baked ham	3 ounces at all levels of the diet				
Escalloped potatoes	½ cup at all levels of the diet				
Creole Green Beans	½ cup at all levels of the diet				
Tossed vegetable salad	as desired at all levels of the diet				
Vinaigrette Dressing	2 tablespoons at all levels of the diet				
Stewed Cranberries	½ cup at all levels of the diet				
Relish tray	as desired at all levels of the diet				
Skim milk				4 oz	4 oz
Margarine				1 tsp	1 tsp
Lemon Pie	⅛ pie at all levels of the diet				
Coffee or tea	as desired at all levels of the diet				

Menu notes: Beans were included because it is considered lucky to eat them on New Year's Day in some parts of the country.

*See Index.

Labor Day Picnic

at noon

Hamburger on a bun with lettuce, catsup,
mustard, and pickle relish
Potato Salad*
Pickled Vegetables*
Tossed salad with Vinaigrette Dressing*
Cubed fresh watermelon
Skim milk, coffee, tea, or Sparkling Punch*
Buttermilk Cookies*

Food Item	1200	1400	1600	1800	2000
Hamburger, raw weight	4 ounces at all levels of the diet				
Hamburger bun	1 small at all levels of the diet				
Margarine				1 tsp	1 tsp
Lettuce	as desired at all levels of the diet				
Catsup	1 tablespoon at all levels of the diet				
Mustard	1 teaspoon at all levels of the diet				
Pickle relish	1 teaspoon at all levels of the diet				
Potato Salad	½ cup at all levels of the diet				
Pickled Vegetables	½ cup at all levels of the diet				
Tossed vegetable salad	as desired at all levels of the diet				
Vinaigrette Dressing	2 tablespoons at all levels of the diet				
Cubed watermelon	1 cup at all levels of the diet				
Skim milk				4 oz	4 oz
Buttermilk cookies					2
Coffee, tea, or Sparkling Punch	as desired at all levels of the diet				

Menu notes: The tossed salad should be something beautiful, with fresh vegetables that are low in carbohydrate so everyone can eat all they want of it. It might include broccoli spears, cauliflower slices, mushrooms, green peppers julienne, a little red cabbage—anything that is colorful, fresh, and low in calories—along with fresh crisp lettuce or other greens such as escarole or spinach.

*See Index.

Thanksgiving

Dinner at noon

Tomato Bouillon*
Roast Turkey*
Bread Dressing*
Turkey Gravy*
Baked sweet potato
Broccoli
Cranberry Gelatin Salad* with Kay's Cooked Dressing*
Relish plate (green pepper strips, dill pickles,
carrot and celery strips)
Skim milk, coffee, or tea
Pumpkin Scotch Pie* with Whipped Topping*

Food Item	1200	1400	1600	1800	2000
Tomato Bouillon	1 cup at all levels of the diet				
Roast Turkey	3 ounces cooked weight at all levels of the diet				
Bread Dressing					1 square
Turkey Gravy	¼ cup at all levels of the diet				
Baked sweet potato	1 small at all levels of the diet				
Broccoli	½ cup at all levels of the diet				
Cranberry Gelatin Salad	1 square at all levels of the diet				
Kay's Cooked Dressing	1 tablespoon at all levels of the diet				
Relish plate	as desired at all levels of the diet				
Margarine				1 tsp	
Skim milk				4 oz	4 oz
Pumpkin Scotch Pie	⅛ pie at all levels of the diet				
Whipped Topping	2 tablespoons at all levels of the diet				
Coffee or tea	as desired at all levels of the diet				
Fruit exchange for afternoon snack	1 at all levels of the diet				

*See Index.

Christmas Day

Dinner at noon

Hot Beef Bouillon*
Roast Beef*
Mashed potatoes
Brown Gravy*
Stewed Cranberries*
Cauliflower
Relish plate (Mrs. Riley's Pickles*, carrot and celery sticks)
Banana gelatin with Kay's Cooked Dressing*
Small plain roll
Margarine
Skim milk, coffee, or tea
Strawberry Chiffon Pie*

Food Item	1200	1400	1600	1800	2000
Hot Beef Bouillon	1 cup at all levels of the diet				
Roast Beef	3 ounces at all levels of the diet				
Mashed potatoes	½ cup at all levels of the diet				
Brown Gravy	¼ cup at all levels of the diet				
Stewed Cranberries	½ cup at all levels of the diet				
Cauliflower	½ cup at all levels of the diet				
Relish plate	as desired at all levels of the diet				
Banana gelatin	1 serving at all levels of the diet				
Kay's Cooked Dressing	1 tablespoon at all levels of the diet				
Small plain roll					1
Margarine				1 tsp	1 tsp
Skim milk				4 oz	4 oz
Strawberry Chiffon Pie	⅛ pie at all levels of the diet				
Coffee or tea	as desired at all levels of the diet				

Menu notes: Prepare banana gelatin by using ½ banana per person in Fruit-Flavored Gelatin.*

Use recipe for Beef Broth* to prepare Beef Bouillon.

*See Index.

Breakfast

Orange or grapefruit juice
Cereal
Skim milk
Bran Muffin*
Coffee or tea

Food Item	1200	1400	1600	1800	2000
Orange or grapefruit juice	4 ounces at all levels of the diet				
½ cup cooked or ¾ cup unsweetened prepared cereal	1 serving at all levels of the diet				
Skim milk	8 ounces at all levels of the diet				
Bran Muffin	1 at all levels of the diet				
Coffee or tea	as desired at all levels of the diet				
Fruit exchange for morning snack			1	1	1

Menu notes: The Bran Muffin may also be saved for a morning snack, if desired. If you choose a bran muffin that includes only ½ fat exchange, the remaining ½ fat exchange could be margarine or ½ serving of Cinnamon Spread.*

*See Index.

Breakfast

Orange juice
Sliced fresh peaches
Shredded wheat
Cinnamon Roll*
Margarine
Skim milk
Coffee or tea

Food Item	1200	1400	1600	1800	2000
Orange juice			4 oz	4 oz	4 oz
Sliced unsweetened fresh, frozen, or canned peaches	½ cup at all levels of the diet				
Shredded wheat	1 large biscuit at all levels of the diet				
Cinnamon Roll	1 at all levels of the diet				
Margarine	½ teaspoon at all levels of the diet				
Skim milk	8 ounces at all levels of the diet				
Coffee or tea	as desired at all levels of the diet				

Menu notes: 1 slice whole wheat toast and 1 teaspoon margarine may be substituted for the Cinnamon Roll and ½ teaspoon margarine.

*See Index.

Vegetable Beef Soup

evening

Vegetable Beef Soup* with melba toast rounds
Lettuce salad with Spicy Tomato Dressing*
Mrs. Riley's Pickles*
Plain roll
Vanilla ice milk
Chocolate Sauce*
Unsweetened pineapple
Skim milk
Coffee or tea

Food Item	1200	1400	1600	1800	2000
Vegetable Beef Soup	¾ cup	¾ cup	1 cup	1 cup	1 cup
Melba toast rounds	5	8	8	8	8
Lettuce salad	as desired at all levels of the diet				
Spicy Tomato Dressing	2 tablespoons at all levels of the diet				
Mrs. Riley's Pickles	up to ¼ cup at all levels of the diet				
Small plain roll				1	1
Vanilla ice milk		½ cup	½ cup	½ cup	½ cup
Chocolate Sauce		2 tbsp	2 tbsp	2 tbsp	2 tbsp
Unsweetened pineapple	½ cup at all levels of the diet				
Skim milk				4 oz	4 oz
Coffee or tea	as desired at all levels of the diet				

*See Index.

Soup and Sandwich

at noon

Tomato Bouillon* with melba toast rounds
Chicken Sandwich Spread* on Rich Whole Wheat Bread*
Relish plate (sliced dill pickles,
green pepper sticks, radishes)
Three-Bean Salad*
Fresh pear
Skim milk, coffee, or tea

Food Item	1200	1400	1600	1800	2000
Tomato Bouillon	1 cup at all levels of the diet				
Melba toast rounds					5
Chicken Sandwich Spread	⅓ cup at all levels of the diet				
Rich Whole Wheat Bread	2 slices at all levels of the diet				
Miracle Whip salad dressing		2 tsp	2 tsp	2 tsp	4 tsp	4 tsp
Lettuce for sandwich	as desired at all levels of the diet				
Relish plate	as desired at all levels of the diet				
Three-Bean Salad	½ cup at all levels of the diet				
Pear	1 small fresh or canned at all levels of the diet				
Skim milk				4 oz	4 oz
Coffee or tea	as desired at all levels of the diet				

Menu notes: Three ounces of sliced turkey or chicken with fat and gristle removed may be substituted for the Chicken Sandwich Spread, if desired. Two teaspoons of Miracle Whip salad dressing is equal to 1 teaspoon margarine; margarine may be substituted, if desired.

*See Index.

Salad Luncheon

at noon

Hot Beef Bouillon* with melba toast rounds
Chef's Salad*
Raisin Bread*
Cinnamon Spread*
Coleslaw*
Skim milk
Pineapple Gelatin*
Whipped Topping*
Coffee or tea

Food Item	1200	1400	1600	1800	2000
Hot Beef Bouillon	as desired at all levels of the diet				
Melba toast rounds					5
Chef's Salad with 1 extra ounce meat or chicken	1 serving at all levels of the diet				
Raisin Bread	1 slice at all levels of the diet				
Cinnamon Spread or	2 tsp	2 tsp	2 tsp	1½ T	1½ T
Margarine	1 tsp	1 tsp	1 tsp	2 tsp	2 tsp
Coleslaw	½ cup at all levels of the diet				
Skim milk				4 oz	4 oz
Pineapple Gelatin	1 serving at all levels of the diet				
Whipped Topping	2 tablespoons at all levels of the diet				
Coffee or tea	as desired at all levels of the diet				

Menu notes: Prepare Pineapple Gelatin using ½ cup crushed, canned unsweetened pineapple per serving in Fruit-Flavored Gelatin* or sugar-free gelatin. As much gelatin as desired may be used per serving.

Use recipe for Beef Broth* to prepare Beef Bouillon.

Raisin Bread may be toasted or served at room temperature.

*See Index.

Fish for Dinner or Supper

evening

Baked Halibut Steak* with Tartar Sauce*
Broccoli Rice Casserole*
Steamed carrots
Baked potato
Plain roll
Unsweetened fresh or frozen strawberries
Skim milk, coffee, or tea

Food Item	1200	1400	1600	1800	2000
Baked Halibut Steak, cooked weight	2 oz	2 oz	3 oz	3 oz	3 oz
Tartar Sauce	up to 2 tablespoons at all levels of the diet				
Broccoli Rice Casserole		½ cup	½ cup	½ cup	½ cup
Steamed carrots	½ cup				
Baked potato	1 sm	1 med	1 med	1 med	1 med
Small plain roll				1	1
Unsweetened fresh or frozen strawberries	1¼ cups at all levels of the diet				
Skim milk				4 oz	4 oz
Coffee or tea	as desired at all levels of the diet				

Menu notes: Strawberries may be molded in unsweetened fruit gelatin, if desired, at all levels of the diet.

Use recipe for Baked Fish Steak* to prepare Baked Halibut Steak.

*See Index.

Minestrone Soup

evening

Minestrone Soup* with melba toast rounds
Coleslaw*
Blueberries or blackberries
Plain roll
Key Lime Pie*
Skim milk, coffee, or tea

Food Item	1200	1400	1600	1800	2000
Minestrone Soup	1 cup at all levels of the diet				
Melba toast rounds	2	5	5	5	5
Extra ounce(s) of lean meat to be added to each serving of soup	1 oz	1 oz	2 oz	2 oz	2 oz
Coleslaw	½ cup at all levels of the diet				
Unsweetened fresh or frozen blueberries or blackberries	¾ cup at all levels of the diet				
Small plain roll				1	1
Key Lime Pie		⅛ pie	⅛ pie	⅛ pie	⅛ pie
Skim milk				4 oz	4 oz
Coffee or tea	as desired at all levels of the diet				

*See Index.

Breakfast

Orange juice
Cereal
Skim milk
Coffee or tea

Morning Coffee with Friends

Chocolate Nut Bread*
Pastel Cookie*
Fresh fruit cup with Orange Liqueur*
Coffee or tea

Food Item	1200	1400	1600	1800	2000
Breakfast					
Orange juice			4 oz	4 oz	4 oz
½ cup cooked or ¾ cup unsweetened prepared cereal		1 serving at all levels of the diet			
Skim milk		8 oz at all levels of the diet			
Coffee or tea		as desired at all levels of the diet			

Morning Coffee with Friends	
Chocolate Nut Bread	½ slice at all levels of the diet
Pastel Cookie	1 at all levels of the diet
Fresh fruit cup	½ cup fruit with ½ teaspoon Orange Liqueur at all levels of the diet
Coffee or tea	as desired at all levels of the diet

Menu notes: The Chocolate Nut Bread and 1 Pastel Cookie give you 1 starch and 1 fat exchange. You can substitute any other foods that total 1 starch and 1 fat exchange for your morning coffee, if desired.

*See Index.

I have included the Morning Coffee with Friends and the Lunch or Dinner (and) Afternoon Tea menus to show that you can save food from a meal to use as a snack in the morning, afternoon, or evening. However, this is meant to be a guide and should be changed according to your own schedule. Non–insulin-dependent persons have more leeway in their diet than do insulin-dependent persons. If you are insulin dependent, you should check with your doctor or dietitian before attempting any drastic reduction in any of your menus.

Lunch or Dinner

at noon

Broiled round steak
Stir-Fry Tomatoes*
Lettuce salad with Creamy Garlic Dressing*
Applesauce
Skim milk, coffee, or tea

Afternoon Tea

Devil's Food Cake* with Fluffy Frosting*
High-Fiber Cookies*
Graham crackers
Sparkling Punch*
Coffee or tea

Food Item	1200	1400	1600	1800	2000
Lunch or Dinner at Noon					
Broiled round steak	3 ounces cooked weight at all levels of the diet				
Stir-Fry Tomatoes	about ¾ cup at all levels of the diet				
Lettuce salad	as desired at all levels of the diet				
Creamy Garlic Dressing	up to 2 tablespoons at all levels of the diet				
Unsweetened applesauce	½ cup at all levels of the diet				
Skim milk				4 oz	4 oz
Coffee or tea	as desired at all levels of the diet				

*See Index.

(Afternoon Tea is continued on page 76.)

Food Item	1200	1400	1600	1800	2000
Afternoon Tea					
Devil's Food Cake	1 square at all levels of the diet				
Fluffy Frosting	1½ tablespoons at all levels of the diet				
High-Fiber Cookies				1	1
Graham crackers	3	3	3		3
Sparkling Punch	as desired at all levels of the diet				
Coffee or tea	as desired at all levels of the diet				

Menu notes: This menu does not have to be followed exactly but can serve as a guide. You can substitute other foods with the same exchange values for any food in the menu or you can add free foods such as a relish plate of free food in the afternoon as long as you stay within the guidelines for your diet.

It is easier to control the menu when you serve it in your own home, but you can remember food exchanges and maintain your own diet if you are careful when you go to parties.

If finger sandwiches are served, pick ones with a plain filling and consider each finger sandwich as ½ bread exchange if it is a double sandwich with the crusts trimmed off and with a plain filling.

5

Cholesterol

Research indicates that about 75 percent of all diabetics die of atherosclerosis or related diseases. Since the American Medical Association, the American Diabetes Association, the American Dietetic Association, and the American Heart Association all stress the importance of keeping your cholesterol count below 200, along with regular exercise and a sensible diet, we need to make every effort to do so, and a good way to help lower your blood cholesterol level is to eat less saturated fatty acids and control your weight.

It isn't hard to follow a low-cholesterol diet, and it is simple to plan your diabetic diet using low-cholesterol guidelines. They both emphasize decreased sugar and fat with a moderate amount of meat, fruit and vegetables, and complex carbohydrates.

I have been following low-cholesterol guidelines for years since our doctor put my husband Chuck on a low-cholesterol diet when we were first married. Since I liked the food prepared according to the low-cholesterol guidelines, I always ate what I had prepared for him and didn't need to change to a low-cholesterol diet after I became a diabetic.

Because it is important for anyone with diabetes to follow a low-cholesterol diet, I am including the following information from the American Heart Association's brochure *The American Heart Association Diet: An Eating Plan for Healthy Americans*.

> Reducing your "controllable" risk factors—those you can change—may prevent a heart attack in the future.

Better food habits can help you reduce one of the major risk factors for heart attack—high blood cholesterol. This eating plan from the American Heart Association describes the latest advice of medical and nutrition experts. The best way to help lower your blood cholesterol level is to eat less saturated fatty acids and cholesterol, and control your weight. The AHA Diet gives you an easy-to-follow guide to eating with your heart in mind.

The eating plan is based on these AHA dietary guidelines:

- Total fat intake should be less than 30 percent of calories.
- Saturated fatty acid intake should be less than 10 percent of calories.
- Polyunsaturated fatty acid intake should be no more than 10 percent of calories.
- Monounsaturated fatty acids make up the rest of total fat intake, about 10 to 15 percent of total calories.
- Cholesterol intake should be no more than 300 milligrams per day.
- Sodium intake should be no more than 3000 milligrams (3 grams) per day.

. . .

It's important to select a variety of foods within each food group. . . .

If you eat the *lower* number of servings from each food group, you will get enough protein, vitamins and minerals—nutrients that your body needs each day. Eat moderate amounts of foods from the meat, fish, poultry, egg, and fat groups. You may choose more servings of foods from the other groups if you don't need to lose weight or if you wish to gain weight.

The American Heart Association suggests this plan for all healthy Americans two years of age and older. Growing children and teenagers have special needs. You must be sure they get enough energy (calories) and nutrients each day. If you or others in your family are pregnant or breastfeeding, or have a medical disorder such as diabetes, talk to your doctor, a Registered Dietitian, or a licensed dietitian or nutritionist about your special dietary needs.

EATING PLAN TIPS

To control the amount and kind of fat, saturated fatty acids, and dietary cholesterol you eat:

- Eat no more than 6 ounces (cooked) per day of lean meat, fish, and skinless poultry.
- Try main dishes featuring pasta, rice, beans, and/or vegetables. Or create "low-meat" dishes by mixing these foods with small amounts of lean meat, poultry, or fish.
- The approximately 5 to 8 teaspoon servings of fats and oils per day may be used for cooking and baking, and in salad dressings and spreads.
- Use cooking methods that require little or no fat— boil, broil, bake, roast, poach, steam, sauté, stir-fry, or microwave.
- Trim off the fat you can see before cooking meat and poultry. Drain off all fat after browning. Chill soups and stews after cooking so you can remove the hardened fat from the top.
- The 3 to 4 egg yolks per week included in your eating plan may be used alone or in cooking and baking (including store-bought products).
- Limit your use of organ meats such as liver, brains, chitterlings, kidney, heart, gizzard, sweetbreads, and port maws.
- Choose skim or 1% fat milk and nonfat or low-fat yogurt and cheeses.

To round out the rest of your eating plan:

- Eat 5 or more servings of fruits or vegetables per day.
- Eat 6 or more servings of breads, cereals or grains per day.

We as diabetics have very little trouble following the low-cholesterol diet because it fits into our diabetic diet perfectly. We will eat the exchanges allowed on our diet, which will almost automatically give us the 6 or less ounces of meat, poultry, or fish per day, and our exchanges will give us the right amount of fruits and vegetables, and most of us have at least 6 bread/starch exchanges per day. Of course a diabetic diet doesn't eliminate coconut and coconut oil or anything with palm oil in it, but since that is a part of the low-cholesterol diet, we only have to real labels carefully to be sure that we don't buy anything containing coconut, coconut oil, or palm oil.

If you choose your meat exchanges from the "lean meat" exchanges as shown in Chapter 2, you will have no trouble choosing the right meat, fish, or poultry entrées. The high-fat and even the medium-fat exchanges contain too much fat for a good low-cholesterol diet.

The American Heart Association, the American Dietetic Association, and the American Diabetes Association have all contributed background information for the following guidelines to help you keep the fat content of your diabetic diet at a manageable level.

- Bake, roast, or grill meats rather than fry them with added fat.
- Use a nonstick cooking spray or a nonstick pan to brown or fry these foods.
- Trim off all visible fat before cooking.
- Do not add flour, bread crumbs, coating mixes, or fat to the foods when preparing them.
- Weigh meat after removing bones and fat and after it is cooked. Three ounces of cooked meat is about equal to 4 ounces of raw meat.
- Organ meats are very high in cholesterol. However, liver is rich in iron and vitamins, and a 3-ounce serving is OK about once a month.
- Use whole turkeys that have not been injected with fat or broth. Remove the skin and fat from poultry before it is cooked. However, if you are roasting a chicken or turkey,

the skin can be left on during baking to help keep the meat from getting too dry while it is cooking. The skin should be removed before the meat is carved.

- If dried beans, peas, or lentils are used as a meat substitute, 1 cup of them cooked provides 2 starches, 1 lean meat exchange, and 3 grams of fiber.
- Shrimp and crayfish are higher in cholesterol than most other types of fish, but lower in fat and cholesterol than most meat and poultry. I suggest that you restrict yourself to one serving of them per month.

Some examples of meat portions are:

- 2 ounces (2 meat exchanges) are equal to 1 small chicken leg or thigh or ½ cup cottage cheese or tuna.
- 3 ounces (3 meat exchanges) are equal to 1 medium pork chop, 1 small hamburger, ½ of a whole chicken breast, 1 unbreaded 4-ounce fish fillet, or cooked meat about the size of a deck of cards.

Of course you know that whole eggs or egg yolks are restricted to 3 per week because of their high cholesterol count (213 mg each), and remember you should count any egg yolks used in cooking or in purchased, prepared baked items in your total for the week. I haven't used any egg yolks in this book. I have used only egg whites or liquid egg substitute, so you can feel free to use your egg allotment as you see fit. If you want to use your egg allotment in baked goods, substitute 1 large whole egg for ¼ cup liquid egg substitute or 2 large egg whites.

You should also watch the fat content of dairy products. It is best to choose 1 percent milk, nonfat or low-fat dry milk powder, evaporated skim milk, buttermilk made from skim milk, and low-fat or nonfat yogurt, fresh or frozen. There are also some low-fat cheeses such as dry-curd, skim, or low-fat cottage cheese, and natural or processed cheese with no more than 5 grams of fat per ounce.

Vegetables and fruits are high in vitamins and fiber. They contain no cholesterol and are low in fat, calories, and sodium. You should include at least one serving high in vitamin C such as orange, tomato, or grapefruit juice, citrus fruits, or tomatoes every day and one serving of foods high in Vitamin A such as broccoli, squash, or other dark-colored vegetables several times weekly according to your diet plan.

Breads, cereals, pasta, and starchy vegetables are high in complex carbohydrates and low in fat and cholesterol. They are also a good source of Vitamin B, iron, and fiber and aren't all that high in calories. It's the fatty sauces we add to them that make them high in calories. Good choices in this group include:

- Low-fat breads such as whole wheat, rye, raisin, and white. Italian and French breads are traditionally made with very little fat.
- Low-fat rolls such as English muffins, pita bread, frankfurter and hamburger rolls, and bagels, except for egg bagels.
- Low-fat crackers and snacks such as saltines, ginger snaps, matzos, bread sticks, melba toast, flat bread, and pretzels.
- Yeast or quick breads made at home using approved ingredients such as instant nonfat dry milk, egg whites or liquid egg substitute, or vegetable oil or margarine.
- Hot or cold cereals, all kinds except granola-type cereals with coconut, coconut oil, or palm oil.
- Rice and pasta of all kinds except those made with egg yolks. Read the labels when purchasing them to be sure they have only approved ingredients. Try to get them with whole wheat flour and no egg yolks.

Fats and oils are high in vitamins A and E, but are also high in fat and calories. (There are 9 calories per gram of fat and only 4 calories per gram of carbohydrate and protein.) Remember to count the hidden fats in bakery products and snack foods, in cooking, and in vegetables and breads. Try to use cooking styles that use little or no fat, and use a nonstick frying pan that only needs to be brushed with fat or sprayed with vegetable pan spray. The following guidelines should help you choose the best sources of fat for your diet.

• *Avoid* solid fats and shortenings, butter, bacon fat, lard, salt pork, ham hocks, meat fat and drippings, shortening, and margarines based on lard or other unacceptable fats.

• *Avoid* chocolate (cocoa is OK), coconut, coconut oil, palm oil, and palm kernel oil. These are often used in bakery products, nondairy creamers, whipped toppings, candy, and commercially fried foods. Read your labels carefully to see if the product includes any of these ingredients.

• *Use* light, tube, or soft margarine based on safflower, sunflower, corn, or soybean oil. Partially hydrogenated soybean or cottonseed oils may also be used but use regular stick margarine, not soft or light margarine, in recipes that include stick margarine.

Oils in order of their increasing saturated fatty acid content are: safflower, sunflower, corn, and partially hydrogenated soybean and cottonseed oils.

Seeds and nuts may be used except cashew, macadamia, and pistachio. Peanut butter may be used within the limits of your diabetic diet but remember it is very high in fat.

Most of our diabetic diets allow for snacks at some time or other, and it is a good idea to follow our low-cholesterol diet as well as our diabetic diet when we are eating those snacks. The following lists, which are based on information from the American Heart Association, should help you make wise choices.

First-choice items that are low in calories include raw vegetables, fresh fruit, fruit canned or frozen without sugar, sugar-free gelatin, tea, coffee, cocoa powder, and sugar-free soft drinks.

Second-choice foods that are low in saturated fat and fairly low in calories include dried fruit, seeds, approved nuts, plain popcorn, pretzels, crackers, cookies, or cake without egg yolks, sherbet, ice milk, frozen or fruited low-fat yogurt, and angel food cake.

Other choices include diabetic desserts made with little or no sugar (see Introduction) and low-fat milk products.

Alcoholic beverages should be consumed in moderation and within the framework of your diabetic diet.

Avoid any foods not acceptable on your diabetic diet including baked goods and mixes that you think might include forbidden ingredients (always read the ingredient list, if available), coconut, high-fat foods such as deep-fried chips and rich crackers, ice cream, cream, or whole milk, and desserts or snacks containing cheese.

If you are on a low-cholesterol diet, you may use any of the recipes in this book, secure in the knowledge that they are suitable for a low-cholesterol diet as well as your diabetic diet.

6

Equipment and Ingredients

EQUIPMENT

Having and using the right equipment is a plus when you are preparing your low-cholesterol diabetic diet.

Knives

Sharp knives to prepare fruits and vegetables and to cut away all visible fat from meat and chicken are important—and I also like a good chopping knife and a knife with a serrated edge for slicing bread. One knife that has a specialized use is a rather round, thin, serrated knife, which is excellent for cutting fresh tomatoes. I don't use it for anything except slicing tomatoes but it is wonderful to have when I need it. A good boning knife and a knife for slicing are also important. If you have any doubt about the kinds of knives that you want, any good hardware store can recommend the types and kinds of knives that would be helpful to you.

Scales

I also find I need two different scales—a small one for weighing diabetic portions and a large one for weighing pounds and ounces when I'm cooking. I don't believe that diabetics should weigh everything they eat, but it is a good idea to weigh out portions occasionally to keep the feel of what is correct. So many times people will give themselves smaller portions than they are allowed because they think that something weighs more than it actually does.

Measuring Cups and Spoons

Standardized measuring cups and spoons are also essential equipment. I like to keep several sets of measuring cups and spoons on hand so I can cook as I like without stopping to wash them. One set of measuring cups that I particularly like has ⅔-cup and ¾-cup measures in addition to the standard cup, ½-cup, ⅓-cup, and ¼-cup measures. Some sets have a coffee measure that holds 2 tablespoons and I find that very handy for measuring 2 tablespoons of an ingredient. It is not a good idea to ever use regular kitchen spoons for measuring, so please don't use them. Most teaspoons hold about 1½ times the amount that measuring teaspoons hold and can wreak havoc with a cake or other baked item when substituted for a measuring spoon. Two-cup measures are also helpful, and I don't think I could do without my quart measure. If I have 2 cups of flour and some salt and baking powder as ingredients, I measure the flour in the quart measure up to the 2-cup line, and then add the salt and baking powder and stir it well before adding it to the other ingredients. Of course I also have the large glass measure for use in the microwave, and that also is a must—you can use it for so many things in the microwave as well as using it for measuring liquids.

Pots and Pans

There is such a variety of pots and pans that it is hard to recommend any one kind to the exclusion of the others. I like to use stainless steel with a copper bottom or core. However, I also have a set of glass pots and pans that I enjoy using, and I wouldn't want to try to get along without nonstick pans. I like to use them for baking as well as frying. They need very little fat for frying and are so easy to clean that it is a pleasure to use them. I keep a special pan for crepes and blintzes, several large pans for soups and spaghetti sauce, and, of course, I also use my iron frying pan, which I've had for years. If you are happy with the pans you have now, don't feel you need to change them, but if you don't have nonstick frying and baking pans, do try them if you need to replace any of your pans.

Casseroles

Casseroles are important and I use a variety of them—mostly Corning Ware and Pyrex, although there are some beautiful ones in enamelware these days. My friend Jessie Johnson was a home economist for Corning for many years and I have a rather complete set of Corning Ware because of her influence. Whenever something new came out and she told me about it, I generally went right out and bought it; I must say I've never been disappointed in any of it.

I like Corning Ware for refrigerator storage and use it a lot; but I also have a set of stainless steel refrigerator dishes with lids that are very handy, and I couldn't be without my stainless steel mixing bowls. My husband Chuck gave me the set of mixing bowls as an Easter gift the first year we were married. Though I thought it was a very unusual gift, they have been so handy that I wouldn't ever be without them now.

Thermometers

I use thermometers frequently. I have a good meat thermometer for testing roasts and turkey, a candy thermometer I use when I make candy for my family and friends, and now I have a yeast thermometer for testing the temperature of the liquid in which I dissolve the yeast when I'm making bread. If you can't find these thermometers at your local hardware store, try a good kitchen supply shop, which can get them for you if they don't have them in stock.

Mixers

One of my favorite pieces of equipment is my KitchenAid mixer. I have the largest size, which I think is best. Frances Nielsen has the middle size and she thinks that hers is the greatest, so I'm sure they are both wonderful. Several recipes in this book use the dough hook attachment on a mixer. If you don't have a dough hook on your mixer, use the mixer as long as you can and then pour the batter into a mixing bowl and do the rest of the bread mixing by hand. If you don't have a dough hook attachment for your mixer, I suggest you get one; you'll never be sorry that you did because it makes bread baking at home a cinch.

Food Processors

A food processor is also a big help. A low-cholesterol diabetic diet includes a lot of vegetables and fruits, and the food processor saves so much time preparing them that I don't know how we ever got along without one. I don't use it for a tablespoonful of chopped onions or other small quantities of food. However, I do use it to chop a cup or so of onions or celery to keep on hand in the refrigerator, because I use them so often.

Microwaves

I like to use a microwave oven to prepare vegetables. Most vegetables taste better, at least to us, when prepared in the microwave. You aren't losing a lot of vitamins and minerals in the water as you do when you cook the vegetables conventionally. I know that home economists and dietitians always tell you to save the vegetable cooking water for soups and sauces, but how many people actually bother to do that? I use the microwave oven to do so many things. I don't cook a lot of meat in it (although the makers say that you can) but I do use it to melt margarine, reheat foods, cook casseroles and vegetables, and bake apples and other fruits. I even use it to dehydrate parsley, and to dry bread when I want to make dry bread crumbs in a hurry.

Chopping Boards

A good chopping board is a must. There are some very good plastic ones that don't dull the knife when you use them. They should be dishwasher-safe, easy to wipe off, and large enough to be efficient. I know that wooden chopping boards are hard to keep clean but sometimes they are worth it. I have a big bread board that Chuck made for his mother when he was taking woodworking in school; she used it for many years before I got it. It is such a help when I'm making bread, rolling out cookies, or shaping a coffee cake that I wouldn't be without it even if it is too big to fit into the dishwasher, and I do have to scrub it by hand whenever I use it.

Steamer

I like to use a stainless-steel steamer with a double-boiler top and a steamer basket. Steamers help preserve vitamins and minerals in vegetables. Find a handy-sized one that will hold a bunch of broccoli or enough carrots for two meals (I like them hot the first meal and cold with diabetic dressing the second meal). It is best to get one that will steam only the amount of food you need. There is no sense using a big one and wasting the extra heat and water.

Dishwasher

I like my dishwasher, but the only way I can see how it helps my diet is that it washes all of those dishes and pots and pans that I get dirty when I'm cooking. It really isn't essential—in fact I suppose it could be called a luxury—but I love it and intend to go right on using it. A friend of mine and I continue to argue over whether it is worthwhile or not. She insists that she can wash dishes in the same amount of time I spend cleaning off the table, getting the dishes ready for the dishwasher, and then putting them away. I'm afraid that it is an argument that will never be resolved—but we will go on being friends anyway.

Bread Makers or Machines

These bread machines can be a mixed blessing. It is hard to resist that extra slice of fresh baked bread. However, the machines are easy to use and will allow you to bake your own bread and analyze the recipe so you know the exact nutritive values in each slice. You can also make specialty breads which you shouldn't buy at a bakery because you might not know the exact ingredients and nutritive values.

Ice Cream Dippers

I also buy and use ice-cream dippers for many things. I particularly like them for muffins, cupcakes, and cookies. A level No. 16 dipper provides ¼ cup batter, which is used for larger muffins, and a level No. 20, 3 tablespoons of batter, which is used for regular-size muffins. A level No. 60 dipper provides

1 tablespoon cookie dough while a level No. 40 dipper is just right for 1½ tablespoons dough. I have indicated the right size dipper to use in recipes for muffins, cupcakes, and cookies. You may be able to get them in your hardware store, but if you can't get them there a good specialty kitchen shop will have them or can get them for you.

The numbers on the inside of the dipper tell you the capacity of the dipper, e.g., a No. 16 dipper is ¼ cup because the yields are based on that portion of a quart. When I refer to the capacity of the dipper, I mean a level dipper, not the way they use them to dip ice cream with lots of ice cream hanging over the sides. The following sizes are the ones I find most useful.

No. 8 . . . . .½ cup
No. 12 . . . . .⅓ cup
No. 16 . . . . .¼ cup
No. 20 . . . . .3 tablespoons
No. 40 . . . . .1½ tablespoons
No. 60 . . . . .1 tablespoon

Other Equipment

Of course I have all of the other usual equipment—spaghetti maker, toaster-oven, electric frying pan, etc.—but I try always to keep the use of equipment to a minimum in any cookbook I write. I feel that if you have specialized equipment and want to use it, you will know how to use it—and the recipe will still be practical for anyone who doesn't want to use any more equipment than necessary.

INGREDIENTS

It is important to understand which foods have cholesterol and which are cholesterol-free, as well as the cholesterol count of the foods that do contain cholesterol. The following table includes average cholesterol counts for various foods. The information is based on that found in the following references:

Nutritive Value of Foods. Home and Garden Bulletin no. 72. U.S. Department of Agriculture, Washington, D.C., 1981.

Composition of Foods, Raw, Processed, and Prepared. Agriculture Handbook no. 8. U.S. Department of Agriculture, Washington, D.C., 1963 and all current revisions.

Information on the cholesterol counts of many more foods can be found in Chapter 5.

INGREDIENTS

Item	Milligrams of cholesterol
DAIRY PRODUCTS	
1 cup whole milk	33
2 tablespoons sour cream	12
½ cup ice cream	29
½ cup soft-serve ice cream or ice milk	10
½ cup sherbet	5
Cheese (per ounce)	
Brie	28
Cheddar	30
Colby	27
Cream	31
Feta	25
Gouda	32
Mozzarella made with part-skim milk or Cheese spread	16
Neufchâtel or Parmesan	22
Romano	29
Roquefort or Swiss	26
EGGS	
1 egg yolk	213
FATS	
1 tablespoon butter	31
¼ cup lard	49

Item	Milligrams of cholesterol
MEATS (100 grams, about 3½ ounces)	
Beef, T-bone steak, lean only, broiled	80
Beef, ground, extra lean, cooked	82
Beef, ground, regular, cooked	87
Beef brains, cooked, simmered	2,054
Beef heart, cooked, simmered	193
Beef kidneys, cooked, simmered	387
Beef liver, pan cooked, fried	482
Beef tongue, cooked, simmered	107
Beef tripe, raw	95
Lamb liver, cooked	501
Lamb tongue, cooked	189
Veal liver, cooked	561
Veal kidneys, cooked	791
Pork, fresh, Italian sausage, cooked	78
Pork, fresh, country-style sausage, cooked	83
Pork liver, cooked	355
Pork, cured, bacon, raw	67
Pork, braunschweiger	156
Pork ham, cured, boneless, cooked	59
Buffalo, composite of cuts, cooked, roasted	58
Deer, cooked, roasted	112
Rabbit, domestic, composite of cuts, cooked	82
Squirrel, cooked, roasted	121
POULTRY (100 grams, about 3½ ounces)	
Chicken giblets, cooked	357
Duck, domestic, flesh only, cooked	89
Goose, domestic, flesh only, cooked	96
Turkey giblets, cooked	418
Turkey bologna	99
Turkey frankfurter	60
Turkey salami	82
FISH (100 grams, about 3½ ounces)	
Sardines in oil	142

Item	Milligrams of cholesterol
SHELLFISH (100 grams, about 3½ ounces)	
Crab, blue, cooked	100
Lobster, northern, cooked	72
Shrimp, mixed species, cooked	195
Shrimp, mixed species, canned	173
Abalone, mixed species, cooked	94
Squid, mixed species, cooked	200

I have discussed which foods are a plus and which shouldn't be used in the low-cholesterol diet at much greater length in Chapter 5, "Cholesterol."

Sugar Substitutes

Even though we can now use a small amount of sugar, I still use sugar substitutes in many of my recipes. We need the sugar for texture, but then I add sugar substitutes to make it taste sweeter, if necessary. If you would like to do so, feel free to increase or decrease the amount of sugar substitute if you think you'd like it better that way. You don't generally need to worry about changing the food exchange values if you add sugar substitute because there would need to be a big increase in sweetness to add enough carbohydrate to change any of the values.

I use a variety of sugar substitutes. I prefer Weight Watchers Smart Options for cooking and baking and I really like Equal for sweetening things that don't need a prolonged cooking time. However, some of my friends prefer Sweet'n Low for their beverages and others like Sprinkle Sweet and Sugar Twin because they are simpler to use.

One thing to remember is that most of the sugar substitutes have some carbohydrate in them, so you need to include their values in your daily diet plan. I wouldn't worry about a couple of packets of sweetener but I would count them if you are going to use several of them at a time.

I hesitate to use tables because they are so dull, but I do think a table of sugar substitutes and their equivalents in sugar might be handy.

Sugar Substitute	Amount	CHO (gm)	Calories	Sugar Equivalent
Equal Measure	½ teaspoon	2	8	1 tablespoon
	1¾ teaspoons	7	28	¼ cup
	2½ teaspoons	10	40	⅓ cup
	3½ teaspoons	14	56	½ cup
Equal Packets	1½ packets	1	6	1 tablespoon
	6 packets	4	24	¼ cup
	8 packets	6	32	⅓ cup
Equal Tablets	1	0	0	1 teaspoon
	10	1	4	3 tablespoons
Weight Watchers Smart Options	1 teaspoon	3	12	2 tablespoons
	2 teaspoons	6	24	¼ cup
	2⅔ teaspoons	8	32	⅓ cup
	4 teaspoons	12	48	½ cup
Sprinkle Sweet	Use an equal measure as a sugar substitute.			
Sugar Twin	Use an equal measure as a sugar substitute.			
Sweet'n Low and Liquid Sucaryl	⅓ teaspoon			1 tablespoon
	1⅓ teaspoons			¼ cup
	1¾ teaspoons			⅓ cup
Adolph's Sugar Substitute	1 teaspoon			¼ cup
	1⅓ teaspoons			⅓ cup
	2 teaspoons			½ cup

Milk Products and Substitutes

Instant nonfat dry milk is also used frequently in these recipes. I have been using large quantities of instant nonfat dry milk for years. When I was working as a dietitian for the Army, one of the other dietitians in our department told me I should be known as "The Dry Milk Kid" because I was always preaching the value of dry milk. I wrote a small booklet on the proper use of dry milk, with recipes and methods in it, since I thought it was a good product and should be used whenever possible. I have also advocated its use in the nursing homes where I work as a dietary consultant. I was so pleased at a meeting to hear one of our dietary employees tell someone from another nursing home what a wonderful product instant nonfat dry milk is when it is used properly.

I like to use dry milk because it has all of the nutrients of whole milk except for the fat. It keeps well without refrigeration, is easy to store, is low in calories, and costs about the same as fresh milk. I have branched out over the last few years and now also use dry buttermilk because it is simpler to keep a can of dry buttermilk in the refrigerator than to keep liquid buttermilk on hand. I used to buy a quart of buttermilk, use a cup of it, and the rest would spoil—and then, too, it isn't always all that easy to buy low-fat buttermilk in our area. The regular instant dry milk whips easily with an equal measure of milk or fruit juice, partially set gelatin, or egg whites to add more variety to the diet.

Instant nonfat dry milk is particularly good in yeast breads—when using it you no longer need to scald the milk, it helps form a good brown crust, and it yields bread with a softer texture. Dry milk can be reconstituted and used as a beverage or in a recipe that needs liquid milk, or it can be used dry along with the flour or other ingredients.

Most packages of instant nonfat dry milk direct you to use ⅓ cup of instant nonfat dry milk to 1 cup of water. I use this as a regular measure, but you will find that some recipes in this book have only ¼ cup of instant dry milk to 1 cup of water. That is because when I am working on a diabetic recipe, I want to cut down on the carbohydrate as much as possible and therefore I use only as much of the milk as necessary to get good results.

Low-fat cottage cheese is usually available. If it isn't available, buy the regular cottage cheese and wash it off with lukewarm water to get rid of the cream, then put it back in the container with a little skim milk if you like it creamy.

If you are accustomed to using cream in your coffee, you can use instant nonfat dry milk or one of the coffee whiteners that list a vegetable oil as their main ingredient. Be careful not to buy a coffee whitener that includes palm oil, coconut oil, or hydrogenated vegetable oil as an ingredient. Better yet, drink your coffee black—or best of all, stop drinking coffee. Tests and research seem to be telling us that coffee isn't all that good for us.

Vegetable Oils and Margarine

Learning to use vegetable oil and margarine instead of lard and butter seems to be one of the hardest things for most cooks to do when they start following a low-cholesterol diet plan. I found it helpful to tell myself that I melted fats before frying anything and now it is already melted. You don't really need all of that butter in a frying pan anyway, especially if it is a nonstick pan. A tablespoon of fat is generally enough to fry almost anything and the oil doesn't burn and turn brown quickly like butter does. If you think you absolutely have to have that butter flavor in baked goods, try adding some butter flavoring.

The type of fat used makes a difference in the texture and flavor of baked goods. You can substitute margarine for butter in baked goods, but use the regular stick margarine, not the soft or "lite" margarine. You can use vegetable oil as a substitute for melted fat in recipes, but if the recipe directs you to cream the fat with sugar, it is always best to use stick margarine.

Vegetable oil should be kept in a cool spot, out of sunlight, because you don't want it to get rancid. It shouldn't be refrigerated unless you expect to keep it for a long time, and then it should be brought back to room temperature before it is used. I keep my reserve oil in the fruit room in the basement and oil I use every day in the kitchen.

It is always a good idea to read the ingredient list of any item, and it is particularly important when you are buying margarine. You need to know what kind of fat has been used in the margarine. Vegetable oil should be the first ingredient in the margarine. Fat is fat in a diabetic diet but the type of fat is very important to anyone on a low-cholesterol diet. You don't want to even consider margarine that contains lard or other animal fat, palm oil, cocoa butter, or coconut oil. If you are in doubt about your local brands, call your Heart Association and ask them to recommend the best ones available. Remember, a fat exchange is a fat exchange, no matter what brand of margarine you use, although you may get more volume for your exchange with the new soft and/or light margarines.

Eggs and Egg Substitutes

Liquid egg substitute is based on egg whites and is a wonderful substitute for whole eggs. It is more expensive than egg whites so I try to use egg whites whenever possible; however, there are certain recipes that need whole eggs and liquid egg substitute works very well when you aren't supposed to be using egg yolks.

People often ask me what to do with leftover egg yolks that aren't used. I freeze mine with 1 teaspoon of salt or 2 teaspoons of sugar per cup and give them to a friend whose family doesn't have any problem with cholesterol. At first it was difficult for me to throw away egg yolks, but now I find myself doing it often when I have only one or two yolks. I tell myself how wonderful it is that I can so easily dispose of all that cholesterol without worrying about it and just toss it down the garbage disposal. If you like, you can buy dehydrated egg whites and then you won't have to toss away the yolks. It costs about the same over a period of time.

Oat Bran

Oat bran has proved to be a very valuable source of water-soluble fiber, which helps reduce sugar and cholesterol in the blood. I am convinced that oat bran should be a part of every diabetic's diet. Oat bran can be used alone or you can use ½ oat bran and ½ oatmeal as a cooked cereal. Either way, cook them as you would oatmeal (add the cereal to boiling water, using twice as much water as cereal. Cook and stir for 1 minute, cover the cereal, remove it from the heat, and let stand for 5 minutes). I serve it hot with skim milk and sugar substitute. You can also use ½ oat bran and ½ bread flour in most baked recipes. You need the bread flour because it has more gluten than all-purpose flour and oat bran doesn't have an appreciable amount of gluten. You can also add 2 teaspoons of wheat gluten for each cup of oat bran if you want to use it in equal proportions with all-purpose flour for most recipes. Wheat gluten is available at health food stores and many supermarkets. If your store doesn't have it, you can ask them to order it for you. It can also be used to add gluten to flours like whole wheat and rye when you want to use them for baking. I keep oat bran and wheat gluten with my other baking supplies. (Keep reserve supplies in airtight containers in the freezer.) I also try to keep a supply of Oat Bran Muffins (see Index) in the freezer so I can have one every day for breakfast or a snack.

Fiber

We have known for a long time that a high-fiber diet with plenty of liquid will help control constipation, and now research has shown that a high-fiber diet with a good proportion of water-soluble fiber will also help control blood sugar and cholesterol.

Dietary fiber is a general term for the indigestible carbohydrates including pectin, cellulose, hemicellulose, and lignin, which make up the cell walls of plants. Many foods contain fiber but it is found most abundantly in raw leafy, root, and tough-skinned vegetables; edible seeds; nuts; fruits; and the outer layer of grains. Because our digestive system does not contain the essential bacteria that breaks down this fiber, it remains more or less unchanged and is passed out of the body through the gastrointestinal system. Dietary fibers have a large capacity to hold water, which gives bulk and softness to the stool and enables food to pass more quickly through the digestive system.

There are two main types of fiber, water-soluble and water-insoluble. Water-soluble fiber forms a gel in water and is found in oats, beans, seeds, and fruits, especially apples and citrus fruits. Water-soluble dietary fiber helps control cholesterol and blood sugar. Water-insoluble dietary fiber is the kind we generally associate with the word fiber and is found in wheat, corn and oat bran, whole grains, and vegetables. It, along with liquid, forms bulky stools that travel faster through the intestines and help prevent constipation.

Most doctors agree you need 30 to 40 grams of dietary fiber each day for the best results, but the average is about 20 grams per day. Many diabetics are on a moderately high-fiber diet already because of all of the vegetables and fruit we eat. If you eat whole grain bread and at least five servings of fruits and vegetables each day, you are probably getting most of your fiber already, but it is a good idea to check on your consumption of fiber because of the very positive results achieved from eating it. Also don't forget to drink six to eight glasses of water every day because fiber needs a lot of water to expand.

Please be cautious when adding more fiber to your diet if you aren't using much of it now. Although it helps lower cholesterol and blood sugar and aids in relieving diverticulitis and preventing cancer of the lower bowel, it is best to add fiber gradually until you are up to 30 to 40 grams per day. Cereal boxes and food packages are a good source of information about the fiber content of foods not found in Chapter 3.

Dr. James Anderson, professor of medicine and clinical nutrition at the University of Kentucky and chief of the metabolic-endocrine section of the Veteran's Administrative Medical Center in Lexington, Kentucky, has pioneered new avenues of research using the High-Carbohydrate High-Fiber (HCF) diet for diabetics and others. If you want further information, you can write to HCF Nutrition Research Foundation, Inc., Box 22124, Lexington, Kentucky 40522. Information on fiber in this book is based on the work of Dr. Anderson and the USDA.

Other Ingredients

There is only one ingredient used in this book that doesn't fit into a low-cholesterol diabetic diet. All of the other ingredients are acceptable on the diet, but I did include a recipe for chocolate chip cookies. There isn't that much cholesterol in the chips, and they can be fit into the typical doctor-recommended limit of 300 milligrams of cholesterol per day—so I used them. After all, chocolate chip cookies are a part of the American way—we would hate to have to get along without them completely!

If you have a question about some ingredient that I haven't used in a recipe, check the tables of nutritive values in Chapter 3, "Calculating Food Exchanges," and if the ingredient is listed you will know that it is acceptable for your diet.

Fruits, vegetables, and cereals are all free of cholesterol and are mostly complex carbohydrates that are recognized to be good for us. Vegetables and fruits should be used as much as possible because they are high in fiber and most of them are low in carbohydrates. A vegetable plate has most of the nutrients we need for a well-balanced meal along with a little cottage cheese, lean meat, or fish.

Since fiber is so good for us, I have used oat bran, whole wheat flour, and other whole grains as often as possible in these recipes. Whole wheat flour and graham flour have the same nutrients except that graham flour has been ground to yield a finer texture and therefore is more suitable in some recipes.

Bread flour is also used several times. Bread flour has a higher gluten content than all-purpose flour and helps make really good bread. It takes more liquid than all-purpose flour, but the final product has a finer texture and greater strength.

Since you will no longer be buying commercial mixes because of the fat and sugar in them, you can make your own or mix up a fresh batch each time. Angel food cake mix or mixes to which you add the egg and fat are acceptable if you add oil and liquid egg substitute to them; however, beware of using most mixes because they usually have ingredients that you shouldn't use.

Cocoa is used in these recipes instead of chocolate because chocolate contains cocoa butter, which isn't good for a low-cholesterol diet. Three tablespoons of cocoa plus one tablespoon of fat is equal to 1 ounce of baking chocolate. The cocoa can also be mixed with boiling water without any fat and used as a chocolate substitute with very good results. (Use only enough boiling water to make a smooth paste.)

Low-sodium variations are included for the recipes whenever practical. I haven't stressed using salt substitutes because not all doctors approve of them for all patients. If you want to use them, it is best to discuss them with your doctor. Each patient is different and no doctor will make a blanket statement that everyone can use salt substitutes.

The low-sodium diet notes in these recipes are planned for low-sodium diets, not salt-free diets. I discussed these variations with Mary Agnes Jones, R.D., formerly of Holy Cross Hospital in Chicago and with Muriel Urbashich, R.D., former head of the dietary department of South Chicago Community Hospital. They both agreed that the low-sodium diet is more liberal than it used to be. Therefore I have used regular milk on the low-sodium diet, rather than salt-free milk. Salt-free margarine is available in most stores now and several packagers are now offering low-sodium canned vegetables that also may be used. Low-sodium soups are also available. Anyone on a "no added salt" diet can use the basic recipes in this book by deleting the salt when salt is specified. Some recipes that contain soy sauce or other highly salted ingredients cannot be changed successfully so they are not recommended for use on a low-sodium diet.

Ice milk, fruit ices, and sherbet can be used on the low-cholesterol diet, so feel free to use them within the limits of your diabetic diet.

The most important thing to remember when planning your low-cholesterol diabetic diet is that you have many food items left that you can use. It is best to work with those and see what interesting and tasty dishes you can develop rather than mourning the loss of those few foods that are no longer available to you.

7

Understanding the New Food Labels

The new food labels are a big help for anyone who is concerned about the contents of cans or packages, as we are. However, they can be hard to understand if you aren't used to reading them so I thought it would be worthwhile to take some time to understand what each part of the label means.

The following discussion of the new label is based on information from the American Heart Association, the American Dietetic Association, and the Food and Drug Administration.

Nutrition Facts: If the label is titled "Nutrition Facts," it meets the 1993 government nutrition labeling requirements.

Serving Size: Is the serving size on the label the one you use? If you use twice as much, double the calories and other information for your size serving. If you only use half as much as the serving listed, divide the calories and other information by 2 to fit your serving.

Calories from Fat: Try to limit your calories from fat. Most people need to cut back on their total fat intake. Try to choose foods that don't get their main percentage of calories from fat.

Calories: This lists the total calories for the size serving shown on the label. If you need to cut your calories, consider cutting the serving size or buying another item that would fit into your meal plan more easily.

% Daily Value: The percentage of the total amount you need daily of each of the items listed.

Total Fat: The total amount of fat in each serving and the percentage of the daily amounts needed for a normal diet. (A

Nutrition Facts

Serving Size ½ cup (114g)
Servings Per Container 4

Amount Per Serving

Calories 90   Calories from Fat 30

% Daily Value*

Total Fat 3g	**5%**
Saturated Fat 0g	**0%**
Cholesterol 0mg	**0%**
Sodium 300mg	**13%**
Total Carbohydrate 13g	**4%**
Dietary Fiber 3g	**12%**
Sugars 3g	
Protein 3g	

Vitamin A	80%	Vitamin C	60%
Calcium	4%	Iron	4%

* Percent Daily Values are based on a 2,000 calorie diet. Your daily values may be higher or lower depending on your calorie needs:

	Calories	2,000	2,500
Total Fat	Less than	65g	80g
Sat Fat	Less than	20g	25g
Cholesterol	Less than	300mg	300mg
Sodium	Less than	2,400mg	2,400mg
Total Carbohydrate		300g	375g
Fiber		25g	30g

Calories per gram:
Fat 9 • Carbohydrate 4 • Protein 4

More nutrients may be listed on some labels.

5'4", 138-pound active woman needs about 2,200 calories each day. A 5'10", 174-pound active man needs about 2,900 calories per day. You will know how many you need according to your diet.) Each fat exchange contains 5 grams of fat (see table, Composition of Food Groups or Exchanges per Serving, in Chapter 3, "Calculating Food Exchanges.")

Saturated Fat: This is the kind of fat that helps raise your blood cholesterol. Avoiding it whenever you can is an important part of your low-cholesterol diet.

Cholesterol: Too much cholesterol can lead to heart problems. Try to eat less than 300 milligrams a day. (See table, Ingredients, in Chapter 6, "Equipment and Ingredients."

Sodium: An excess amount of sodium can aggravate high blood pressure for some people. Try to keep your sodium intake below 2,400 to 3,000 (mg) milligrams of salt per day.

Total Carbohydrates: The amount of carbohydrate per serving is very important to anyone on a diabetic diet. We must count our carbohydrate, so it is important to know how much carbohydrate we would get in a serving of food. (There are 15 grams of carbohydrate, 3 grams of protein, and a trace of fat in a bread/starch exchange.)

Dietary Fiber: We need both soluble and insoluble fiber in our diets. Fruits, vegetables, whole-grain cereals, beans, and peas are all high in fiber and can help reduce the risk of cancer, heart trouble, and constipation. Thirty to 40 grams of fiber per day is about the right amount for most of us. However, we must remember that it is also important to drink enough liquid, preferably water, to rehydrate the fiber. Six to eight glasses of water per day should be your goal. Another important thing to remember is to start increasing, if necessary, your fiber, gradually adding a little more every few days until you have reached your goal.

Sugars: You will notice there is no percentage of Daily Value for sugar. We are now allowed a little sugar, but it isn't considered a necessary part of our diet.

Protein: It is important to have enough protein in our diet to maintain our bodily structure. However, we don't need as much protein as many people think we need. You will know how much protein you need for your diet from the number of meat exchanges you are allowed. Each meat exchange contains 7 grams of protein and 3 to 8 grams of fat depending upon whether you choose lean meat (3 grams of fat and 7 grams of protein), medium-fat meat (5 grams of fat and 7 grams of protein), or high-fat meat (8 grams of fat and 7 grams of protein). It is advisable to choose the lean meat with less fat because it will also have less cholesterol in it.

Vitamins and Minerals: Our goal here is to reach 100% of the daily requirements.

Daily Values: Let the daily values be your guide to what you need but always concentrate on your own food plan. Daily values are listed for people with a 2,000- or 2,500-calorie intake. Your daily values will be determined by your own food plan.

There are some key words used on labels that are important to us. They have been defined by the government, and you can be confident that if the label uses the following phrases, it can be proved to the government's satisfaction that the phrase is justified:

Fat Free: Less than 0.5 gram of fat per serving.

Low Fat: 3 grams or less of fat per serving.

Reduced Fat: At least 25% less fat when compared with a similar food.

Lean: Less than 10 grams of fat, 4 grams of saturated fat, and 95 milligrams of cholesterol per serving.

Light or Lite: ⅓ less calories or no more than ½ the fat of the higher-calorie, higher-fat version, or no more than ½ the sodium of the higher sodium version.

Low Saturated Fat: 1 gram or less saturated fat per serving and no more than 15% calories from saturated fat.

Cholesterol Free: Less than 2 milligrams cholesterol per serving and 2 grams or less saturated fat per serving.

Low Cholesterol: Less than 20 milligrams cholesterol per serving and 2 grams or less saturated fat per serving.

Reduced Cholesterol: At least 25% less cholesterol when compared with a similar food, and 2 grams or less saturated fat per serving.

Sodium or Salt Free: Less than 5 milligrams sodium per serving.

Very Low Sodium: 35 milligrams or less sodium per serving.

Low Sodium: 140 milligrams or less sodium per serving.

Reduced Sodium: At least 25% less sodium when compared with a similar food.

Light in Sodium: 50% less sodium per serving; restricted to foods with more than 40 calories or 3 grams of fat per serving.

Excellent Source of: Contains more than 20% of the Daily Value per serving.

8

Soups

Soup is always a good addition to a low-cholesterol diabetic diet. For the diabetic diet you are interested only in the amount of carbohydrate, protein, and fat in the soup; however, for the low-cholesterol diet you also want to substitute polyunsaturated fats for animal fats, so you need to find substitutes for the animal fat, egg yolks, cream, whole milk, or butter often used in soup recipes.

There are all sorts of tricks you can use to change a high-cholesterol soup into one suitable for a low-cholesterol diet. Liquid egg substitute can be used instead of egg yolks, margarine or oil instead of butter, a double amount of instant dry milk instead of evaporated milk, and a little more margarine in the soup along with the milk instead of cream. Of course this changes the flavor a little bit (but not too much) and the soups are still good in their own right.

I would have liked to have been able to include more soups in this chapter based on dried peas, beans, and lentils. I wasn't able to include too many of them, since they are so high in carbohydrate that one bowl of soup takes up most of a meal's allowance. Therefore, I concentrated on vegetable soups that provide fiber with less carbohydrate.

Because many soups are based on a good, rich chicken or beef broth, and because a low-cholesterol diet needs broth without any animal fat in it, I use a great deal of the fat-free chicken and beef broth concentrates available in the stores. These concentrates generally have a large amount of salt in them so the sodium count is very high when they are used. If you are on a low-sodium diet, you can handle this by buying low-sodium bouillon cubes or by preparing your own low-sodium, fat-free broth. When buying low-sodium soup concentrates, check the list of ingredients carefully, because several of them are based on animal fats instead of salt, which aren't acceptable on a low-cholesterol diet.

If you decide to make your own low-sodium, fat-free broth, start by buying (if you don't have one) a heavy stainless steel or aluminum stock pot with a 2- or 3-gallon capacity and a tight-fitting lid. The broth needs to cook for a long time to develop flavor and it isn't worth doing unless you can cook a large amount. The broth freezes well and can be frozen in containers holding the right amount for future soups or casseroles. I have a heavy stainless steel 3-gallon pot that I bought when we were first married. I couldn't count the amount of soup, spaghetti sauce, and other things that I have cooked in that pot and it still looks as bright and shiny as it did the day we bought it.

I used very little salt in most of the soup recipes containing broth because I used the commercial bouillon cubes that are high in salt in making the broth. If you use your own broth you will probably have to add salt (if you can) or a salt substitute if your doctor approves.

Fat-Free, Low-Sodium Beef Broth

Although we class it as beef broth, veal bones are also very good and may be used whenever available. I don't care for lamb or pork bones in broth although the British do make a lamb broth that they prize very much.

Any beef or veal bones are acceptable. You can get soup bones or soup meat from your butcher, save any bones from roasts, and collect any available bones from your family until you have enough to make a good, big pot of broth. It just isn't worthwhile unless you save enough bones.

> **Beef or veal bones, any kind**
> **1 onion**
> **2 carrots**
> **1–2 celery stalks**
> **Water to cover, at room temperature**

The broth will have a better flavor if you roast the bones and trimmings in an open roaster in the oven at 350°F until they are well browned. Cool the bones to room temperature and place in a stock pot. Add onion, a couple of carrots, and a stalk or so of celery. Add water. Cover and simmer for 4–6 hours. Scum will rise to the top when the liquid first begins to simmer and it is a good idea to skim most of this off. (It is almost impossible to get it all off; I know, I've tried it often enough.) The broth may look done to you long before the cooking time is ended, but it won't have the flavor and body it will have if cooked the full length of time.

Remove from heat. Strain well, putting the broth in a pan and leaving the bones out. Refrigerate the broth until the fat has risen to the top and solidified. Remove the fat, place the clear broth in another container, and freeze or refrigerate until needed. At this stage I add any broth, with the fat removed, that

I have gathered from roasts. The broth from the roasts also has a good flavor and seems to add something to the broth. (Throw away the murky part at the bottom of the broth.)

As soon as the bones are cool enough to handle, remove any meat from them and refrigerate or freeze until needed. This meat is excellent for future use in soups. Discard the bones and any bits of overcooked vegetables with them.

Since this broth is considered free on a diabetic diet, it may be used for soups or other recipes without adding any nutritive values that need to be counted.

Fat-Free, Low-Sodium Chicken or Turkey Broth

Chicken or turkey bones, necks, wings
1 onion
2 carrots, small
2 celery stalks
A little parsley
1 quart cold water for each pound of bones

Weigh the chicken or turkey bones, necks, and wings, place in a stock pot, and add 1 quart cold water for each pound of bones. Don't add any giblets, skin, or fat because they are all forbidden on a low-cholesterol diet. Bring the water to a boil, reduce heat, and simmer 5 minutes. Drain well. Replace with the same amount of cold water. Add 1 onion, 2 small carrots, a couple of stalks of celery, and a little parsley. Cover tightly and simmer for 2½–3 hours. If you are using a precooked carcass of a turkey or chicken with no raw bones, it isn't necessary to discard the first liquid. Just cover with cold water and simmer an hour or so or until the meat is falling off the bones. If the carcass is still whole, you will get a richer broth if you crush the bones or separate them so they won't need as much water to cover them.

After the cooking period, strain the broth, setting aside the chicken or turkey bones to cool. Chill the broth until the fat has risen to the top and solidified. Discard the fat. Remove the clear broth to another container and freeze or refrigerate until used. (Throw away the murky part at the bottom of the pot.)

Pick any chicken or turkey meat off the bones as soon as they are cool enough to handle and refrigerate or freeze it for future use in soups, discarding the bones.

Since this broth is considered free on a diabetic diet, it may be used for soups or other recipes without adding any nutritive values that need to be counted.

Chunky Split Pea Soup

This soup has little bits of vegetable in it. If you want a smoother soup, it can be puréed in the blender or food processor before it is served.

1 cup dried split peas
6 cups water
6 chicken bouillon cubes
1 cup finely chopped onions
¼ cup finely chopped celery
¼ cup finely chopped fresh green peppers
¼ cup finely chopped fresh carrots
2 tablespoons margarine
¼ teaspoon ground thyme
Salt and pepper to taste

Wash split peas and put in a saucepan. Add water and bouillon cubes; cover and simmer 1½ hours, stirring frequently.

Add onions, celery, peppers, and carrots to split peas; cover and simmer ½ hour, stirring frequently.

Add margarine and seasonings to soup and continue to simmer for 10 minutes. Remove from heat and serve hot. Serve ¾ cup per serving. (The amount of salt needed will depend upon the saltiness of the bouillon cubes. The recipe is calculated using chicken bouillon cubes instead of low-sodium chicken broth.)

Yields 6 cups—8 servings

Nutritive Values Per Serving

CAL	CHO (g)	PRO (g)	TOTAL FAT (g)	SAT. FAT (g)	CHOL (mg)	FIBER (g)	NA (mg)
125	18	7	3	.5	0	2	762

Food exchanges per serving: 1 starch, 1 lean meat
Low-sodium diets: Use low-sodium broth instead of the water and chicken bouillon cubes or delete the chicken bouillon cubes and use only water. Use salt-free margarine and don't add any salt to the soup.
Sugar content per serving: None.

Barley Mushroom Soup

"Chef Dave" Hutchins gave me this recipe. It is kosher as long as you use vegetable stock, which you can buy in a health food store or some supermarkets. I'm happy to say that Chef Dave is very careful to follow low-cholesterol guidelines when cooking or planning menus. This low-cholesterol food is greatly appreciated by his many older patrons who are attempting to keep their cholesterol count under 200.

¾ cup pearl barley
¼ cup vegetable oil
2 pounds sliced fresh mushrooms
2 cups diced celery
2 cups julienne onions
4 minced garlic cloves
3 quarts vegetable stock
Salt to taste
⅛ to ¼ teaspoon freshly ground black
    pepper
½ cup plain yogurt
¼ cup soy sauce

Put barley in a food processor, preferably a small one, and give it a couple of pulses to chop barley into grits. Set aside.

Preheat a 4- or 6-quart heavy pot on medium heat for 1 minute. Swirl oil around the bottom of pot. Add mushrooms and cook, stirring frequently, until mushrooms are well browned. Add celery, onions, and garlic and continue to cook and stir until onions are soft. Add vegetable stock and barley and bring to a rolling boil. (If you don't have vegetable stock, you can use fat-free beef stock, in which case the soup will no longer be kosher.) Decrease heat, cover, and simmer until barley is tender. Add salt and pepper (the amount of salt you need will depend upon the saltiness of the stock).

Remove soup from heat and stir ½ cup of it into yogurt. Add yogurt mixture and soy sauce to soup. Serve hot, but don't boil after adding yogurt. Use 1 cup per serving.

Yields 3 quarts—12 servings

Nutritive Values Per Serving

CAL	CHO (g)	PRO (g)	TOTAL FAT (g)	SAT. FAT (g)	CHOL (mg)	FIBER (g)	NA (mg)
147	21	4	6	.8	1	4	1,370

Food exchanges per serving: 1 starch, 1 vegetable, 1 fat
Low-sodium diets: Omit salt and use low-sodium vegetable or beef broth and soy sauce.
Sugar content per serving: None.

Cabbage and Rice Soup

---

1 tablespoon vegetable oil
1 pound (about 5 cups) shredded cabbage
1 cup thinly sliced onions
4 cups fat-free beef broth
4 cups fat-free chicken broth
Sprinkle of pepper
¼ teaspoon grated nutmeg
½ cup long-grain rice

Preheat a heavy saucepan on medium heat for 1 minute. Swirl oil around bottom of pan. Add cabbage and onions and cook, stirring frequently, over medium heat until cabbage and onions are soft. Add broths, pepper, nutmeg, and rice. Cover and simmer about 20 minutes, or until rice is tender. Do not overcook. Serve hot, using 1 cup soup per serving.

Yields 2 quarts—8 servings

Nutritive Values Per Serving

CAL	CHO (g)	PRO (g)	TOTAL FAT (g)	SAT. FAT (g)	CHOL (mg)	FIBER (g)	NA (mg)
96	15	5	2	.3	0	2	648

Food exchanges per serving: 1 starch, 1 vegetable
Low-sodium diets: Omit salt. Use salt-free broth.
Sugar content per serving: None.

Cream of Tomato Soup

This recipe came from Vera Wilson, a friend of mine from here in Wadena. She made it with home-canned tomato juice, but it is also good made with commercially canned tomato juice.

> 1 tablespoon finely chopped onion
> 3 tablespoons margarine
> 3 tablespoons all-purpose flour
> 1 teaspoon salt
> ⅛ teaspoon pepper
> 2 cups tomato juice
> 2 cups milk at room temperature
> 1 1-gram packet Equal (aspartame) sugar
>   substitute

Fry onion in margarine in a saucepan, stirring constantly, until soft but not brown. Add flour and seasonings to onion and cook and stir over moderate heat until bubbly but not browned.

Add tomato juice to flour mixture. Bring to a boil, stirring constantly, for 1 minute. Stir tomato mixture into milk. Place soup in the top of a double boiler. Return to heat and heat to serving temperature. Remove from heat.

Stir Equal into soup and serve hot, ¾ cup per serving.

Yields about 4 cups—6 servings

Nutritive Values Per Serving

CAL	CHO (g)	PRO (g)	TOTAL FAT (g)	SAT. FAT (g)	CHOL (mg)	FIBER (g)	NA (mg)
130	11	4	8	2.6	11	1	767

Food exchanges per serving: 1 skim milk, 1 fat
Low-sodium diets: Omit salt. Use salt-free margarine and tomato juice canned without salt.
Sugar content per serving: None.

Gazpacho

This is refreshing on a warm summer day—a good way to cele-brate the first ripe tomatoes in summer, although it is equally tasty later in the fall.

> **3 cups fat-free beef broth**
> **¾ cup tomato juice**
> **2 tablespoons lemon juice**
> **3 tablespoons Spicy Tomato Dressing (see Index)**
> **⅓ cup finely chopped onions**
> **⅓ cup finely chopped fresh green peppers**
> **2 tablespoons finely chopped celery**
> **1 cup diced, peeled, and cored fresh tomatoes**
> **¼ teaspoon garlic powder**
> **1 teaspoon salt**
> **1 tablespoon chopped parsley**
> **¼–½ cup thinly sliced or diced cucumbers**

Combine all ingredients except cucumbers; mix lightly and refrigerate overnight or at least 4 hours.

Serve soup in chilled cups garnished with cucumbers, using ¾ cup soup per serving.

Yields about 4½ cups—6 servings

Nutritive Values Per Serving

CAL	CHO (g)	PRO (g)	TOTAL FAT (g)	SAT. FAT (g)	CHOL (mg)	FIBER (g)	NA (mg)
30	6	2	trace	0	0	1	842

Food exchanges per serving: 1 vegetable
Low-sodium diets: Omit salt. Use low-sodium broth and low-sodium version of the salad dressing.
Sugar content per serving: None.

Goulash Soup

Muriel Urbashich, a dietitian who was the head of the Dietary Department at South Chicago Community Hospital, tells me that this soup was a great favorite in its employees' cafeteria. The cafeteria sold gallons of it whenever it was on the menu. Muriel and I have done three large-quantity cookbooks together and spend a lot of time talking recipes and food preparation when we get together.

> **2 cups chopped onions**
> **3 tablespoons vegetable oil**
> **1 pound beef round**
> **8 cups fat-free broth**
> **¼ teaspoon garlic powder**
> **2 teaspoons paprika**
> **½ cup drained, crushed, canned tomatoes**
> **Salt to taste**
> **1½ cups diced fresh white potatoes**

Brown onions in 2 tablespoons vegetable oil in a heavy frying pan over moderate heat, stirring occasionally. Transfer onions with a slotted spoon to a heavy saucepan.

Add remaining tablespoon of oil to frying pan. Trim all visible fat from the beef and cut it into ¾-inch cubes. (This is easier if the meat is slightly frozen.) Brown beef in the frying pan over moderate heat, stirring occasionally. Transfer meat with a slotted spoon into saucepan with the onions. Discard as much fat as possible from the frying pan.

Add broth to frying pan and cook and stir over low heat to get as many of the brown particles in the pan as possible into the broth. Pour the hot broth into the saucepan with the onions and meat.

Add seasonings and tomatoes to meat and broth. Cover and simmer over low heat until meat is tender. Remove from heat. Cool to room temperature. Refrigerate until thoroughly chilled and the fat has risen to the top. Remove the fat and discard it.

Return the soup to heat. Taste for seasoning and add salt, if necessary.

Add potatoes to soup. Cover and simmer 15–20 minutes or until the potatoes are tender. Serve 1 cup hot soup per serving.

Yields 2 quarts—8 servings

Nutritive Values Per Serving

CAL	CHO (g)	PRO (g)	TOTAL FAT (g)	SAT. FAT (g)	CHOL (mg)	FIBER (g)	NA (mg)
183	11	17	8	1.6	33	1	688

Food exchanges per serving: 2 lean meat, ⅓ starch, 1 vegetable, ½ fat
Low-sodium diets: Use low-sodium broth and fresh tomatoes or tomatoes canned without salt.
Sugar content per serving: None.

Fruit Soup

I can never decide if this is a soup or a fruit. I generally serve it as a dessert, so I calculated it using a ½-cup serving. If you want to serve it chilled or hot as a soup, it would be 2 fruit exchanges for a 1-cup portion.

> 4 cups water
> 2 whole cinnamon sticks
> 1 teaspoon whole cloves
> 3 tablespoons instant tapioca
> ⅓ cup white raisins
> 1 cup drained, canned unsweetened
>   mandarin oranges
> 1 cup drained, canned unsweetened
>   pineapple tidbits
> 1 cup drained, canned unsweetened diced
>   peaches
> Sugar substitute equal to ⅔ cup sugar

Combine water, cinnamon, and cloves in a saucepan. Cover and bring to a boil. Reduce heat and simmer for 5 minutes. Remove from heat and allow to marinate overnight. Drain spices from the liquid and discard spices.

Add tapioca and raisins to liquid and let stand at room temperature for 5 minutes. Place in saucepan, cover, and simmer until clear. Remove from heat.

Add fruits and sweetener to soup and refrigerate at least overnight before serving. If you want to serve it warm, it can be reheated after it has marinated. Serve ½ cup per serving.

Yields 6 cups—12 servings

Nutritive Values Per Serving

CAL	CHO (g)	PRO (g)	TOTAL FAT (g)	SAT. FAT (g)	CHOL (mg)	FIBER (g)	NA (mg)
56	15	trace	trace	trace	0	.5	54

Food exchanges per serving: 1 fruit
Low-sodium diets: May be served as written.
Sugar content per serving: None.

Golden Squash Soup

This recipe is a memento of my trip to Argentina. They use squash much more frequently than we do as a vegetable as well as in soups and stews. I loved their food, but I never did get used to having dinner at ten o'clock in the evening.

> **2 tablespoons margarine**
> **¾ cup finely chopped onion**
> **⅓ cup all-purpose flour**
> **½ cup instant nonfat dry milk**
> **2 cups hot water**
> **6 cups fat-free chicken broth at room temperature**
> **2 cups cooked, puréed winter squash**
> **⅛ teaspoon white pepper**
> **½ teaspoon celery salt**
> **¼ to 1 teaspoon curry powder**
> **½ teaspoon salt**
> **2 tablespoons chopped chives or parsley**

Preheat a heavy saucepan over medium heat for 1 minute. Melt margarine in pan, add onions, and cook and stir over medium heat until onions are soft and lightly browned. Sprinkle flour evenly over onions and continue to cook and stir until flour is lightly browned. Dissolve milk in hot water, combine with broth (combined liquid should be lukewarm), and add to onions and flour. Cook and stir over medium heat until smooth and thickened. Add puréed squash, pepper, celery salt, curry powder, and salt. Simmer 5 minutes. Serve hot, garnished with chives or parsley, using 1 cup soup per serving.

Yields 2 quarts—8 servings

Nutritive Values Per Serving

CAL	CHO (g)	PRO (g)	TOTAL FAT (g)	SAT. FAT (g)	CHOL (mg)	FIBER (g)	NA (mg)
99	13	5	3	.5	1	2	718

Food exchanges per serving: 1 starch, ½ fat
Low-sodium diets: Omit salt and use salt-free broth.
Sugar content per serving: None.

Minestrone Soup

This is a hearty Italian vegetable soup that is high in fiber. I think it is my favorite soup. I generally make a double batch and freeze most of it in containers to use later. It is high in sodium because I calculated it with commercial beef concentrate for the beef broth. If you are watching your salt, you should prepare it with homemade or low-sodium beef broth. Most minestrone contains pasta in some form but I leave that out because I want to use my bread exchanges for crackers with my soup.

3 quarts fat-free beef broth
1 cup peeled, diced fresh white potatoes
½ cup chopped onions
½ cup chopped carrots
¼ cup diced celery
¼ cup diced fresh green peppers
1 tablespoon chopped parsley
1 cup diced canned tomatoes and juice
½ cup coarsely chopped cabbage
2 cups (16-ounce can) cooked navy or great northern beans
½ teaspoon garlic powder
Salt to taste
¼ teaspoon pepper
1½ teaspoons Italian seasoning
1 teaspoon leaf oregano
½ teaspoon basil
1½ cups diced cooked beef without visible fat
Water as necessary

Place first six ingredients in a large soup kettle, at least 6 quarts; cover and simmer for 15 minutes.

Add all remaining ingredients except meat to soup, cover, and simmer for another 15 minutes.

Add meat to soup. Add enough water, if necessary, to make 3 quarts soup. Serve hot, 1 cup per serving.

Yields 3 quarts—12 servings

Nutritive Values Per Serving

CAL	CHO (g)	PRO (g)	TOTAL FAT (g)	SAT. FAT (g)	CHOL (mg)	FIBER (g)	NA (mg)
121	14	12	2	.6	18	3	682

Food exchanges per serving: ½ starch, 1 lean meat, 1 vegetable
Low-sodium diets: Use salt-free broth. Omit salt.
Sugar content per serving: None.

Tomato Bouillon

1 cup chopped celery
1 cup chopped onions
2 cups fat-free chicken broth
3 cups fat-free beef broth
3 cups tomato juice
1 teaspoon Worcestershire sauce
¼ teaspoon basil
Whisper of black pepper

Place celery, onions, and chicken broth in saucepan. Cover and simmer 30 minutes. Drain well. Discard vegetables and return broth to saucepan.

Add beef broth, tomato juice, and seasonings to chicken broth. Cover and simmer for about 5 minutes. Taste for seasoning and add more, if necessary. Serve ¾ cup hot or cold bouillon per serving.

Yields 2 quarts—10 servings

Nutritive Values Per Serving

CAL	CHO (g)	PRO (g)	TOTAL FAT (g)	SAT. FAT (g)	CHOL (mg)	FIBER (g)	NA (mg)
30	6	3	trace	0	0	1	598

Food exchanges per serving: 1 vegetable
Low-sodium diets: Use low-sodium broths and tomato juice. Delete Worcestershire sauce and add ¼ teaspoon ground thyme or dried oregano.
Sugar content per serving: None.

Green and Gold Cream Soup

This is a basic cream soup. Other vegetables in the same vegetable food group may be substituted for the carrots and broccoli. The vegetables may also be puréed before they are added to the soup—but I like the small bits of vegetables in the soup.

1 cup frozen or fresh broccoli stems and pieces
1 cup finely chopped carrots
3 tablespoons flour
2 tablespoons margarine
4 cups fat-free chicken broth
2 tablespoons instant nonfat dry milk
¼ teaspoon salt

Chop broccoli into small pieces. They should be large enough to have a little texture but not very large. Place in a small container, cover, and cook for 2 minutes on high in the microwave or cook until barely tender in a small amount of water. Drain well and set aside.

Place carrots in a small container. Add 1 tablespoon water, cover, and cook on high in the microwave for 6–8 minutes or until tender, or cook until barely tender in a small amount of water. Drain well and set aside.

Place flour and margarine in a 1½- or 2-quart saucepan over moderate heat. Cook and stir until smooth. Stir broth, dry milk, and salt together and add to flour mixture. Cook and stir over moderate heat until smooth and thickened. Continue to cook, stirring frequently, over low heat for 1 more minute. Add vegetables and reheat to serving temperature. Serve ¾ cup soup per serving.

Yields 4 cups—6 servings

Nutritive Values Per Serving

CAL	CHO (g)	PRO (g)	TOTAL FAT (g)	SAT. FAT (g)	CHOL (mg)	FIBER (g)	NA (mg)
76	7	4	4	.6	trace	1	582

Food exchanges per serving: 1 vegetable, 1 fat
Low-sodium diets: Omit salt. Use salt-free margarine and low-sodium broth.
Sugar content per serving: None.

Potage Pierre

This luscious soup is from Beverly Wolfrum of Aurora, Colorado. She and I share a crusading fervor aimed at helping people lower their cholesterol counts. She told me she has been using this recipe since her husband was a seminarian and she needed to use economical recipes. Don't change a thing in this recipe; it is wonderful just as it is written. You may think it is ready after 2 hours, but please simmer it for at least 4 hours because the flavor continues to improve.

> **1 pound lean beef with fat and gristle removed**
> **1 29-ounce can whole tomatoes and juice**
> **¾ cup finely chopped onions**
> **¾ cup finely chopped celery**
> **¾ cup finely chopped carrots**
> **4 cups fat-free beef broth**
> **1 teaspoon thyme**
> **10 whole peppercorns**

Place meat in a 4-quart pot. Chop tomatoes and add with their juice to meat. Add onions, celery, carrots, broth, thyme, and peppercorns. Cover and simmer 4 to 5 hours. Add hot water if necessary to keep yield at 10½ cups. Serve hot, using 1½ cups per serving.

Yields 10½ cups—7 servings

Nutritive Values Per Serving

CAL	CHO (g)	PRO (g)	TOTAL FAT (g)	SAT. FAT (g)	CHOL (mg)	FIBER (g)	NA (mg)
132	9	17	3	1	39	2	610

Food exchanges per serving: 2 very lean meat, 2 vegetable
Low-sodium diets: Use low-sodium canned tomatoes and salt-free broth.
Sugar content per serving: None.

Mulligatawny Soup

This soup is delicious and I think it is well worth the bread exchange it costs me.

¼ cup chopped onions
¼ cup chopped fresh green pepper
¼ cup diced celery
2 tablespoons vegetable oil
⅓ cup flour
5 cups fat-free chicken broth at room temperature
1 small (4 to the pound) tart apple
¾ cup drained, crushed canned tomatoes
¼ teaspoon curry powder
⅛ teaspoon ground cloves
Whisper of white pepper
1 cup diced cooked chicken with fat and
skin removed
1 cup cooked rice

Fry onions, pepper, and celery in oil in a heavy saucepan over moderate heat, stirring frequently, until the onions are limp but not browned. Remove vegetables from the pan with a slotted spoon and reserve for later use.

Add flour to oil in pan and stir over moderate heat until smooth and lightly browned. Add broth to flour mixture and stir over moderate heat until thickened. Add the reserved vegetables.

Wash and core apple and cut into small pieces as though you were going to make Waldorf salad. Add to soup. Add tomatoes and seasonings to soup. Cover and simmer for 45 minutes or until the vegetables are tender.

Add chicken and rice to the soup just before it is served. Reheat soup if necessary and serve 1 cup hot soup per serving.

Yields 7 cups—7 servings

Nutritive Values Per Serving

CAL	CHO (g)	PRO (g)	TOTAL FAT (g)	SAT. FAT (g)	CHOL (mg)	FIBER (g)	NA (mg)
163	18	10	6	1	18	1	524

Food exchanges per serving: 1 starch, 1 lean meat
Low-sodium diets: Use low-sodium broth and rice cooked without salt.
Sugar content per serving: None.

Swiss Soup

I like having a soup that is only 1 vegetable exchange. You can place 1–2 ounces of lean, cubed cooked beef in a soup bowl and add this soup for a good vegetable-beef soup that only costs you the meat and 1 vegetable exchange.

1 tablespoon margarine
¼ cup chopped onions
½ cup chopped celery
¼ cup chopped carrots
¼ cup chopped fresh green pepper
6 cups fat-free beef broth
2 cups shredded cabbage
¹⁄₁₆ teaspoon black pepper (optional)
Salt to taste
¼ teaspoon ground nutmeg

Melt the margarine in the bottom of a saucepan. Add onions, celery, carrots, and peppers and stir over moderate heat about 4 minutes or until the vegetables are limp but not browned.

Add broth to vegetables; cover and simmer 15 minutes.

Add cabbage and seasonings to soup. Cover and simmer another 5 minutes. Serve soup hot, 1 cup per serving.

Yields 7 cups—7 servings

Nutritive Values Per Serving

CAL	CHO (g)	PRO (g)	TOTAL FAT (g)	SAT. FAT (g)	CHOL (mg)	FIBER (g)	NA (mg)
41	4	3	2	.3	0	1	571

Food exchanges per serving: 1 vegetable
Low-sodium diets: Do not add salt. Use salt-free margarine.
Sugar content per serving: None.

Vegetable Beef Soup

1½ pounds beef stew meat
Cold water as necessary
2 quarts cold water
1½ teaspoons salt
⅛ teaspoon black pepper
1 cup diced fresh white potatoes
½ cup diced carrots
1 cup coarsely chopped onions
½ cup shredded cabbage
1 cup canned tomatoes and juice
½ cup fresh or frozen green string beans
    cut into ½-inch pieces

Trim any gristle and visible fat from meat with a sharp knife. Place meat in a saucepan. Cover with cold water, bring to a boil, and boil 1 minute. Remove meat from broth and discard broth. Return meat to saucepan.

Add 2 quarts cold water, salt, and pepper to meat. Bring to a boil. Reduce heat, cover, and simmer for about 1½ hours or until meat is tender. Drain the broth from the meat. Strain the broth, cover, and refrigerate meat and broth separately. After the broth is chilled, remove the hard fat from the top of the broth.

Measure the broth and add cold water to the broth to equal 7 cups of liquid. Add vegetables to stock. Cover and simmer 30–45 minutes or until vegetables are tender. Taste for seasoning and add more if desired. (Nutritive values are calculated using 1½ teaspoons salt.) Add meat to soup. Reheat to serving temperature, if necessary, and serve hot using 1 cup per serving.

Yields 2 quarts—8 servings

Nutritive Values Per Serving

CAL	CHO (g)	PRO (g)	TOTAL FAT (g)	SAT. FAT (g)	CHOL (mg)	FIBER (g)	NA (mg)
145	8	19	4	1.4	51	1	523

Food exchanges per serving: 2 very lean meat, 1½ vegetable, 1 fat
Low-sodium diets: Omit salt. Use fresh tomatoes or tomatoes canned
    without salt.
Sugar content per serving: None.

Vegetable Chowder

2 tablespoons margarine
½ cup chopped onions
¼ cup chopped carrots
¼ cup chopped fresh green peppers
1 cup diced fresh white potatoes
1 cup cream-style corn
1 teaspoon salt
¹⁄₁₆ teaspoon black pepper
3 cups water
4 ounces sliced fresh or frozen Brussels
  sprouts
⅓ cup instant dry milk
2 tablespoons flour
1 cup cold water

Melt margarine in the bottom of a saucepan. Add onions, carrots, and peppers and cook and stir over moderate heat until onions are soft but not browned.

Add potatoes, corn, seasonings, and water to vegetables. Bring to a boil. Reduce heat and simmer 20 minutes. Add Brussels sprouts to soup. Cover and simmer 10 minutes.

Stir milk, flour, and cold water together until smooth. Add to soup and stir to mix. Simmer, stirring frequently, for 3 minutes. Remove from heat and serve hot, 1 cup per serving.

Yields 7 cups—7 servings

Nutritive Values Per Serving

CAL	CHO (g)	PRO (g)	TOTAL FAT (g)	SAT. FAT (g)	CHOL (mg)	FIBER (g)	NA (mg)
106	17	3	4	.6	1	2	482

Food exchanges per serving: 1 starch, ½ fat
Low-sodium diets: Omit salt. Use salt-free margarine.
Sugar content per serving: None.

9

Fish

Fish is a wonderful food. It is low in calories and saturated fat and easy and quick to prepare. With so many different kinds of fish available and so many different ways to prepare them, it is easy to have fish two or three times a week (as doctors and dietitians recommend) without repeating yourself very often. If you live along the coasts or in the Great Lakes area, you are probably used to serving a great deal of fish. If you live inland and aren't used to using all that much fish, you are going to be very pleasantly surprised as you try the various recipes and different kinds of fish available across the country.

Fish is available in the following forms:

- *Whole fish* are fish as they are caught. The fish needs to be scaled, eviscerated, and cut into portions, if necessary. The head and tail are generally removed although they may be left on some of the smaller fish.
- *Dressed fish* have had the scales and entrails removed. The head, tail, and fins are generally also removed although the head and tail may be left on smaller fish. These are called pan-dressed fish, such as trout or catfish. The fish may also be cut into fillets, steaks, or chunks.
- *Fillets* are ready to be cooked when they are purchased. They are the sides of fish cut from the backbone.
- *Steaks* are generally cut ⅝ to 1 inch thick and are cross sections cut from larger fish. The only bone in them is the cross section of the backbone. They are ready to be cooked when purchased.

- *Chunks* are cross section pieces of larger fish. The only bone that might be in them would be a cross section of the backbone, but most of the pieces are without bone. They are ready to be cooked when they are purchased.
- *Sticks and squares* are generally cut from frozen fish blocks. They are coated with a batter or breading. They are not recommended for a low-cholesterol diabetic diet unless you are sure the batter does not include whole eggs and the package includes nutritive information to help you determine the exchanges for them.
- *Fish portions* are generally individual pieces of fish that have been dipped in batter or breading and frozen so they can be cooked or reheated without further preparation. They, too, are not recommended for a low-cholesterol diabetic diet unless you are sure the batter does not contain whole eggs and the package includes nutritive information to help you determine the exchanges for them.
- *Canned fish* includes many varieties of fish. They are ready to be used as purchased. The ones packed in water are lower in calories than the ones packed in oil. The most readily available canned fish are salmon, tuna, mackerel, and sardines. Several species of fish are marketed as tuna and all of them are equally desirable.

When you are buying fresh fish, it should be really fresh. Fresh fish should have the following characteristics:

- *Flesh* should be firm and not separated from the bones.
- *Odor* should be fresh and mild. Fish with a strong odor is probably older since the fish odor becomes more apparent with age.
- *Eyes* should be bright and clear. The eyes become sunken as the fish becomes stale.
- *Gills* should be red and free of slime.
- *Skin* should be shiny with the color unfaded. Older fish lose their iridescence and the color is faded.
- *Fish steaks or fillets* should be firm and have a fresh-cut appearance. There should be no trace of brown or drying around the edges.

When you are buying frozen fish, the following points are important:

- *Flesh* should be frozen solid when purchased. There should not be any discoloration or freezer burn.
- *Odor* should not be apparent. Fish that is frozen properly should have little or no odor. A strong fish odor indicates poor quality.
- *Wrappings* should be of moisture- and vapor-retardant materials. There should be little or no space between the fish and the wrappings. Wrappings should not be torn, dirty, or discolored.

After fish are purchased, they must be stored correctly to avoid loss of quality and possible food spoilage or poisoning.

- *Fresh fish* should be placed in the refrigerator immediately after they are purchased. They should be stored in the refrigerator at 35–40°F and should be used within 48 hours after they are purchased.
- *Frozen fish* should be placed in the freezer in their original wrappings and stored at zero degrees or below. Fish should always be dated so you can use the oldest fish first and not have to contend with freezer burn on some package that got shoved to the back of the freezer. It is important to thaw fish correctly. A 1-pound package of fish should thaw in the refrigerator in about 24 hours, or in 1–2 hours under cold running water. I thaw fish in the microwave, placing it at defrost for 5–10 minutes for a 1-pound package. Fish should never be defrosted at room temperature because of the danger of food spoilage or food poisoning. Frozen fillets or steaks may be cooked without thawing if you allow a little more cooking time, but if they are to be breaded or baked, they should always be thawed before they are prepared.

Fish is cooked to develop flavor, soften the small amount of connective tissue, and make it easier to digest. Fish cooked at too high a temperature or for too long will be tough and dry and the flavor will be poor.

Deep-fat-fried fish is a favorite with many people, but it isn't all that good on a low-cholesterol diabetic diet—you can't be sure exactly how much fat the fish has absorbed or what ingredients are in the batter. If you are eating in a restaurant, it is a good idea to order plain broiled or baked fish, and if it is served with a sauce ask them to serve the fish with the sauce on the side. If you can, you should ask what they have used to baste the fish; it might be an oil-based marinade, but then again it might be lemon butter, which you wouldn't want to eat.

I have tried to include recipes in this chapter to illustrate the various methods for preparing fish. If you have a favorite recipe you want to use that doesn't contain cholesterol, you can calculate the exchanges from the information in Chapter 3.

Some fish do contain some fat, although most of the different kinds of fish are very lean. Fish that are considered lean include the following: catfish, cod, flounder, haddock, halibut, lake perch, ocean perch, pike, red snapper, sole, swordfish, and whiting.

Some recipes for preparing fish are methods more than individual recipes. These include the following:

Broiled fish. This is a form of dry heat cooking but the heat is more direct and intense than when fish is baked. It is best to use steaks, fillets, or pan-dressed fish about 1 inch thick because the intense heat will dry out thinner fish. The fish should be thawed and patted dry with a paper towel and should be brushed with an oil-based marinade or sauce while it is being broiled. The directions for your own broiler should be followed; however, it is a general rule that fish should be broiled about 3–4 inches from the source of heat. Thicker cuts should be broiled further from the heat than thinner cuts. The length of time for broiling depends upon the thickness of the fish to be broiled and the distance from the heat. It generally takes about 10–15 minutes before the fish flakes easily when tested with a fork. Fish do not generally need to be turned while they are being broiled, but thicker pieces such as whole fish should be turned and brushed with more marinade when they are about half-cooked. Always serve broiled fish very hot.

Charcoal-broiled fish. Fish are good for this type of cooking because they cook so quickly. Pan-dressed fish, fillets, and steaks are all suitable for broiling. The fish should be thawed and patted dry before it is broiled; and because it flakes easily, it is a good idea to use a well-greased, long-handled, hinged wire grill for your fish. Thicker cuts of fish are best because they will dry out less than the thinner cuts, but all of them should be basted generously before and during the cooking period. Fish are generally cooked about 4 inches from moderately hot coals for 15–20 minutes depending upon the thickness of the fish. French or Italian style dressings that are based on oil are good for basting the fish. It is not a good idea to baste fish with a sauce high in sugar because it burns easily—but since we would never do that anyway we won't need to worry about that type of marinade. Marinades used for both types of broiling should be calculated when food exchanges for the fish are calculated.

Poached fish. Poaching means to cook in a simmering liquid. The fish should be placed in a single layer in a shallow, wide pan such as a large frying pan and barely covered with liquid. The liquid can be fish stock, lightly salted water, white wine and water, or water with various herbs in it. It is important not to let the water boil and not to overcook the fish. The fish should cook in a simmering liquid, in a covered pan, about 10–15 minutes or until the fish flakes easily when tested with a fork. It can then be served warm or cold with a sauce, in a salad, or used for a casserole.

Steamed fish. Steamed fish is generally cooked with steam from hot water although some people like to add herbs to the water. It is a good way to cook fish to retain its natural flavor and juices. A steamer is best, but any deep pan with a tight cover may be used if you have a rack that fits in the pan. The rack is to keep the fish out of the water. The fish is placed on a rack over rapidly boiling water and allowed to steam for 10–15 minutes or until the fish flakes easily when tested with a fork. Steamed fish is generally served the same way as poached fish.

Fish cooked in foil. Individual fish portions may be baked in the oven or prepared on an outside grill in foil. Put a single portion of fish in a foil packet along with some sauce or margarine and thinly sliced vegetables. It cooks beautifully this way without getting any pans dirty and tastes delicious when it is finished. It takes longer on the grill than in the oven but either method is satisfactory. The fish should be cooked until it flakes easily when tested with a fork.

Of course, all of the above methods yield fish that should be calculated using 1 ounce of the cooked fish as 1 lean meat exchange plus whatever sauce you use on the fish.

The sauces served with fish can be murder. I generally ask for the sauce on the side when ordering fish. If I can see that it is based on sour cream or is high in egg yolks or some other forbidden ingredient, I ask for lemon juice—or if all else fails, I ask for just plain vinegar. You would be surprised at the difference between those sauces and herb-flavored vinegar or lemon juice when you are calculating the exchanges for a fish recipe.

I first discovered the advantages of vinegar with fish when I was eating fish and chips in Great Britain. When I came home, I tried it again and liked it as well as I did over there. I guess I had thought that maybe it was the atmosphere over there which made me like it; however, it worked just as well here, so I experimented with different types of vinegar and discovered I could make my own herb vinegar very easily. I steep about a tablespoon of herbs (fresh if possible) in a cup of vinegar for a few days or until it is as strong as I like it. Then I strain off the herbs, put my vinegar in a cruet, and keep it for the next time we have fish. I even like to use the pickle juice from Mrs. Riley's Pickles (see Index) on fish.

Baked Fish with Mustard Sauce

6 3-ounce fillets of codfish, haddock,
  perch, flounder, or whiting
Margarine
1 tablespoon lemon juice
1 tablespoon vegetable oil
1 teaspoon paprika
1 teaspoon salt
¼ cup all-purpose flour
2 tablespoons margarine
2 tablespoons instant nonfat dry milk
2 cups cool water
1 tablespoon chopped parsley
2 teaspoons salad mustard
Whisper of white pepper

Defrost fish if necessary. Pat dry with paper towels and place in a shallow baking pan lined with aluminum foil and greased with margarine.

In a small cup mix together lemon juice, oil, paprika, and ½ teaspoon of the salt. Using a pastry brush, brush the tops and sides of the fillets with the mixture. Bake at 350°F for 30–40 minutes depending upon the thickness of the fillets, or until the fish flakes easily when tested with a fork.

While the fish is baking, in a small saucepan cook the flour, margarine, dry milk, and remaining ½ teaspoon salt. Stir over low heat until smooth. Add 2 cups water to flour mixture and cook and stir until smooth and thickened.

Add remaining seasonings to sauce and stir to mix well. Serve ⅓ cup hot sauce over 1 hot fish fillet per serving.

Yields 6 fillets—6 servings

Nutritive Values Per Serving

CAL	CHO (g)	PRO (g)	TOTAL FAT (g)	SAT. FAT (g)	CHOL (mg)	FIBER (g)	NA (mg)
157	5	16	7	1	37	trace	495

Food exchanges per serving: 2 very lean meat, 1 vegetable, 1½ fat
Low-sodium diets: Omit salt and use salt-free margarine.
Sugar content per serving: None.

Baked Fish Steak

**1 pound halibut or salmon steak cut
⅝-1 inch thick
⅓ cup Spicy Tomato Dressing (see Index)**

Defrost fish if necessary. Pat dry with paper towels. Line a small pan with aluminum foil. Grease the foil with margarine and place the steak on the pan. The steak can be cut into 4 equal portions at this time or after it is baked.

Brush steak generously with dressing using a pastry brush. Bake 25–35 minutes at 350°F or until fish flakes easily when tested with a fork. Cut into 4 equal portions, if not already cut, and serve hot using 1 portion per serving.

Yields 1 pound—4 servings

Nutritive Values Per Serving

CAL	CHO (g)	PRO (g)	TOTAL FAT (g)	SAT. FAT (g)	CHOL (mg)	FIBER (g)	NA (mg)
107	1	19	2	trace	29	trace	167

Food exchanges per serving: 3 very lean meat
Low-sodium diets: Use low-sodium variation of the salad dressing.
Sugar content per serving: None.

Oven-Fried Fish Fillets

3 tablespoons margarine at room
   temperature
½ cup dry bread crumbs
1 teaspoon paprika
¼ teaspoon garlic powder
½ teaspoon salt
2 tablespoons Parmesan cheese
8 4-ounce codfish fillets
½ cup skim milk

Line a 9" × 13" cake pan with aluminum foil. Grease the foil using part of the margarine. Set the remaining margarine aside for later use.

Place bread crumbs, seasonings, and Parmesan in a pie pan. Mix well to blend and set aside for later use.

Defrost fish if necessary. Pat dry with a paper towel. Place milk in an individual salad bowl. Dip fish fillets in milk and then in the bread crumb mixture. Place evenly on the foil in the pan.

Using all the remaining margarine, spread a small amount of the margarine on top of each of the fillets. Bake at 500°F for 10–15 minutes or until lightly browned and firm. (The length of time will depend upon the thickness of the fillets.) Let stand 5 minutes and serve hot, using 1 fillet per serving.

Yields 8 fillets—8 servings

Nutritive Values Per Serving

CAL	CHO (g)	PRO (g)	TOTAL FAT (g)	SAT. FAT (g)	CHOL (mg)	FIBER (g)	NA (mg)
170	6	22	6	1	50	trace	338

Food exchanges per serving: 3 very lean meat, ⅓ starch, 1 fat
Low-sodium diets: Omit salt. Use salt-free margarine.
Sugar content per serving: None.

Shrimp Etouffée

This is another Cajun recipe I developed, with the help of Della Andreassen, R.D., from Lafayette, Louisiana, for a magazine article about Cajun cooking.

> **1 tablespoon vegetable oil**
> **¾ cup chopped onions**
> **½ cup chopped fresh green peppers**
> **½ cup chopped celery**
> **½ cup tomato sauce**
> **¼ cup water**
> **2 teaspoons cornstarch**
> **⅛–¼ teaspoon cayenne pepper**
> **¼ teaspoon salt**
> **8 ounces cooked, cleaned shrimp**
> **¼ cup chopped fresh green onion tops**

Preheat ½-quart saucepan over medium heat for 1 minute. Swirl oil in bottom of pan. Add onions, green peppers, and celery and cook, stirring frequently, over medium heat until onions are soft but not browned.

In a separate bowl combine tomato sauce, water, cornstarch, cayenne pepper, and salt and stir until smooth. Add tomato sauce mixture to vegetables and cook and stir until sauce is clear. Add shrimp and heat to serving temperature. Stir chopped onion tops into mixture and serve hot using 1 cup per serving. *Note:* This is good over rice, but rice is not included in the nutritive analysis.

Yields 3 cups—3 servings

Nutritive Values Per Serving

CAL	CHO (g)	PRO (g)	TOTAL FAT (g)	SAT. FAT (g)	CHOL (mg)	FIBER (g)	NA (mg)
158	10	17	6	.8	147	2	615

Food exchanges per serving: 2 very lean meat, 2 vegetable, 1 fat
Low-sodium diets: Omit salt. Use low-sodium tomato sauce.
Sugar content per serving: None.

Grecian Shrimp and Baby Artichoke Brochette

Since shrimp is permitted once a week on a low-cholesterol diet, I like to use a really good recipe when I prepare it, especially when I'm in Arizona and can pick fresh lemons off the tree.

12 baby artichokes
½ cup olive or vegetable oil
¼ cup fresh lemon juice
1 clove garlic, minced
1 teaspoon oregano
1 teaspoon Dijon mustard
½ teaspoon rosemary
⅛–¼ teaspoon crushed red pepper flakes
¼ teaspoon salt
Whisper of freshly ground black pepper
16 peeled, raw jumbo shrimp with tails left
    intact
1 fresh lemon, cut into wedges

Cook artichokes in boiling, salted water just until tender, 8–12 minutes, depending on their size. Drain well and hold under cold running water until cool to the touch. They can be cooked a day in advance and refrigerated until needed, if desired.

Combine oil, lemon juice, garlic, oregano, mustard, rosemary, red pepper flakes, salt, and pepper in a large plastic food bag. Add shrimp, seal tightly, and refrigerate 1 hour or longer before cooking.

If artichokes are very small, leave them whole. Larger ones should be cut in half lengthwise and the choke removed. Trim pointed tips of leaves if they are sharp. Thread artichokes and shrimp alternately onto 4 metal or wooden skewers, using 4 shrimp and 3 artichokes for each skewer. (If you are using wooden skewers, soak them in water for 10 minutes before using them.) Brush them with any remaining marinade.

Grill brochettes over a hot fire, turning once, for 7–9 minutes or until shrimp is cooked through. Garnish with lemon wedges. Serve hot, using 1 brochette per serving.

Note: Baby artichokes, which are about 2 inches long, are too young to have developed the prickly inside choke, so you can eat the whole artichoke. If they are not available, use the smallest mature ones you can find.

Yields 4 brochettes—4 servings

Nutritive Values Per Serving

CAL	CHO (g)	PRO (g)	TOTAL FAT (g)	SAT. FAT (g)	CHOL (mg)	FIBER (g)	NA (mg)
410	19	23	29	4	140	7	423

Food exchanges per serving: 3 very lean meat, 4 fat, 4 vegetable
Low-sodium diets: Omit salt.
Sugar content per serving: None.

Tuna Fish, Mushrooms, and Celery

If you have wondered why I use mushrooms and celery so often, it is not only because we like them but also because they add bulk and flavor to a recipe without adding much carbohydrate or many calories.

> **2 6½-ounce cans of chunk-style tuna fish packed in water**
> **3 tablespoons margarine**
> **1 cup thinly sliced celery**
> **1 4-ounce can mushroom stems and pieces, drained**
> **3 tablespoons all-purpose flour**
> **2 cups water at room temperature**
> **½ cup instant nonfat dry milk**
> **½ teaspoon salt**
> **Whisper of white pepper**

Drain tuna well. Discard liquid. Set tuna aside for later use.

Place margarine in a 1½-quart saucepan. Melt over moderate heat. Add celery and mushrooms and cook, stirring occasionally, over moderate heat until celery is limp. Add flour to vegetables and cook and stir until flour is absorbed.

With a fork, mix water, dry milk, salt, and pepper to blend. Add to vegetables and cook and stir over moderate heat until smooth and thickened. Add tuna fish. Mix very lightly and serve hot using ¾ cup per serving.

Yields 4 cups—6 servings

Nutritive Values Per Serving

CAL	CHO (g)	PRO (g)	TOTAL FAT (g)	SAT. FAT (g)	CHOL (mg)	FIBER (g)	NA (mg)
163	7	19	6	1	24	trace	536

Food exchanges per serving: 3 lean meat, 1 vegetable
Low-sodium diets: Omit salt. Use salt-free margarine.
Sugar content per serving: None.

Fish Creole

**4 4-ounce fillets of codfish, haddock,
    perch, flounder, or whiting**
2 tablespoons vegetable oil
¼ cup chopped fresh green peppers
¼ cup chopped onions
1 tablespoon all-purpose flour
1 cup chopped canned tomatoes and juice
½ teaspoon salt
½ teaspoon sugar
⅛ teaspoon ground cloves
Whisper of pepper

Defrost fish, if necessary. Pat dry with paper towels and place in a shallow 1-quart casserole.

Place oil in a small saucepan. Bring to a cooking temperature. Add peppers and onions and cook, stirring frequently, over moderate heat until onions are soft but not browned. Add flour to vegetables. Cook and stir until flour is absorbed by the vegetables.

Add tomatoes and seasonings to vegetables. Cook and stir over moderate heat for 2 minutes. Pour the hot sauce over the fish. Bake, uncovered, at 350°F for 35–40 minutes or until the fish flakes easily when tested with a fork. Serve hot using 1 fillet and ¼ of the sauce per serving.

Yields 4 fillets—4 servings

Nutritive Values Per Serving

CAL	CHO (g)	PRO (g)	TOTAL FAT (g)	SAT. FAT (g)	CHOL (mg)	FIBER (g)	NA (mg)
180	6	21	8	1	49	1	433

Food exchanges per serving: 3 lean meat, 1 vegetable
Low-sodium diets: Omit salt. Use fresh tomatoes or low-sodium canned
    tomatoes.
Sugar content per serving: .1 teaspoon.

Salmon Patties with Creamed Peas

---

1 1-pound can red salmon
2 large egg whites
1 tablespoon finely chopped onions
¼ teaspoon salt
Whisper of pepper
1 cup crushed white soda crackers or
  saltines
1 cup fat-free chicken broth
1 tablespoon cornstarch
1 tablespoon margarine
1½ cups drained canned peas

Drain salmon and place the juice in a mixing bowl. Remove bones and dark skin from the salmon and set aside. Add egg whites, onions, salt, and pepper to salmon juice and mix together with a fork.

Crush the crackers with your hands. Don't substitute cracker crumbs. Add to the egg white mixture along with the salmon. Mix well with a fork to blend. (The cracker pieces and small chunks of salmon should still be visible.) Shape into patties about ¾ inch thick using about ⅓ cup of the mixture per patty. Place patties on a small cookie sheet that has been greased with margarine. Bake at 350°F for 35–40 minutes or until firm and lightly browned.

Stir broth and cornstarch together until smooth. Cook and stir over moderate heat in a small saucepan until thickened and smooth. Continue to cook and stir for another minute. Add margarine and peas to sauce and mix lightly. Reheat to serving temperature. Serve 1 patty with ⅙ of the sauce (about ⅓ cup) per serving.

Yields 6 patties—6 servings

CAL	CHO (g)	PRO (g)	TOTAL FAT (g)	SAT. FAT (g)	CHOL (mg)	FIBER (g)	NA (mg)
211	15	18	8	4	29	2	833

Food exchanges per serving: 1 starch, 2 lean meat
Low-sodium diets: Omit salt. Use salt-free margarine, low-sodium crackers, and fresh or frozen peas. Discard salmon juice and substitute an equal amount of water.
Sugar content per serving: None.

Codfish with Mushroom Sauce

1 4-ounce can mushroom stems and pieces
2 tablespoons margarine
2 tablespoons all-purpose flour
¼ teaspoon salt
Whisper of white pepper
1 cup fat-free chicken broth
4 4-ounce codfish fillets

Drain mushrooms. Discard juice. Chop mushrooms into small pieces. Place in small saucepan. Add margarine, flour, and seasonings to mushrooms and cook and stir over moderate heat until lightly browned. Add broth to mushrooms. Cook and stir over moderate heat until smooth and thickened.

Thaw fish if necessary. Pat dry with a paper towel and place in a 1½-quart casserole. Cover with the hot sauce, using a fork to ease the sauce around the fish. Bake uncovered at 350°F for 30–35 minutes or until the fish flakes easily when tested with a fork. Serve 1 fillet and ¼ of the sauce per serving.

Yields 4 fillets—4 servings

Nutritive Values Per Serving

CAL	CHO (g)	PRO (g)	TOTAL FAT (g)	SAT. FAT (g)	CHOL (mg)	FIBER (g)	NA (mg)
167	4	22	7	1	49	.5	490

Food exchanges per serving: 3 lean meat, 1 vegetable
Low-sodium diets: Omit salt. Use salt-free margarine, low-sodium broth, and fresh mushrooms.
Sugar content per serving: None.

Tartar Sauce

---

1 cup Kay's Cooked Dressing (see Index)
2 tablespoons finely chopped Mrs. Riley's
  Pickles (see Index)
1 tablespoon finely chopped onions
1 tablespoon chopped pimientos
1 tablespoon chopped parsley

Mix all ingredients well to blend. Refrigerate until served, using 2 tablespoons per serving.

Yields 1¼ cups—10 servings

Nutritive Values Per Serving

CAL	CHO (g)	PRO (g)	TOTAL FAT (g)	SAT. FAT (g)	CHOL (mg)	FIBER (g)	NA (mg)
24	2	1	1	trace	0	trace	117

Food exchanges per serving: 2 tablespoons may be considered free. ¼ cup is
   1 vegetable exchange
Low-sodium diets: Use low-sodium variation of salad dressing.
Sugar content per serving: None.

10

Poultry

Chicken and turkey are both important in the low-cholesterol diabetic diet because they are low in calories, easily available, and comparatively inexpensive. It is also relatively simple to remove the skin and fat from them before they are cooked. Goose is a little too fat and I never use it, but I depend upon chicken and turkey for many of our meals.

Chicken and turkey are interchangeable in many recipes and especially so when you are using cubed or diced, raw or cooked chicken or turkey with the fat and skin removed. When they are used interchangeably in recipes the nutritive values are based upon the first one listed. However, the food exchanges do not vary when one or the other is used.

Giblets should never be used on a low-cholesterol diet. If you don't have someone in your family who can use them, save them for a friend or neighbor who doesn't have to worry about cholesterol, or give them to your cat or dog—they'll probably love them.

All poultry is perishable and you should be careful when you are buying or storing it. It is a good idea to always observe the following precautions:

1. Buy frozen or chilled poultry only from freezers or refrigerated cases.
2. Inspect the wrappers to be sure they are not torn or damaged.
3. Keep fresh poultry in the coldest part of your refrigerator;

147

use it within two days after it is purchased or freeze it for later use.

Chicken or turkey parts may be purchased and they are often a better buy than the whole chicken or turkey. Turkey breast makes a very good roast and has less waste than the whole turkey. One ounce of the cooked turkey roast, without any skin, is of course 1 lean meat exchange. You can also buy turkey legs or thighs. I cook them all afternoon in the Crock-Pot and then use the meat for turkey sandwiches, à la king, casseroles, or salads if I have any left after dinner. Turkey frankfurters are available in most stores, but they still aren't all that good for you because they do have fat in them. Turkey ham is lean and I buy that occasionally because it is generally lower in fat than regular ham.

I haven't included directions for roasting a turkey because most of the turkeys you buy include that information on the wrapper. However, I want to caution you not to cook the dressing inside the chicken or turkey for a low-cholesterol diet. It picks up too much fat that way—saturated fat that is not acceptable on a low-cholesterol diet. I know it is good that way, and that is probably how your grandmother did it, but it is better to cook the dressing in a separate pan where you can control the amount and kind of fat in the dressing. If you cook dressing inside the chicken or turkey, give it to someone who doesn't need to worry about cholesterol—and prepare yours in a separate pan.

I remove the skin from a chicken before I roast it, but I don't when I roast a turkey. It is simple to serve a slice of the turkey breast with very little of the fat from the skin on it, but it isn't all that easy on the smaller chicken.

In my role as dietary consultant, every year I discussed with the dietary staff at the Lutheran Home in Strawberry Point, Iowa, the sanitation measures to be taken when preparing poultry. One year one of the ladies told me she thought she could give the lecture because she had heard it so many times—so I asked each of them to give the group a point that they remembered. I was pleased to find that they were all well aware of the precautions we should take when preparing poultry. The points we covered included the following:

1. *Be careful that everything is scrubbed* including table tops, chopping boards, knives, pans, and anything which might touch the poultry—both before and after you work with raw poultry.

2. *Do not defrost poultry at room temperature.* It should be defrosted in the refrigerator even if it does take several days for a large turkey. If you don't have refrigerator space sufficient to keep a large turkey in the refrigerator for that long, it can be defrosted, still in its plastic bag, in the sink in cold running water. This will take several hours but can be done the day before you want to cook the turkey.

3. *Do not stuff chicken or turkey the night before it is to be cooked,* or stuff it and cook it partially one day and finish cooking it the next day. Prestuffing gives bacteria a chance to multiply and could cause food poisoning.

4. *As soon as possible after dinner, refrigerate leftover chicken or turkey, dressing, and gravy in a shallow pan.* Food stored in a deep pan takes too long to cool to the correct temperature and bacteria can develop while it is chilling. Don't let chicken or turkey, dressing, or gravy stay on the table at room temperature for nibbling after dinner. Refrigerate everything as soon as possible and if anyone wants a snack, let him or her go to the refrigerator for it, or set it out for guests to help themselves later.

5. *Leftover chicken or turkey should be frozen if it is not to be used within the next couple of days.* Divide it into serving-size portions and freeze it for future use. It is a big help when you have unexpected company or want to make yourself a different entrée than you are serving to others in the family. I don't like to carry a chicken or turkey sandwich for lunch because of the danger of bacterial contamination, but if you freeze the sandwich and wrap it in foil it will be cold enough to be safe several hours later when you need it.

I hope you will enjoy the recipes in this chapter. Chicken

and turkey are a very special treat in many parts of the world and you can make them a special treat in your home, too. If you have a recipe of your own that you want to use, calculate the nutritive values in the recipe using the information in Chapter 3, and then go on from there. Remember to remove the skin and fat before the chicken is cooked and don't use any butter, cream, eggs, or other no-nos in your recipe.

Roast Chicken

I like leftovers. They are so nice to have on hand and I especially like leftover roast chicken—it makes such good sandwiches, salads, or casseroles. It is almost impossible these days to get an old-fashioned roasting chicken, which is good because those heavier chickens have a very high percentage of the fat we are trying to avoid on a low-cholesterol diabetic diet. Look for the heavier broiler-fryers and you should be able to find one weighing 3½ pounds, big enough for roasting.

1 3½-pound broiler-fryer chicken

Wash chicken well. Remove all skin and visible fat with a sharp knife. (Give the giblets to your cat or cook for someone who isn't on a low-cholesterol diet.) Place the chicken on a rack in a small roaster, breast side down. Cover and roast at 325°F for 1½–1¾ hours or until tender and lightly browned. Remove from the oven and let set 15 minutes before it is carved into portions. (*Note*: If you want to serve ¼ of a chicken, start out with a 2½-pound broiler-fryer and roast it about 1½ hours, cut it into 4 equal portions, and serve ¼ of the chicken per serving.) Serve 3 ounces of boneless cooked chicken per serving.

Yields 6 3-ounce servings plus leftovers

Nutritive Values Per Serving

CAL	CHO (g)	PRO (g)	TOTAL FAT (g)	SAT. FAT (g)	CHOL (mg)	FIBER (g)	NA (mg)
162	0	25	6	1.7	76	0	73

Food exchanges per serving: 3 lean meat
Low-sodium diets: May be used as written.
Sugar content per serving: None.

Oven-Browned Chicken

This is the chicken that Chuck and our friend Garrieth "Butch" Franks preferred, and they especially liked it with rice cooked in chicken broth.

> **1 2½-pound broiler-fryer chicken**
> **¾ cup dry bread crumbs**
> **1 teaspoon salt**
> **2 teaspoons paprika**
> **¹⁄₁₆ teaspoon black pepper**
> **½ teaspoon rubbed sage or thyme**
> **1 large egg white**
> **½ cup water**
> **1 tablespoon margarine**
> **1 tablespoon vegetable oil**

Wash chicken well. Remove skin and all visible fat with a sharp knife and cut into serving-size pieces. You should have 2 breast halves, 2 thighs, and 2 legs. (Freeze the neck, wings, and back to use later to make chicken broth.)

Mix bread crumbs and seasonings well and place in a pie pan. (You won't need but about half of this amount, but you need a certain amount in order to be able to dredge the chicken in it successfully. Discard the remainder. Nutritive values are calculated using ½ of the bread crumb mixture.)

Mix egg white and water well and put into an individual salad bowl. Spread a small rimmed cookie sheet with aluminum foil and spread the margarine on the aluminum foil. Dip each piece of chicken in the egg white mixture and then dredge it in the bread crumb mixture and place on the aluminum foil.

Dribble ½ teaspoon oil on the top of each piece of chicken. Bake at 350°F for 30 minutes. Remove the chicken from the oven. Turn it over and continue to bake for another 30 minutes. Serve hot or cold using 1 breast half or 1 leg and 1 thigh per serving.

Yields 1 chicken—4 servings

Nutritive Values Per Serving

CAL	CHO (g)	PRO (g)	TOTAL FAT (g)	SAT. FAT (g)	CHOL (mg)	FIBER (g)	NA (mg)
238	9	28	11	2	79	1	773

Food exchanges per serving: 4 lean meat, ½ starch
Low-sodium diets: Omit salt. Use salt-free margarine.
Sugar content per serving: None.

Poached Chicken

The poaching liquid can be changed to suit your favorite season-ings without changing the nutritive values, as long as it is based on chicken broth and no fat is added.

1 2½-pound broiler-fryer chicken
1 cup fat-free chicken broth
¼ teaspoon thyme or sage
¼ teaspoon salt
1 teaspoon chopped parsley
2 tablespoons orange juice
¼ cup dry white wine

Wash chicken well; remove skin and all visible fat with a sharp knife and cut into 4 equal portions. Place chicken in a shallow casserole. Discard the giblets, or give them to someone who isn't worried about cholesterol.

Mix together remaining ingredients and pour over chicken. Cover tightly with aluminum foil and bake at 325°F for about 1 hour or until the chicken is tender. Remove from oven and serve ¼ chicken per serving. (Discard the poaching liquid. It is too highly spiced to be good for soup and it isn't thick enough or flavorful enough for a sauce on the chicken.)

Yields 1 chicken—4 servings

Nutritive Values Per Serving

CAL	CHO (g)	PRO (g)	TOTAL FAT (g)	SAT. FAT (g)	CHOL (mg)	FIBER (g)	NA (mg)
152	trace	23	6	1.5	71	0	133

Food exchanges per serving: 3 lean meat
Low-sodium diets: Omit salt. Use salt-free chicken broth.
Sugar content per serving: None.

Emperor Chicken Breasts

This recipe comes from the multitalented "Chef Dave".

- ¼ teaspoon Chinese Five Spice seasoning (found in the ethnic food section of most stores)
- 1 cup soy sauce
- 4 4-ounce boneless, skinless chicken breast halves
- 1 tablespoon stick margarine
- ¼ cup cornstarch
- ¼ cup all-purpose flour
- 2½ cups fat-free chicken broth
- ¼ cup soy sauce
- 2 tablespoons cornstarch
- 2 tablespoons brown sugar
- 3 finely chopped garlic cloves
- 1 tablespoon peanut oil
- 1 teaspoon finely minced fresh ginger
- ½ cup chopped onions
- ½ cup chopped fresh green peppers
- ½ cup chopped celery
- ½ cup coarsely grated carrots
- 1 8-ounce can sliced bamboo shoots
- 1 cup coarsely chopped Chinese cabbage or bok choy
- 1 to 2 teaspoons Weight Watchers dry sugar substitute

Combine Chinese Five Spice seasoning and 1 cup soy sauce in a shallow baking pan. Wash chicken, drain well, and marinate overnight in soy sauce mixture. Drain well. Use ¼ of the margarine to grease a 9-inch-square nonstick pan. Set aside.

Blend ¼ cup cornstarch and flour in a shallow dish. Dredge chicken in flour mixture. Shake off any excess flour mixture and place chicken in the greased pan. Divide remaining margarine into 4 equal portions and put 1 portion on top of each breast half. Bake, uncovered, at 375°F for 30–40 minutes, or until browned.

While chicken is baking, combine chicken broth, ¼ cup soy sauce, 2 tablespoons cornstarch, brown sugar, and garlic. Blend well and set aside.

Preheat a nonstick frying pan, add the peanut oil and the ginger and cook and stir over medium heat until you can smell the ginger. Add onions, green peppers, celery, carrots, bamboo shoots, and Chinese cabbage or bok choy. Cook and stir over medium heat about 5 minutes or until thickened and lightly browned. Mix lightly and pour over browned chicken.

Bake, uncovered, at 325°F for 30 minutes or until chicken is lightly browned. Serve hot, using ½ breast topped with ¼ of chicken broth mixture and ¼ of vegetable mixture for each serving.

Yields 4 chicken breast halves with sauce—4 servings

Nutritive Values Per Serving

CAL	CHO (g)	PRO (g)	TOTAL FAT (g)	SAT. FAT (g)	CHOL (mg)	FIBER (g)	NA (mg)
318	29	32	8	1.4	66	3	2,137

Food exchanges per serving: 3 lean meat, 1 starch, 3 vegetable
Low-sodium diets: Omit salt and use salt-free broth and low-sodium soy sauce.
Sugar content per serving: 1½ teaspoons.

Chicken or Turkey Mushroom Casserole

---

1 4-ounce can mushroom stems and pieces
1 10¾-ounce can Campbell's Cream of Chicken soup
½ cup fat-free chicken broth
1 cup diced cooked chicken or turkey without skin or visible fat
½ cup long-grain rice
1 teaspoon chopped parsley

Combine mushrooms, soup, and broth in a small saucepan. Cook and stir over moderate heat until smooth and bubbling.

Add chicken, rice, and parsley to hot soup mixture. Stir to mix well and place in a 1½-quart casserole. Cover tightly and bake at 325°F for 40 minutes or until rice is tender. Serve ¾ cup hot casserole per serving.

Yields 3 cups—4 servings

Nutritive Values Per Serving

CAL	CHO (g)	PRO (g)	TOTAL FAT (g)	SAT. FAT (g)	CHOL (mg)	FIBER (g)	NA (mg)
240	26	15	8	2.6	37	1	781

Food exchanges per serving: 2 very lean meat, 1 fat, 1 starch, 2 vegetable
Low-sodium diets: Use low-sodium soup and broth.
Sugar content per serving: None.

Microwave Chicken

This recipe from Dr. Crockett is simple to prepare but it has an intriguing flavor. It can also be baked in a conventional oven, if you prefer.

1 2½-pound broiler-fryer chicken
½ teaspoon salt
¼ teaspoon ground sage
¾ cup orange juice
½ cup dry white wine

Wash chicken well. Remove all skin and visible fat with a sharp knife and cut into pieces. You should have 2 breast halves, 2 thighs, 2 wings, 2 legs, and the back. Freeze the wings, back, and neck for use for making broth later. Discard the giblets or give them to someone who isn't worried about cholesterol. Place the remaining pieces in an 8- or 9-inch dish suitable for use in the microwave.

Sprinkle salt and sage evenly over the chicken. Pour orange juice and wine over chicken pieces. Cover with plastic wrap or wax paper and cook on high for 5 minutes. Reduce heat to simmer and cook for 15–20 minutes or until tender. Serve hot with a little bit of the juice. Serve 1 breast half or 1 leg and 1 thigh per serving.

Note: If you prefer to use a conventional oven, cover the pan tightly with aluminum foil and bake at 325°F for 45 minutes–1 hour or until the chicken is tender. If you prefer, you can remove the foil the last 15 minutes to allow the chicken to brown a little.

Yields 1 chicken—4 servings

Nutritive Values Per Serving

CAL	CHO (g)	PRO (g)	TOTAL FAT (g)	SAT. FAT (g)	CHOL (mg)	FIBER (g)	NA (mg)
184	5	25	6	1.7	76	trace	349

Food exchanges per serving: 3 lean meat, 1 vegetable
Low-sodium diets: Omit salt.
Sugar content per serving: None.

Jambalaya

This is a recipe I developed with help from my friend Della Andreassen for a magazine article.

1 tablespoon vegetable oil
½ cup chopped onions
½ cup chopped fresh green peppers
½ cup chopped celery
1 16-ounce can tomatoes and juice
1 cup fat-free chicken broth
½ cup long-grain rice
½ teaspoon salt
⅛–¼ teaspoon cayenne pepper, to taste
1 tablespoon chopped parsley
½ teaspoon thyme
1½ cups boneless, chopped, cooked chicken
    with fat and skin removed
½ cup chopped cooked ham with all visible
    fat removed

Preheat a 2-quart saucepan over medium heat for 1 minute. Swirl oil in bottom of pan. Add onions, green peppers, and celery. Cook, stirring frequently, over medium heat until onions are soft but not browned. Add tomatoes and juice, broth, rice, salt, cayenne pepper, parsley, and thyme. Cook, uncovered, over low heat, stirring frequently, for 20–25 minutes, or until rice is tender. If mixture gets too dry, add hot water, ¼ cup at a time. Add chicken and ham and continue to cook until meat is heated through. Serve hot, using 1 cup per serving.

Yields 5 cups—5 servings

Nutritive Values Per Serving

CAL	CHO (g)	PRO (g)	TOTAL FAT (g)	SAT. FAT (g)	CHOL (mg)	FIBER (g)	NA (mg)
226	22	18	7	1.5	45	1.5	715

Food exchanges per serving: 2 lean meat, 1 starch, 1 vegetable
Low-sodium diets: Omit salt. Use low-sodium canned tomatoes and broth.
    Omit ham and use 2 cups chicken.
Sugar content per serving: None.

Chicken or Turkey à la King

1 4-ounce can mushroom stems and pieces
2 tablespoons vegetable oil
3 cups fat-free chicken broth
3 tablespoons cornstarch
¼ cup instant nonfat dry milk
⅛ teaspoon white pepper
2 cups cooked diced chicken or turkey with
    fat and skin removed
¼ cup chopped drained pimiento

Drain mushrooms well. Discard juice. Place oil in the bottom of a saucepan. Add the mushrooms and cook and stir over moderate heat until mushrooms are lightly browned.

Mix together broth, cornstarch, dry milk, and pepper until smooth. Add all at once to mushrooms and oil and stir, cooking over moderate heat until thickened. Continue to cook and stir another 2 minutes or until the starchy taste is gone.

Add chicken and pimiento to sauce. Mix lightly. Reheat to serving temperature and serve 1 cup per serving.

Yields 4 cups—4 servings

Nutritive Values Per Serving

CAL	CHO (g)	PRO (g)	TOTAL FAT (g)	SAT. FAT (g)	CHOL (mg)	FIBER (g)	NA (mg)
280	10	29	13	2.6	77	trace	648

Food exchanges per serving: 3 lean meat, 1 skim milk
Low-sodium diets: Use low-sodium chicken broth.
Sugar content per serving: None.

Chicken and Broccoli

This recipe is based on one from Judy Ballantine of Madison, Wisconsin. Judy is my cousin Virginia Ballantine's daughter-in-law. Judy is a diabetic, also, and does such interesting things with vegetables, and with her life—she is a marvelous artist. We were all so proud of her when she took a trip to China with her husband, Dr. Larry Ballantine, in spite of the fact that she is a Type I diabetic and had to manage her insulin, diet, and exercise to fit their schedule while they toured China.

> 1 tablespoon cornstarch
> 1 tablespoon sherry or fat-free chicken
>   broth
> 2 tablespoons soy sauce
> ½ cup fat-free chicken broth
> ⅛ teaspoon ground ginger
> ⅛ teaspoon garlic powder
> 2 medium-size chicken breast halves
>   without skin or visible fat
> 1 tablespoon vegetable oil
> ½ cup sliced onions
> 2 cups (6 ounces) frozen broccoli cuts
> ½ cup fat-free chicken broth

Combine first 6 ingredients and mix until smooth to form a marinade. Bone chicken breasts. Freeze bones for later use in broth and cut chicken into bite-size pieces. Place in marinade and refrigerate for 1–4 hours. Drain well, reserving marinade for later use.

Fry chicken in vegetable oil in heavy frying pan until clear and firm. Remove chicken from frying pan with a slotted spoon, leaving as much of the fat as possible still in the frying pan. Add onions and broccoli to the fat in the frying pan. Slice any larger pieces of broccoli to about ½-inch thickness. Cook and stir about 1 minute or until broccoli is thawed.

Add broth to vegetables, mix lightly, cover, and simmer for 5 minutes or until the broccoli is crisp-tender. Add marinade and cook and stir over moderate heat until sauce is thickened and clear. Add chicken and reheat to serving temperature. Serve ⅔ cup per serving over hot rice.

Yields 2 cups—3 servings

Nutritive Values Per Serving (without rice)

CAL	CHO (g)	PRO (g)	TOTAL FAT (g)	SAT. FAT (g)	CHOL (mg)	FIBER (g)	NA (mg)
179	10	21	6	.9	44	1.4	965

Food exchanges per serving: 2½ very lean meat, 1 vegetable, 1 fat
Low-sodium diets: Use low-sodium soy sauce and broth.
Sugar content per serving: None.

Tomato Chicken Sauce for Spaghetti

6 ounces raw boneless chicken without
  skin or visible fat
2 tablespoons vegetable oil
½ cup chopped onions
½ cup chopped fresh green peppers
½ cup chopped celery
2 cups canned tomato sauce
¼ teaspoon Italian seasoning
¼ teaspoon salt
¼ teaspoon leaf oregano
¼ teaspoon basil
½ teaspoon paprika
Whisper of white pepper

Cut chicken in ½-inch cubes and set aside for later use.

Place oil in the bottom of a saucepan. Heat over moderate
heat for 1 minute. Add onions, peppers, celery, and chicken and
cook and stir about 5 minutes or until chicken is white and firm,
and vegetables are softened but not browned.

Add remaining ingredients to vegetables and chicken and
cook, stirring almost constantly, for 5 minutes. Serve hot, ½ cup
per serving, over hot spaghetti or hot, thin, homemade noodles.

Yields 3 cups—6 servings

Nutritive Values Per Serving

CAL	CHO (g)	PRO (g)	TOTAL FAT (g)	SAT. FAT (g)	CHOL (mg)	FIBER (g)	NA (mg)
108	8	8	6	.8	20	1.7	614

Food exchanges per serving: 1 lean meat, 1½ vegetable, 1 fat
Low-sodium diets: Omit salt. Use low-sodium tomato sauce.
Sugar content per serving: None.

Chicken or Turkey Chop Suey

2 tablespoons cornstarch
1⅓ cups cold fat-free chicken broth
2 tablespoons soy sauce
1 teaspoon sugar
1 cup celery cut into ½-inch pieces
½ cup sliced onions
1 4-ounce can mushroom stems and pieces
    with juice
2 cups (16-ounce can) drained bean
    sprouts
2 cups diced, cooked chicken or turkey
    with skin and fat removed

Place cornstarch, broth, soy sauce, and sugar in saucepan and mix until smooth. Add celery, onions, and mushrooms to chicken broth mixture. Bring to a boil. Reduce heat and simmer, stirring frequently, for 20 minutes. Add bean sprouts to vegetables and simmer another 5 minutes, stirring frequently.

Add chicken to vegetables. Reheat to serving temperature, if necessary, and serve over hot rice, using ⅙ of the recipe (about 1 cup) per serving.

Yields about 6 cups—6 servings

Nutritive Values Per Serving (without rice)

CAL	CHO (g)	PRO (g)	TOTAL FAT (g)	SAT. FAT (g)	CHOL (mg)	FIBER (g)	NA (mg)
148	8	19	4	1	50	1.7	666

Food exchanges per serving: 2 lean meat, 1 vegetable
Low-sodium diets: Use low-sodium soy sauce and chicken broth.
Sugar content per serving: .2 teaspoon.

Chicken and Bean Sprouts with Mushrooms

---

1 4-ounce can mushroom pieces
Fat-free chicken broth as necessary
3 tablespoons soy sauce
1 teaspoon sugar
1½ tablespoons cornstarch
1 tablespoon sherry
2 large chicken breast halves without skin
or visible fat
2 tablespoons vegetable oil
1 16-ounce can bean sprouts

Drain mushrooms. Set drained mushrooms aside. Place the mushroom juice in a 1 cup measure and add enough broth to total 1 cup liquid. Set aside.

Mix together soy sauce, sugar, cornstarch, sherry, and 2 tablespoons of broth mixture in a small bowl until smooth, and set aside. Bone chicken breasts. You should have about 8 ounces chicken. Discard bones and cut chicken into ¾-inch cubes. Place chicken into the soy sauce mixture and let marinate for 10 minutes. Drain well, reserving the marinade for later.

Place oil in a heavy frying pan and heat over moderate heat until oil has a haze over it. Add the chicken to the hot oil and fry over moderate heat until chicken is firm and white, stirring frequently. Push chicken to the side of the frying pan. Add mushrooms and cook and stir until mushrooms are hot but not browned. Mix lightly with chicken. Add remainder of marinade and chicken broth mixture and cook and stir over moderate heat until the sauce is thickened and clear.

Drain bean sprouts well and stir into chicken and sauce. Cook and stir until hot and the sprouts are covered with sauce. Serve hot over rice, using ¾ cup per serving.

Yields 3 cups—4 servings

Nutritive Values Per Serving (without rice)

CAL	CHO (g)	PRO (g)	TOTAL FAT (g)	SAT. FAT (g)	CHOL (mg)	FIBER (g)	NA (mg)
197	8	22	8	1	49	1	1,090

Food exchanges per serving: 3 lean meat, 1 vegetable
Low-sodium diets: Use low-sodium soy sauce and broth.
Sugar content per serving: .3 teaspoon.

Chicken or Turkey Sandwich Spread

This is a favorite of my friend Jan Franks. Beef may be substituted for the chicken with no change in the food exchanges. This spread is also good for appetizers, and 1 tablespoon (about 3 appetizers) may be eaten without counting the spread.

**1 cup diced, cooked chicken or turkey
without skin or visible fat
3 tablespoons Kay's Cooked Dressing
(see Index)
2 tablespoons Mrs. Riley's Pickles, finely
chopped (see Index)**

Chop chicken rather fine in a food processor or grind in a food grinder, using the coarse blade.

Add dressing and pickles to chicken and mix well. Refrigerate until served using ¼ cup per serving for a sandwich.

Yields 1 cup—4 servings

Nutritive Values Per Serving

CAL	CHO (g)	PRO (g)	TOTAL FAT (g)	SAT. FAT (g)	CHOL (mg)	FIBER (g)	NA (mg)
121	1	17	5	1.3	50	trace	222

Food exchanges per serving: 2 lean meat -
Low-sodium diets: Use low-sodium variation of the dressing.
Sugar content per serving: None.

Chicken or Turkey Loaf

This makes excellent sandwiches, hot or cold.

> **2 pounds ground raw chicken or turkey**
> **1 cup dry bread crumbs**
> **2 large egg whites**
> **2 chicken bouillon cubes dissolved in ½ cup**
> **water**
> **1 tablespoon Worcestershire sauce or ½**
> **teaspoon rubbed sage or thyme**
> **1 tablespoon chopped parsley**
> **Dash of white pepper**
> **½ cup finely chopped onions**

It is best to grind the meat yourself since the ground chicken and turkey you buy generally has the skin and some fat in it. If your market will grind it for you without skin or fat you are in luck; but if not, figure that you will need about 3 pounds raw chicken or turkey for each pound of ground meat. Remove all skin and visible fat with a sharp knife. Bone the chicken or turkey, and then grind it in a meat grinder or chop it in a food processor. (Freeze the bones, wings, and neck to use to make broth later.) Refrigerate until needed. The ground poultry can also be used to make chicken or turkey patties.

Place remaining ingredients in mixing bowl. Mix well. Add chicken and mix lightly but thoroughly. Form into a loaf and place in a 9″ × 5″ × 3″ loaf pan that has been greased with margarine. Bake at 325°F about 1½ hours or until firm and lightly browned. Remove from oven and let set for 15 minutes. Slice into 12 equal slices and serve 1 slice per serving.

Yields 1 loaf—12 servings

Nutritive Values Per Serving

CAL	CHO (g)	PRO (g)	TOTAL FAT (g)	SAT. FAT (g)	CHOL (mg)	FIBER (g)	NA (mg)
136	8	18	3	.8	53	trace	323

Food exchanges per serving: 2 lean meat, ½ starch
Low-sodium diets: Use ½ cup strong low-sodium, fat-free chicken broth
    instead of the bouillon cubes and water. Use sage or thyme instead of
    Worcestershire sauce.
Sugar content per serving: None.

Chicken or Turkey Gravy

2¼ cups fat-free chicken or turkey
    drippings or broth
2 tablespoons cornstarch
⅛ teaspoon rubbed sage or thyme
1½ teaspoons margarine
Whisper of white pepper

Combine all ingredients in a small saucepan and cook and stir
over moderate heat, stirring constantly, until thickened and
smooth. Continue to cook and stir for another 2 minutes over
low heat until the starchy taste is gone. Serve hot using ¼ cup
gravy per serving. (The flavor of the gravy will depend upon the
flavor of the drippings or broth, so it is a good idea to use the
most flavorful drippings or broth possible for this gravy.)

Yields 2 cups—8 servings

Nutritive Values Per Serving

CAL	CHO (g)	PRO (g)	TOTAL FAT (g)	SAT. FAT (g)	CHOL (mg)	FIBER (g)	NA (mg)
19	2	1	1	trace	0	trace	190

Food exchanges per serving: 1 serving may be considered free. ½ cup is
    1 vegetable exchange
Low-sodium diets: Use low-sodium drippings or broth.
Sugar content per serving: None.

Bread Dressing

This costs a lot in bread exchanges but I included it because it illustrates how to adapt bread dressing to a low-cholesterol diet. I like it well enough to consider it worth the bread exchanges it costs me.

2 tablespoons vegetable oil
¾ cup finely chopped celery
½ cup finely chopped onions
2 cups fat-free chicken or beef broth
¾ teaspoon ground sage or thyme
Whisper of black pepper
12 slices day-old white bread
2 egg whites

Place oil in the bottom of a saucepan. Add celery and onions and cook over moderate heat for 5 minutes, stirring frequently. Remove from heat. Add broth and seasonings to vegetables. Mix well and cool to lukewarm, if necessary.

Cut bread into cubes. It is a good idea to leave the bread spread out on a tray overnight before it is used—the bread won't absorb enough liquid to give it a good flavor if it isn't somewhat dry. Place cubes in a large mixing bowl.

Add egg whites to lukewarm vegetables and broth. Mix well and pour over bread cubes. Toss lightly but thoroughly. Spread evenly in an 8-inch square cake pan or 1-quart shallow casserole that has been well greased with margarine. Bake at 375°F for 45 minutes. Cut 3 × 4 into 12 equal servings, allowing 1 square per serving.

Yields 8-inch square pan—12 servings

Nutritive Values Per Serving

CAL	CHO (g)	PRO (g)	TOTAL FAT (g)	SAT. FAT (g)	CHOL (mg)	FIBER (g)	NA (mg)
105	15	4	3	.5	trace	.9	276

Food exchanges per serving: 1 starch
Low-sodium diets: Use low-sodium broth.
Sugar content per serving: None.

11

Meats

Planning and preparing meat dishes is probably the hardest part of the low-cholesterol diabetic diet. Most of us are used to using a lot of plain roast meat, and this is still a good idea as long as we pick the leanest cuts and prepare them so that we remove as much of the remaining fat as possible.

Specific cuts with a lower fat content that are good for the low-cholesterol diabetic diet include the following:

- *Beef*—round, rump, sirloin, tenderloin, and dried beef
- *Pork*—loin, center cut roasts or chops, tenderloin, lean ham, center cut ham, and Canadian bacon
- *Veal*—round, rump, leg, sirloin, cutlets, and loin chops
- *Lamb*—sirloin, leg, cutlets, and sirloin chops

Baking, boiling, broiling, and roasting are all good methods for preparing meat because they help remove any remaining fat after all of the visible fat has been removed with a sharp knife. Baked or roasted meats should be placed on a rack so that the liquids will drip down in the bottom of the pan and the meat won't be cooking in its own fat. If necessary, the meat can be basted with broth or a marinade. Drippings in the bottom can be chilled and used for gravy or soups after the fat is removed.

Meats can be pan-broiled if salt or only a small amount of fat is used in the bottom of the frying pan—and you will be surprised how little fat is really needed for pan-broiling. I like to do it by sprinkling the pan first with salt; but if you can't do that, you can use just a tablespoon of oil in the bottom of the frying pan with excellent results. Oil is better than margarine for pan-frying because it doesn't get brown and burn as easily as margarine does.

Roasts should be cooked at about 325°F. There is a classic example I use when teaching meat cookery to illustrate the advantages of using the lower temperature: We take two identical roasts, roasting one at 325°F and the other at 400°F—the one cooked at 400°F is always obviously shrunken and less tender. All roasting time is approximate because of the variability of the tenderness of the meat, thickness, and whether the roast has been in the refrigerator or is at room temperature. A meat thermometer should be used for accuracy. It should be inserted in the thickest part of the roast without touching any fat or bone. Rare meat is more tender than well done.

My favorite roast is round of beef. It has the lowest fat content, so you don't have to worry about the amount of fat left in the cooked roast. In fact, round of beef is about my favorite cut of meat. Round of beef is found in many different forms in your supermarket. You can get a boneless top round roast, eye of round roast, and the less tender bottom round pot roast. You can find thick round steaks for broiling and thinner round steaks for grilling or pan-frying. There are thinly sliced minute steaks for sandwiches, and top round can be found that has been cut into cubes for stews or broiling on skewers. The less tender bottom round can be cut into cubes or ground for use in spaghetti sauce, stew, or chili. Bottom round is also the top choice ground for hamburgers.

I must admit that roast round of beef requires a little extra care to make it tender. Top round or eye of round are best for roasting. Roast it, uncovered, at 300°F to about 130–140°F internally for rare or medium rare. Don't overcook it. Well done round of beef will be tough unless you pot-roast it until it is falling apart (which is the way I really prefer it, but that's another recipe). It is better if it is soaked in a marinade for several hours or overnight in the refrigerator—or a commercial tenderizer can be used according to the directions on the package. (Never use tenderizer on hamburger; it makes it mushy.) Don't bother to include oil in your marinade. It doesn't help tenderize the meat and adds calories and fat exchanges. Wine, vinegar, and tomato juice contain natural acids that tenderize meat without the addition of many calories.

Flank steak, rump, round, or sirloin tip are best used for stews and casseroles. If you must use stew meat, remove all visible fat before it is cooked. All stew meat should be browned first in as little fat as possible, covered with liquid, and simmered until tender. It can then be drained and the broth refrigerated until it is cool and the fat has risen to the top. I'm sure you will be surprised at the amount of fat you will be able to skim off the broth before it is recombined with the meat and the stew or casserole finished. This is a time-consuming task, so I generally do several pounds of meat at once and then freeze what I'm not going to use that day in portions for future use.

Recipes including ground beef should be prepared so that you get as much of the fat as possible out of the meat. Buy lean ground beef, ground round of beef or veal, or ground leg of lamb. I try to use recipes that allow the meat to be browned, drained, and rinsed with hot water before it is combined with other ingredients. Meat loaves aren't all that good for you if they contain much filler such as bread crumbs or oatmeal, because the fillers absorb the saturated fat from the meat while the loaf is cooking. This is too bad because meat loaves are handy to have for sandwiches—besides, I really like a good meat loaf, and you probably do, too! Because meat loaves tend to hold fat, it is a good idea to use only the leanest meat in them, or chicken or turkey, which also make a good meat loaf (see Index). The best way to do it when you want to make a beef meat loaf is to buy round steak, have the butcher remove any visible fat, and then grind the meat for you. If you don't have a butcher who will do it for you, a food processor will do a good job. Most heavy-duty mixers have good grinders, or you can buy an electric or hand grinder to use. If you grind the meat yourself you can be sure that you have removed all possible visible fat before grinding.

Hamburgers are good and we all love them, but it isn't a good idea to buy them out because the fat content is generally very high. If you do have to buy them at a hamburger stand, take a paper napkin and blot the fat off both sides of the hamburger before you eat it. When you cook hamburgers at home be sure to use lean ground meat and the seasonings you like; however, it is best not to add bread crumbs or other fillers to the meat because they trap the fat that you are trying to get rid of. It will taste good but it will have more saturated fat than you really should be using. Hamburgers can be prepared according to one of the following methods:

- *Grilled.* Rub a grill lightly with oil or sprinkle with salt (if permissible), heat until it is sizzling hot, and brown the burgers on both sides. Cook them 2–8 minutes on each side depending upon whether you like them rare or well done.
- *Pan-fried.* Heat a heavy frying pan until sizzling hot, rub lightly with oil or sprinkle with salt (if permissible), and brown the burgers on both sides. Reduce the heat and cook them over medium heat 2–8 minutes on each side depending upon whether you like them rare or well done.
- *Broiled.* Arrange hamburger patties on a cold broiler rack. Broil 3–4 inches from the heat, turning once, for about 4–6 minutes on each side depending upon how thick they are and how well done you like them to be.

It is a good idea to stick to the *good* grade of beef. *Choice* beef may be a little more tender, but that is because it has more marbling of fat and this is what you want to avoid. Check the grade of beef before you buy it, and if you are in doubt always check with the butcher or salesperson behind the counter. If it is practical for you, it is a good idea to buy your meat at a store where you can be sure you are getting the *good* grade of beef, and then instruct them to remove every bit of fat possible before the meat is ground. This is what we do in our small town and it is really best if it is also possible in your area.

Swine breeders have developed much leaner hogs in the last few years, so that pork is no longer as fat as it used to be and may be used occasionally on a low-cholesterol diabetic diet. However, it is still wise to use the leanest cuts, avoiding spareribs, pork sausage, and other cuts, such as the shoulder, with a higher fat content. The tenderloin is particularly good and is luscious when cut thick and broiled. Fresh ham and center cut loin are also good for roasting after all the visible fat has been removed. Pork chops should be center cut and have all visible fat removed before cooking, and they should not be cooked with dressing or stuffing because the dressing or stuffing picks up too much fat from the pork chops while they are baking.

Ham can be very lean, and if you don't have to worry about salt restrictions can be a very good buy, particularly some of the low-fat hams. Most hams available are precooked so you only need to reheat them to an interior temperature of 130°F. This should take about 15–20 minutes per pound at 325°F or you can do it in the microwave, according to directions with your microwave. The center cut of smoked ham is generally acceptable also if all of the visible fat is removed. It may be broiled or pan-broiled.

- *Broiled.* Remove all visible fat from a center cut of ham about 1 inch thick. Broil about 15 minutes for precooked ham and about 25 minutes for uncooked ham, turning it once while it is broiling.
- *Pan-Broiled.* Remove all visible fat from a center cut of ham about ¼–½ inch thick. Rub a frying pan with a little oil and cook over medium heat, turning at least once while it is frying. Cook about 6–8 minutes for precooked ham and about 12–16 minutes for uncooked ham.

Here in Iowa we have what they call Iowa Pork Chops. These are lean chops that weigh about 8–9 ounces each. One chop is far too much for our meat allowance, but I like to brown them, put them in a small roaster with a rack, and continue cooking them, covered, in the oven at 325°F for about an hour or until they are tender. I cut off the amount of meat that I am allowed for that meal and save the rest for another meal. It tastes like luscious roast pork and is really very good. If they aren't available in your area, I'm sure your butcher would be happy to cut some for you from the center loin. Of course, I cut off all visible fat before preparing them, and they are really very lean when prepared that way.

Properly cooked lamb has a delicious, mild flavor and an

appetizing aroma. It should be served hot or cold—never luke-warm. In the past, recipes generally specified well-done lamb; however, today the accepted procedure is to cook it to 165°F, which is slightly rare. This gives you a more flavorful and juicy roast. Lamb is good for a low-cholesterol diet because it is lower in fat than many of the beef cuts. The leg is the leanest part of the lamb and it can be cut into a leg of lamb roast or a sirloin roast. The sirloin may also be cut into chops or ground. Lamb patties, which are traditionally lean, are often wrapped in bacon. We can't do this but I find that if I add a little seasoning and broil the patty until it is medium well done, it will be moist and juicy. If you buy the whole leg of lamb you will find it is covered with a whitish, brittle fat that is called the fell. This should be removed before the roast is cooked because it tends to make the flavor of the meat strong, as well as adding additional fat that you don't need.

Veal has a delicate flavor when it is cooked properly. Good veal is light pink in color rather than red and has a small amount of very white fat. It is not suited for broiling because of the small amount of fat, but that small amount of fat makes it an excellent choice for a low-cholesterol diabetic diet. Veal cutlets are very lean and may be pan-broiled. They are often dipped in egg white and then cracker crumbs and deep fat fried. This method would be satisfactory except that it does add more fat exchanges. The veal cutlets may also be dipped in egg white and then crumbs and pan-broiled using a very little oil, which uses fewer fat exchanges and still tastes like a good veal cutlet. Veal is a good choice for stews and casseroles because of its low fat content—and roast leg of veal is an excellent entrée for a dinner or special occasion.

If you have a favorite meat recipe that isn't included in this book, you can calculate the nutritive values for it using the information in Chapter 3. Roast meats are calculated using nutritive values of 1 meat exchange per 1 ounce serving of meat. If gravy is used it will have to be figured separately. I have not included many roast recipes in this book—there are so many of them in other cookbooks. I have used the space for casseroles and other combination dishes. When we were first talking about this book, Sister Rosemary, who was a dietitian at Holy Cross Hospital in Chicago, told me that she hoped I'd use mostly casseroles and similar recipes because that is what most of her patients want. I have tried to illustrate different methods of preparation hoping that you could use them as a basis for your own recipes—but remember, if you add or subtract something, unless it is very, very low in food value like celery or mushrooms, you must recalculate the recipe to arrive at the correct exchanges for your diet pattern.

Broiled Round Steak

Who says we can't have steak on a low-cholesterol diet? I think you will be surprised when you taste this broiled steak.

It is really a method more than an exact recipe. You can vary the marinade to suit yourself, which will change the flavor a little bit. The steak will be more tender if it is rare or, at the least, medium done. This method also will work for a round bone pot roast, although the round is better for a low-cholesterol diet.

> **2 pounds round of beef, 2 inches thick,**
> **with all visible fat removed**
> **¼ cup vegetable oil**
> **¼ cup red wine vinegar**
> **¼ cup red wine**
> **¼ to ½ teaspoon garlic powder**
> **1 teaspoon leaf thyme**
> **1 teaspoon leaf oregano**
> **3 tablespoons chopped parsley**
> **Salt and pepper to taste**

Place steak in a shallow dish. Mix together all remaining ingredients except salt and pepper and pour over the round steak. Cover tightly and let it marinate at room temperature for about 2 hours, or overnight in the refrigerator. Remove meat from the marinade. Pat it dry with a paper towel and discard the marinade. Broil 3–4 minutes on each side about 4 inches from the heat for rare, or more as desired.

Season meat with salt and pepper and serve hot. It can be carved in thin slices across the grain or served in large pieces for each person to cut his or her own. Food exchanges will depend upon the serving size, with 1 ounce cooked meat counted as 1 lean meat exchange. Low-sodium diets should omit salt.

Yields 21 to 24 ounces

Nutritive Values Per 3-Ounce Serving

CAL	CHO (g)	PRO (g)	TOTAL FAT (g)	SAT. FAT (g)	CHOL (mg)	FIBER (g)	NA (mg)
180	trace	25	8	2.4	66	0	55

Food exchanges per 3-ounce serving: 3 lean meat
Low-sodium diets: May be used as written.
Sugar content per serving: None.

Beef with Green Beans

I find this easier to prepare in an electric frying pan. I'm not sure why but I always prepare it that way.

**8 ounces round of beef with all visible fat
    removed before it is weighed
2 tablespoons soy sauce
1 tablespoon cornstarch
½ teaspoon salt
1 tablespoon sherry or beef broth
1 tablespoon vegetable oil
¼ cup water
1 pound frozen green beans cut into 1-inch
    lengths**

Cut beef into pieces about ⅛–¼ inch thick and about 1 inch long. (This is easier if the meat is slightly frozen.) Refrigerate until needed.

Mix soy sauce, cornstarch, salt, and sherry well. Pour over the meat. Mix lightly and let stand at room temperature for about ½ hour, or refrigerate for several hours or overnight. Drain well, reserving the marinade.

Spread oil over the bottom of a frying pan. Heat to a frying temperature. Drain the meat well and fry, stirring frequently, until the meat is no longer pink. Add ¼ cup water to the meat along with the reserved marinade. Stir lightly over medium heat.

Add green beans to meat mixture. Cook and stir until beans and meat are both well coated with the sauce. Cover and cook, stirring occasionally, until beans are crisp-tender. Serve about ¾ cup per serving over rice or noodles.

Yields 3 cups—4 servings

Nutritive Values Per Serving (without rice or noodles)

CAL	CHO (g)	PRO (g)	TOTAL FAT (g)	SAT. FAT (g)	CHOL (mg)	FIBER (g)	NA (mg)
164	12	15	6	1.4	33	2	824

Food exchanges per serving: 2 lean meat, 1 other carbohydrate
Low-sodium diets: Omit salt and use low-sodium soy sauce.
Sugar content per serving: None.

Texas Round Steak

½ cup all-purpose flour
1 teaspoon salt
1½ teaspoons chili powder
1 pound 2 ounces round of beef about ½
    inch thick (weighed after fat and bone
    are removed), cut into 6 3-ounce steaks
2 tablespoons vegetable oil
½ cup chopped fresh green peppers
½ cup chopped onions
1 cup fat-free beef broth
½ cup tomato sauce
½ cup tomato juice
1 teaspoon chili powder
¼ teaspoon garlic powder
¼ teaspoon ground cumin

Blend flour, salt, and 1½ teaspoons chili powder well and place in a pie pan. Dredge meat in the flour mixture. You should use about half of the mixture. (You can discard the rest; however, it is necessary to have this amount to make dredging practical.)

Place oil in a heavy frying pan and heat to frying temperature over moderate heat. Add meat and brown on both sides. Transfer steaks to a 1½-quart casserole.

Fry peppers and onions over moderate heat in the pan in which the meat was browned, stirring frequently. Remove vegetables with a slotted spoon and spread over the meat. Pour out any remaining fat. Add beef broth to frying pan and cook and stir over moderate heat to absorb any brown particles remaining in the pan.

Add remaining ingredients to broth. Mix well and pour over meat. Stir the meat and vegetables lightly with a fork to distribute the broth and vegetables. Cover tightly and bake at 325°F for about 1–1½ hours or until the meat is tender. Serve 1 piece of steak with some of the sauce per serving.

Yields 6 steaks—6 servings

Nutritive Values Per Serving

CAL	CHO (g)	PRO (g)	TOTAL FAT (g)	SAT. FAT (g)	CHOL (mg)	FIBER (g)	NA (mg)
220	13	21	9	2	50	1.4	728

Food exchanges per serving: 3 lean meat, 1 other carbohydrate
Low-sodium diets: Omit salt. Use low-sodium broth, tomato sauce, and tomato juice.
Sugar content per serving: None.

Beef Mushroom Spaghetti Sauce

**12 ounces round of beef weighed and
ground after fat is removed
1 tablespoon vegetable oil
½ cup finely chopped onions
2 4-ounce cans mushroom stems and pieces
3½ cups (29-ounce can) tomato purée
2 cups tomato juice
2 tablespoons chopped parsley
1 teaspoon salt
½ teaspoon dehydrated garlic
½ teaspoon basil
½ teaspoon leaf oregano
1 teaspoon Italian seasoning**

Place beef in a 5- or 6-quart Dutch oven or heavy pot. Cook and stir over moderate heat until it is separated and lightly browned. Place in a strainer and strain off any fat. Set aside to drain. Rinse out the pan with hot water and return it to the heat.

Place oil in Dutch oven. Add onions. Drain mushrooms well. Discard juice and add mushrooms to onions. Cook and stir over moderate heat until onions are soft.

Add remaining ingredients along with meat to onions and mushrooms. Cook over low heat for 30 minutes, stirring frequently. Serve hot over cooked, well-drained spaghetti, ½ cup sauce per serving.

Yields 7 cups—14 servings

Nutritive Values Per Serving (without spaghetti)

CAL	CHO (g)	PRO (g)	TOTAL FAT (g)	SAT. FAT (g)	CHOL (mg)	FIBER (g)	NA (mg)
78	9	7	2	.5	14	1.7	570

Food exchanges per serving: 1 lean meat, 2 vegetable
Low-sodium diets: Omit salt. Use low-sodium tomato purée and tomato juice.
Sugar content per serving: None.

Vegetable-Beef Stew

**1 pound round of beef or veal weighed
    after fat and bone are removed
1 tablespoon vegetable oil
3 cups hot fat-free beef broth
¼ teaspoon thyme
⅛ teaspoon pepper
¼ teaspoon garlic powder
1 teaspoon salt
1 cup carrots cut into 1-inch pieces
4 large stalks celery cut into 1-inch lengths
½ cup coarsely chopped onions
¼ cup chopped fresh green peppers
10-ounce package frozen Brussels sprouts
2 tablespoons cornstarch
¼ cup water**

Cut meat into ¾-inch cubes. (This is easier if the meat is slightly frozen.) Place oil on the bottom of a heavy pot. (I use a deep iron frying pan with a glass cover.) Bring to a frying temperature. Add meat and cook, stirring occasionally, until meat is browned.

Add broth and seasonings to meat. Cover and simmer 45 minutes–1 hour or until meat is tender.

Add carrots, celery, onions, and peppers to meat. Cover and simmer 10 minutes. Add Brussels sprouts to stew. Cover and simmer another 12 minutes.

Mix cornstarch and water until smooth. Add to stew and cook and stir until thickened. Continue to simmer for another 2–3 minutes or until starchy taste is gone. Serve hot, 1 cup stew with gravy per serving.

Yields 6 cups—6 servings

Nutritive Values Per Serving

CAL	CHO (g)	PRO (g)	TOTAL FAT (g)	SAT. FAT (g)	CHOL (mg)	FIBER (g)	NA (mg)
181	11	21	6	1.6	44	2.3	767

Food exchanges per serving: 2 lean meat, 2 vegetable
Low-sodium diets: Omit salt. Use low-sodium broth.
Sugar content per serving: None.

Stir-Fry Beef and Vegetables

This stir-fry recipe is an adaptation of a Chinese recipe. Probably no good Chinese cook would recognize it, but we like it and I serve it, or a variation of it, frequently.

> **8 ounces beef sirloin with fat and gristle
>   removed**
> **¼ cup dry red wine or fat-free beef broth**
> **3 tablespoons soy sauce**
> **1 teaspoon sugar**
> **1½ tablespoons cornstarch**
> **Water**
> **1 tablespoon vegetable oil**
> **2 cups coarsely chopped onions**
> **½ cup thinly sliced celery**
> **½ cup coarsely chopped fresh green
>   peppers**
> **2 tablespoons chopped roasted cashews**

Place meat in freezer until it is firm but not frozen. Cut across the grain into bite-size pieces and set aside. Place wine or broth, soy sauce, sugar, and cornstarch in a 2-cup measure. Add enough water to total 1 cup. Stir until smooth and set aside.

Preheat a 10-inch, nonstick-surfaced frying pan. (I use a wok frying pan with a T-Fal lining.) Swirl oil around bottom of frying pan, add onions, celery, and green peppers, and cook, stirring frequently, over medium heat until onions are soft but not browned.

Push vegetables to one side of pan, add meat, and cook, stirring the meat frequently, until the meat is rare to well done, as you prefer. Pour wine sauce over meat and vegetables and cook and stir until sauce is clear and thickened. Serve hot over rice or noodles using 1 cup per serving. Garnish each serving with 2 teaspoons of cashews. *Note:* Nutritive information does not include rice or noodles.

Yields 3 cups—3 servings

Nutritive Values Per Serving

CAL	CHO (g)	PRO (g)	TOTAL FAT (g)	SAT. FAT (g)	CHOL (mg)	FIBER (g)	NA (mg)
264	20	19	11	2.3	46	2.5	1,096

Food exchanges per serving: 2 medium fat meat, 1 vegetable, 1 other carbohydrate
Low-sodium diets: Use low-sodium soy sauce.
Sugar content per serving: .3 teaspoon.

Mary's Meatballs

This recipe is based on one from Mary Hinkle here in Wadena. She is my friend Vera Wilson's daughter and a very good cook. I wouldn't dare eat many of her recipes, but she makes the very best cookies, cakes, and other desserts.

¼ cup catsup
¼ cup tomato juice
1 tablespoon liquid smoke
½ teaspoon Durkee's barbecue seasoning
1 teaspoon sugar
½ cup oatmeal
¼ cup dry bread crumbs
3 tablespoons grated onions
½ teaspoon salt
¼ teaspoon black pepper
1 cup skim milk
1½ pounds round of beef weighed and
    ground after fat is removed

Blend first 5 ingredients together well to form a barbecue sauce and set aside at room temperature for later use.

Place oatmeal, crumbs, onions, salt, pepper, and milk in a mixer bowl and mix together at low speed to mix well. Add beef to milk mixture and mix at low speed until blended. Do not overmix. Shape into balls using 2 tablespoons of the mixture for each meatball. Place on a cookie sheet and broil 2–4 minutes. Remove from cookie sheet and place in a casserole, brushing the balls with the barbecue sauce as you put them in the casserole. Pour any remaining sauce over the meatballs, cover, and bake at 325°F for about 45 minutes or until done. Serve hot, 2 meatballs per serving.

Yields 28 meat balls—14 servings

Nutritive Values Per Serving

CAL	CHO (g)	PRO (g)	TOTAL FAT (g)	SAT. FAT (g)	CHOL (mg)	FIBER (g)	NA (mg)
99	6	12	3	.9	29	.5	208

Food exchanges per serving: 1¼ lean meat, 1 vegetable
Low-sodium diets: Omit salt. Use low-sodium catsup.
Sugar content per serving: Trace.

Norwegian Meatballs

This recipe is based on one from Doris Walker of Grinnell, Iowa, who was living in Wadena when we first moved here.

> **2 tablespoons cornstarch**
> **¾ teaspoon salt**
> **½ teaspoon nutmeg**
> **2 large egg whites**
> **¾ cup skim milk**
> **1 pound ground round of beef weighed and ground after fat is removed**
> **⅔ cup Campbell's Cream of Mushroom soup**

Place first 4 ingredients and ¼ cup of the milk in mixer bowl and mix at low speed to blend well. Add beef to mixer bowl and mix at low speed to blend well. Shape 18 meatballs using about 1½ tablespoons mix per meatball. (The mixture will be soft.) Place in a 9″ × 13″ cake pan that has been lined with aluminum foil or sprayed with pan spray. Bake 30 minutes at 375° F. Remove from pan while still hot and place in a 1½-quart casserole.

Mix soup and remaining ½ cup milk well and pour over meatballs. Cover and bake at 350°F for 30 minutes. Serve 3 meatballs per serving with ⅙ of the sauce.

Yields 18 meatballs—6 servings

Nutritive Values Per Serving

CAL	CHO (g)	PRO (g)	TOTAL FAT (g)	SAT. FAT (g)	CHOL (mg)	FIBER (g)	NA (mg)
156	6	19	5	1.9	45	trace	546

Food exchanges per serving: 3 lean meat, 1 vegetable
Low-sodium diets: Omit salt. Use low-sodium soup.
Sugar content per serving: None.

Chicago Chili

This is the recipe Chuck developed when he owned a restaurant in Chicago. He always served it in a bowl with the beans on the side. If you add canned beans to your chili, add 1 bread exchange for each ⅓ cup hot, cooked, drained kidney or pinto beans that you stir into a bowl of chili.

   1 tablespoon vegetable oil
   1 cup chopped onions
   1 pound ground round of beef weighed and
      ground after bone and fat are removed
   2 cups chopped solid-pack canned
      tomatoes with juice
   1 cup tomato purée
   1 cup tomato juice
   3 cups fat-free chicken broth
   1 teaspoon sugar
   1½ teaspoons salt
   ¼ teaspoon pepper
   ½ teaspoon garlic powder
   ¼ teaspoon ground cumin
   ½ teaspoon ground oregano
   1 teaspoon chili powder

Pour the oil into a heavy pot. Bring to frying temperature over moderate heat. Add the onions and cook and stir over moderate heat until onions are soft but not golden.

Add beef to onions. Cook and stir over moderate heat until meat is well browned and broken into small pieces. Pour meat and onions into a colander and drain off any fat and liquid. Discard fat and liquid, rinse the pot out with hot water, and then return the meat and onions to the pot.

Add remaining ingredients to meat mixture. Bring to a boil, reduce heat, and simmer, uncovered, for 1¼ hours, stirring occasionally. Serve hot using 1 cup chili per serving.

Yields 6 cups—6 servings

Nutritive Values Per Serving

CAL	CHO (g)	PRO (g)	TOTAL FAT (g)	SAT. FAT (g)	CHOL (mg)	FIBER (g)	NA (mg)
189	13	21	6	1.6	44	2.4	1,363

Food exchanges per serving: 2 lean meat, 2 vegetable
Low-sodium diets: Omit salt. Use low-sodium tomatoes, tomato purée,
    tomato juice, and broth.
Sugar content per serving: .2 teaspoon.

Barbecue Meat Loaf

¼ cup finely chopped onions
¼ cup finely chopped celery
¼ cup catsup
2 large egg whites
¼ cup dry bread crumbs
1 teaspoon liquid smoke
1 teaspoon salt
Whisper of black pepper
1 pound round of beef weighed and ground
    after fat is removed

Place all ingredients except beef in mixer bowl and mix at low speed to blend well.

Add beef to catsup mixture and mix at low speed until blended. Do not overmix. Shape into a loaf about 3½" × 7". Place in a pan that has been sprayed with pan spray or lined with aluminum foil. Bake at 325°F about 1 hour or until browned and firm. Pour off any fat and drippings and let stand for 10 minutes before cutting into 6 equal slices. Serve 1 slice per serving.

Yields 1 loaf—6 servings

Nutritive Values Per Serving

CAL	CHO (g)	PRO (g)	TOTAL FAT (g)	SAT. FAT (g)	CHOL (mg)	FIBER (g)	NA (mg)
143	7	19	4	1.3	44	.5	591

Food exchanges per serving: 2 very lean meat, 1 fat, 1 vegetable
Low-sodium diets: Omit salt. Use low-sodium catsup.
Sugar content per serving: None.

Meat Loaf with Fiber

1 cup All-Bran, Bran Buds, or 100% Bran
¼ cup finely chopped onions
3 large egg whites
1 cup tomato sauce
1 teaspoon Worcestershire sauce
1 teaspoon dry mustard
½ teaspoon salt
¹⁄₁₆ teaspoon pepper
1 pound 4 ounces round of beef weighed
   and ground after fat is removed

Place all ingredients except beef in mixer bowl and mix at low speed to blend.

Add beef to bran mixture and blend at low speed. Do not overmix. Shape into a loaf and place in a pan that has been sprayed with pan spray or lined with aluminum foil. Bake at 325°F about 1¼ hours or until browned and firm. Pour off any fat and drippings and let stand for 10 minutes. Cut into 8 equal slices. Serve 1 slice per serving.

Yields 1 loaf—8 servings

Nutritive Values Per Serving

CAL	CHO (g)	PRO (g)	TOTAL FAT (g)	SAT. FAT (g)	CHOL (mg)	FIBER (g)	NA (mg)
137	8	18	4	1.2	41	3	459

Food exchanges per serving: 2 very lean meat, 1 vegetable
Low-sodium diets: Omit salt. Use low-sodium tomato sauce.
Sugar content per serving: None.

Baked Pork and Rice

**12-ounces pork tenderloin weighed after
 visible fat is removed**
1 cup thinly sliced celery
½ cup chopped onions
1½ cups fat-free chicken broth
½ cup long-grain rice
2 tablespoons soy sauce
Whisper of black pepper
3 tablespoons chopped pimientos

Cut pork into ½-inch cubes. Place in a shallow pan and bake at
350°F about 30 minutes or until browned. Remove from pan
with a slotted spoon and place in a 1½-quart casserole.

Place celery, onions, and broth in a small saucepan. Bring to
a boil, reduce heat, cover, and simmer for 10 minutes. Add rice,
soy sauce, and pepper to hot broth. Mix lightly and add to meat
in casserole. Mix lightly. Cover tightly and bake at 350°F about
40 minutes or until rice is tender. Remove from oven.

Stir pimientos into hot pork and rice. Serve hot, using ¼ of
the total (about ¾ cup) per serving.

Yields about 3 cups—4 servings

Nutritive Values Per Serving

CAL	CHO (g)	PRO (g)	TOTAL FAT (g)	SAT. FAT (g)	CHOL (mg)	FIBER (g)	NA (mg)
212	23	22	3	1	55	1	828

Food exchanges per serving: 2½ very lean meat, 1 starch, 1 vegetable
Low-sodium diets: Use low-sodium soy sauce and broth.
Sugar content per serving: None.

Sweet Sour Pork

---

1 pound lean pork from fresh ham or
    tenderloin weighed after bone and fat are
    removed
1 tablespoon vegetable oil
2 cups fat-free chicken broth
1½ cups thinly sliced celery
½ cup coarsely chopped onions
¼ cup soy sauce
2 tablespoons cornstarch
⅓ cup vinegar
¼-⅓ cup Brown Sugar Twin granulated
    sugar substitute
1 large tomato cut into wedges
1 cup drained, canned unsweetened
    pineapple tidbits

Cut pork into small pieces about 1" × ¼". (It is easier to cut the pork this thin if it is slightly frozen.) Place oil in the bottom of a heavy frying pan or saucepan. Bring to frying temperature. Add pork and cook and stir over moderate heat until pork is browned and cooked through. Remove pork with slotted spoon and set aside for later use. Pour off as much of the fat as possible from the pan and then blot up any remaining fat with a paper towel.

Add broth to frying pan. Cook and stir over low heat to get up the browned bits in the bottom of the pan. Add celery and onions to hot chicken broth. Cover and simmer 10 minutes.

Mix soy sauce, cornstarch, and vinegar until smooth. Add to vegetables and cook and stir over moderate heat until thickened. Add sweetener to vegetables to taste and mix lightly.

Add tomatoes and pineapple to vegetables along with the pork. Cook over low heat until serving temperature, stirring occasionally. Do not allow to boil. The tomato wedges should be hot but not cooked. Serve hot over cooked rice using 1 cup per serving.

Yields 5 cups—5 servings

Nutritive Values Per Serving (without rice)

CAL	CHO (g)	PRO (g)	TOTAL FAT (g)	SAT. FAT (g)	CHOL (mg)	FIBER (g)	NA (mg)
228	18	22	8	2	62	1.6	1,166

Food exchanges per serving: 2½ lean meat, 2 vegetable, ½ fruit
Low-sodium diets: Use low-sodium broth and soy sauce.
Sugar content per serving: None.

Brown Gravy

The flavor of this gravy depends upon the flavor of the drippings or broth that you use as a base. It can be luscious or it can be blah. I prefer to use drippings from roasts. I chill them and remove the fat and the murky stuff at the bottom and then save them for gravy.

2¼ cups cold fat-free drippings or broth
2 tablespoons cornstarch
Whisper of pepper
½ teaspoon Kitchen Bouquet
Salt to taste

Place drippings, cornstarch, and pepper in a small saucepan and mix together until smooth. Place over moderate heat and cook and stir until smooth and thickened, using a wire whisk. Taste for flavoring and add salt and Kitchen Bouquet if necessary. Serve hot, using ¼ cup per serving.

Yields 2 cups—8 servings

Nutritive Values Per Serving

CAL	CHO (g)	PRO (g)	TOTAL FAT (g)	SAT. FAT (g)	CHOL (mg)	FIBER (g)	NA (mg)
13	2	1	0	0	0	0	178

Food exchanges per serving: ¼ cup may be considered free
Low-sodium diets: Omit salt. Use salt-free broth or drippings.
Sugar content per serving: None.

Pan Gravy

This gravy is a great favorite in the Midwest. It is served often and in large quantities. I have never lived down the time we were visiting my cousin Virginia Ballantine in Clarion, Iowa, when we were still living in Chicago. She was busy getting dinner and asked me to make the gravy. I made about this much, which is what I make at home. When her husband and two grown sons looked at that tiny bowl of gravy—well, you wouldn't believe how they teased me about starving them, and city cooks, and above all dietitians! I'm still hearing about it years later, even though I have made it in larger quantities for them many times since then.

> 1 tablespoon vegetable oil
> ¼ cup all-purpose flour
> 2½ cups cold water
> ½ teaspoon salt
> Whisper of pepper

Pour all of the fat out of a pan in which you have pan-fried steak, chicken, pork chops, or other meats. Blot out remaining fat with a paper towel. Add the oil to the pan and bring the pan to a frying temperature. Add flour to oil and cook and stir until browned and smooth.

Add the water to the flour mixture; cook and stir over moderate heat until thickened and you have scraped all of the brown bits from the pan. Add salt and pepper to the gravy. Mix lightly and serve hot, using ¼ cup gravy per serving.

Yields 2 cups—8 servings

Nutritive Values Per Serving

CAL	CHO (g)	PRO (g)	TOTAL FAT (g)	SAT. FAT (g)	CHOL (mg)	FIBER (g)	NA (mg)
29	3	trace	2	trace	0	trace	137

Food exchanges per serving: ½ vegetable
Low-sodium diets: Omit salt.
Sugar content per serving: None.

Brown Rice Dressing

1 cup raw brown rice
2½ cups fat-free chicken broth
1 tablespoon vegetable oil
2 cups thinly sliced celery
1 cup chopped onions
1 4-ounce can drained mushroom stems
  and pieces
1 8-ounce can water chestnuts
½ teaspoon leaf thyme
½ teaspoon rosemary
⅟₁₆ teaspoon black pepper
¼ teaspoon salt
½ teaspoon sage

Combine rice and broth in a saucepan. Heat to boiling. Stir, cover, and reduce heat. Simmer 45–50 minutes or until tender.

Place oil in saucepan. Bring to frying temperature. Add celery, onions, and mushrooms to hot oil. Cook, stirring frequently, over moderate heat, until onions are just tender. Drain chestnuts well. Slice into thin slices and add to hot vegetables.

Add remaining seasonings to vegetables and cook over low heat for 4 minutes, stirring frequently. Add rice and toss lightly. Reheat, if necessary, stirring gently over low heat. Serve hot using ½ cup per serving.

Yields 6 cups—12 servings

Nutritive Values Per Serving

CAL	CHO (g)	PRO (g)	TOTAL FAT (g)	SAT. FAT (g)	CHOL (mg)	FIBER (g)	NA (mg)
87	16	2	2	trace	0	1.4	221

Food exchanges per serving: 1 starch
Low-sodium diets: Omit salt. Use low-sodium broth.
Sugar content per serving: None.

12

Vegetables, Etc.

There is such an abundance of interesting fresh, frozen, dried, and canned vegetables available these days that we shouldn't ever complain that we don't know what vegetable to have for dinner that day. They can be prepared very simply or they can be the star of the menu—and you can eat your fill of vegetables without adding all that much carbohydrate to the meal. Vegetables don't contain any cholesterol so we should really appreciate them from both the low-cholesterol and the low-calorie viewpoints.

Vegetables contain a great deal of fiber, vitamins, and minerals; they even have a little protein, although only a trace of fat. They also taste delicious, which is a definite plus.

Vegetables fresh from the garden are wonderful in the summer. I always enjoyed seeing how much Frances Nielsen and Chuck relished fresh vegetables. Both of them were so pleased with the first ripe tomato, the first fresh green beans, those little potatoes fresh from the garden and the green onions.

If you can't get vegetables fresh from the garden, frozen ones are next best. Sometimes frozen vegetables can be even better than fresh because they are picked and frozen at the peak of their perfection (and haven't stayed in the refrigerator until you get around to using them).

It is best to use fresh or frozen vegetables on a low-sodium diet because most canned vegetables have salt added to them when they are processed. If you can't get either fresh or frozen vegetables for your low-sodium diet, drain the liquid off the vegetables (except for tomatoes or some other vegetable where the liquid is important) and replace it with water. This will lower the sodium content somewhat. There are also vegetables available now that are canned without added salt, and they are a good buy on a low-sodium diet—or you can can your own vegetables (see Chapter 20) without adding any salt when you process them.

If you aren't on a low-sodium diet, canned vegetables are an excellent source of fiber, vitamins, and minerals. There is such a variety of them and they are always available. We like to keep a good supply of them on hand in our fruit room so we have them when we want them. If you do keep some canned vegetables on hand, they should be kept in a cool place (around 70°F or lower), out of direct light, and should be rotated. Use the oldest cans first. In fact, Chuck dated the cans of vegetables as we bought them so we would know which to use first. It is disconcerting to discover some canned vegetables a couple of years old that got shoved to the back of the shelf and not used when they were fresh.

If the cans show any signs of spoilage they should be discarded. If they are bulging or leaking or have a bad smell when you open them, discard them immediately. Don't ever taste them to see if they are good. Just tasting them, if there is botulism in the cans, can cause death. Very few cases of botulism have been reported in this country in this century, but it still pays to be cautious.

Although many vegetables are very low in carbohydrate, some vegetables are higher in carbohydrate and need to be included under the bread exchanges on a diabetic diet. I would have liked to have included more beans, brown rice, peas, and other starchy vegetables in this chapter because of their good fiber content; however, we will get sufficient fiber in our diet if we eat a good supply of the other vegetables. Most dietitians will tell you that if you eat whole wheat bread, an occasional special bran bread or muffin, and five or more servings of fruits and vegetables daily, you will get enough fiber.

I do enjoy beans in any form. I usually consider them a special treat that I can have when the carbohydrate content of my meal is very low—or I use a couple of tablespoons of them in a lettuce salad to add interest to the salad (2 tablespoons of baked beans is 1 vegetable exchange). If you have a liberal diabetic diet and can afford it, I highly recommend that you use a good quantity of beans and other starchy vegetables because of their taste and good fiber content.

All of our diabetic lists include the values for vegetables, so I haven't included many plain vegetables in this chapter. I have tried to show you how to add a little zing to a few of them. I hope you'll try them, and perhaps adapt some of your own vegetable recipes using the information in Chapter 3, "Calculating Food Exchanges," and also develop some of your own special recipes.

Green Bean and Mushroom Casserole

This recipe was given to me by M. J. Smith, a registered dietitian from Guttenberg, Iowa. She is an innovative dietitian who has written several cookbooks for people on low-fat diets.

> 1 10-ounce package frozen French-cut
>   green beans
> 1 teaspoon liquid margarine
> 8 ounces fresh mushrooms, sliced
> ½ cup plain low-fat yogurt
> 1 tablespoon all-purpose flour
> 1 tablespoon dry sherry
> 2 teaspoons Worcestershire sauce

Thaw the green beans. Preheat a small (8-inch) nonstick-surfaced frying pan over medium heat for 1 minute. Swirl margarine in it, add mushrooms, and cook and stir over medium heat until mushrooms are tender.

Combine yogurt, flour, sherry, and Worcestershire sauce in a 1½-quart casserole and stir until smooth. Fold mushrooms and beans into sauce and bake at 350°F for 35–40 minutes. Serve hot, using 1 cup per serving.

Yields 4 cups—4 servings

Nutritive Values Per Serving

CAL	CHO (g)	PRO (g)	TOTAL FAT (g)	SAT. FAT (g)	CHOL (mg)	FIBER (g)	NA (mg)
76	12	4	2	.5	2	2	62

Food exchanges per serving: 2 vegetable
Low-sodium diets: May be used as written.
Sugar content per serving: None.

Creole Green Beans

1 tablespoon vegetable oil
¼ cup chopped onions
¼ cup thinly sliced celery
1 tablespoon flour
1 cup tomato juice
¼ teaspoon salt
Whisper of pepper
2 16-ounce cans green string beans

Place oil in a saucepan and heat to frying temperature over moderate heat. Add onions and celery to oil and cook and stir over moderate heat until the onions are soft but not browned. Add flour to vegetables and cook and stir until the flour is absorbed by the vegetables. Add tomato juice, salt, and pepper to the vegetables and cook and stir over moderate heat until slightly thickened and smooth.

Drain beans well. Add to hot sauce and simmer 2 minutes over moderate heat. Serve hot, using ½ cup per serving.

Yields 4 cups—8 servings

Nutritive Values Per Serving

CAL	CHO (g)	PRO (g)	TOTAL FAT (g)	SAT. FAT (g)	CHOL (mg)	FIBER (g)	NA (mg)
40	6	1	2	trace	0	1.2	352

Food exchanges per serving: 1 vegetable
Low-sodium diets: Omit salt. Drain green beans and wash them well before using them.
Sugar content per serving: None.

Broccoli Rice Casserole

1 tablespoon vegetable oil
1 cup chopped onions
1 pound fresh or frozen broccoli pieces
1 can cream of mushroom soup
¼ cup milk
1 cup cooked rice
2 tablespoons grated Parmesan cheese

Place oil in a saucepan and bring to a frying temperature. Add onions to oil and cook and stir over moderate heat until soft but not browned. Add broccoli to onions and cook and stir over moderate heat until hot but not cooked. Mix soup and milk together to blend and add to broccoli mixture.

Add rice to vegetables. Cook and stir over low heat until hot and mixed. Place in a 1½- or 2-quart casserole that has been greased with margarine.

Sprinkle Parmesan evenly over the top of the broccoli mixture. Bake, uncovered, at 350°F for 35–40 minutes or until the casserole is bubbly and the broccoli is cooked. Serve hot using ½ cup per serving.

Yields 5 cups—10 servings

Nutritive Values Per Serving

CAL	CHO (g)	PRO (g)	TOTAL FAT (g)	SAT. FAT (g)	CHOL (mg)	FIBER (g)	NA (mg)
96	12	3	4	1	2	1.6	276

Food exchanges per serving: 2 vegetable, 1 fat
Low-sodium diets: Cook rice without salt and use low-sodium soup.
Sugar content per serving: None.

Chinese Vegetables

We like this served as a vegetable with plain roast pork or baked chicken. My sister says it tastes like chop suey and I guess she is right—but I like chop suey very much so that doesn't bother me.

> 1 tablespoon vegetable oil
> ½ cup coarsely chopped onions
> 1 cup thinly sliced celery
> 1 4-ounce can of well-drained mushrooms
> 1 cup water
> 1½ tablespoons cornstarch
> ¼ cup soy sauce
> 1 14-ounce can of well-drained bean
> 　sprouts
> 2 tablespoons chopped cashew nuts roasted
> 　in oil

Place oil in a saucepan and bring to a frying temperature. Add onions, celery, and mushrooms to hot oil. Cook and stir over moderate heat for 2–3 minutes or until onions are softened. Add ¼ cup water to vegetables. Cover and cook over low heat about 8 minutes or until vegetables are tender.

Mix together ¾ cup water, cornstarch, and soy sauce until smooth. Add to vegetables and cook and stir over moderate heat until thickened and clear. Add sprouts and nuts to vegetables and heat to serving temperature. Serve hot using ½ cup per serving.

Yields 3 cups—6 servings

Nutritive Values Per Serving

CAL	CHO (g)	PRO (g)	TOTAL FAT (g)	SAT. FAT (g)	CHOL (mg)	FIBER (g)	NA (mg)
65	7	2	4	.5	0	1	781

Food exchanges per serving: 1 vegetable, 1 fat
Low-sodium diets: Use low-sodium soy sauce.
Sugar content per serving: None.

Shredded Cabbage

---

1 pound white cabbage
¼ cup water
½ teaspoon salt
1 tablespoon margarine
Whisper of pepper

Trim and wash cabbage. Shred coarsely or cut into slices about ⅛ inch wide. Place water and salt in a saucepan and bring to a boil. Add cabbage. Mix lightly and cover tightly. Simmer over low heat for 12 minutes, stirring once during the cooking period. Drain well. Add margarine and pepper to cabbage. Toss lightly and serve hot, using ½ cup cabbage per serving.

Yields 2 cups—4 servings

Nutritive Values Per Serving

CAL	CHO (g)	PRO (g)	TOTAL FAT (g)	SAT. FAT (g)	CHOL (mg)	FIBER (g)	NA (mg)
50	6	1	3	.5	0	2.5	187

Food exchanges per serving: 1 vegetable, ½ fat
Low-sodium diets: Omit salt. Use salt-free margarine.
Sugar content per serving: None.

Cauliflower Parmesan

Chuck's cousin Dave Cavaiani's wife Etta cooked this for us when we visited them in Iron Mountain and we really liked it. The cheese adds to the flavor of the cauliflower in a most attractive way.

1 pound frozen cauliflower
2 cups boiling water
1 teaspoon salt
1 tablespoon margarine
2 tablespoons grated Parmesan cheese

Place cauliflower, water, and salt in a saucepan, cover, and simmer about 8 minutes or until the cauliflower is tender; or cook in the microwave oven according to directions on the package. Drain well.

Sprinkle margarine and cheese over the cauliflower. Toss lightly to coat the cauliflower and serve hot, using ¼ of the cauliflower (about ½ cup) per serving.

Yields about 2 cups—4 servings

Nutritive Values Per Serving

CAL	CHO (g)	PRO (g)	TOTAL FAT (g)	SAT. FAT (g)	CHOL (mg)	FIBER (g)	NA (mg)
64	5	3	4	1	2	3	381

Food exchanges per serving: 1 vegetable, 1 fat
Low-sodium diets: Omit salt. Use salt-free margarine.
Sugar content per serving: None.

Eggplant and Tomatoes

1 1-pound eggplant
¼ cup vegetable oil
½ cup coarsely chopped onions
½ cup coarsely chopped fresh green
   peppers
1 finely minced garlic clove
2 cups (1-pound can) Italian plum
   tomatoes
¼ cup chopped fresh parsley
⅛ teaspoon pepper
1 teaspoon salt
1 teaspoon sugar

Wash eggplant and remove ends. Cut into ½-inch cubes without removing the skin. Place oil in the bottom of a heavy pot or frying pan. Add eggplant along with onions, peppers, and garlic and fry over moderate heat, stirring occasionally, until eggplant is transparent and tender.

Add remaining ingredients to eggplant mixture and cook, stirring frequently, over moderate heat for about 5 minutes. Serve hot or at room temperature, using ½ cup per serving.

Yields 6 cups—12 servings

Nutritive Values Per Serving

CAL	CHO (g)	PRO (g)	TOTAL FAT (g)	SAT. FAT (g)	CHOL (mg)	FIBER (g)	NA (mg)
64	5	1	5	.6	0	1	251

Food exchanges per serving: 1 vegetable, 1 fat
Low-sodium diets: Omit salt. Use low-sodium canned or fresh tomatoes.
Sugar content per serving: Trace.

Sauerkraut with Tomatoes

I wish you could meet Dave Christen, who gave me this recipe. To me, he represents all the best in small-town residents. He truly cares about the town and his neighbors. He is a quiet family man who enjoys cooking occasionally. He and his wife, Dorothy, are active in their church and in the First Responders, who quickly arrive in an emergency in a small town. He has been commander of his American Legion Post, is active in the fire department, and was president of his state professional organization, the Iowa Blacksmith and Welder's Association.

1 29-ounce can sauerkraut
1 16-ounce can whole tomatoes with juice
½ cup cooked, diced, very lean ham with
    all visible fat removed
½ cup chopped onions
2 tablespoons packed brown sugar
½ teaspoon brown Sweet'n Low sugar
    substitute

Place sauerkraut in a colander, rinse with 2 quarts cold water, and drain well. Place sauerkraut in a large bowl, add tomatoes and juice, ham, onions, and brown sugar, and mix well. Place in a 2-quart casserole. Cover and bake at 325°F for 1 hour.

Remove cover, stir lightly, and bake 1 more hour. (Dave says he sometimes does this in a Crock-Pot for picnics.) Stir sugar substitute into sauerkraut mixture and serve hot, using ½ cup per serving.

Yields 1 quart—8 servings

Nutritive Values Per Serving

CAL	CHO (g)	PRO (g)	TOTAL FAT (g)	SAT. FAT (g)	CHOL (mg)	FIBER (g)	NA (mg)
52	9	3	1	trace	5	1.9	431

Food exchanges per serving: ¼ lean meat, 1½ vegetable
Low-sodium diets: Use low-sodium canned or fresh tomatoes and rinse and
    drain sauerkraut very well.
Sugar content per serving: .8 teaspoon.

Southern-Style Greens

---

1 pound frozen mustard or turnip greens
4 ounces chopped center-cut ham with fat,
bone, and skin removed
Whisper of black pepper
1½ cups boiling water

Greens should be almost completely thawed before cooking. Place greens in a saucepan. Add ham, pepper, and water to greens. Bring to a boil, reduce heat, and simmer uncovered for 30 minutes or until tender, adding more hot water if necessary. Cut through the greens several times with a sharp knife. Serve hot with some of the juice using ½ cup greens per serving.

Yields about 2 cups—4 servings

Nutritive Values Per Serving

CAL	CHO (g)	PRO (g)	TOTAL FAT (g)	SAT. FAT (g)	CHOL (mg)	FIBER (g)	NA (mg)
60	4	8	2	.5	13	3	438

Food exchanges per serving: 1 very lean meat, 1 vegetable
Low-sodium diets: May be used as written as part of a menu with low-sodium items.
Sugar content per serving: None.

Pickled Vegetables

These vegetables can be canned but I never bother to do so. I prepare them one recipe at a time and keep them in the refrigerator where they keep well for several weeks.

3 cups vinegar
3 cups water
3 tablespoons pickling spices
1 pound fresh carrots
1 10-ounce package frozen Brussels sprouts
2 cups celery cut into thin slices
2 cups (1-pound can) drained canned green beans
2 cups (1-pound can) drained canned yellow wax beans
2 cups julienne-cut fresh green peppers
2 cups coarsely chopped onions
Sugar substitute equal to 2 cups sugar

Combine vinegar, water, and pickling spices in a saucepan. Bring to a boil and simmer, covered, for 3 minutes. Remove from heat, cover, and let stand at room temperature for about a week or until the vinegar mixture tastes spicy according to your taste. Discard spices.

Clean carrots and cut into julienne pieces. Combine carrots, Brussels sprouts, and celery. Cover with boiling water and cook 3 minutes. Remove from heat; drain. Cover with cold water and drain again. Place in a large kettle with the vinegar mixture. Drain beans well and add to carrot and vinegar mixture.

Add peppers and onions to vegetables. Bring to a boil but remove immediately from heat. The vegetables should not be allowed to boil. Add sweetener to vegetable mixture. Mix lightly. Cover and allow to come to room temperature. Refrigerate at least 3 days before serving (½ cup per serving) as a salad or vegetable.

Yields about 1 gallon—32 servings

Nutritive Values Per Serving

CAL	CHO (g)	PRO (g)	TOTAL FAT (g)	SAT. FAT (g)	CHOL (mg)	FIBER (g)	NA (mg)
23	6	1	trace	0	0	1.2	56

Food exchanges per serving: 1 vegetable
Low-sodium diets: Rinse canned vegetables thoroughly.
Sugar content per serving: None.

Sautéed Vegetables

2 teaspoons vegetable oil
2 cups coarsely shredded cabbage
1 cup coarsely shredded carrots
1½ cups thinly sliced celery
¼ cup chopped fresh green peppers
½ cup coarsely chopped onions
½ teaspoon salt
¼ cup water
Soy sauce as desired

Place oil in the bottom of a heavy saucepan and heat to frying temperature. Add vegetables and salt to oil. Cook over medium heat for 5 minutes stirring frequently.

Add ¼ cup water to vegetables, cover, and cook over low heat for 5–7 minutes or until vegetables have reached the desired tenderness. Serve vegetables hot, using ½ cup per serving with soy sauce to be added as desired.

Yields 3 cups—6 servings

Nutritive Values Per Serving (without soy sauce)

CAL	CHO (g)	PRO (g)	TOTAL FAT (g)	SAT. FAT (g)	CHOL (mg)	FIBER (g)	NA (mg)
38	6	1	2	trace	0	1.9	219

Food exchanges per serving: 1 vegetable
Low-sodium diets: Omit salt. Use low-sodium soy sauce.
Sugar content per serving: None.

Spinach Frittata

I'm very fond of frittatas and make them frequently. I use a variety of vegetables, and sometimes I use ¼ cup cooked rice instead of bread.

2½ ounces frozen chopped spinach
¼ cup finely chopped onions
1 tablespoon imitation bacon bits
⅛ teaspoon salt
Whisper of pepper
Whites from 2 large or 3 medium eggs
½ slice whole wheat bread cut into cubes
½ teaspoon margarine

Cut a 10-ounce package of frozen chopped spinach into quarters. Defrost one quarter and return the rest to the freezer. Press any liquid out of spinach. Put spinach into a small bowl with onions, bacon bits, salt, pepper, and egg whites. Mix well with a fork. Add bread cubes and mix lightly, until they are covered with egg mixture but not soaked.

Preheat a small (8-inch) nonstick-surfaced frying pan over medium heat for 1 minute. Swirl margarine around bottom of pan. Add spinach mixture and fry over medium heat until bottom is lightly browned. Turn frittata over and cook until firm and bottom is lightly browned. Serve hot, using 1 frittata per serving. *Note:* If you want to make several frittatas, it is best to make them individually.

Yields 1 frittata—1 serving

Nutritive Values Per Serving

CAL	CHO (g)	PRO (g)	TOTAL FAT (g)	SAT. FAT (g)	CHOL (mg)	FIBER (g)	NA (mg)
143	16	14	4	.5	0	3.6	717

Food exchanges per serving: 2 very lean meat, 1 starch
Low-sodium diets: Omit salt. Use salt-free margarine.
Sugar content per serving: None.

Creamed Spinach with Peanuts

My husband Chuck developed this recipe when we lived in Chicago to persuade a friend who insisted he didn't like spinach that it could be very good.

1 10-ounce package frozen chopped
  spinach
1 quart boiling water
1½ cups fat-free chicken broth
2 tablespoons instant nonfat dry milk
3 tablespoons all-purpose flour
¼ teaspoon salt
⅛ teaspoon nutmeg
Whisper of white pepper
2 tablespoons chopped salted peanuts

Defrost spinach, break it up with a fork, and place it in a bowl. Add boiling water and let it sit for 5 minutes. Drain well and set aside.

Place broth, dry milk, flour, salt, nutmeg, and pepper in a small saucepan. Stir until smooth and then cook, stirring over medium heat until smooth and thickened. Add spinach and peanuts to the sauce. Stir lightly and serve hot, using ½ cup per serving.

Yields 2½ cups—5 servings

Nutritive Values Per Serving

CAL	CHO (g)	PRO (g)	TOTAL FAT (g)	SAT. FAT (g)	CHOL (mg)	FIBER (g)	NA (mg)
63	8	5	2	.3	trace	1.6	368

Food exchanges per serving: 1 vegetable
Low-sodium diets: Omit salt. Use low-sodium broth and unsalted peanuts.
Sugar content per serving: None.

Summer Squash with Ginger

I've never cared much for summer squash but when Chef Dave Hutchins served this to us at a luncheon, I knew I had finally found a recipe for summer squash I could enjoy. He is a very interesting person with an excellent professional background. His extensive knowledge about food and its preparation is reflected in the wonderful and varied food he serves in his restaurant.

> **1 tablespoon vegetable oil**
> **3 cups ¼-inch slices of summer squash (about 6 small zucchini)**
> **1½ teaspoons finely chopped fresh ginger**
> **4 crushed garlic cloves**
> **1 cup peeled, seeded, and chopped fresh tomatoes**
> **1 teaspoon grated Parmesan cheese**
> **½ teaspoon salt**
> **Whisper of pepper**

Preheat a large (12-inch) nonstick-surfaced frying pan. Swirl oil around pan, add squash, ginger, and garlic, and cook, stirring frequently, until squash is soft but not transparent. Add tomato to the sauce and continue to cook over medium heat, stirring frequently, until squash is transparent. Stir in Parmesan, salt, and pepper. Serve hot, using ½ cup per serving.

Yields 3 cups—6 servings

Nutritive Values Per Serving

CAL	CHO (g)	PRO (g)	TOTAL FAT (g)	SAT. FAT (g)	CHOL (mg)	FIBER (g)	NA (mg)
40	4	1	3	trace	trace	.8	193

Food exchanges per serving: 1 vegetable, ½ fat
Low-sodium diets: Omit salt.
Sugar content per serving: None.

Fran's Butternut Squash Casserole

This recipe was a favorite of my friend Frances Nielsen. She always fixed it for us when she came to visit every fall. You can use 1 cup canned tomatoes and juice instead of the fresh tomatoes, but the fresh tomatoes are the best.

> **2 pounds butternut squash**
> **2 medium-size fresh tomatoes**
> **1 cup coarsely chopped onions**
> **1 cup coarsely chopped fresh green peppers**
> **1 teaspoon Italian seasoning**
> **¾ teaspoon salt**
> **2 tablespoons (¼ stick) margarine**

Peel squash, remove seeds and fiber, and cut into slices about ½-inch thick. Wash and peel tomatoes and slice. Layer vegetables with the squash on the bottom, then tomatoes, onions, and peppers. Add seasoning and dot with margarine. Cover and bake at 350°F for 1½ hours. Remove the cover, stir lightly, and continue to bake about another ½ hour or until lightly browned and almost dry. Stir lightly and serve hot using ½ cup per serving.

Yields 3 cups—6 servings

Nutritive Values Per Serving

CAL	CHO (g)	PRO (g)	TOTAL FAT (g)	SAT. FAT (g)	CHOL (mg)	FIBER (g)	NA (mg)
115	20	2	4	.7	0	3.5	332

Food exchanges per serving: 1 starch, 1 fat, 1 vegetable
Low-sodium diets: Omit salt. Use fresh tomatoes or low-sodium canned
    tomatoes and salt-free margarine.
Sugar content per serving: None.

Monk's Rice

Margaret "Monk" Sellers prepared this rice when we both visited her sister and brother-in-law, Frances and Bud Gunsallus, in Miami. Monk said that she likes this version because the rice and vegetables aren't soupy or gummy as they are when you cook them all in the same pot. She prepared a big roaster full of it for the family party that night and we ate every bite of it.

½ cup long-grain rice
1 cup chicken broth
1 tablespoon vegetable oil
2 cups broccoli ends and pieces
1 cup coarsely chopped onions
1 cup coarsely grated carrots
½ cup chopped fresh green peppers
½ cup thinly sliced celery
1 4-ounce can well-drained mushroom
    stems and pieces
¼ teaspoon salt

Combine rice and broth and bring to a boil. Pour in a small casserole, cover tightly, and bake at 350°F for 30 minutes. Remove cover and set aside for later use.

Spread oil in a heavy 9- or 10-inch frying pan. Bring to a cooking temperature over moderate heat. Add vegetables and salt to hot oil in frying pan. Cook, stirring frequently, over moderate heat 10 to 15 minutes or until vegetables are crisp-tender (or soft if you prefer them that way). Add rice and mix lightly. Serve ½ cup per serving.

Yields 5 cups—10 servings

Nutritive Values Per Serving

CAL	CHO (g)	PRO (g)	TOTAL FAT (g)	SAT. FAT (g)	CHOL (mg)	FIBER (g)	NA (mg)
67	12	2	2	trace	0	1.4	160

Food exchanges per serving: ½ starch, 1 vegetable
Low-sodium diets: Omit salt. Use low-sodium broth.
Sugar content per serving: None.

Baked Tomato Halves

Frances Nielsen taught me to make these when she lived here in Wadena. The tomatoes are best right out of the garden. They should be fully ripe but still firm. The seasoning can be varied using basil, oregano, or any other favorite seasoning instead of the garlic.

4 fresh, ripe, medium-size tomatoes
2 tablespoons melted margarine
1 teaspoon garlic salt
¹⁄₁₆ teaspoon pepper
4 teaspoons grated Parmesan cheese
2 teaspoons dried parsley flakes

Wash tomatoes and remove the stems. Cut the tomatoes in half crosswise and place the halves on a rimmed cookie sheet that has been greased with margarine or sprayed with pan spray. Brush the tomato halves with margarine using a pastry brush.

Sprinkle the garlic salt and pepper on the tops of the tomato halves and then sprinkle the halves with the Parmesan cheese and parsley flakes, using ½ teaspoon of cheese for each tomato half. Bake at 350°F for 35–45 minutes or until tender and lightly browned. Serve hot using 2 halves per serving.

Yields 8 halves—4 servings

Nutritive Values Per Serving

CAL	CHO (g)	PRO (g)	TOTAL FAT (g)	SAT. FAT (g)	CHOL (mg)	FIBER (g)	NA (mg)
85	6	2	7	1.3	1	1.6	470

Food exchanges per serving: 1 vegetable, 1 fat
Low-sodium diets: Omit garlic salt. Sprinkle with garlic powder.
Sugar content per serving: None.

Stir-Fry Tomatoes

1 tablespoon vegetable oil
1 cup thinly sliced celery
1 cup julienne-cut fresh green peppers
1 6- to 8-inch zucchini cut into ¼-inch slices
4 medium-size tomatoes at room temperature
1 cup fat-free chicken broth
1 tablespoon cornstarch
¼ teaspoon salt
½ teaspoon ground ginger
1 teaspoon pepper

Place oil in heavy saucepan or deep, heavy frying pan and bring to frying temperature. Add celery, peppers, and zucchini to frying pan. Cook and stir over moderate heat about 5 minutes, or until crisp-tender. Wash tomatoes and remove stems. Cut into wedges and add to vegetable mixture. Cook and stir until tomatoes are hot.

Stir together broth, cornstarch, and seasonings until smooth. Add to vegetables and cook and stir about 2 minutes or until thickened. Serve hot using about ¾ cup per serving.

Yields about 6 cups—8 servings

Nutritive Values Per Serving

CAL	CHO (g)	PRO (g)	TOTAL FAT (g)	SAT. FAT (g)	CHOL (mg)	FIBER (g)	NA (mg)
45	6	2	2	trace	0	1.4	168

Food exchanges per serving: 1 vegetable
Low-sodium diets: Omit salt. Use low-sodium broth.
Sugar content per serving: None.

Zucchini Scramble

My sister-in-law, Josephine Serevino of Chicago, said this was one of her favorite summer vegetable combinations.

1 tablespoon vegetable oil
1 6- to 8-inch zucchini cut into ¼-inch slices
1 cup julienne-cut fresh green pepper
½ cup diced fresh potatoes
½ cup coarsely chopped onions
1 large fresh tomato cut into wedges
¼ teaspoon garlic powder
½ teaspoon salt
1 bay leaf

Place oil in a heavy saucepan or deep, heavy frying pan and bring to frying temperature.

Add vegetables and seasonings to hot oil. Cook and stir over moderate heat for about 3 minutes. Reduce heat to low, cover, and cook, stirring occasionally, about 20 minutes or until vegetables are tender. Remove bay leaf and serve hot, using about ½ cup per portion.

Yields about 4 cups—8 servings

Nutritive Values Per Serving

CAL	CHO (g)	PRO (g)	TOTAL FAT (g)	SAT. FAT (g)	CHOL (mg)	FIBER (g)	NA (mg)
38	5	1	2	trace	0	.9	140

Food exchanges per serving: 1 vegetable
Low-sodium diets: Omit salt.
Sugar content per serving: None.

Pandy's Zucchini and Corn

This recipe came from my friend Pandy Williams of Ajo, Arizona, where I spend the winter months. She isn't on a low-cholesterol diet, so she sprinkles it with 8 ounces grated Longhorn or Monterey Jack cheese just before she serves it. The cheese melts and it is absolutely luscious. Since she is diabetic she counts the 8 ounces of cheese as 1 meat exchange per serving.

1 pound fresh 6- to 8-inch zucchini
1 tablespoon vegetable oil
1 cup coarsely chopped onions
1 cup coarsely chopped fresh green pepper
   or 4-ounce can diced green chilies
2 cups fresh or canned chopped tomatoes
   and juice
1 cup canned or fresh whole kernel corn
1 teaspoon garlic salt
Whisper of pepper

Wash and trim the ends from zucchini. Cut crosswise into ¼-inch slices and set aside.

Heat oil in a nonstick-surfaced frying pan, add onions and peppers, and stir over medium heat until the onions begin to soften. Add tomatoes and cook 2 minutes. Add zucchini and cook, stirring occasionally, for 10 minutes. Add corn, salt, and pepper, cover, and cook, stirring occasionally, 10 to 12 minutes or until the zucchini are transparent. Serve hot, using ½ cup per serving.

Yields 4 cups—8 servings

Nutritive Values Per Serving

CAL	CHO (g)	PRO (g)	TOTAL FAT (g)	SAT. FAT (g)	CHOL (mg)	FIBER (g)	NA (mg)
64	11	2	2	trace	0	1.7	258

Food exchanges per serving: 2 vegetable
Low-sodium diets: Use fresh tomatoes, fresh or frozen peppers and corn,
   and ¼ teaspoon garlic powder instead of salt.
Sugar content per serving: None.

Vegetable Purées

This is a method, not a recipe, but I urge you to try it. The vegetable purées are very flavorful and attractive—a whole new taste sensation. Since they are more concentrated than the regular vegetables, ⅓ of a cup of puréed vegetable is equal to ½ cup of the same vegetable—but it is worth it. I add margarine and other seasonings after the vegetables are puréed, except for the salt that I add when cooking the vegetable. If you add 1 tablespoon of margarine per cup of cooked puréed vegetables, you will have 1 vegetable exchange and 1 fat exchange per ⅓ cup of puréed vegetable.

Start with good fresh vegetables. Wash them, and peel them if necessary. Cook them until tender but not mushy. I prefer to cook vegetables in the microwave, but you can also cook them in water if you prefer. If you have cooked them in water, drain them well and shake the pan over low heat for a few seconds to get rid of as much moisture as possible. If you have cooked them in the microwave, drain them well and cover them with a clean napkin or dishtowel for a few minutes to absorb as much of the steam as possible.

Vegetables can be sieved or put into the food processor. I prefer the food processor because it is much simpler. I don't recommend the blender because you have to add a little water and the results aren't firm enough. Remove any seeds or skin you don't want to be in the purée before you put the food in the food processor because it will process everything together.

The vegetable purée will probably be cold after it is finished. I add seasonings then along with the margarine. The purée can be reheated by placing it in the microwave, or it can be stirred over low heat in a saucepan until it is at serving temperature. If I'm having guests, I like to put it in a casserole and put it in the oven to be lightly browned before it is served. You can also freeze the purées in ⅓ cup portions to add interest to some other meals in the future. If you do this, it is better not to add the margarine until you are ready to defrost and reheat the vegetables.

Potatoes should not be prepared in the food processor because the action of the food processor will make the potatoes gummy. However, winter squash and carrots both react well in the food processor. I also like to combine vegetables, puréeing them separately or together, such as adding onions to winter squash or broccoli, or a little green pepper to carrots. One of my favorites is to add some dill seed to puréed winter squash. There are so many good combinations to explore that your vegetable exchanges should never be dull.

Baked Beans

These are my sister Shirley's favorite. I wish I could use more of them in my diet because I also like them and they are a good source of fiber, but they are so high in carbohydrate that I don't use them too often. Sometimes I add a couple of tablespoons of them to a big lettuce salad—which is very good and only costs me a vegetable exchange.

> 1 pound dry great northern beans
> Cold water as necessary
> 4 ounces chopped center-cut ham with fat,
>   bone, and skin removed
> 1 cup chopped onions
> 6 ounces tomato paste
> 1½ teaspoons salt
> 2 tablespoons salad mustard
> ¾ cup Brown Sugar Twin granulated sugar
>   substitute

Wash beans and discard any imperfect ones. Add cold water, cover, and bring to a boil. Simmer for 5 minutes. Remove from heat and let stand for 2–3 hours. Drain well. Cover again with cold water to about ½ inch over the top of the beans. Bring to a boil, reduce heat, cover, and let simmer for about 2½ hours or until the beans are soft.

Thoroughly mix beans with remaining ingredients. Place in a shallow baking dish and bake, uncovered, at 325°F for 2 to 3 hours or until the beans are rather dry, stirring every hour. Serve hot or cold, using ⅓ cup beans per serving.

Yields 6 cups—18 servings

Nutritive Values Per Serving

CAL	CHO (g)	PRO (g)	TOTAL FAT (g)	SAT. FAT (g)	CHOL (mg)	FIBER (g)	NA (mg)
109	19	7	1	trace	3	10.6	373

Food exchanges per serving: 1 starch, 1 very lean meat
Low-sodium diets: Omit salt.
Sugar content per serving: None.

Red Beans and Rice

Judy Ballantine from Madison, Wisconsin, loves this combination. It takes a lot of exchanges but she says it is worth it even though it takes most of the exchanges for a meal.

> **1 pound dry kidney beans**
> **Water as necessary**
> **1 cup chopped onions**
> **¾ cup chopped fresh green peppers**
> **1 cup finely chopped celery**
> **4 ounces chopped center-cut ham with fat, skin, and bone removed**
> **2 teaspoons salt**
> **½ teaspoon cayenne pepper**
> **¼ teaspoon black pepper**
> **3 tablespoons thinly sliced green onion tops**
> **1½ tablespoons parsley flakes**
> **6 cups hot fluffy cooked rice**
> **Fresh onion slices**

Wash and sort beans. Add 2 quarts hot water. Cover and soak overnight. Drain well. Discard the liquid and add cold water to cover the beans to about ½ inch over the top.

Add onions, peppers, celery, ham, salt, cayenne, and black pepper to beans. Bring to a boil. Reduce heat, cover, and simmer 2½ hours, stirring occasionally. Add onion tops and parsley to beans. Simmer uncovered about 30 minutes, stirring occasionally.

Serve ½ cup of the hot beans over ½ cup of the rice per serving. Garnish the beans with a few onion slices, if desired.

Yields 6 cups—12 servings

Nutritive Values Per Serving (including rice)

CAL	CHO (g)	PRO (g)	TOTAL FAT (g)	SAT. FAT (g)	CHOL (mg)	FIBER (g)	NA (mg)
280	53	14	1	trace	5	4.8	501

Food exchanges per serving: 3 starch, 1 vegetable, ⅓ lean meat
Low-sodium diets: Omit salt.
Sugar content per serving: None.

Creamy Brown Rice

I never really liked brown rice until Dr. Karen Kuenzel of the Rice Research and Extension Center at the University of Arkansas told me that I wasn't using enough liquid and I wasn't cooking it long enough. She gave me these proportions to use and now I like it very well and use it more often. Dr. Kuenzel is the daughter of Zella Kuenzel, a friend of mine who is a dietitian in Guttenberg, Iowa, a town on the Mississippi. Dr. Kuenzel was in Guttenberg so I asked Zella if she would help me with my difficulties with brown rice—and she helped me a lot!

1 cup brown rice
2½ cups boiling water
½ teaspoon salt

Place rice, water, and salt in a Crock-Pot. Turn on high and cook for about 2 hours or until soft and creamy. Serve hot using ⅓ cup per serving.

Note: If you like brown rice more firm, use less liquid. It can also be cooked in a saucepan over low heat for about 50–60 minutes if you don't like to use the Crock-Pot. Remove the lid and fluff the rice with a fork, cover with a napkin or terry cloth dish towel, and let stand 5–10 minutes to fluff before it is served, using ⅓ cup per serving.

Yields 3 cups—9 servings

Nutritive Values Per Serving

CAL	CHO (g)	PRO (g)	TOTAL FAT (g)	SAT. FAT (g)	CHOL (mg)	FIBER (g)	NA (mg)
76	16	2	1	trace	0	.7	123

Food exchanges per serving: 1 starch
Low-sodium diets: Omit salt.
Sugar content per serving: None.

Medium White Sauce

---

2 tablespoons all-purpose flour
¼ cup instant nonfat dry milk
½ teaspoon salt
Whisper of white pepper (optional)
1 tablespoon vegetable oil
1 cup cold water

Stir together flour, milk, salt, and pepper until blended. Place oil in a small saucepan. Add the flour mixture and cook and stir over moderate heat until smooth but not browned. Remove from heat.

Add 1 cup water to flour mixture. Return to heat and cook and stir over medium heat until sauce is thickened and smooth. (1 cup fat-free chicken broth may be substituted for the cold water, if desired, to make a Velouté sauce with no change in food exchanges. However, the sodium will be increased to 546 mg per serving.) Use for creamed vegetables or meats using ¼ cup per serving.

Yields 1 cup—4 servings

Nutritive Values Per Serving

CAL	CHO (g)	PRO (g)	TOTAL FAT (g)	SAT. FAT (g)	CHOL (mg)	FIBER (g)	NA (mg)
60	5	2	4	trace	1	trace	297

Food exchanges per serving: ½ skim milk
Low-sodium diets: Omit salt.
Sugar content per serving: None.

Mock Sour Cream

This recipe from Esther Smith, a home economist from near Wadena, is great on baked potatoes. I also like to add some garlic powder to it and use it as a dip or for salad dressing.

> **1½ cups well-drained cottage cheese,**
> **preferably large curd**
> **2 tablespoons dry buttermilk**
> **½ cup skim milk**
> **1 tablespoon lemon juice**
> **½ teaspoon salt**

Place all ingredients in bowl of food processor and process until thick and smooth. Refrigerate until needed using ¼ cup per serving.

Yields 2 cups—8 servings

Nutritive Values Per Serving

CAL	CHO (g)	PRO (g)	TOTAL FAT (g)	SAT. FAT (g)	CHOL (mg)	FIBER (g)	NA (mg)
36	2	6	trace	trace	4	0	158

Food exchanges per serving: 1 very lean meat, ¼ skim milk
Low-sodium diets: Omit salt.
Sugar content per serving: None.

Blintzes

This recipe is from Anita Kane of Shorewood, Wisconsin. Anita served them with unsweetened applesauce or other fruit. I like them with Cinnamon Shake or Apple Butter (see Index).

FILLING
1 pound well-drained low-fat cottage
  cheese
¼ cup liquid egg substitute
2 teaspoons sugar

PANCAKE
¾ cup liquid egg substitute
1 cup water
¾ cup all-purpose flour
2 tablespoons vegetable oil
Margarine or oil as necessary

Mix cottage cheese, ¼ cup egg substitute, and sugar together lightly and refrigerate until needed.

Beat together ¾ cup egg substitute, 1 cup water, flour, and 2 tablespoons oil until smooth.

Heat a little margarine or oil in a 6-inch frying pan (I like oil best). Use a shallow frying pan as you would for frying crepes. Pour about 2 tablespoons batter into the frying pan, tilting the pan so that the batter coats as much of the pan surface as possible. It should make a very thin pancake. Cook over medium heat 1 to 2 minutes or until the bottom of the pancake is lightly browned and the sides are curled up. Carefully turn the pancake out onto a clean dish towel. The pancakes can be stacked like shingles.

When all of the pancakes are cooked, spread about a tablespoon of filling in the center of each pancake. Fold in both sides and then the ends so that you have a neat little package. Place the blintzes seam side down in a baking dish that has been greased with margarine. Brush lightly with melted margarine and bake at 375°F for 30–40 minutes or until browned and puffy. Serve hot with fruit, Apple Butter, or Cinnamon Shake (see Index), using 3 blintzes per serving.

These freeze very well. I put them individually on a cookie sheet until they are frozen and then I keep them in a bag in the freezer until I need them. I grease a baking dish well with margarine and let them defrost before I bake them.

Yields 18 blintzes—6 servings

Nutritive Values Per Serving (without fat for frying or topping)

CAL	CHO (g)	PRO (g)	TOTAL FAT (g)	SAT. FAT (g)	CHOL (mg)	FIBER (g)	NA (mg)
190	17	16	6	1.5	6	.4	374

Food exchanges per serving: 1 starch, 1½ lean meat, ¼ skim milk
Low-sodium diets: Use salt-free margarine.
Sugar content per serving: None.

Stewed Cranberries

I like cranberries very much and like to keep a supply of them in the freezer. I always buy several packages when they first come to our stores in the fall and stew them, or freeze them whole, to have all winter.

1 pound fresh cranberries
1 cup water
Sugar substitute equal to ½ cup sugar

Wash cranberries well under running water. Pick them over and discard any imperfect berries. Place cranberries and water in a small saucepan. Simmer about 5 minutes or until the cranberries have burst.

Remove from heat. Add sugar substitute, mix lightly, and cool to room temperature. Taste for flavor and add more sugar substitute, if desired. Refrigerate until used, using ½ cup per serving.

Yields 3 cups—6 servings

Nutritive Values Per Serving

CAL	CHO (g)	PRO (g)	TOTAL FAT (g)	SAT. FAT (g)	CHOL (mg)	FIBER (g)	NA (mg)
45	12	trace	trace	0	0	2.8	61

Food exchanges per serving: ¾ fruit (2 tablespoons may be considered free)
Low-sodium diets: May be used as written.
Sugar content per serving: None.

13

Salads and Salad Dressings

Salads are an important part of a diabetic diet. A chef's salad is easy to order when you are eating out, and a bowl of lettuce added to your lunch or dinner makes you feel as though you have dined well—which you have. Salads offer bulk, fiber, vitamins and minerals, satisfaction, and good taste, all of which are very important. However, you need to be careful even when ordering or making a salad because some salads can hide a lot of cholesterol and carbohydrate, and the most innocent-looking fruit salad can hide a lot of fat in the dressing. So always analyze a salad (quietly to yourself, of course) before you eat it.

Some salad ingredients are so low in calories that you can eat up to a cup of them without counting them, so I always try to include them in salads whenever possible. They include chinese cabbage, cucumbers, endive, escarole, lettuce, parsley, dill pickles, radishes, and watercress.

A good tossed salad begins with clean, crisp greens. They lose texture and nutrients even when properly refrigerated so it is best to be careful when you are preparing them. They are also fragile and must be stored carefully. It is a good idea not to wash them until shortly before they are used. Everyone has different ideas about how to keep greens fresh. I like to clean them and remove as much of the water as possible, and then store them in a plastic container in the refrigerator until I need them. Some cooks like to wash them and wrap them in a damp towel and refrigerate them until used. If they are wilted you can sometimes bring them back to a manageable state by soaking them in cold water for a short time and then drying them before they are used. Remember, you shouldn't add the dressing until just before the salad is served because the dressing will wilt the greens.

Hard-cooked egg yolks should not be used in a salad on a low-cholesterol diabetic diet because of the cholesterol in the egg yolks. If you want chopped whole eggs in your salad, you can cook liquid egg substitute in the microwave oven or the top of a double boiler, let it return to room temperature, and then chop it into cubes for use in salads. I generally just hard-cook the eggs, discard the egg yolks, and chop the whites for salad. You can use the egg yolks to garnish the salad, and anyone who doesn't need to watch their cholesterol intake can eat them. Don't feel guilty if you throw away the yolks. Just tell yourself you are discarding cholesterol and it gets easier every time you do it.

There are some good low-calorie salad dressings on the market that are suitable for a low-cholesterol diabetic recipe. However, they hardly ever contain vegetable oil because of the calories, and you do need some polyunsaturated vegetable oils in your diet. Anyone on a low-cholesterol diabetic diet has a hard time balancing the amount of vegetable oil needed for a low-cholesterol diet with the number of fat exchanges on the diabetic diet. I suggest that you talk to your doctor about it and see which is the most important—getting the polyunsaturated vegetable oil or restricting your fat intake.

Sour cream is also a no-no on a low-cholesterol diet and a lot of very good dressings contain sour cream. You can generally substitute low-fat yogurt for sour cream in most recipes with good results. Again, it is a good idea to read the list of ingredients on the container before you buy salad dressing to be sure they don't contain anything that shouldn't be used on a low-cholesterol diet—as well as honey, or sugar, or other things that shouldn't be used on a diabetic diet. I'm happy to say that Miracle Whip, made by Kraft, is satisfactory on a low-cholesterol diet—it is very low in cholesterol and is low enough in carbohydrate that it can also be used on a diabetic diet (within reason, of course). If you are in doubt about your favorite dressing, read the label; you may be happily surprised.

Fruits and vegetables—except for coconut and coconut oil

and palm oil—do not have any cholesterol. You are free to use any fruits and vegetables in a salad that will fit into your diabetic diet pattern. I haven't used any avocados because they are so high in fat exchanges that they are hard to fit into a diabetic diet pattern. However, if you like them well enough that you are willing to use your fat exchanges for them, feel perfectly free to use them; they are a good source of fiber, which is a plus. I also have not used grapefruit or oranges because I feel that most diabetics use them so often and are so used to eating them that I should concentrate on salads that might be a little different. Grapefruit sections or orange sections on a lettuce leaf is a perfect salad for both the low-cholesterol and diabetic diets.

Equal (aspartame) sugar substitute has been used a great deal in this chapter because I like to use it whenever possible, but feel free to use your own favorite sugar substitute. Each packet of Equal is equal to 2 teaspoons sugar—use your own favorite sugar substitute accordingly.

Basic Salad Gelatin

This gelatin base is free and doesn't need to be counted. However, you will need to count any other ingredients that you add to the gelatin unless they, too, are free.

> **1¾ cups water**
> **1 ¼-ounce packet Knox Unflavored**
> **Gelatine**
> **2 tablespoons lemon juice or white vinegar**
> **Sugar substitute equal to 2 tablespoons**
> **sugar**

Place 1 cup water in pan. Sprinkle gelatin over it and let stand for 5 minutes. Heat and stir over low heat until clear and gelatin is dissolved. Remove from heat.

Add remaining ¾ cup water, lemon juice, and sweetener to gelatin mixture. Stir to dissolve sugar substitute, if necessary. Pour into mold or dish and refrigerate until firm. Serve about ½ cup per serving. (Up to 1½ cups vegetables or fruit may be added to the gelatin. First chill the gelatin until it is the consistency of unbeaten egg whites. Then fold in vegetables and pour into mold or bowl. Chill until firm.)

Yields about 2 cups—4 servings

Nutritive Values Per Serving

CAL	CHO (g)	PRO (g)	TOTAL FAT (g)	SAT. FAT (g)	CHOL (mg)	FIBER (g)	NA (mg)
11	1	2	trace	0	0	0	28

Food exchanges per serving: May be considered free
Low-sodium diets: May be used as written.
Sugar content per serving: None.

Fruit-Flavored Gelatin

You can use any flavor unsweetened drink mix with this recipe, but we prefer strawberry or cherry. Of course, you will have to calculate any fruit or other ingredients you add to the gelatin. If you add 1 cup drained, unsweetened fruit to the gelatin, each serving will be ½ fruit exchange.

2 cups water
1 ¼-ounce packet Knox Unflavored
   Gelatine
1 .20-ounce packet Wyler's unsweetened
   flavored soft drink mix or Kool-Aid
   unsweetened soft drink mix
8 1-gram packets Equal (aspartame) sugar
   substitute

Sprinkle gelatin over water. Heat over low heat or in the microwave oven until water is hot and gelatin is dissolved. Add drink mix and sweetener to hot gelatin mixture and stir until dissolved. Pour into mold or dish and refrigerate until firm. Serve ½ cup per serving.

Yields 2 cups—4 servings

Nutritive Values Per Serving

CAL	CHO (g)	PRO (g)	TOTAL FAT (g)	SAT. FAT (g)	CHOL (mg)	FIBER (g)	NA (mg)
14	1	3	0	0	0	0	62

Food exchanges per serving: May be considered free
Low-sodium diets: May be used as written.
Sugar content per serving: None.

Apple Salad

This recipe is from Kay Knochel of Phoenix, Arizona. It is a typically Midwestern one that she gave me when we were room-mates in Chicago.

Diabetic lemon gelatin to prepare 2 cups
  gelatin
1¾ cups water
½ cup low-fat cottage cheese
2 small (4 to the pound) tart apples
½ cup chopped nuts

Prepare gelatin according to directions, using 1¾ cups water instead of 2 cups. Refrigerate until it begins to thicken. Drain cottage cheese well and mash with the back of a large spoon. Fold into slightly thickened gelatin. Wash and core apples but do not peel them. Cut into small pieces and stir into the gelatin.

Stir nuts into gelatin and pour into a 9-inch square pan that has been rinsed with cold water. Chill until firm. Cut 3 × 4 into 12 equal portions. Serve 1 portion on a lettuce leaf per serving. The salad may be garnished with 1 tablespoon Kay's Cooked Dressing (see Index) without adding any exchanges, if desired.

Yields 1 9-inch square pan—12 servings

Nutritive Values Per Serving

CAL	CHO (g)	PRO (g)	TOTAL FAT (g)	SAT. FAT (g)	CHOL (mg)	FIBER (g)	NA (mg)
54	4	2	3	trace	trace	.6	57

Food exchanges per serving: ¼ fruit, ½ fat
Low-sodium diets: Use low-sodium variation of the salad dressing.
Sugar content per serving: None.

Molded Spicy Apricot Salad

This salad is excellent for buffets. It is colorful, and the sur-prising, spicy taste is a good accent to cold roast meats, chicken, and turkey.

  1 16-ounce can apricot halves in light
    syrup
  ¼ cup white vinegar
  2 tablespoons sugar
  1 stick cinnamon
  4 whole cloves
  Water
  1 .3-ounce package apricot or peach sugar-
    free gelatin
  3 1-gram packets Equal (aspartame) sugar
    substitute

Drain apricots well and reserve liquid. Refrigerate apricots. Combine apricot juice, vinegar, sugar, cinnamon, and cloves. Add enough water to yield 2 cups liquid. Pour into a saucepan, cover, and simmer for 10 minutes. Immediately strain spices from liquid and dissolve gelatin in liquid while still hot. Add enough cold water to total 2 cups, if necessary. Stir Equal into gelatin mixture and mix lightly. Cool until syrupy, add apricots, mix lightly, and pour into an 8-inch-square glass dish and refrig-erate until set. Cut into 6 equal portions, using 1 portion per serving. (The gelatin can also be molded and ½ cup of the salad used per serving.)

Yields 1 8-inch square—6 servings

Nutritive Values Per Serving

CAL	CHO (g)	PRO (g)	TOTAL FAT (g)	SAT. FAT (g)	CHOL (mg)	FIBER (g)	NA (mg)
73	18	1	trace	0	0	0	44

Food exchanges per serving: 1 fruit
Low-sodium diets: May be used as written.
Sugar content per serving: None.

Nectarine Salad

If nectarines aren't available, you can use ½ cup well-drained, sliced, juice-packed peaches instead.

> ¼ **cup Miracle Whip salad dressing**
> ¼ **cup 2% milk**
> **1 1-gram packet Equal (aspartame) sugar substitute**
> **2 cups diced crisp, fresh apples (about 2 medium-size)**
> **1 cup sliced, washed but not peeled, fresh nectarine (about 1 medium)**
> **1 cup diced celery**

Place Miracle Whip, milk, and Equal in a bowl and mix until smooth. Let sit at room temperature for 15 minutes to thicken. Add apples, nectarine, and celery. Mix lightly and refrigerate. Serve cold, using ½ cup per serving.

Yields 3 cups—6 servings

Nutritive Values Per Serving

CAL	CHO (g)	PRO (g)	TOTAL FAT (g)	SAT. FAT (g)	CHOL (mg)	FIBER (g)	NA (mg)
89	11	1	5	.8	4	1.5	79

Food exchanges per serving: ⅔ fruit, 1 fat
Low-sodium diets: May be used as written.
Sugar content per serving: None.

Cranberry Gelatin Salad

**Diabetic strawberry gelatin to yield 4 cups
  gelatin**
1¾ cups water
1¼ cups cooked cranberries, unsweetened
½ cup finely chopped celery
¼ cup Kay's Cooked Dressing (see Index)
¼ cup chopped nuts
Sugar substitute

Prepare gelatin as directed on the package, but use only 1¾ cups water. Cool for 5 minutes. Add cranberries, celery, dressing, and nuts to gelatin mixture. Mix lightly.

Add sweetener to salad to taste. Pour salad into a 9-inch square glass pan. Refrigerate until firm. Cut 3 × 4 into 12 equal portions. Serve 1 square on a lettuce leaf per serving. The salad may be garnished with 1 teaspoon Kay's Cooked Dressing without changing the exchange values.

Yields 1 9-inch square mold—12 servings

Nutritive Values Per Serving

CAL	CHO (g)	PRO (g)	TOTAL FAT (g)	SAT. FAT (g)	CHOL (mg)	FIBER (g)	NA (mg)
34	2	1	2	trace	0	.6	53

Food exchanges per serving: One serving may be considered free
Low-sodium diets: May be used as written. Use low-sodium variation of the
  salad dressing.
Sugar content per serving: None.

Molded Cabbage Salad

I know it sounds unusual but I like to serve this salad with stir-fry meals. The tartness of the salad complements the sauce on the stir-fry food.

1 .3-ounce package sugar-free lemon
   gelatin
1¼ cups boiling water
2 tablespoons Kay's Cooked Dressing
   (see Index)
2 tablespoons white vinegar
1 tablespoon instant dry milk
¼ teaspoon salt
1 cup finely chopped cabbage
¼ cup finely chopped celery
¼ cup finely chopped onions
2 tablespoons finely chopped fresh green
   peppers

Dissolve gelatin in water and let cool to room temperature. Add salad dressing, vinegar, dry milk, and salt to gelatin and refrigerate until syrupy. Beat with a whip at medium speed until thickened, creamy, and slightly increased in volume. Stir cabbage, celery, onions, and peppers into the gelatin mixture and pour into a shallow 1-quart casserole or mold. Chill until firm and then cut into 6 equal portions. Use 1 portion per serving.

Yields 1 mold—6 servings

Nutritive Values Per Serving

CAL	CHO (g)	PRO (g)	TOTAL FAT (g)	SAT. FAT (g)	CHOL (mg)	FIBER (g)	NA (mg)
21	2	1	trace	trace	trace	.5	149

Food exchanges per serving: ½ vegetable
Low-sodium diets: Omit salt.
Sugar content per serving: None.

Broccoli Salad

This recipe is based on one from Esther Smith. Esther is a home economist who lives out in the country near Wadena. She plays the organ at our church. This tremendously talented person is also a marvelous seamstress and a wonderful program chairman for our women's group at church—the sort of person that every small town needs.

2 cups sliced fresh cauliflower
2 cups sliced fresh broccoli
⅓ cup sliced Bermuda onion
1 teaspoon garlic salt
1 cup sliced fresh mushrooms
3 tablespoons Miracle Whip salad dressing
1 tablespoon milk

Clean the cauliflower, broccoli, and onion and slice them evenly. I like to trim the skin from the stalks of the broccoli and use the stalks, saving the flowerets for a vegetable. However, I do use the cauliflower flowerets, slicing them lengthwise—they look so pretty together that way.

Sprinkle the garlic salt over the vegetables. Toss them lightly and place them in a covered container in the refrigerator overnight.

Drain broccoli mixture well and add sliced mushrooms. Thoroughly mix together salad dressing and milk and pour over the vegetables. Mix lightly and serve ½ cup per serving.

Yields 4½ cups—9 servings

Nutritive Values Per Serving

CAL	CHO (g)	PRO (g)	TOTAL FAT (g)	SAT. FAT (g)	CHOL (mg)	FIBER (g)	NA (mg)
39	4	1	3	.4	2	1.3	199

Food exchanges per serving: 1 vegetable, ½ fat
Low-sodium diets: Omit garlic salt. Sprinkle vegetables with ½ teaspoon garlic powder before placing them in the refrigerator overnight.
Sugar content per serving: None.

Marinated Broccoli and Mushrooms

My godchild, Vicki Glastetter, from Redlands, California, shared this recipe with me. She arranges the broccoli flowerets around the edge of the platter and piles the mushrooms in the center for an appetizer that she says she and her friends enjoy. I use it as a salad because it is so pretty and tastes so good. She uses ½ teaspoon pepper, but I use only ⅛ teaspoon pepper. Our taste buds aren't used to the hot Southwestern food that she and her friends enjoy.

> 1½ pounds fresh broccoli
> 8 ounces fresh mushrooms
> ½ cup tarragon vinegar
> 1 tablespoon chopped parsley
> ⅛-½ teaspoon pepper
> ½ teaspoon salt
> 1 tablespoon lemon juice
> ¼ cup vegetable oil
> 1 tablespoon sugar
> 2 large cloves garlic

Wash broccoli and cut into bite-size pieces. Place in a plastic or stainless-steel refrigerator container that has a tight cover. Wash or wipe off mushrooms, thinly slice them, and place on top of broccoli.

In a separate bowl, combine vinegar, parsley, pepper, salt, lemon juice, oil, and sugar. Mash or chop garlic very fine and add to dressing. Mix well and pour over vegetables. Cover container tightly and refrigerate, turning container over several times a day, for 2 or 3 days. Drain well and serve, using ¾ cup per serving.

Yields 6 cups—8 servings

CAL	CHO (g)	PRO (g)	TOTAL FAT (g)	SAT. FAT (g)	CHOL (mg)	FIBER (g)	NA (mg)
102	9	3	7	.9	0	2.8	162

Food exchanges per serving: 2 vegetable, 1 fat
Low-sodium diets: Omit salt.
Sugar content per serving: .4 teaspoon.

Special Broccoli Salad

This is another broccoli salad from Esther Smith.

¼ cup **Miracle Whip salad dressing**
¼ cup **skim milk**
1 tablespoon **white vinegar**
3 1-gram packets **Equal (aspartame) sugar substitute**
¼ teaspoon **salt**
1 quart fresh **broccoli flowerets and sliced, peeled stems**
2 tablespoons **raisins**
2 tablespoons **salted sunflower kernels**
½ cup **chopped onions**

Combine Miracle Whip and milk in a mixing bowl and stir until smooth. Add vinegar, sugar substitute, and salt and mix well. Let sit at room temperature for 15–30 minutes.

Prepare broccoli and set aside. Add raisins, sunflower kernels, and onions to Miracle Whip mixture. Mix lightly, pour over broccoli, mix lightly again, and refrigerate 2–8 hours before serving. Serve chilled using ⅔ cup salad per serving.

Yields 4⅔ cups—7 servings

Nutritive Values Per Serving

CAL	CHO (g)	PRO (g)	TOTAL FAT (g)	SAT. FAT (g)	CHOL (mg)	FIBER (g)	NA (mg)
85	8	3	5	.7	3	2	162

Food exchanges per serving: 1 vegetable, 1 fat
Low-sodium diets: Omit salt, use unsalted sunflower kernels.
Sugar content per serving: None.

Chef's Salad

I'm sure I don't need to tell you about chef's salad. We so often order them in restaurants since it is the easiest thing to order to count our exchanges and not go over. They come in all varieties and forms, but this version is my favorite for preparing at home.

> 1 cup chopped or shredded fresh crisp
> lettuce
> ¼ medium-size fresh tomato, washed,
> cored, and sliced or diced
> ¼ cup chopped celery
> ¼ cup chopped onions
> ½ cup sliced fresh cauliflower
> 1 ounce (about 3 tablespoons) diced or
> chopped cooked chicken with all visible
> fat removed
> 1 ounce (about 3 tablespoons) diced or
> chopped lean ham with all visible fat
> removed
> ¼ cup Garlic Dressing, Creamy (see Index)

Place lettuce evenly in the bottom of a shallow salad bowl. (I often use a shallow soup bowl for my salad.) Sprinkle tomato, celery, onions, and cauliflower evenly over chopped lettuce.

Sprinkle chicken and ham evenly over chopped vegetables. (You can use sliced chicken and ham, if desired, and cut the slices into strips instead of dicing them.) Pour dressing evenly over salad, or keep on the side and use as needed. Serve salad chilled. Serve all of the salad for 1 serving.

Yields 1 salad—1 serving

CAL	CHO (g)	PRO (g)	TOTAL FAT (g)	SAT. FAT (g)	CHOL (mg)	FIBER (g)	NA (mg)
192	15	20	6	1.7	42	3.3	504

Food exchanges per serving: 2 lean meat, 3 vegetable
Low-sodium diets: Delete ham and use 2 ounces chicken, and use low-sodium variation of the salad dressing.
Sugar content per serving: None.

Carrot and Pineapple Salad

This is the salad I make for my sister Shirley when she is here because she likes it so well.

2 cups shredded carrots
½ cup canned unsweetened crushed
pineapple with juice
1 tablespoon raisins
¼ cup Kay's Cooked Dressing (see Index)
1 tablespoon lemon juice
⅛ teaspoon salt
1 1-gram packet Equal (aspartame) sugar
substitute

Place carrots, pineapple, and raisins in small mixing bowl.

Stir together dressing, lemon juice, salt, and sweetener to blend and add to carrot mixture. Toss lightly to coat carrot mixture with dressing and refrigerate until served. Serve ¼ of the salad (about ½ cup) for each serving.

Yields about 2 cups—4 servings

Nutritive Values Per Serving

CAL	CHO (g)	PRO (g)	TOTAL FAT (g)	SAT. FAT (g)	CHOL (mg)	FIBER (g)	NA (mg)
65	14	2	1	trace	0	2	126

Food exchanges per serving: 1 vegetable, ½ fruit
Low-sodium diets: Omit salt. Use low-sodium variation of the salad dressing.
Sugar content per serving: None.

Coleslaw

Coleslaw has always been a favorite of ours so I generally make a pretty good-sized batch of it. You can make it the day before a party or a picnic because it is even better the second day.

> 1½ pounds cabbage, cleaned, cored, and
>   shredded (about 3 quarts)
> 1½ cups shredded carrots
> ¼ cup chopped fresh green peppers
> ¼ cup finely chopped onions
> 2 tablespoons chopped parsley
> ¾ cup Kay's Cooked Dressing (see Index)
> ¼ cup vinegar
> 1 tablespoon celery seed
> 2 teaspoons salt
> Sugar substitute equal to ⅓ cup sugar

Place cabbage in the bottom of a big mixing bowl. Add remaining vegetables and toss lightly.

Mix together dressing, vinegar, celery seed, salt, and sweetener until smooth and pour over the vegetables. Mix lightly, cover, and refrigerate at least 2 hours. Toss salad and dressing again just before it is served. Drain excess liquid from the salad and allow ½ cup salad per serving.

Yields about 1½ quarts—12 servings

Nutritive Values Per Serving

CAL	CHO (g)	PRO (g)	TOTAL FAT (g)	SAT. FAT (g)	CHOL (mg)	FIBER (g)	NA (mg)
44	8	2	1	trace	0	2.2	442

Food exchanges per serving: 1½ vegetable
Low-sodium diets: Omit salt. Use low-sodium variation of the salad dressing.
Sugar content per serving: None.

Traditional Cabbage Salad

This recipe is from M. J. Smith, a registered dietitian from Guttenberg, Iowa, a lovely little town on the Mississippi. She has published several good low-fat cookbooks.

> 1½ teaspoons salad mustard
> Dry sugar substitute equal to ¼ cup sugar
> 1 tablespoon vegetable oil
> ¼ teaspoon salt
> ¼ teaspoon celery seed
> 2 tablespoons white vinegar
> 3 cups shredded cabbage
> 1½ cups shredded carrot
> ¼ cup shredded onions
> ½ cup chopped fresh green peppers

Combine mustard, sugar substitute, oil, salt, celery seed, and vinegar and set aside.

Place cabbage, carrots, onions, and green peppers in a mixing bowl. Shake dressing well and pour over vegetables. Mix lightly and refrigerate. Serve cold using ⅔ cup per serving.

Yields 4 cups—6 servings

Nutritive Values Per Serving

CAL	CHO (g)	PRO (g)	TOTAL FAT (g)	SAT. FAT (g)	CHOL (mg)	FIBER (g)	NA (mg)
51	7	1	3	trace	0	2	153

Food exchanges per serving: 1 vegetable, ½ fat
Low-sodium diets: Omit salt.
Sugar content per serving: None.

Snappy Coleslaw

2 quarts shredded cabbage
½ cup shredded carrots
½ cup shredded red onions
½ cup finely chopped jalapeño peppers
½ cup vegetable oil
¼ cup white vinegar
1 tablespoon sugar
2 teaspoons salt
½ teaspoon celery seed
¼ teaspoon black pepper

Place cabbage, carrots, onions, and jalapeño peppers in a bowl and toss lightly to mix well. In a separate bowl, stir together oil, vinegar, sugar, salt, celery seed, and black pepper to mix well. Add to vegetables and toss again. Cover and refrigerate for 3 hours before serving. Drain well and serve, using ½ cup per serving.

Yields 1 quart—8 servings

Nutritive Values Per Serving

CAL	CHO (g)	PRO (g)	TOTAL FAT (g)	SAT. FAT (g)	CHOL (mg)	FIBER (g)	NA (mg)
96	8	1	7	.8	trace	2	567

Food exchanges per serving: 1½ vegetable, 1 fat
Low-sodium diets: Omit salt.
Sugar content per serving: .4 teaspoon.

Cucumber Salad

Frances Sonitzky who gave me this recipe says it is a basic Hungarian recipe. You can add a little more or less onion, make it a little sweeter, or add a whisper of white pepper according to your tastes.

2 small cucumbers 6-7 inches long
¾ teaspoon salt
2 tablespoons finely chopped onions
2 tablespoons white vinegar
2 tablespoons evaporated skim milk
2 1-gram packets Equal (aspartame) sugar
   substitute
Paprika

Slice cucumbers as thin as possible. Sprinkle with salt and let stand at room temperature for 1–2 hours. Drain well and with your hands, squeeze as much juice as possible out of the cucumbers.

Mix onions, vinegar, milk, and sweetener together lightly. Add cucumbers and mix lightly. Refrigerate until ready to serve, using about ⅔ cup (⅓ of the finished recipe) per serving. Sprinkle each portion with paprika just before it is served.

Yields about 2 cups—3 servings

Nutritive Values Per Serving

CAL	CHO (g)	PRO (g)	TOTAL FAT (g)	SAT. FAT (g)	CHOL (mg)	FIBER (g)	NA (mg)
30	6	2	trace	trace	trace	1.3	292

Food exchanges per serving: 1 vegetable
Low-sodium diets: Press as much of the juice out of the cucumbers as you
   can to eliminate as much of the salt as possible.
Sugar content per serving: None.

Farmer's Salad

I like to use warm, freshly cooked potatoes and green beans for this salad. They seem to absorb the flavor of the dressing better that way.

> 1 pound new potatoes
> 1 pound fresh green beans cut into 1-inch
>   pieces
> ½ cup Vinaigrette Dressing (see Index)
> 1½ cups (6 ounces) lean cubed cooked beef
>   with all visible fat removed
> Fresh crisp lettuce leaves as necessary
> 3 medium-size ripe red tomatoes
> ½ cup sliced sweet onions

Cook potatoes and green beans. Peel potatoes and slice them into about ¼-inch-thick slices. Place both potatoes and green beans in a mixing bowl. Pour dressing over potatoes and beans. Mix lightly, cover, and let sit about ½ hour at room temperature. Toss beef with marinated vegetables.

Line a round serving plate with lettuce leaves. Mound the vegetable and meat mixture in the center of the plate and surround it with tomato wedges and onions. Refrigerate if not served immediately (but it is better if served immediately). Serve ⅙ of the salad per serving.

Yields about 7½ cups—6 servings

Nutritive Values Per Serving

CAL	CHO (g)	PRO (g)	TOTAL FAT (g)	SAT. FAT (g)	CHOL (mg)	FIBER (g)	NA (mg)
185	24	12	5	1.1	23	3.6	75

Food exchanges per serving: 1 starch, 1 lean meat, 2 vegetable, ½ fat
Low-sodium diets: Cook potatoes and beans without salt and use low-sodium variation of the salad dressing.
Sugar content per serving: None.

Garden Cottage Cheese Salad

We used this at Health Care Manor Nursing Home in Hampton, Iowa, where I worked as a dietary consultant. The employees liked it as well as the residents did—it was popular with everyone at the home.

½ **cup thinly sliced radishes**
½ **cup finely chopped onions**
½ **cup finely chopped celery**
¼ **cup finely chopped fresh green peppers**
½ **cup thinly sliced cucumbers**
2 **tablespoons Kay's Cooked Dressing (see Index)**
1 **teaspoon salt**
1½ **pounds low-fat cottage cheese**

Combine vegetables and toss lightly. Combine dressing and salt and stir into vegetables.

Drain cottage cheese well and add to vegetable mixture. Mix lightly and refrigerate until served. Drain off any liquid before it is served, using ½ cup of the mixture per serving. This should be prepared as close to serving time as possible.

You can use the same amounts of any other fresh raw vegetables you might prefer—such as chives, slivers of fresh cauliflower, or broccoli—without changing the exchange values.

Yields 5 cups—10 servings

Nutritive Values Per Serving

CAL	CHO (g)	PRO (g)	TOTAL FAT (g)	SAT. FAT (g)	CHOL (mg)	FIBER (g)	NA (mg)
70	4	10	2	.9	5	trace	511

Food exchanges per serving: 1 lean meat, 1 vegetable
Low-sodium diets: Omit salt. Use low-sodium variation of the salad dressing.
Sugar content per serving: None.

Individual Beef Salad

I'm so fond of this salad and served it so often when tomatoes were in season that I think Chuck got tired of it—even though it was his mother's favorite salad and he taught me to make it when we were first married.

> 2 ounces (about ⅓ cup) chopped or cubed cooked lean beef with all visible fat removed
> ¼ cup chopped or sliced fresh sweet onions
> ¼ cup chopped fresh green peppers
> 2 tablespoons Spicy Tomato Dressing (see Index)
> 1 large tomato
> Lettuce leaf
> ½ teaspoon fresh parsley (optional)

Mix beef, onions, peppers, and dressing lightly in a small bowl. Cover and refrigerate 1–8 hours. Wash and core tomato. Cut into cubes or wedges. Add to marinated meat and dressing mixture and toss to coat tomato with dressing.

Line a salad bowl with lettuce. Mound salad in center of the lettuce. Sprinkle parsley on top of salad and serve immediately. Serve all of the salad for 1 serving.

Yields 1 salad—1 serving

Nutritive Values Per Serving

CAL	CHO (g)	PRO (g)	TOTAL FAT (g)	SAT. FAT (g)	CHOL (mg)	FIBER (g)	NA (mg)
168	14	19	5	1.4	46	3.3	230

Food exchanges per serving: 2 lean meat, 3 vegetable
Low-sodium diets: Use low-sodium variation of the salad dressing.
Sugar content per serving: None.

Kidney Bean Salad

The idea of adding apple to a bean or pea salad came from my cousin LaVerle Sniffin of Waterloo, Iowa. We all think it really improves the salad.

⅓ cup Kay's Cooked Dressing (see Index)
1 tablespoon chopped pimiento
¼ cup finely chopped Mrs. Riley's Pickles
    (see Index) or dill pickles
¼ cup finely chopped onions (optional)
1 cup thinly sliced celery
4 chopped hard-cooked large egg whites
1 cup washed and drained canned kidney
    beans
1 small (4 to a pound) tart apple

Place dressing, pimiento, pickle, onion, celery, and egg whites in a mixing bowl and mix lightly. (In order to get the hard-cooked egg whites, I hard-cook 4 eggs and then discard the yolks, or use them to garnish the salad of someone who doesn't need to worry about cholesterol.) Add kidney beans to dressing mix.

Wash, core, and slice apple. Add to salad. Toss lightly and serve ½ cup per serving.

Yields 3 cups—6 servings

Nutritive Values Per Serving

CAL	CHO (g)	PRO (g)	TOTAL FAT (g)	SAT. FAT (g)	CHOL (mg)	FIBER (g)	NA (mg)
72	10	6	1	trace	0	2.6	242

Food exchanges per serving: 2 vegetable
Low-sodium diets: Use only 2 tablespoons chopped pickles and low-sodium
    variation of the salad dressing.
Sugar content per serving: None.

Taco Salad

This recipe makes 6 salads, but I generally just make 2 at a time. I freeze the remaining meat in portions and then reheat them as needed in the microwave. This salad is best when the meat is slightly warm when added to the vegetables.

> 1 tablespoon vegetable oil
> 1 pound lean ground beef
> 2 quarts hot water
> 1 cup taco sauce
> 6 cups shredded lettuce
> 2 cups cubed fresh tomatoes
> ½ cup thinly sliced onions
> ½ cup diced fresh green peppers
> ¾ cup **Spicy Tomato Dressing (see Index)**
> 6 large pitted black olives

Preheat a frying pan over medium heat for 1 minute. Swirl oil around bottom of pan, add meat, and cook and stir over medium heat until meat is well browned and separated.

Place meat in a colander and drain off as much fat as possible. Pour hot water over meat and then discard that liquid also. Rinse the frying pan with hot water, wipe it dry, and return meat to pan. Add taco sauce and cook, stirring frequently, over medium heat until sauce has evaporated. Remove from heat and keep warm until used or refrigerate until needed and then warm again.

Fill 6 salad bowls with 1 cup lettuce each. Divide cooked meat into 6 equal portions and place on top of lettuce. Add ⅓ cup tomato cubes to each salad, and sprinkle each bowl with ⅙ of the onions, peppers, and Spicy Tomato Dressing. Slice each olive into thin slices and use as garnish for each salad. Serve as soon as possible using 1 salad per serving.

Yields 6 salads—6 servings

Nutritive Values Per Serving

CAL	CHO (g)	PRO (g)	TOTAL FAT (g)	SAT. FAT (g)	CHOL (mg)	FIBER (g)	NA (mg)
226	13	16	13	4.5	48	2.1	562

Food exchanges per serving: 2 medium-fat meat, 2 vegetable, ½ fat
Low-sodium diets: Use low-sodium taco sauce and low-sodium variation of
the salad dressing.
Sugar content per serving: None.

Frijole Salad

¾ cup rinsed and drained kidney beans
⅔ cup Spicy Tomato Dressing (see Index)
4 cups shredded cabbage
½ cup thinly sliced sweet onions or green
   onions and tops
1 cup diced tomatoes (1 medium-size
   tomato)
½ cup peeled and thinly sliced cucumbers

Combine beans and dressing, mix lightly, cover, and refrigerate overnight.

Place cabbage in the bottom of a mixing bowl. Place beans with dressing, onions, tomatoes, and cucumbers over the cabbage. Toss lightly just before serving, using ½ cup per serving. Lettuce may be substituted for cabbage, if desired, without changing the exchange values.

Yields about 6 cups—12 servings

Nutritive Values Per Serving

CAL	CHO (g)	PRO (g)	TOTAL FAT (g)	SAT. FAT (g)	CHOL (mg)	FIBER (g)	NA (mg)
29	6	2	trace	0	0	1.7	107

Food exchanges per serving: 1 vegetable
Low-sodium diets: Use low-sodium variation of the salad dressing.
Sugar content per serving: None.

Marinated Vegetable Salad

1 cup water
1 tablespoon cornstarch
1 tablespoon prepared mustard
¼ cup lemon juice
6 1-gram packets Equal (aspartame) sugar
  substitute
2 cups broccoli flowerets
2 cups cauliflower flowerets
1 cup sliced celery
¼ cup chopped fresh green peppers
¼ cup chopped onions
½ cup drained and chopped pimientos
½ cup cooked and drained red beans
9 lettuce leaves

Stir water and cornstarch together until smooth in a small saucepan. Add mustard and cook and stir over moderate heat until thickened. Continue to cook and stir for 2 minutes. Remove from heat. Cool to room temperature. Add lemon juice and sweetener to sauce. Mix lightly and set aside for later use.

Put broccoli, cauliflower, and celery in boiling salted water; cook exactly 6 minutes after the water has returned to a boil. Drain immediately and cool to room temperature. Place in the bottom of a refrigerated bowl. Add peppers, onions, pimientos, and beans to broccoli, cauliflower, and celery. Pour reserved dressing over the vegetables and mix lightly. Refrigerate overnight or all day. Toss lightly again just before serving.

Line each salad bowl with a crisp lettuce leaf. Add ¾ cup marinated vegetables per serving and serve chilled.

Yields 7 cups—9 servings

Nutritive Values Per Serving

CAL	CHO (g)	PRO (g)	TOTAL FAT (g)	SAT. FAT (g)	CHOL (mg)	FIBER (g)	NA (mg)
45	9	3	trace	trace	0	2.4	51

Food exchanges per serving: 2 vegetable
Low-sodium diets: Cook vegetables without salt.
Sugar content per serving: None.

Cucumber and Lettuce Salad

This salad is light with a delicate flavor, a good accompaniment to a strongly flavored casserole.

> 1 small cucumber 6 to 7 inches long
> ½ teaspoon salt
> 1 tablespoon chopped parsley
> 2 tablespoons low-fat yogurt
> ¼ cup Kay's Cooked Dressing (see Index)
> 2 tablespoons skim milk
> 6 cups fresh crisp lettuce

Peel cucumber and grate coarsely. Sprinkle with salt and refrigerate for ½ hour. Drain well, pressing as much juice as possible out of the cucumber. Combine parsley, yogurt, dressing, and milk with drained cucumbers and mix lightly.

Tear lettuce into bite-size pieces. Toss with cucumber mixture just before it is served, using about 1 cup lettuce per serving.

Yields about 6 cups—6 servings

Nutritive Values Per Serving

CAL	CHO (g)	PRO (g)	TOTAL FAT (g)	SAT. FAT (g)	CHOL (mg)	FIBER (g)	NA (mg)
27	4	2	1	trace	trace	.7	127

Food exchanges per serving: 1 vegetable
Low-sodium diets: Press as much of the juice out of the cucumbers as you
  can to eliminate as much of the salt as possible.
Sugar content per serving: None.

Potato Salad

I like to make this several hours before I want to use it so the flavors can develop as the salad marinates.

> 1 cup Kay's Cooked Dressing (see Index)
> 1 teaspoon salad mustard
> 1 1-gram packet Equal (aspartame) sugar
>   substitute
> ½ teaspoon salt
> Whisper of white pepper
> 1 tablespoon chopped parsley
> ¼ cup chopped Mrs. Riley's Pickles (see
>   Index) or dill pickles
> ¼ cup finely chopped onions (optional)
> ¼ cup chopped pimientos
> ½ cup finely chopped celery
> 4 chopped hard-cooked egg whites
> 3 cups cooked, peeled, and diced potatoes

Place dressing, mustard, sweetener, salt, pepper, and parsley in mixing bowl and mix lightly. Add pickles, onion, pimiento, celery, and egg whites to dressing and mix lightly. (That's right, don't use the egg yolks. Hard-cook the eggs, separate the yolks and whites and add the whites to the salad. I use the yolks as a garnish, and those who can have the egg yolks add them to their salad.)

Add potatoes and toss lightly to coat the potatoes well. Refrigerate until needed, serving ½ cup per serving.

Yields 4 cups—8 servings

Nutritive Values Per Serving

CAL	CHO (g)	PRO (g)	TOTAL FAT (g)	SAT. FAT (g)	CHOL (mg)	FIBER (g)	NA (mg)
92	15	4	2	trace	0	1	401

Food exchanges per serving: 1 starch
Low-sodium diets: Omit salt. Use low-sodium variation of the salad dressing
   and cook the potatoes without salt.
Sugar content per serving: None.

Sauerkraut Salad

This recipe is based on one from my cousin Ruth Clapper of Clear Lake, Iowa. I rinse the sauerkraut to make it milder but you can use it without rinsing if you like a stronger flavor.

3½ cups (29-ounce can) sauerkraut
⅓ cup white vinegar
3 tablespoons vegetable oil
½ cup water
8 1-gram packets Equal (aspartame) sugar
   substitute
½ cup chopped fresh green peppers
½ cup chopped onions
½ cup chopped and drained canned
   pimientos
1 cup thinly sliced celery

Drain sauerkraut well. Rinse with cold water and set aside to drain for later use.

Combine vinegar, oil, and water in a small saucepan. Bring to a boil and remove from heat. Add sweetener to hot vinegar and mix lightly.

Place drained sauerkraut in mixing bowl. Add remaining vegetables and mix lightly. Pour hot liquid over vegetables and mix again. Place in container, cover tightly, and refrigerate at least overnight before it is served. Serve ½ cup per serving.

Yields 6 cups—12 servings

Nutritive Values Per Serving

CAL	CHO (g)	PRO (g)	TOTAL FAT (g)	SAT. FAT (g)	CHOL (mg)	FIBER (g)	NA (mg)
47	4	1	4	trace	0	1.2	164

Food exchanges per serving: 1 vegetable, 1 fat
Low-sodium diets: Rinse sauerkraut well.
Sugar content per serving: None.

Sweet Coleslaw

This recipe came from Gena LeVan of Royalton, Illinois. It keeps well in the refrigerator, so I make it ahead of time to take to potluck dinners.

2¾ cups ice water
1½ tablespoons salt
1 quart shredded cabbage
½ cup shredded fresh green peppers
¾ cup vinegar
1½ teaspoons mustard seed
2 cups thinly sliced celery
7 1-gram packets Equal (aspartame) sugar
   substitute
½ cup chopped, canned, drained pimientos

Place 2 cups ice water and salt in bowl and stir to dissolve salt. Add cabbage and peppers, mix well, and let stand ½–1 hour.

Place vinegar, ¾ cup water, and mustard seed in a small saucepan and bring to a boil. Remove from heat. Immediately add celery to hot vinegar mixture. Cover and let cool to room temperature. Drain well, reserving liquid. Add sweetener to cool vinegar liquid.

Drain cabbage mixture well. Combine cabbage mixture, pimientos, and celery and vinegar mixture. Mix well. Refrigerate until needed. Serve ½ cup per serving.

Yields 5 cups—10 servings

Nutritive Values Per Serving

CAL	CHO (g)	PRO (g)	TOTAL FAT (g)	SAT. FAT (g)	CHOL (mg)	FIBER (g)	NA (mg)
22	5	1	trace	0	0	1.1	248

Food exchanges per serving: 1 vegetable
Low-sodium diets: Wash cabbage very well to remove as much salt
   as possible.
Sugar content per serving: None.

Three-Bean Salad

Dried beans are high in fiber and we should try to eat a lot of them. However, they are also high in carbohydrate, so I generally try to mix them with something else that isn't all that high in carbohydrate. This salad recipe comes from my very good friend, Jan Franks, who is a nurse and is very much interested in good nutrition for herself and her family.

**2 cups (16-ounce can) cooked, drained
    yellow wax beans cut into 1-inch lengths
2 cups (16-ounce can) cooked, drained
    green beans cut into 1-inch lengths
½ cup washed and drained cooked kidney
    beans
1 cup thinly sliced onions
1 cup coarsely chopped fresh green peppers
1 cup thinly sliced celery
1 cup vinegar
⅛ teaspoon salt
Sugar substitute equal to ½ cup sugar**

Place beans, onions, peppers, and celery in mixing bowl. Mix together vinegar, salt, and sweetener and pour over vegetables. Mix lightly, cover, and refrigerate at least overnight before serving ½ cup per serving.

Yields 7 cups—14 servings

Nutritive Values Per Serving

CAL	CHO (g)	PRO (g)	TOTAL FAT (g)	SAT. FAT (g)	CHOL (mg)	FIBER (g)	NA (mg)
29	7	1	trace	0	0	1.1	149

Food exchanges per serving: 1 vegetable
Low-sodium diets: Omit salt. Use low-sodium canned vegetables or fresh or
    frozen vegetables cooked without salt.
Sugar content per serving: None.

Walnut Wild Rice

This recipe from Dr. Crockett's niece, Jacalyn Hill of Rancho Palos Verde, California, may be used as a salad or a potato substitute. We like it as a potato substitute with chicken, in which case I serve it lukewarm without chilling it.

1 6-ounce package Uncle Ben's long-grain
　and wild rice
1 cup thinly sliced celery
2 tablespoons chopped celery leaves
1 cup shredded carrots
4 tablespoons vegetable oil, divided
¼ cup chopped English walnuts
2 tablespoons red wine vinegar
1 1-gram packet Equal (aspartame) sugar
　substitute
1 teaspoon salt

Prepare rice according to the directions on the package, omitting the butter. Transfer rice to a large bowl and cool to room temperature. Stir celery, celery leaves, and carrots into cooked rice.

Place 2 tablespoons oil in a small frying pan. Add walnuts and cook and stir over medium heat until walnuts are golden and toasted. Remove from heat. Combine 2 tablespoons oil, vinegar, sweetener, and salt. Add to walnuts; mix lightly and pour over rice mixture. Toss lightly to blend well. Cover and chill well. Serve as a potato substitute or salad using ½ cup per serving.

Yields 5 cups—10 servings

Nutritive Values Per Serving

CAL	CHO (g)	PRO (g)	TOTAL FAT (g)	SAT. FAT (g)	CHOL (mg)	FIBER (g)	NA (mg)
134	15	3	8	.9	0	1	426

Food exchanges per serving: 1 starch, 1½ fat
Low-sodium diets: Omit salt.
Sugar content per serving: None.

Zucchini Salad

This recipe from Thelma VanLaningham of Independence, Iowa, is a delicious way to use those zucchini that grow so profusely in all our gardens.

> ⅔ cup cider vinegar
> 2 tablespoons wine vinegar
> 2 tablespoons vegetable oil
> ½ teaspoon pepper
> 1 teaspoon salt
> Liquid sugar substitute equal to ½ cup
>   sugar
> ½ cup diced onions
> ½ cup diced celery
> ½ cup diced fresh green peppers
> 6 medium (about 6 to 7 inches) zucchini,
>   washed and sliced

Combine vinegars, oil, pepper, salt, and sweetener and set aside for later use. Place vegetables in a mixing bowl and toss lightly. Add dressing and toss again. Cover and allow to marinate in the refrigerator at least 4 hours or overnight before it is served, using ½ cup per serving.

Yields about 2 quarts—16 servings

Nutritive Values Per Serving

CAL	CHO (g)	PRO (g)	TOTAL FAT (g)	SAT. FAT (g)	CHOL (mg)	FIBER (g)	NA (mg)
29	3	1	2	.2	0	.5	143

Food exchanges per serving: 1 vegetable
Low-sodium diets: Omit salt.
Sugar content per serving: None.

Kay's Cooked Dressing

This creamy cooked dressing is from Kay Knochel of Phoenix, Arizona. Kay gave it to me when we were roommates in Chicago. She has always been an excellent cook and I still have several of her very good recipes in my personal file.

> **2 tablespoons cornstarch**
> **2 teaspoons dry mustard**
> **1 cup water**
> **½ cup liquid egg substitute**
> **¼ teaspoon salt**
> **2 tablespoons margarine**
> **½ cup white wine vinegar**
> **6 1-gram packets Equal (aspartame) sugar
>   substitute**

Stir cornstarch, mustard, and water together until smooth in a 2-quart heavy saucepan. Add egg substitute, salt, and margarine to liquid in saucepan and mix well. Cook, stirring constantly, over low heat until thickened and smooth. Continue to simmer for 1 more minute, stirring constantly. Remove from heat.

Add vinegar and sweetener to dressing and mix well. Cover and refrigerate until used. Serve 2 tablespoons per serving.

Yields 1¾ cups—14 servings

Nutritive Values Per Serving

CAL	CHO (g)	PRO (g)	TOTAL FAT (g)	SAT. FAT (g)	CHOL (mg)	FIBER (g)	NA (mg)
27	2	1	2	.3	0	trace	72

Food exchanges per serving: Up to 2 tablespoons may be considered free. ¼ cup is 1 vegetable and 1 fat
Low-sodium diets: Omit salt. Use salt-free margarine.
Sugar content per serving: None.

Creamy Garlic Dressing

You can vary the amount of garlic powder used according to how much you like the taste of garlic. This is rather mild.

½ cup Kay's Cooked Dressing (see Index)
½ cup plain low-fat yogurt
2 tablespoons skim milk
½ teaspoon garlic powder

Place all ingredients in a bowl and mix with a fork until smooth. Refrigerate in a covered container until served. Use 2 tablespoons per serving.

Yields 1 cup—8 servings

Nutritive Values Per Serving

CAL	CHO (g)	PRO (g)	TOTAL FAT (g)	SAT. FAT (g)	CHOL (mg)	FIBER (g)	NA (mg)
25	2	2	1	.3	1	trace	48

Food exchanges per serving: Up to 2 tablespoons may be considered free. ¼ cup is 1 vegetable
Low-sodium diets: Use low-sodium variation of Kay's Cooked Dressing.
Sugar content per serving: None.

French Dressing

---

1 cup vinegar
1 cup water
¼ cup vegetable oil
1 tablespoon paprika
1 teaspoon Worcestershire sauce
1 teaspoon A-1 sauce
½ teaspoon celery seed
1 teaspoon onion powder

Place all ingredients in a bowl and beat with a beater for ½ minute. Pour into a container, cover, and refrigerate until used. Bring back to room temperature and shake well before using. Allow 2 tablespoons per serving.

Yields 2¼ cups—18 servings

Nutritive Values Per Serving

CAL	CHO (g)	PRO (g)	TOTAL FAT (g)	SAT. FAT (g)	CHOL (mg)	FIBER (g)	NA (mg)
31	1	trace	3	.4	0	0	8

Food exchanges per serving: ½ fat
Low-sodium diets: May be used as written.
Sugar content per serving: None.

Chef's French Dressing

This recipe came from Walter Marion, who was executive chef for the Swift and Co. general office food service for many years. He was a wonderful chef who was always willing to share recipes for the foods served there.

⅓ cup catsup
¼ cup white vinegar
½ cup water
1 tablespoon vegetable oil
Sugar substitute equal to 2 tablespoons
  sugar
½ teaspoon onion salt
½ teaspoon garlic salt
1 teaspoon paprika
Sprinkle of cayenne pepper

Place catsup, vinegar, water, oil, sugar substitute, onion salt, garlic salt, paprika, and pepper in a jar and shake vigorously to blend well. Refrigerate until needed. Serve the dressing at room temperature and shake it well just before it is served using 2 tablespoons per serving.

Yields 1¼ cups—12 servings

Nutritive Values Per Serving

CAL	CHO (g)	PRO (g)	TOTAL FAT (g)	SAT. FAT (g)	CHOL (mg)	FIBER (g)	NA (mg)
19	2	trace	1	trace	0	trace	195

Food exchanges per serving: 2 tablespoons may be considered free. ¼ cup is
  1 vegetable
Low-sodium diets: Omit onion and garlic salts. Add ¼ teaspoon garlic
  powder and 1 tablespoon dehydrated onions.
Sugar content per serving: None.

Spicy Tomato Dressing

This recipe is based on one from Anita Kane of Shorewood, Wisconsin. It is excellent on vegetables or lettuce and keeps well. If I intend to keep it more than a few days, however, I strain it to take out the dill weed and the onion.

> **1 cup (8 ounces) canned tomato sauce**
> **½ teaspoon garlic salt**
> **½ cup white vinegar**
> **1 teaspoon dill weed**
> **¼ teaspoon Tabasco sauce**
> **2 tablespoons grated onion**
> **3 1-gram packets Equal (aspartame) sugar**
> **substitute**

Place all ingredients in a small bowl and beat with a wire whip to blend. Refrigerate until needed but bring back to room temperature before it is used. Shake well before using and serve 2 tablespoons per serving.

Yields 1½ cups—12 servings

Nutritive Values Per Serving

CAL	CHO (g)	PRO (g)	TOTAL FAT (g)	SAT. FAT (g)	CHOL (mg)	FIBER (g)	NA (mg)
9	2	trace	trace	0	0	trace	175

Food exchanges per serving: 2 tablespoons may be considered free. ¼ cup is
    1 vegetable
Low-sodium diets: Omit garlic salt. Use low-sodium tomato sauce and
    ¼ teaspoon garlic powder instead of the garlic salt.
Sugar content per serving: None.

Thousand Island Dressing

½ cup **Kay's Cooked Dressing (see Index)**
¼ cup **chopped, drained canned pimientos**
½ cup **chopped, drained dill pickles**
2 tablespoons **chopped fresh green peppers**
¼ cup **chili sauce**
¼ cup **catsup**
4 1-gram **packets Equal (aspartame) sugar substitute**

Place all ingredients in a bowl and mix with a fork until smooth. Place in a covered container and refrigerate until served using 2 tablespoons per serving.

Yields 2¼ cups—18 servings

Nutritive Values Per Serving

CAL	CHO (g)	PRO (g)	TOTAL FAT (g)	SAT. FAT (g)	CHOL (mg)	FIBER (g)	NA (mg)
16	3	1	trace	trace	0	trace	162

Food exchanges per serving: ½ vegetable
Low-sodium diets: Use low-sodium catsup and chili sauce. Use low-sodium
   variation of Kay's Cooked Dressing.
Sugar content per serving: None.

Vinaigrette Dressing

This recipe, which Frances Nielsen made often, is a great favorite with our families. It is good on tossed salads, vegetables, cold meats, and fish. It is best if you make it fresh when you need it, but it can be refrigerated and then brought back to room temperature for serving, if that is more convenient for you.

½ cup vegetable oil
1 cup vinegar
1 tablespoon soy sauce
1 tablespoon chopped parsley
1 tablespoon chopped celery
⅓ cup finely chopped onions
1 cup water
Sugar substitute equal to ½ cup sugar
½ teaspoon vanilla
¼ teaspoon garlic powder

Place all ingredients in a 1-quart container and shake well to mix. Shake well before using. Serve 2 tablespoons per serving.

Yields 3 cups—24 servings

Nutritive Values Per Serving

CAL	CHO (g)	PRO (g)	TOTAL FAT (g)	SAT. FAT (g)	CHOL (mg)	FIBER (g)	NA (mg)
45	1	trace	5	.6	0	trace	59

Food exchanges per serving: 1 fat
Low-sodium diets: May be used as written.
Sugar content per serving: None.

Vinegar and Oil Dressing

You can change the seasonings in this dressing with no change in the exchange values but I like the ones I have included. It tastes like there is a lot of oil in it instead of less than ½ teaspoon per serving.

> ½ cup cider or white vinegar
> ½ cup water
> 1 tablespoon vegetable oil
> 3 1-gram envelopes sugar substitute
> 1 teaspoon paprika
> ¼ teaspoon onion salt
> ¼ teaspoon garlic salt
> Whisper of black pepper

Place vinegar, water, oil, sugar substitute, paprika, onion salt, garlic salt, and pepper in a jar and shake vigorously to blend well. Refrigerate when not in use but return to room temperature and shake vigorously when used, using 2 tablespoons per serving.

Yields 1 cup—8 servings

Nutritive Values Per Serving

CAL	CHO (g)	PRO (g)	TOTAL FAT (g)	SAT. FAT (g)	CHOL (mg)	FIBER (g)	NA (mg)
20	1	trace	2	trace	0	0	81

Food exchanges per serving: Up to 2 tablespoons may be considered free.
  ¼ cup is 1 fat
Low-sodium diets: Omit onion and garlic salts. Add ¼ teaspoon garlic powder and 1 tablespoon dehydrated onions.
Sugar content per serving: None.

Yogurt Topping

I didn't really know where to include this recipe in the book. My friend Jan Franks gave me the recipe and it is a good dip, a good salad dressing, and makes a tasty topping for baked potatoes. It is easy to make and keeps well in the refrigerator for a week or more.

>**2 teaspoons dehydrated minced onions**
>**½ teaspoon salt**
>**1 tablespoon dried parsley flakes**
>**⅛ teaspoon garlic powder**
>**1 cup (8 ounces) plain low-fat yogurt**
>**¼ cup Kay's Cooked Dressing (see Index)**

Stir together onions, salt, parsley, and garlic powder to blend well in a small bowl. Add yogurt and dressing to dry ingredients and mix lightly but thoroughly. Refrigerate until needed. Serve with fresh vegetables as a dip or a dressing, or as a topping for baked potatoes. Serve 2 tablespoons per serving.

Yields 1¼ cups—10 servings

Nutritive Values Per Serving

CAL	CHO (g)	PRO (g)	TOTAL FAT (g)	SAT. FAT (g)	CHOL (mg)	FIBER (g)	NA (mg)
21	2	2	1	trace	1	0	140

Food exchanges per serving: 2 tablespoons may be considered free. ¼ cup is
    1 vegetable
Low-sodium diets: Omit salt. Use low-sodium variation of the salad dressing.
Sugar content per serving: None.

14

Breads

I have always enjoyed making bread and I particularly like to do so now that I'm diabetic. I'm not about to waste my precious bread exchanges. I want to get something really good with them—preferably with fiber, if possible. You can, of course, buy some very good high-fiber breads, and if you don't like to bake that is the way to go. However, if you like to make breads, I'm sure you will enjoy making bread suitable for your diet.

It isn't terribly difficult to find a good bread when you are diabetic, but if it must also be suitable for a low-cholesterol diet, you need to be more careful in your selection. You want to be sure that the bread you buy doesn't include any whole milk, egg yolks, butter, or most shortenings. French, Italian, and Vienna bread are traditionally suitable because they are generally made of flour, oil, water, and a little salt. However, unless you live in or near a city it can be difficult to find them.

It isn't advisable to buy many of the specialty breads in bakeries if you are on a low-cholesterol diet, because most bakeries won't give you a list of the ingredients in their specialty breads. They may not have sugar in them but they might have egg yolks or some other no-nos. Many of the light commercial breads are safe because they contain dry milk and oil for reasons of cost, but if you do buy them be sure to read the list of ingredients on the wrapper. Remember, the ingredients are listed in the order of their importance, so the first ingredients on the list are always the ones that form the greatest percentage of the final product.

269

I've never been able to understand why salt-free bread is so expensive and so scarce. It doesn't cost any more to make than regular bread. Maybe it is because they sell less of it and don't want to bother with it. If you need salt-free bread, it is easy to make one of your favorite recipes using oil or salt-free margarine for the fat, and without salt and other ingredients such as milk and cheese that are high in sodium. Most of the breads in this chapter are low in sodium, and those that aren't can easily be adapted for a low-sodium diet. Salt gives flavor to bread but you can always use salt substitute or add some flavoring such as herbs, spices, or seeds like caraway or sesame if you feel the need for more flavor. I like to add a little cinnamon to low-sodium whole grain bread—not enough to make it taste like cinnamon, but just enough to give it a little flavor, about ¼ teaspoon per loaf. You can also add some sugar substitute to give it a slightly sweet taste that helps compensate for not using salt.

Making bread isn't all that difficult, but it is important to pay close attention to correct temperatures and ingredients. I use a thermometer every time I make bread to check the temperature of the liquid in which I dissolve the yeast. Using liquid that is too hot or too cold can spoil a batch of bread very quickly. I have a friend (who shall be nameless) who could never make good bread. She was thoroughly discouraged because her husband loved homemade bread. In fact, I used to send him over a loaf of bread occasionally because he was always doing something nice for us. Eventually we got together, and I told her that there must be some little thing she was doing wrong and to tell me exactly how she made her bread. The first thing she told me was that she used water that was just barely lukewarm, as her mother always had—and that explained her failures. Her mother had used the old-fashioned yeast cake and my friend was using active dry yeast. Once we got that straightened out, my friend started using a thermometer to check the temperature of the water before she added the yeast and began making excellent bread.

Flour is a very important part of making bread, and it is a good idea to use a good quality flour. I keep all-purpose and bread flour at room temperature because I use them up fast.

However, I keep an assortment of whole grain flours in the refrigerator or freezer, taking care to bring them back to room temperature before I use them, because I don't always use them all that quickly. I like to use bread flour because of its high gluten content, which helps compensate for the lower gluten content of the whole grain flours. However, it does take more liquid than all-purpose flour, and therefore you need to use a recipe specifically written for the bread flour or do some experimenting with it when you are adapting your own recipes. I use whole grain flours whenever possible because I am convinced that a high-fiber regime is good for anyone on a low-cholesterol or diabetic diet.

Instant nonfat dry milk is used in many recipes because it is convenient, economical, easy to use, and easy to store. It gives me a good feeling to know that if I decide to do some baking unexpectedly, I won't need to run down to the store for milk. Also, using dry milk means you don't need to scald it before you add it to the bread, and that is a timesaver. It is free of butterfat and therefore good for a low-cholesterol diet. I also use dehydrated buttermilk in many of the recipes in this book for the same reasons. I very seldom reconstitute the milk when using it for breads because it can be added very easily along with other dry ingredients, and you get the same results as if you had added water to it and then added it to the dough or batter.

It is also very convenient to use liquid egg substitute instead of egg yolks for the low-cholesterol diet. It can get a little expensive if you use a lot of it so I try to use egg whites whenever possible, but there are some recipes that really need those whole eggs. It is wonderful to have the liquid egg substitute to use when egg whites just can't replace those cholesterol-rich whole eggs.

Many people think yeast needs sugar to grow, but it will thrive without any sugar in the recipe. If you have a recipe that you feel absolutely has to have a couple of tablespoons of sugar, go ahead and use it, but include the sugar in your nutritive calculations.

If you want to use your own recipes for baking bread, you can use them if you calculate them according to the information in Chapter 3. You will probably find you will have to adjust the number of slices in each loaf, but you shouldn't have any other difficulties unless you are using ingredients that are not suitable on a low-sodium or low-cholesterol diet.

I find that I can make a much better loaf of bread using the dough hook on my electric mixer. If you don't have a dough hook, you can do the first step in the regular mixer and then put it all in a big bowl to add the final flour to the batter by hand— or you can do the whole process by hand. If you are doing it by hand, you should knead the dough for several minutes to develop the gluten, since you aren't developing it with the dough hook in the mixer.

If you have a bread maker, follow the directions that came with your bread machine. Most of them provide good recipes that you can use if they don't contain egg yolks, other high-cholesterol foods, or sugar in large amounts. Liquid egg substitutes may be used instead of whole eggs, using ¼ cup of most substitutes to replace each egg. If there is a recipe that looks good to you, analyze it according to the directions in Chapter 3 to see if it can fit into your diet.

The number of loaves and the slices per loaf are shown with each recipe. This is very important because it is an essential part of the information used to calculate the food exchanges per serving. The diabetic calculations are accurate only if you follow the recipes exactly and then cut the finished product into the number of servings shown on the recipe.

Any loaf of bread can be used to make rolls, if you roll the dough out into a long roll and then cut it into the same number of pieces that you would cut for a finished loaf. Then each portion can be used to make a roll with the same nutritive values as each slice of bread would have contained. If you want larger rolls, cut the bread dough into half the number of pieces you would cut for a finished loaf, and then shape and bake, with each roll having twice the nutritive values of a slice of bread.

Homemade bread has always been a special treat. Since we have lost so many of our special treats because we are diabetic, I believe in providing myself and other diabetics with fresh homemade bread whenever possible. I hope you feel the same way and that you will enjoy preparing these breads for yourself and others.

Cinnamon Applesauce Muffins

I like to have a variety of oat and wheat bran muffins in the freezer so that I can have a different kind to pop in the microwave for breakfast each morning or with a salad or soup for lunch.

1 cup 100% Bran
2 large egg whites
¼ cup vegetable oil
1 cup unsweetened applesauce
2 tablespoons brown sugar
2 tablespoons water
1 cup all-purpose flour
1 teaspoon Weight Watchers dry sugar
    substitute (optional)
1 teaspoon baking soda
2 tablespoons dry buttermilk
½ teaspoon salt
1 teaspoon ground cinnamon

Place bran, egg whites, oil, applesauce, brown sugar, and water in mixer bowl. Mix lightly to blend and let sit at room temperature for 30–45 minutes.

Stir flour, sugar substitute, soda, dry buttermilk, salt, and cinnamon together to blend well. Add to bran mixture and mix at medium speed only until all flour is moistened. Grease muffin tins with margarine or line with paper cups. Fill tins ½ full (level No. 20 dipper) and bake at 400°F for 20 minutes, or until muffins spring back when touched in the center. Serve hot if possible.

Yields 12 muffins—12 servings

Nutritive Values Per Serving

CAL	CHO (g)	PRO (g)	TOTAL FAT (g)	SAT. FAT (g)	CHOL (mg)	FIBER (g)	NA (mg)
127	17	3	6	.8	1	2.2	263

Food exchanges per serving: 1 starch, 1 fat
Low-sodium diets: Omit salt.
Sugar content per serving: .5 teaspoon

Bran Nut Muffins

1 cup water
1 cup All Bran, Bran Buds, or 100% Bran
Dry sugar substitute equal to
   3 tablespoons sugar (optional)
2 large egg whites at room temperature
⅓ cup (⅔ stick) margarine at room
   temperature
1¼ cups all-purpose flour
¼ cup instant nonfat dry milk
4 teaspoons baking powder
¼ cup chopped nuts

Combine water, bran, sweetener, and egg whites and let sit for 5 to 10 minutes.

Cream margarine at medium speed until light and fluffy.

Stir flour, dry milk, baking powder, and nuts to blend well and add to creamed margarine along with bran mixture. Mix at medium speed only until flour is moistened. Do not overmix. Grease muffin tins with margarine or line with paper liners. Fill muffin tins ½ full (level No. 20 dipper) and bake at 400°F for 20–25 minutes or until muffins spring back when touched in the center. Serve hot, if possible. Serve 1 muffin per serving.

Yields 12 muffins—12 servings

Nutritive Values Per Serving

CAL	CHO (g)	PRO (g)	TOTAL FAT (g)	SAT. FAT (g)	CHOL (mg)	FIBER (g)	NA (mg)
139	15	3	8	1.1	trace	2	297

Food exchanges per serving: 1 starch, 1½ fat
Low-sodium diets: Use salt-free margarine and low-sodium baking powder.
Sugar content per serving: None.

Dark Bran Muffins

1 cup all-purpose flour
1 teaspoon baking soda
1 cup All Bran, Bran Buds, 100% Bran, or
   oat bran
¼ cup dry buttermilk
1 cup water
2 large egg whites at room temperature
2 tablespoons vegetable oil
Liquid sugar substitute equal to 3
   tablespoons sugar (optional)
¼ cup dark molasses

Place flour, soda, bran, and dry buttermilk in mixer bowl and mix at low speed to blend.

Combine water, egg whites, oil, sweetener, and molasses and stir with a fork to blend. Add to flour mixture and mix at medium speed only until flour is moistened. Grease muffin tins with margarine or line with paper liners. Fill muffin tins half full (level No. 20 dipper) and bake at 400°F for 20–25 minutes, or until muffins spring back when touched in the center. Serve hot, if possible. Serve 1 muffin per serving.

Yields 12 muffins—12 servings

Nutritive Values Per Serving

CAL	CHO (g)	PRO (g)	TOTAL FAT (g)	SAT. FAT (g)	CHOL (mg)	FIBER (g)	NA (mg)
108	17	3	4	.5	2	2	189

Food exchanges per serving: 1 starch, 1 fat
Low-sodium diets: May be used as written.
Sugar content per serving: 1 teaspoon.

Refrigerator Bran Muffins

This recipe is based on one from Doris Walker of Grinnell, Iowa. Doris and her husband Denver lived in Wadena when we first moved here, but returned back home to Grinnell when they retired. I like to keep this batter on hand and generally bake 6 muffins at a time. They are dark, rich muffins that I often serve to friends without telling them that it's a low-sugar recipe.

> **3 cups Bran Buds, All Bran, or 100% Bran**
> **3 cups water**
> **⅓ cup vegetable oil**
> **4 large egg whites**
> **Liquid sugar substitute equal to ⅓ cup**
>   **sugar**
> **2½ cups all-purpose flour**
> **½ cup dry buttermilk**
> **¼ cup sugar**
> **1 tablespoon baking soda**
> **½ teaspoon salt**

Place bran, water, oil, egg whites, and sweetener in mixer bowl and mix at low speed to blend.

Stir remaining dry ingredients together to blend well. Add to bran mixture and mix at medium speed only to blend. Line 30 muffin tins with paper cups or spray with pan spray. Fill muffin tins ½ full (level No. 20 dipper) and bake at 375°F for about 20 minutes, or until they spring back when touched in the center. Serve hot if possible, 1 muffin per serving.

Muffins can be baked immediately or batter can be covered and kept in the refrigerator for up to 3 weeks. The batter does not need to be brought to room temperature when it is used. If the batter gets too thick, it can be thinned with a little hot water.

Yields 30 muffins—30 servings

Nutritive Values Per Serving

CAL	CHO (g)	PRO (g)	TOTAL FAT (g)	SAT. FAT (g)	CHOL (mg)	FIBER (g)	NA (mg)
97	17	3	3	.4	1	2.6	232

Food exchanges per serving: 1 starch, ½ fat
Low-sodium diets: Omit salt.
Sugar content per serving: .4 teaspoon.

Raisin Bran Muffins

1 cup water
2 large egg whites at room temperature
¼ cup vegetable oil
¼ cup instant nonfat dry milk
1 cup all-purpose flour
1 tablespoon baking powder
1 cup All Bran, Bran Buds, 100% Bran, or
  oat bran
¼ cup raisins

Place water, egg whites, oil, and dry milk in mixer bowl and mix at low speed to blend.

Stir together flour and baking powder to blend.

Add bran and raisins to liquid along with flour mixture. Mix at medium speed only until flour is moistened. Do not overmix. Grease muffin tins with margarine or line with paper liners. Fill muffin tins ½ full (level No. 20 dipper) and bake at 400°F for 20–25 minutes, or until muffins spring back when touched in the center. Serve hot, if possible. Serve 1 muffin per serving.

Yields 12 muffins—12 servings

Nutritive Values Per Serving

CAL	CHO (g)	PRO (g)	TOTAL FAT (g)	SAT. FAT (g)	CHOL (mg)	FIBER (g)	NA (mg)
117	15	3	6	.7	trace	2.1	197

Food exchanges per serving: 1 starch, 1 fat
Low-sodium diets: Use low-sodium baking powder.
Sugar content per serving: None.

Applesauce Oat Bran Muffins

1 cup bread flour
1 cup oat bran
¼ cup packed brown sugar
4 teaspoons baking powder
1 teaspoon ground cinnamon or pumpkin
   pie spice
½ cup unsweetened applesauce
½ cup water
¼ cup vegetable oil
2 large egg whites

Place flour, oat bran, brown sugar, baking powder, and cinnamon or pumpkin pie spice in bowl and mix well at low speed. In a separate bowl combine applesauce, water, oil, and egg whites and beat with a fork to blend.

Add applesauce mixture to flour mixture and mix at medium speed only until all flour is moistened. Grease muffin tins with margarine or line with paper cups. Fill muffin tins ½ full (level No. 20 dipper) and bake at 400°F for about 20 minutes, or until muffins are browned and spring back when touched in the center. Serve hot, if possible, using 1 muffin per serving.

Yields 12 muffins—12 servings

Nutritive Values Per Serving

CAL	CHO (g)	PRO (g)	TOTAL FAT (g)	SAT. FAT (g)	CHOL (mg)	FIBER (g)	NA (mg)
132	19	3	6	.8	0	1.7	186

Food exchanges per serving: 1 starch, 1 fat, ¼ other carbohydrate
Low-sodium diets: Use low-sodium baking powder.
Sugar content per serving: 1 teaspoon.

Oat Bran Muffins

This muffin isn't very big, and it is plain but very good. The bread flour provides the gluten, which the oat bran needs to give the muffins a good texture.

 1 cup bread flour
 1 cup oat bran cereal
 2 tablespoons sugar
 2 tablespoons instant nonfat dry milk
 1 tablespoon baking powder
 Dry sugar substitute equal to ⅓ cup sugar
 1 cup water
 ½ cup egg whites or liquid egg substitute
 ¼ cup vegetable oil
 1 teaspoon vanilla

Place bread flour, oat bran, sugar, dry milk, baking powder, and sugar substitute in mixer bowl and mix at low speed to blend well. Stir water, egg whites or liquid egg substitute, oil, and vanilla together to blend and add to the flour mixture. Mix at medium speed only until the flour is moistened. Fill muffin cups that have been greased or lined with paper liners ½ full (level No. 20 dipper) and bake at 400°F for 20–25 minutes or until lightly browned. Serve hot, if possible, using 1 muffin per serving.

Yields 12 muffins—12 servings

Nutritive Values Per Serving

CAL	CHO (g)	PRO (g)	TOTAL FAT (g)	SAT. FAT (g)	CHOL (mg)	FIBER (g)	NA (mg)
130	17	4	6	.8	trace	1.4	174

Food exchanges per serving: 1 starch, 1 fat
Low-sodium diets: Use low-sodium baking powder.
Sugar content per serving: .5 teaspoon.

Chocolate Oat Bran Muffins

These muffins can add more variety to the oat bran muffins you take along to work for coffee breaks. If you want them sweeter, you can add two teaspoons dry Weight Watchers sugar substitute along with the flour without changing the food exchange value.

1 cup bread flour
1 cup oat bran
⅓ cup cocoa
¼ cup sugar
1 tablespoon baking powder
½ teaspoon salt
1 cup plus 2 tablespoons water at room
  temperature
¼ cup vegetable oil
2 large egg whites
1 teaspoon vanilla

Place flour, oat bran, cocoa, sugar, baking powder, and salt in a mixer bowl and mix well at low speed. Combine water, oil, egg whites, and vanilla and stir with a fork to blend.

Add liquid mixture to flour mixture and mix at low speed only until all flour is moistened. Grease muffin tins with margarine or line with paper cups. Fill muffin tins ½ full (level No. 20 dipper) and bake at 400°F for about 20 minutes, or until muffins spring back when touched in the center. Serve hot, if possible, using 1 muffin per serving.

Yields 12 muffins—12 servings

Nutritive Values Per Serving

CAL	CHO (g)	PRO (g)	TOTAL FAT (g)	SAT. FAT (g)	CHOL (mg)	FIBER (g)	NA (mg)
132	19	4	7	1	0	2.2	234

Food exchanges per serving: 1 starch, 1 fat
Low-sodium diets: Omit salt. Use low-sodium baking powder.
Sugar content per serving: 1 teaspoon.

Pineapple Bran Muffins

These are a favorite of my sister Shirley and I try to keep them on hand when she comes to visit me.

> 1 cup all-purpose flour
> 1 tablespoon baking powder
> ½ teaspoon baking soda
> 2 tablespoons instant nonfat dry milk
> 2 tablespoons sugar
> Sugar substitute equal to ¼ cup sugar
> 2 large egg whites or ¼ cup liquid egg substitute
> ½ cup water at room temperature
> ¼ cup vegetable oil
> 1 cup All Bran, Bran Buds, 100% Bran, or oat bran
> 1 cup well drained, crushed pineapple canned without sugar

Place flour, baking powder, soda, dry milk, sugar, and sugar substitute in a bowl and mix at low speed to blend well. Stir egg whites or liquid egg substitute, water, and oil together to mix well and add to the flour mixture along with the bran and pineapple. Mix at medium speed only until the flour is moistened. Grease muffin tins with margarine, spray with pan spray, or line with paper liners. Fill muffin tins ½ full (level No. 20 dipper) and bake at 400°F 20–25 minutes or until lightly browned and firm. Serve hot, if possible, using 1 muffin per serving.

Yields 12 muffins—12 servings

Nutritive Values Per Serving

CAL	CHO (g)	PRO (g)	TOTAL FAT (g)	SAT. FAT (g)	CHOL (mg)	FIBER (g)	NA (mg)
128	18	3	6	.7	trace	2	260

Food exchanges per serving: 1 starch, 1 fat
Low-sodium diets: Use low-sodium baking powder.
Sugar content per serving: .5 teaspoon.

Rye Muffins

You can vary the amount of caraway seed without changing the exchange values of the muffins. I like 1½ tablespoonfuls of them but you might like 1 or 2 tablespoonfuls depending upon your own taste.

> 1 cup bread flour
> 1 cup rye flour
> 2 tablespoons brown sugar
> 1 tablespoon baking powder
> ¼ teaspoon salt
> 1½–2 tablespoons caraway seed
> 1 cup water at room temperature
> 4 large egg whites or ½ cup liquid egg
>   substitute at room temperature
> ¼ cup vegetable oil

Stir flours, brown sugar, baking powder, salt, and caraway seed together at low speed to blend. Beat water, egg whites or egg substitute, and oil together with a fork to blend and add to the flour mixture. Mix at medium speed only until the flour is moistened. Grease muffin tins with margarine, spray with pan spray, or line with paper liners. Fill muffin tins half full (level No. 20 dipper) and bake at 400°F for 20–25 minutes or until lightly browned and firm. Serve hot, if possible, using 1 muffin per serving.

Yields 12 muffins—12 servings

Nutritive Values Per Serving

CAL	CHO (g)	PRO (g)	TOTAL FAT (g)	SAT. FAT (g)	CHOL (mg)	FIBER (g)	NA (mg)
131	17	3	6	.7	0	1.5	197

Food exchanges per serving: 1 starch, 1 fat
Low-sodium diets: Omit salt and use low-sodium baking powder.
Sugar content per serving: .5 teaspoon.

Yankee Cornbread

If you like your cornbread thicker, bake it in an 8-inch square pan. I like it thinner and crustier so I bake it in a 9-inch square pan.

> 1 cup cornmeal
> 1 cup all-purpose flour
> 4 teaspoons baking powder
> ¼ cup sugar
> ¼ cup instant nonfat dry milk
> ¼ teaspoon salt
> 1 cup water at room temperature
> ¼ cup liquid egg substitute at room
>   temperature
> ¼ cup vegetable oil

Place dry ingredients in mixer bowl and mix at low speed to blend well. (I find that I get much better results mixing it in a mixer than I do when I mix it by hand.)

Beat together water, egg substitute, and oil with a fork and add all at once to the flour mixture. Beat at low speed only until the flour is moistened. Pour into an 8- or 9-inch pan that has been greased with margarine. Bake at 400°F for about 25 minutes for a 9-inch pan or 30–35 minutes for an 8-inch pan. Serve hot, if possible. Cut 4 × 4 to yield 16 squares. Serve 1 square per serving.

Yields 1 9-inch square—16 servings

Nutritive Values Per Serving

CAL	CHO (g)	PRO (g)	TOTAL FAT (g)	SAT. FAT (g)	CHOL (mg)	FIBER (g)	NA (mg)
109	17	2	4	.5	trace	.7	127

Food exchanges per serving: 1 starch, 1 fat
Low-sodium diets: Omit salt. Use low-sodium baking powder.
Sugar content per serving: .8 teaspoon.

Applesauce Nut Bread

⅓ cup (⅔ stick) margarine at room
  temperature
3 tablespoons sugar
3 large egg whites at room temperature
1 cup all-purpose flour
⅔ cup graham flour
1 teaspoon pumpkin pie spice
1 tablespoon baking powder
½ teaspoon baking soda
½ teaspoon salt
1 cup unsweetened applesauce
Liquid sugar substitute equal to
  3 tablespoons sugar
½ cup chopped nuts

Cream margarine and sugar together until light and fluffy. Add egg whites to creamed mixture and beat at medium speed for ½ minute.

Stir together flours, spice, baking powder, soda, and salt until well blended.

Add applesauce, sweetener, and nuts, along with flour mixture, to creamed mixture. Mix at medium speed only until the flour is moistened. Do not overbeat. Spread evenly in a 9″ × 5″ × 3″ loaf pan that has been greased with margarine. Bake at 375°F for 45 minutes, or until a cake tester comes out clean from the center and the bread pulls away from the sides of the pan. Cool 10 minutes in the pan and turn out onto a wire rack to cool to room temperature. Cut into 16 equal slices. Serve 1 slice per serving.

Yields 1 loaf—16 servings

CAL	CHO (g)	PRO (g)	TOTAL FAT (g)	SAT. FAT (g)	CHOL (mg)	FIBER (g)	NA (mg)
126	15	3	7	.9	0	1.2	266

Food exchanges per serving: 1 starch, 1 fat
Low-sodium diets: Omit salt. Use salt-free margarine and low-sodium baking powder.
Sugar content per serving: .6 teaspoon.

Banana Nut Bread

This recipe is based on one from Florence Jennings who lives here in Wadena. I've always thought that it was the best banana bread I've ever eaten. It isn't terribly rich but it has a wonderful flavor. Florence is a very good cook—and we also share an interest in quilts and quilting.

½ cup (1 stick) margarine at room
    temperature
2 tablespoons sugar
½ cup liquid egg substitute at room
    temperature
Dry sugar substitute equal to ⅓ cup sugar
1 cup all-purpose flour
¾ cup oat bran
2 teaspoons baking powder
½ teaspoon baking soda
1 cup mashed bananas (3 medium
    bananas)
¼ cup chopped nuts

Cream together margarine and sugar at medium speed until light and fluffy. Add egg substitute and sweetener to creamed mixture and beat at medium speed for 1 minute.

Stir together flour, oat bran, baking powder, and soda to blend well. Add bananas to creamed mixture along with the flour mixture and beat 1 minute at medium speed.

Add nuts to batter and mix lightly. Spread evenly in a 9" × 5" × 3" loaf pan that has been greased with margarine. Bake at 375°F for 45 minutes, or until a cake tester comes out clean from the center of the loaf and the loaf starts to pull away from the sides of the pan. Cool in the pan for 10 minutes. Turn out onto a wire rack and cool to room temperature. Cut into 14 equal slices and serve at room temperature. Serve 1 slice per serving.

Yields 1 loaf—14 servings

Nutritive Values Per Serving

CAL	CHO (g)	PRO (g)	TOTAL FAT (g)	SAT. FAT (g)	CHOL (mg)	FIBER (g)	NA (mg)
146	17	3	9	1.3	0	1.4	209

Food exchanges per serving: 1 starch, 1¾ fat
Low-sodium diets: Use salt-free margarine and low-sodium baking powder.
Sugar content per serving: .4 teaspoon.

Zucchini Bread

This recipe is based on one from Delores LeMaster of Strawberry Point, Iowa. Delores, who is also diabetic, works at the nursing home where I worked as a dietary consultant. She is quite clever about adapting recipes for her own use and she often shares them with me.

> 2 cups all-purpose flour
> 1½ teaspoons cinnamon
> ¼ teaspoon salt
> 1 teaspoon baking soda
> ½ teaspoon baking powder
> 3 large egg whites
> ⅓ cup vegetable oil
> 1½ teaspoons vanilla
> Dry sugar substitute equal to ¾ cup sugar
> 1½ cups well-packed shredded fresh
>   zucchini

Place flour, cinnamon, salt, soda, and baking powder in a mixer bowl and mix at low speed to blend well.

Place egg whites, oil, vanilla, and sweetener in a cup and mix well with a fork to blend.

Add zucchini to flour mixture along with oil mixture and mix at medium speed until well blended and creamy. Pour into a 9″ × 5″ × 3″ loaf pan that has been greased with margarine. Bake at 375°F for 45 minutes, or until a cake tester comes out clean from the center and the bread pulls away from the sides of the pan. Cool in the pan for 10 minutes. Turn out onto a wire rack and cool to room temperature. Cut into 18 equal slices and serve 1 slice per serving.

Yields 1 loaf—18 servings

Nutritive Values Per Serving

CAL	CHO (g)	PRO (g)	TOTAL FAT (g)	SAT. FAT (g)	CHOL (mg)	FIBER (g)	NA (mg)
99	13	2	4	.6	0	.5	156

Food exchanges per serving: 1 starch, 1 fat
Low-sodium diets: Omit salt. Use low-sodium baking powder.
Sugar content per serving: None.

Chocolate Nut Bread

If you are a chocoholic (and it seems to me that most diabetics are), this bread is for you. Even nondiabetics love it. I like to serve it with peanut butter. It sounds unusual, but chocolate and peanut butter go well together.

1¾ cups all-purpose flour
⅓ cup cocoa
¼ cup dry buttermilk
¼ cup sugar
1 teaspoon cinnamon
1 teaspoon baking soda
1 teaspoon baking powder
1 cup water
¼ cup vegetable oil
¼ cup liquid egg substitute at room
   temperature
Dry sugar substitute equal to ⅓ cup sugar
1 teaspoon vanilla
½ cup chopped nuts

Place first 7 ingredients in mixer bowl and mix at low speed to blend well.

Mix water, oil, egg substitute, sweetener, and vanilla with a fork to blend. Add to flour mixture and mix at medium speed only until flour is moistened. Do not overbeat.

Add nuts to dough and spread evenly in a 9″ × 5″ × 3″ loaf pan that has been greased with margarine. Bake at 375°F for 45 minutes or until a cake tester comes out clean from the center and the bread pulls away from the sides of the pan. Let cool in the pan for 10 minutes and then turn out onto a wire rack to cool to room temperature. Cut into 16 equal slices. Serve 1 slice per serving.

Yields 1 loaf—16 servings

Nutritive Values Per Serving

CAL	CHO (g)	PRO (g)	TOTAL FAT (g)	SAT. FAT (g)	CHOL (mg)	FIBER (g)	NA (mg)
135	17	3	6	.9	1	1	144

Food exchanges per serving: 1 starch, 1 fat
Low-sodium diets: Use low-sodium baking powder.
Sugar content per serving: .8 teaspoon.

Graham Scones

Scones can be, and often are, made from all-white flour, but I like to think that this is more like the way they were made in Scotland before white flour was so readily available.

> 1 cup graham flour
> 1 cup all-purpose flour
> 4 teaspoons baking powder
> 2 tablespoons brown sugar
> 1 teaspoon cinnamon
> ¼ teaspoon salt
> ½ cup (1 stick) margarine
> ¼ cup raisins or currants
> ¼ cup liquid egg substitute at room
> temperature
> ⅔ cup skim milk

Place flours, baking powder, sugar, cinnamon, and salt in a mixing bowl and stir with a spoon to blend well. Cut margarine into the flour mixture with a pastry blender until it resembles coarse meal. Stir raisins or currants into the flour and margarine mixture to coat them with flour.

Mix together egg substitute and milk and add as much as necessary of the mixture to the flour mixture to make a soft dough like a baking powder biscuit dough. Knead several times in the bowl and then turn out onto a lightly floured working surface. Shape into a 9-inch round and place on a baking sheet that has been lightly greased with margarine. Crease the top of the round about ¼ inch deep to form 16 equal pie-shaped wedges. The scones may be baked as they are or the wedges may be cut through and separated to form a crustier scone. If left whole, the scones should be baked at 400°F for 25–30 minutes, then broken apart and served hot. If separated, the wedges should be baked at 400°F about 15 minutes or until browned and crisp. Serve 1 wedge per serving.

Yields 1 9-inch round—16 servings

Nutritive Values Per Serving

CAL	CHO (g)	PRO (g)	TOTAL FAT (g)	SAT. FAT (g)	CHOL (mg)	FIBER (g)	NA (mg)
128	16	3	6	1	trace	1	239

Food exchanges per serving: 1 starch, 1 fat
Low-sodium diets: Omit salt. Use low-sodium baking powder and salt-free margarine.
Sugar content per serving: .4 teaspoon.

Challah

This Jewish bread makes marvelous French toast or bread pudding if you have any of it left over.

> 1⅓ cups water at 110–115°F
> 2 packages (1½ tablespoons) active dry yeast
> 7 cups all-purpose flour, divided
> 1 cup liquid egg substitute at room temperature
> 2 teaspoons salt
> ¼ cup (½ stick) margarine at room temperature
> 1 egg white at room temperature
> ¼ cup water at room temperature
> 2 teaspoons sesame seeds

Place 1⅓ cups water and yeast in mixer bowl. Mix lightly and let stand for 5 minutes. Add 3 cups flour to liquid and beat at low speed, using dough hook, for 4 minutes.

Add egg substitute, salt, margarine, and 3 cups flour to dough and mix, using dough hook, at low speed for another 2 minutes or until a smooth dough is formed.

Turn dough out onto a working surface and knead, using as much of the remaining flour as necessary to form a smooth resilient dough. Form into a ball and place in a bowl that has been well greased with margarine. Turn the ball over to cover the top with margarine. Cover and let stand in a warm place until doubled in volume.

Turn the dough out onto a lightly floured working surface. Divide the dough into 2 equal portions. Round each portion into a ball. Cover with a cloth and let rest for 10 minutes. Divide each ball into 3 equal portions. Roll each portion gently to form a roll about 14 inches long. Braid 3 rolls to form a loaf. Place the loaves on 1 or 2 cookie sheets that have been greased lightly with margarine. Cover with a cloth and let stand in a warm place until doubled in volume.

Beat egg white and ¼ cup water together with a fork until smooth. Brush each loaf with the egg white mixture and sprinkle with sesame seeds. Bake at 400°F for 30 minutes or until the loaves sound hollow and are lightly browned. Transfer loaves to wire rack to cool to room temperature. Cut each loaf into 20 equal slices and serve 1 slice per serving.

Yields 2 loaves—40 servings

Nutritive Values Per Serving

CAL	CHO (g)	PRO (g)	TOTAL FAT (g)	SAT. FAT (g)	CHOL (mg)	FIBER (g)	NA (mg)
98	17	3	2	.3	0	.7	138

Food exchanges per serving: 1 starch
Low-sodium diets: Omit salt. Use salt-free margarine.
Sugar content per serving: None.

Note: This bread can be baked in regular loaf pans, if desired. If the dough is baked in 3 equal loaves and each loaf is cut into 14 slices, each slice will provide the following:

Nutritive Values Per Serving

CAL	CHO (g)	PRO (g)	TOTAL FAT (g)	SAT. FAT (g)	CHOL (mg)	FIBER (g)	NA (mg)
93	16	3	2	.2	0	.7	131

Food exchanges per serving: 1 starch
Low-sodium diets: Omit salt. Use salt-free margarine.
Sugar content per serving: None.

Whole Wheat Italian Bread

This bread dough makes excellent hard rolls. We like to divide the dough into 18 equal portions, shape it into long hard rolls, and bake them to eat with hot beef sandwiches. Each roll is equal to 2 bread exchanges with double the nutritive values for each slice of bread.

**2 cups water at 110–115°F
2 packages (1½ tablespoons) active dry
   yeast
4 cups all-purpose flour
¼ cup vegetable oil
2 teaspoons salt
2 cups whole wheat flour, divided
1 egg white
1 tablespoon cold water**

Combine 2 cups water and yeast and let stand 5 minutes in mixer bowl. Add 4 cups all-purpose flour to liquid and beat 4 minutes at medium speed, using dough hook. Add oil, salt, and 1½ cups whole wheat flour to batter and beat, using dough hook, at low speed for 4 minutes.

Use as much of the remaining flour as necessary to make a smooth, resilient loaf. Turn dough out onto a lightly floured working surface and knead a few times. Form into a ball and place in a bowl that has been greased with margarine. Turn the ball over so the top will be greased with the margarine. Cover with a cloth and set in a warm place until doubled in volume.

Turn dough out onto a lightly floured working surface, knead lightly, and divide into 2 equal portions. Form each portion into a ball and let rest, covered with a cloth, for 10 minutes. Shape each roll into a long, thin loaf tapered at the end. Place loaves diagonally, seamed side down, on greased baking sheets. Cut slits about ⅛-inch deep, about 2 inches apart on tops of loaves.

Beat egg white and 1 tablespoon water together and brush

tops and sides of loaves with this mixture. Cover with a cloth and let rise again until doubled in volume.

Bake at 400°F for 10 minutes; reduce heat to 350°F and bake another 10 minutes. Brush tops and sides of loaves again with egg white mixture. Continue baking for another 30 minutes for a total of 50 minutes, or until loaves are golden brown. Turn out on a wire rack and cool to room temperature. Cut each loaf into 18 equal slices and serve 1 slice per serving.

Yields 2 loaves—36 servings

Nutritive Values Per Serving

CAL	CHO (g)	PRO (g)	TOTAL FAT (g)	SAT. FAT (g)	CHOL (mg)	FIBER (g)	NA (mg)
91	16	3	2	.3	0	1.3	127

Food exchanges per serving: 1 starch
Low-sodium diets: Omit salt.
Sugar content per serving: None.

Raisin Bread

I have always loved raisin bread. I just wish that raisins weren't so high in carbohydrate so we could double the amount of them in the bread.

> 1½ cups hot water
> ⅓ cup instant nonfat dry milk
> 2 packages (1½ tablespoons) active dry yeast
> 5 cups all-purpose flour, divided
> Dry sugar substitute equal to ½ cup sugar (optional)
> 2 teaspoons salt
> ¼ cup liquid egg substitute at room temperature
> ¼ cup vegetable oil
> ½ cup raisins

Place water and dry milk in mixer bowl and mix at slow speed only to dissolve milk. Let cool to 110–115° F. Add yeast to liquid and let stand for 5 minutes. Add 2 cups flour to liquid and mix at low speed, using dough hook, for 3 minutes.

Add sweetener, salt, egg substitute, oil, and 2 cups flour to batter and mix at low speed, using dough hook, for another 2 minutes. Add raisins to dough and mix at low speed for another minute.

Turn dough out onto a working surface spread with 1 cup flour and knead, using as much of the remaining flour as necessary to form a smooth, elastic dough. Form dough into a ball and place in a bowl that has been well greased with margarine. Turn the ball over so the top will be greased with the margarine, cover, and let stand in a warm place until doubled in volume.

Turn the dough out onto a lightly floured working surface. Knead lightly. Divide into 2 equal parts. Form each half into a ball, cover, and let rest for 10 minutes. Form each ball into a loaf and place each loaf in a 9" × 5" × 3" loaf pan that has been greased with margarine. Cover and let rise in a warm place until doubled in volume.

Bake at 375°F for about 45 minutes or until browned. As soon as the bread is removed from the oven, turn it out onto a wire rack and brush it with margarine. Slice each loaf into 18 equal slices and serve 1 slice per serving.

Yields 2 loaves—36 servings

Nutritive Values Per Serving

CAL	CHO (g)	PRO (g)	TOTAL FAT (g)	SAT. FAT (g)	CHOL (mg)	FIBER (g)	NA (mg)
91	16	2	2	trace	trace	.7	133

Food exchanges per serving: 1 starch
Low-sodium diets: Omit salt.
Sugar content per serving: None.

Country Loaf

This bread is also good for a low-sodium diet. Without the salt, it contains only 3 mg sodium per serving.

2½ cups hot water
2 tablespoons brown sugar
1 cup cornmeal
2 packages (1½ tablespoons) active dry
   yeast
3½ cups bread flour, divided
¼ cup liquid egg substitute
¼ cup vegetable oil
2 teaspoons salt
2 cups graham or whole wheat flour

Place water, sugar, and cornmeal in a mixer bowl. Mix to dissolve the sugar and let cool to 110–115°F. Add yeast to liquid mixture and let stand for 5 minutes. Add 3 cups bread flour to liquid and beat at medium speed, using dough hook, for 4 minutes. Add egg substitute, oil, salt, and 2 cups graham flour to batter and beat at low speed, using dough hook, for another 4 minutes.

Use as much of the remaining bread flour as necessary to make a smooth, resilient loaf. Turn dough out onto a lightly floured working surface and knead a couple of times. Form into a ball and place in a bowl that has been greased with margarine. Turn the ball over to coat the top of it with margarine. Cover with a cloth and set in a warm place until doubled in volume.

Turn dough out onto a lightly floured working surface, knead lightly, and divide into 3 equal portions. Form each portion into a ball and let rest, covered with a cloth, for 10 minutes. Form each ball into a loaf and place in a 9″ × 5″ × 3″ loaf pan that has been greased with margarine.

Cover and let rise until doubled in volume. Bake at 475°F for 45 minutes or until browned and firm. Turn out onto a wire rack and cool to room temperature. Cut each loaf into 14 equal slices and serve 1 slice per serving.

Yields 3 loaves—42 servings

Nutritive Values Per Serving

CAL	CHO (g)	PRO (g)	TOTAL FAT (g)	SAT. FAT (g)	CHOL (mg)	FIBER (g)	NA (mg)
93	16	3	2	trace	0	1.2	112

Food exchanges per serving: 1 starch
Low-sodium diets: Omit salt.
Sugar content per serving: Trace.

Rich Whole Wheat Bread

This is a good bread for a low-sodium diet. Without the salt, it contains only 3 mg sodium per slice. However, I included the salt because if you aren't on a low-sodium diet, it adds to the flavor of the bread.

> **2 cups hot water**
> **¼ cup brown sugar**
> **2 packages (1½ tablespoons) active dry yeast**
> **3½ cups bread flour, divided**
> **⅓ cup vegetable oil**
> **¼ cup liquid egg substitute**
> **2 teaspoons salt**
> **3 cups whole wheat flour**

Place water and sugar in mixer bowl and stir to dissolve sugar. Cool to 110–115°F. Add yeast to liquid and let stand for 5 minutes. Add 3 cups bread flour to liquid and mix, using dough hook, for 4 minutes at medium speed.

Add oil, egg substitute, salt, and 3 cups whole wheat flour to dough and mix, using dough hook, for 4 minutes at low speed.

Add as much of the remaining bread flour as necessary to the dough to make a smooth, resilient dough. Turn out onto a lightly floured working surface and knead a few times. Form into a ball and place in a bowl that has been greased with margarine. Turn the ball over to coat the top of the ball with margarine. Cover with a cloth and set in a warm place until doubled in volume.

Turn dough out onto a lightly floured working surface, knead lightly, and divide into 3 equal portions. Form each portion into a ball and let rest, covered with a cloth, for 10 minutes. Form each ball into a loaf and place each loaf in a 9" × 5" × 3" loaf pan that has been greased with margarine. Cover and let rise in a warm place until doubled in volume. Bake at 375°F for 45 minutes, or until browned and firm. Turn bread out onto wire rack and let cool to room temperature. Cut each loaf into 14 equal slices and serve 1 slice per serving.

Yields 3 loaves—42 servings

Nutritive Values Per Serving

CAL	CHO (g)	PRO (g)	TOTAL FAT (g)	SAT. FAT (g)	CHOL (mg)	FIBER (g)	NA (mg)
96	16	3	2	trace	0	1.4	113

Food exchanges per serving: 1 starch
Low-sodium diets: Omit salt.
Sugar content per serving: .3 teaspoon.

Panettone

This bread has been a favorite of mine since Chuck's cousin sent us a loaf from Milan, Italy, as a Christmas gift one year. I tried to duplicate it but couldn't until I added anise flavoring and used bread flour. It is frequently baked in a round shape on a cookie sheet or in a special panettone pan that I have, but it is easier to cut into the right portions when it is baked in a loaf pan.

¾ cup water at 110–115°F
2 tablespoons instant nonfat dry milk
1 package (2¼ teaspoons) active dry yeast
2¼ cups bread flour, divided
Dry sugar substitute equal to
    3 tablespoons sugar
2 drops yellow food coloring
¼ teaspoon anise extract
⅛ teaspoon ground ginger
¼ cup liquid egg substitute at room
    temperature
½ teaspoon salt
2 tablespoons margarine at room
    temperature
¼ cup chopped candied cherries

Combine water, dry milk, and yeast and let stand for 5 minutes in a mixer bowl. Add 1 cup flour to liquid and beat at low speed, using a dough hook, for 4 minutes.

Add sweetener, food coloring, anise, ginger, egg substitute, salt, margarine, and 1 cup flour to batter and mix at low speed, using a dough hook, for another 4 minutes. Add candied cherries to dough and mix, using a dough hook, only until fruit is mixed into the dough.

Use as much additional flour as necessary to form a smooth, resilient loaf. Turn dough out onto lightly floured working surface and knead a couple of times. Form into a ball and place in a bowl that has been well greased with margarine. Turn the ball over to coat the top of it with margarine. Cover with a cloth and set in a warm place until doubled in volume.

Turn dough out onto a lightly floured working surface, knead lightly, and form into a ball. Cover with a cloth and let rest for 10 minutes. Form into a loaf and place in a 9" × 5" × 3" loaf pan that has been greased with margarine. Cover and let rise again until doubled in volume. Bake at 375°F for 45 minutes until well browned and firm. Turn out onto a wire rack and cool to room temperature. Cut into 18 equal slices and serve 1 slice per serving.

Note: It is important to use bread flour in this recipe. However, if you do use all-purpose flour (3¼ cups) and cut each loaf into 18 equal slices, each slice will have a nutritive value of 1⅓ bread exchanges (114 calories); or you can cut it into 24 thin slices with a nutritive value of 1 bread exchange (85 calories) per serving.

Yields 1 loaf—18 servings

Nutritive Values Per Serving

CAL	CHO (g)	PRO (g)	TOTAL FAT (g)	SAT. FAT (g)	CHOL (mg)	FIBER (g)	NA (mg)
88	15	3	2	trace	trace	.4	87

Food exchanges per serving: 1 starch
Low-sodium diets: Omit salt. Use salt-free margarine.
Sugar content per serving: None.

Three-Grain Bread

½ cup cornmeal
2 teaspoons salt
¼ cup (½ stick) margarine
2 cups boiling water
2 packages (1½ tablespoons) active dry
   yeast
½ cup water at 110–115°F
3 cups bread flour, divided
1 cup light rye flour
1 cup graham or whole wheat flour

Place cornmeal, salt, margarine, and 2 cups boiling water in mixer bowl and mix at low speed to melt margarine. Cool to room temperature. Stir together yeast and ½ cup warm water and let rest for 5 minutes. Add to lukewarm mixture and mix lightly. Add 2¾ cups bread flour to liquid mixture and mix at medium speed, using dough hook, for 4 minutes. Add rye and graham flours to dough and mix, using dough hook, for another 4 minutes at low speed.

Turn dough out onto lightly floured working surface and knead, using as much of the remaining bread flour as necessary to form a smooth, resilient dough. Form into a ball and place in a bowl that has been greased with margarine, turning the dough so it is greased on top. Cover with a cloth and let rise in a warm place until it is doubled in volume.

Turn the dough out onto a lightly floured working surface. Divide the dough into 2 equal portions. Round each portion into a ball. Cover with a cloth and let rest for 10 minutes. Shape each ball into a loaf and place each loaf in a 9″ × 5″ × 3″ loaf pan that has been greased with margarine. Cover and let rise until doubled in volume. Bake at 375°F for 45 minutes, or until browned and firm. Turn bread out onto wire rack and let cool to room temperature. Cut each loaf into 18 equal slices and serve 1 slice per serving.

Note: It is important to use bread flour in this recipe.

Yields 2 loaves—36 servings

Nutritive Values Per Serving

CAL	CHO (g)	PRO (g)	TOTAL FAT (g)	SAT. FAT (g)	CHOL (mg)	FIBER (g)	NA (mg)
86	15	2	2	trace	0	1.2	142

Food exchanges per serving: 1 starch
Low-sodium diets: Omit salt. Use salt-free margarine.
Sugar content per serving: None.

Whole Wheat Bread

2½ cups water at 110–115°F
½ cup instant nonfat dry milk
2 packages (1½ tablespoons) active dry yeast
3 cups bread flour
¼ cup (½ stick) margarine at room temperature
2 teaspoons salt
2¾ cups whole wheat flour, divided

Combine water, dry milk, and yeast and let stand 5 minutes in a mixer bowl. Add 3 cups bread flour to liquid and beat at medium speed, using dough hook, for 4 minutes.

Add margarine, salt, and 2½ cups whole wheat flour to batter and mix at low speed, using dough hook, for another 4 minutes.

Use as much of the remaining whole wheat flour as necessary to make a smooth, resilient loaf. Turn dough out onto a lightly floured working surface and knead a couple of times. Form into a ball and place in a bowl that has been well greased with margarine. Turn the ball over to coat the top of it with margarine. Cover with a cloth and set in a warm place until doubled in volume.

Turn dough out onto a lightly floured working surface, knead lightly, and divide into 2 equal portions. Form each portion into a ball and let rest, covered with a cloth, for 10 minutes. Form each ball into a loaf and place in a 9" × 5" × 3" loaf pan that has been greased with margarine. Cover and let rise again until doubled in volume. Bake at 375°F for 45 minutes, or until browned and firm. Turn out onto a wire rack and cool to room temperature. Cut each loaf into 18 equal slices and serve 1 slice per serving.

   Note: It is important to use bread flour in this recipe. The gluten in the bread flour helps give texture to the finished loaf of bread.

Yields 2 loaves—36 servings

Nutritive Values Per Serving

CAL	CHO (g)	PRO (g)	TOTAL FAT (g)	SAT. FAT (g)	CHOL (mg)	FIBER (g)	NA (mg)
92	16	3	2	trace	trace	1.4	147

Food exchanges per serving: 1 starch
Low-sodium diets: Omit salt. Use salt-free margarine.
Sugar content per serving: None.

Cinnamon Rolls

These rolls are a great favorite of my friend John Franks. I've known him to eat four of them at one time, washed down with a couple of glasses of milk. He knows what he likes for between-meal snacks, and I agree with him that there is nothing like a hot, fresh cinnamon roll, right from the oven.

> 1 cup water at 110–115°F
> ¼ cup instant nonfat dry milk
> 1 package (2¼ teaspoons) active dry yeast
> 3½ cups all-purpose flour, divided
> ⅛ teaspoon ground ginger
> ¼ cup vegetable oil
> 1 teaspoon salt
> 1 teaspoon cinnamon
> Dry sugar substitute equal to
>   2 tablespoons sugar
> 1 tablespoon margarine at room
>   temperature
> ¼ cup brown sugar
> Dry brown sugar substitute equal to ¼ cup
>   brown sugar
> ½ teaspoon cinnamon
> 1½ tablespoons margarine at room
>   temperature

Place water, dry milk, and yeast in mixer bowl; mix lightly and let stand for 5 minutes. Add 1½ cups flour to liquid. Mix at medium speed, using dough hook, for 4 minutes. Add ginger, oil, salt, 1 teaspoon cinnamon, dry sugar substitute, and 1½ cups flour and mix at low speed, using dough hook, for another 4 minutes.

Spread the remaining ½ cup flour on a mixing board. Turn the dough out onto the flour and use as much of it as necessary to make a smooth, resilient dough. Shape the dough into a ball and place it in a bowl that has been greased with margarine.

Turn the ball over to coat the top of it with margarine. Cover with a cloth and let stand in a warm place until doubled in volume.

Use 1 tablespoon margarine to grease the sides and bottom of a 9″ × 13″ cake pan. Set aside for later use.

Stir brown sugar, brown sugar substitute, and ½ teaspoon cinnamon to blend well and set aside for later use.

Turn dough out onto a lightly floured working surface. Knead lightly and form into a ball. Cover with a cloth and let rest for 10 minutes. Roll dough out to form a 9″ × 13″ rectangle. Spread 1½ tablespoons of margarine evenly over the dough. Sprinkle evenly with the brown sugar mixture. Roll into a long roll like a jelly roll and cut into 24 equal slices. Place the slices, cut side down, in the cake pan, spacing them evenly. Cover with a cloth and let rise until doubled in volume. Bake at 375°F for 25–30 minutes, or until golden brown. Turn rolls out of the pan onto a wire rack and serve warm, if possible. Serve 1 roll per serving.

Yields 24 rolls—24 servings

Nutritive Values Per Serving

CAL	CHO (g)	PRO (g)	TOTAL FAT (g)	SAT. FAT (g)	CHOL (mg)	FIBER (g)	NA (mg)
111	17	2	4	.5	trace	.6	111

Food exchanges per serving: 1 starch, 1 fat
Low-sodium diets: Omit salt. Use salt-free margarine.
Sugar content per serving: 1 teaspoon.

Oat Bran Pancakes

½ cup all-purpose flour
½ cup oat bran
2 tablespoons sugar
½ teaspoon baking soda
¼ teaspoon salt
¼ cup dry buttermilk
1 cup water at room temperature
2 large egg whites or ¼ cup liquid egg
  substitute
2 tablespoons vegetable oil

Place flour, oat bran, sugar, soda, salt, and dry buttermilk in mixer bowl and mix well at low speed. Beat water, egg whites or liquid egg substitute, and oil together with a fork to blend well. Add to flour mixture and beat until almost smooth.

Lightly grease a griddle and preheat to 375°F (the fat on the griddle has been included in your fat exchange). Pour ⅓ cup batter onto griddle and cook about 3 minutes on one side, or until bubbles begin to form on surface and edges of pancake are dry. Turn and cook 2–3 minutes on other side, or until nicely browned. Repeat with remaining batter and serve hot using 1 pancake per serving.

Yields 7 pancakes—7 servings

Nutritive Values Per Serving

CAL	CHO (g)	PRO (g)	TOTAL FAT (g)	SAT. FAT (g)	CHOL (mg)	FIBER (g)	NA (mg)
130	17	5	6	.9	3	1.3	205

Food exchanges per serving: 1 starch, 1 fat
Low-sodium diets: Omit salt.
Sugar content per serving: .9 teaspoon.

Buttermilk Pancakes

Frances Nielsen used to make these as a special treat for Chuck when we visited her. He ate them with lots of margarine and syrup but I liked them with unsweetened applesauce sprinkled with cinnamon and sugar substitute.

> **2 cups all-purpose flour**
> **1 teaspoon baking powder**
> **1 teaspoon baking soda**
> **1 tablespoon sugar**
> **¼ cup dry buttermilk**
> **2 cups water at room temperature**
> **½ cup liquid egg substitute**
> **½ teaspoon vanilla**
> **2 tablespoons vegetable oil**

Stir flour, baking powder, soda, sugar, and dry buttermilk together to blend well. Beat water, egg substitute, vanilla, and oil together and add to the flour and beat with a large spoon until smooth.

Pour ¼ cup (level No. 16 dipper) batter onto a lightly greased griddle that has been preheated to 375° F. Cook about 3 minutes on one side or until bubbles form on the surface and the edges of the pancake are dry. Turn and cook 2–3 minutes on the other side or until nicely browned. Repeat with remaining batter. Serve hot using 1 pancake per serving.

Yields 16 pancakes—16 servings

Nutritive Values Per Serving

CAL	CHO (g)	PRO (g)	TOTAL FAT (g)	SAT. FAT (g)	CHOL (mg)	FIBER (g)	NA (mg)
97	14	3	3	.4	1	.4	132

Food exchanges per serving: 1 starch, ½ fat
Low-sodium diets: May be used as written.
Sugar content per serving: Trace.

Cinnamon Spread

This counts as a regular fat exchange but it adds something special to toast or hot breads. I keep some in the refrigerator most of the time and I have given it, in a pretty little ceramic pot, to other diabetics for Christmas or birthday presents. You can vary it using other spices but I prefer cinnamon.

8 ounces soft margarine at room
  temperature
2 teaspoons ground cinnamon
Granulated sugar substitute equal to ½ cup
  sugar

Combine ingredients and mix well. Return to container and refrigerate except when it is being used. Yields 24 servings of 2 teaspoons each.

Yields 1 cup—24 servings

Nutritive Values Per Serving

CAL	CHO (g)	PRO (g)	TOTAL FAT (g)	SAT. FAT (g)	CHOL (mg)	FIBER (g)	NA (mg)
70	1	trace	8	1.3	0	0	117

Food exchanges per serving: 1½ fat
Low-sodium diets: Use salt-free margarine.
Sugar content per serving: None.

Cinnamon Shake

This is good to shake on hot buttered toast, cereal, baked apples, or other fruit, or as directed in recipes in this book.

**Granulated sugar substitute equal to ½ cup
  sugar**
1 teaspoon ground cinnamon

Mix sugar substitute and cinnamon well. Put in a shaker and use as desired.

Yields ½ cup

Nutritive Values Per Serving

CAL	CHO (g)	PRO (g)	TOTAL FAT (g)	SAT. FAT (g)	CHOL (mg)	FIBER (g)	NA (mg)
3	1	0	0	0	0	0	23

Food exchanges per serving: May be used as desired without adding any
  nutritive value
Low-sodium diets: May be used as written.
Sugar content per serving: None.

Noodles

I call this noodle *dough, the Italians call it* pasta, *and the Polish call it* kluski. *It can be cut wide for lasagna, square for manicotti, thin and narrow for fettucini, or in small squares for some types of southern noodles. I also use it for ravioli or cut it thin and narrow to use with spaghetti sauce.*

Remember, when you're deciding which noodles to use, keep in mind that oat bran noodles are very chewy, and wheat noodles have a nutty taste. These characteristics may keep you from using them in various recipes.

Ingredients	Basic	Oat Bran	Wheat
Bread flour	2¼ cups	2 cups	1 cup
Oat bran cereal	none	1 cup	none
Whole wheat flour	none	none	1 cup
Salt	1 teaspoon for all recipes		
Liquid egg substitute	¾ cup	½ cup	½ cup
Lukewarm water	¼ cup	½ cup	½ cup
Vegetable oil	1 tablespoon for all recipes		
Yellow food coloring	2 drops	2 drops	none
Raw yield	20 ounces	24 ounces	20 ounces
Cooked yield	10 cups	12 cups	10 cups

Place dry ingredients in mixer bowl and mix at low speed for ½ minute to blend well. Beat liquid ingredients together with a fork to blend well. Add to dry ingredients and beat, using dough hook, at medium speed for 4 minutes. Turn out onto lightly floured working surface and knead a few times. Form into a ball, place on lightly floured working surface, cover with a cloth, and let stand for 30 minutes to 1 hour.

Divide dough into 3 equal portions. Work with 1 portion at a time, keeping the other 2 portions covered with the cloth. Roll each portion into a very thin rectangle (I like to use my marble rolling pin) on a floured surface. As you roll out the dough, lightly sprinkle the surface with flour to keep it from sticking to the rolling pin. The dough can be cut immediately with a noodle cutter or allowed to dry flat for about 1 hour and then rolled up like a jelly roll and cut with a sharp knife into noodles as wide as you like. You can also use a noodle machine, as I do, for more uniform noodles. Shake out the strips and lay them on a lightly floured towel if you are not going to use them immediately. If the room is sufficiently warm and dry, they should dry in a few hours or overnight; then they can be used right away or stored in the freezer or an airtight container until you need them.

Noodles can also be frozen without drying first. Spread a layer of noodles on a piece of waxed paper, sprinkle with a little flour, and repeat, stacking layers of waxed paper and noodles on top of one another. Wrap the layers in an airtight package and freeze until needed. *Do not defrost noodles before you use them.* Just drop into boiling liquid, as you would fresh noodles, stir until separated, and cook about 20 minutes, or until tender.

When you are ready to cook the noodles, drop them into boiling water or broth, add 1 tablespoon vegetable oil to the pot, and simmer for 10–20 minutes depending on the thickness of the noodles. Drain well. Toss with a little margarine and serve hot, or prepare as directed by recipe in which you are using them.

NUTRITIVE VALUES PER CUP OF COOKED NOODLES

VALUES	BASIC	OAT BRAN	WHEAT
Calories	132	115	107
CHO (g)	24	23	19
PRO (g)	5	5	4
TOTAL FAT	3	3	3
SAT. FAT	trace	trace	trace
CHOL (mg)	0	0	0
FIBER (g)	.5	2.3	2
NA (mg)	238	193	222

Food exchanges per cup of cooked noodles
   Basic: 1⅔ starch
   Oat bran: 1⅔ starch
   Wheat: 1⅓ starch
Low-sodium diets: Omit salt.

15

Pies

Man lives not by bread alone. Most people want an occasional piece of pie along with their bread, and if we have to give up some bread to have our pie, well, isn't it worth it once in a while? I, for one, think it is better to enjoy a small piece of pie occasionally and know I can have it once in a while than to feel deprived and think I'll never be able to eat pie again.

It isn't advisable to buy already prepared pie, even if it is advertised as low calorie, because you don't know what kind of fat is used in the crust and filling—and this is very important on a low-cholesterol diet. It is best to make the crust and filling at home and then you will know it is prepared correctly.

It is difficult to make a good crust without a certain amount of fat. We can cut the fat back a little bit, but it still requires a fair amount of fat to have a tender crust. Since the crust is necessarily high in fat and calories, it is better to serve one-crust pies rather than double-crust pies and to use a filling that is lower in calories.

The pie crust recipes in this chapter yield just enough dough for a single crust. If you want to make a double-crust pie, double the recipe and it will be the correct amount of dough for a double crust. It won't be enough for the elaborate edges and fancy decorations that some good cooks like to add to their pies, but it will be enough for a generous crust.

If you want to make a pie filling using your own recipe, you can calculate the exchanges for the filling according to Chapter 3 and then use it in one of the crusts in this chapter. Sometimes you may have to work with your filling a little bit to get it down to where you can afford it, but if it is a family favorite it can be worthwhile to work on it.

Of course, we use unsweetened fruits and sugar substitutes routinely, and don't forget that diabetic puddings make good pie fillings. You can use a diabetic pudding and a couple of fresh bananas to make a very good banana pie, and you can always garnish it with a couple of tablespoons of Whipped Topping (see Index).

I have included the exchange values of the pie crust in the pie recipes. If you need to know the values of the filling, you can subtract the values of the crust from the total values of the pie.

Mom's Pie Crust

This is the crust that my mother always made. She used lard until we started following a low-cholesterol meal pattern; then she changed to margarine. She always said that she couldn't make good pie crust until she started using this recipe—and then she never had a failure.

> ⅓ cup (⅔ stick) margarine
> 2 tablespoons water
> 1 cup all-purpose flour
> ¼ teaspoon baking powder
> ¼ teaspoon salt
> Warm water

Heat margarine and 2 tablespoons water together until margarine is melted. Set aside to cool to room temperature. Place flour, baking powder, and salt in mixing bowl and stir to blend well. Mix margarine mixture with a fork to blend and then add to flour mixture.

Add warm water by the tablespoonful to crust mixture, if necessary. (It will depend upon the type of flour, but I've never needed to add more than 2 tablespoons to any flour that I have used.) Round dough into a ball and let stand, covered, at room temperature for 15–30 minutes. Roll crust out on a lightly floured working surface to form a circle. Fit into 9-inch pie pan and prick the bottom 6 or 7 times with the tines of a fork. Bake at 425°F for 12–15 minutes or until lightly browned. Cool and fill with desired filling; or fill the unbaked crust with desired filling and bake according to directions with the filling.

I use two pie pans when I'm making a single crust. I place the crust in the bottom pan, prick it with a fork, and then put another pan exactly the same size on top of the crust, and bake it about 15 minutes or until lightly browned. I then remove it from the oven and remove the top pan, cool to room temperature, and use as desired.

Serve ⅛ of the crust per serving.

Yields 1 9-inch crust—8 servings

Nutritive Values Per Serving

CAL	CHO (g)	PRO (g)	TOTAL FAT (g)	SAT. FAT (g)	CHOL (mg)	FIBER (g)	NA (mg)
124	12	2	8	1.3	0	.4	171

Food exchanges per serving: ¾ starch, 1½ fat
Low-sodium diets: Omit salt. Use low-sodium baking powder and salt-free
   margarine.
Sugar content per serving: None.

Graham Cracker Crust

I like to bake this crust because that makes it crisp. If you want a softer crust, refrigerate it after it is prepared instead of baking it.

**8 crushed graham crackers (2½-inch
   squares)
3 tablespoons melted margarine
2 tablespoons sugar**

Combine ingredients in 9-inch pie tin and mix well with your fingers. Press crumbs evenly around the edges and on the bottom of the pie tin. Bake at 350°F for 6 minutes. Cool and fill as desired. Cut into 8 even portions, using 1 portion per serving.

Yields 1 9-inch crust—8 servings

Nutritive Values Per Serving

CAL	CHO (g)	PRO (g)	TOTAL FAT (g)	SAT. FAT (g)	CHOL (mg)	FIBER (g)	NA (mg)
80	9	1	5	.9	0	trace	93

Food exchanges per serving: ½ starch, 1 fat
Low-sodium diets: Use salt-free margarine.
Sugar content per serving: .8 teaspoon.

Southern Pie Crust

This crust isn't as yellow as it is when it is made with egg yolks. If you like the yellow color, you can add a drop or two of yellow coloring to the ice water when you are mixing the crust.

½ cup cake flour
½ cup all-purpose flour
⅓ cup (⅔ stick) margarine from the
   refrigerator
¼ cup ice water
¼ teaspoon salt
1 egg white
1½ teaspoons white vinegar

Place flours in bowl and stir to blend. Cut margarine into the flour until the mixture resembles coarse meal.

Combine water, salt, egg white, and vinegar in a cup. Mix well with a fork and then add to the flour mixture. Mix lightly with a fork until you can round the pastry into a ball. Refrigerate, or cover and let stand at room temperature for 15–30 minutes. Roll crust out on a lightly floured working surface to form a circle. Fit into 9-inch pie tin and prick the bottom 6 or 7 times with the tines of a fork. Bake at 425°F for 12–15 minutes, or until lightly browned. Cool and fill with the desired filling; or fill the unbaked crust with the desired filling and bake according to directions with the filling. Serve ⅛ of the pie per portion.

Yields 1 9-inch crust—8 servings

Nutritive Values Per Serving

CAL	CHO (g)	PRO (g)	TOTAL FAT (g)	SAT. FAT (g)	CHOL (mg)	FIBER (g)	NA (mg)
123	12	2	8	1.2	0	trace	163

Food exchanges per serving: ¾ starch, ½ fat
Low-sodium diets: Omit salt. Use salt-free margarine.
Sugar content per serving: None.

Apple Pie

FILLING
7 tart medium (4 to the pound) apples
¾ cup Brown Sugar Twin
2 tablespoons flour
⅛ teaspoon nutmeg or mace
1 teaspoon cinnamon
¼ teaspoon salt

2 unbaked 9-inch Mom's Pie Crusts (see Index)
2 tablespoons margarine

Peel and core apples and slice thin. Stir together Sugar Twin, flour, nutmeg, cinnamon, and salt to blend and then mix lightly with apples.

Fill bottom crust evenly with apple mixture. Dot with margarine. Cut slits in upper crust and place over filling. Seal pie crust at the edges and bake at 400°F for 50 minutes, or until pie is browned and well done. Cool to room temperature on wire rack. Cut into 8 equal pieces and serve 1 piece per serving.

Yields 1 9-inch pie—8 servings

Nutritive Values Per Serving

CAL	CHO (g)	PRO (g)	TOTAL FAT (g)	SAT. FAT (g)	CHOL (mg)	FIBER (g)	NA (mg)
336	40	4	19	3	0	2.5	443

Food exchanges per serving: 1½ starch, 1 fruit, 3½ fat
Low-sodium diets: Omit salt. Use salt-free margarine and low-sodium variation of the pie crust.
Sugar content per serving: None.

Cherry Pie

This was my husband's favorite pie. He always looked for it when we went to church dinners in this area because the women who live here in Iowa are such wonderful cooks and their pies are fabulous. In the fall it seems as though we go to a church dinner at least once a week—and all of them are good.

FILLING
2 16-ounce cans unsweetened red cherries
1 cup liquid from the cherries
1 tablespoon cornstarch
Sugar substitute equal to 1 cup sugar
¼ teaspoon almond flavoring

1 prebaked 9-inch Mom's Pie Crust (see Index)
Whipped Topping (see Index)

Drain cherries well, reserving 1 cup liquid. Set cherries aside and combine 1 cup liquid and cornstarch. Cook and stir over moderate heat until thickened and transparent and the starchy taste is gone. Remove from heat and add sugar substitute, almond flavoring, and cherries. Taste and add more sweetener, if desired. Cool to room temperature.

Spread filling evenly in crust. Let stand at least 15 minutes. Cut into 8 equal portions and serve 1 portion per serving. Garnish each serving of pie with 1 or 2 tablespoons Whipped Topping, if desired.

Yields 1 9-inch pie—8 servings

Nutritive Values Per Serving

CAL	CHO (g)	PRO (g)	TOTAL FAT (g)	SAT. FAT (g)	CHOL (mg)	FIBER (g)	NA (mg)
181	26	3	8	1.3	0	.4	269

Food exchanges per serving: ¾ starch, 1 fruit, 1½ fat
Low-sodium diets: Use low-sodium variation of the pie crust.
Sugar content per serving: None.

Custard Pie

This recipe is from Vera Wilson, a friend of mine in Wadena. Vera has been a great help to me in writing this—she gave me several recipes, listened to me when I was troubled over parts of the book, and rejoiced with me when everything came out OK.

FILLING
1 cup liquid egg substitute
2 tablespoons sugar
Sugar substitute equal to ⅓ cup sugar
1 teaspoon vanilla
¼ teaspoon salt
1 teaspoon cornstarch
¾ cup instant nonfat dry milk
2 cups water

1 unbaked 9-inch Mom's Pie Crust (see Index)
Ground nutmeg as desired

Combine all filling ingredients and mix thoroughly. Pour filling into unbaked pie crust.

Sprinkle nutmeg over filling and bake at 475°F for 10 minutes. Reduce heat to 425°F without opening the oven door and bake another 15 minutes. Test to see if it is done by sticking a knife in the center of the pie—if the knife doesn't come out clean, bake another 5 minutes. (It has always been done for me at the end of 15 minutes but Vera said to be sure and include that caution.) Cool to room temperature out of drafts. Cut into 8 pieces and serve 1 piece per serving.

Yields 1 9-inch pie—8 servings

Nutritive Values Per Serving

CAL	CHO (g)	PRO (g)	TOTAL FAT (g)	SAT. FAT (g)	CHOL (mg)	FIBER (g)	NA (mg)
181	21	7	8	1.3	1	.4	354

Food exchanges per serving: 1 starch, ½ skim milk, 1 fat
Low-sodium diets: Omit salt. Use low-sodium variation of the pie crust.
Sugar content per serving: .8 teaspoon.

Key Lime Pie

When I was in Key West with Bud and Frances Gunsallus, she ordered Key Lime Pie and gave me a bite of it. It was delicious and I decided I'd like to be able to make it for myself. Fortunately for me, Searle's published a recipe for it in one of their advertisements and I was quick to try it and serve it back here in Iowa. You can make it with lemon juice, but it is the lime juice that makes it authentic.

FILLING
1 packet Knox Unflavored Gelatine
3 tablespoons lime juice
½ cup boiling water
9 1-gram packets Equal (aspartame) sugar substitute
1 cup evaporated skim milk
1 teaspoon vanilla
Juice of 1½ limes
2 drops green food coloring

1 9-inch graham cracker crust (see Index)
Lime zest
Thin lime slices

Sprinkle gelatin over lime juice and let it stand for 1 minute. Add boiling water and sweetener to gelatin mixture and stir until gelatin is dissolved. Refrigerate about 45 minutes or until slightly thickened.

Combine milk and vanilla and freeze 30 minutes. Remove from freezer and whip at high speed until stiff. Stir lime juice and food coloring into whipped milk. (Save remaining ½ lime for garnish.) Slowly blend gelatin mixture into whipped milk.

Spoon pie filling into crust. Chill until firm. Garnish with lime zest and lime slices. Cut into 8 even portions and serve 1 portion per serving.

Yields 1 9-inch pie—8 servings

Nutritive Values Per Serving

CAL	CHO (g)	PRO (g)	TOTAL FAT (g)	SAT. FAT (g)	CHOL (mg)	FIBER (g)	NA (mg)
117	14	4	5	1	1	trace	132

Food exchanges per serving: 1 starch, 1 fat
Low-sodium diets: Use low-sodium variation of the pie crust.
Sugar content per serving: .8 teaspoon in the crust.

Lemon Pie

FILLING
2 large egg whites at room temperature
¼ teaspoon cream of tartar
¼ cup sugar
1 cup water
3 tablespoons lemon juice
2 tablespoons cornstarch
Grated rind of 1 lemon
1 tablespoon margarine
3 drops yellow food coloring
8 1-gram packets Equal (aspartame)

1 9-inch graham cracker crust (see Index)

Beat egg whites until frothy. Add cream of tartar and continue to beat at high speed, gradually adding sugar until meringue is stiff.

Combine water, lemon juice, and cornstarch in a small saucepan and stir until smooth. Add lemon rind, margarine, and food coloring to cornstarch mixture and cook and stir over moderate heat until thickened and the starchy taste is gone. Remove from heat. Mix sweetener into hot cooked mixture. Fold hot cooked mixture into meringue and mix lightly but thoroughly.

Pour filling into crust and refrigerate until firm. Cut into 8 equal pieces and serve 1 piece per serving.

Yields 1 9-inch pie—8 servings

Nutritive Values Per Serving

CAL	CHO (g)	PRO (g)	TOTAL FAT (g)	SAT. FAT (g)	CHOL (mg)	FIBER (g)	NA (mg)
134	18	2	6	1.1	0	trace	124

Food exchanges per serving: 1 starch, 1 fat
Low-sodium diets: Use salt-free margarine and low-sodium variation of the pie crust.
Sugar content per serving: 2.3 teaspoons including crust.

Pumpkin Pie

Every year when we have our annual church dinner in the fall, I cut and serve the pies, and it keeps me busy. I have noticed that pumpkin and sour cream raisin pies are the most popular, with cherry and apple right behind them. I've really tried, but I can't manage a sour cream raisin pie that fits into our diets—but we can have pumpkin, apple, and cherry, so let's enjoy them!

FILLING
1 16-ounce can solid-pack pumpkin
½ cup liquid egg substitute
2 tablespoons sugar
Sugar substitute equal to ⅓ cup sugar
½ teaspoon salt
2 teaspoons pumpkin pie spice
1⅔ cups water
½ cup instant nonfat dry milk

1 unbaked 9-inch Mom's Pie Crust (see Index)

Combine filling ingredients and mix until smooth.

Pour filling into the unbaked pie crust. Be careful to build up the crust around the edges of the pan because the pie will puff while it is baking. Bake at 425°F for 15 minutes. Reduce the temperature of the oven to 350°F without opening the oven door and continue to bake for another 45 minutes, or until a knife inserted in the center of the pie comes out clean. Cool to room temperature. Cut into 8 even portions and serve 1 piece per serving.

Yields 1 9-inch pie—8 servings

Nutritive Values Per Serving

CAL	CHO (g)	PRO (g)	TOTAL FAT (g)	SAT. FAT (g)	CHOL (mg)	FIBER (g)	NA (mg)
184	24	5	8	1.3	1	1.4	389

Food exchanges per serving: 1 starch, ⅔ skim milk, 1 fat
Low-sodium diets: Omit salt. Use low-sodium variation of the pie crust.
Sugar content per serving: .8 teaspoon.

Pumpkin Scotch Pie

This recipe is from Dorothea Odekirk of Fayette, Iowa. Dorothea and I both belong to the Fayette County Branch of the American Association of University Women and she gave me this recipe after I had talked about my new book one night at a meeting.

FILLING
1 2⅛-ounce package sugar-free
   butterscotch pudding
1¾ cups skim milk
1 cup precooked canned pumpkin
¼ cup Brown Sugar Twin sugar substitute
1 teaspoon pumpkin pie spice

1 9-inch graham cracker crust (see Index)
Whipped Topping (see Index)

Empty package of pudding mix into small saucepan. Add milk gradually. Cook and stir over moderate heat until pudding comes to a boil. Remove from heat. Add pumpkin, sweetener, and spice to cooked pudding. Mix well.

Pour filling into prepared crust. Refrigerate until served. Cut into 8 equal portions and serve 1 portion per serving. Garnish with whipped topping just before pie is served, if desired (2 tablespoons topping is free).

Yields 1 9-inch pie—8 servings

Nutritive Values Per Serving

CAL	CHO (g)	PRO (g)	TOTAL FAT (g)	SAT. FAT (g)	CHOL (mg)	FIBER (g)	NA (mg)
124	17	3	5	1	1	.7	292

Food exchanges per serving: 1 starch, 1 fat
Low-sodium diets: Use low-sodium variation of the pie crust.
Sugar content per serving: .8 teaspoon in crust.

Strawberry Chiffon Pie

This pie it is as good as it looks. You can use different flavors of soft drink mix if you like, with different garnishes.

FILLING
1 cup water
1 envelope Knox Unflavored Gelatine
1 .20-ounce packet Wyler's unsweetened
  strawberry flavored soft drink mix or
  Kool-Aid unsweetened soft drink mix
8 1-gram packets Equal (aspartame) sugar
  substitute
1 recipe Whipped Topping (see Index)
2 tablespoons instant nonfat dry milk

9-inch Graham Cracker Crust (see Index)
9 fresh strawberries (optional)

Combine water and gelatin. Let stand for 5 minutes and then heat until gelatin is melted. Add soft drink mix and sweetener to gelatin. Mix well and refrigerate until slightly thickened.

Prepare Whipped Topping while gelatin is thickening. Refrigerate until needed. Add dry milk to thickened gelatin and whip at high speed until creamy and stiff. Remove beater and gently fold whipped topping into whipped gelatin.

Spread filling evenly in graham cracker crust. Garnish each serving with a fresh strawberry, placing a fresh strawberry in the center of the pie. Refrigerate until firm. Cut into 8 equal pieces and serve 1 piece per serving.

Yields 1 9-inch pie—8 servings

Nutritive Values Per Serving

CAL	CHO (g)	PRO (g)	TOTAL FAT (g)	SAT. FAT (g)	CHOL (mg)	FIBER (g)	NA (mg)
120	15	4	5	.9	1	trace	154

Food exchanges per serving: 1 starch, 1 fat
Low-sodium diets: Use low-sodium variation of the pie crust.
Sugar content per serving: .8 teaspoon in crust.

Whipped Topping

This topping may be spread on top of a pie or used as a garnish for pies, puddings, or gelatins. It should be prepared as close to serving time as possible since it loses volume after a period of time.

½ cup instant nonfat dry milk
⅓ cup cold water
2 tablespoons lemon juice
2 tablespoons sugar
Dry sugar substitute equal to ¼ cup sugar
  (optional)
½ teaspoon vanilla

Combine dry milk and water and refrigerate for 30 minutes. Beat at high speed for 4 minutes.

Add lemon juice to whipped milk and beat at high speed for 4 minutes. Stir the sugar and sugar substitute together and add gradually to the whipped milk while it is being beaten. Add vanilla to whipped topping and refrigerate until used. Yields 24 servings of 2 tablespoons each.

Yields 3 cups topping—24 servings

Nutritive Values Per Serving

CAL	CHO (g)	PRO (g)	TOTAL FAT (g)	SAT. FAT (g)	CHOL (mg)	FIBER (g)	NA (mg)
10	2	1	trace	0	trace	0	8

Food exchanges per serving: 2 tablespoons may be considered free. ⅓ cup is
  1 vegetable exchange
Low-sodium diets: May be used as written.
Sugar content per serving: .3 teaspoon.

16

Cakes

Most diabetics long for the cakes and cookies that we used to enjoy so much. In fact, when I asked my friends and other diabetics what recipes they would like to see in this book, most of them started out with, "Some really good cakes and cookies." That is a tough request for a diabetic cookbook and gets even tougher when the recipes also need to be suitable for a low-cholesterol diet.

We all know that we can't have cake and cookies for every meal, because we need to save the exchanges for more important foods—but there are times such as birthdays when you really would like to be able to eat a piece of cake along with everyone else. Another time I like to have diabetic cake or cookies on hand is when we have unexpected guests and I want to offer them cake or cookies along with their coffee or tea. This is a great area for coffee and a sweet, but until I started to make my own cake or cookies, I always just sat there and sipped coffee. Now I can have something with it and I'm much happier and more relaxed when we have guests. I also have learned to slip a couple of my diabetic cookies in my purse (well-wrapped, of course) and take them along with me when we are invited out for afternoon coffee. Hostesses don't seem to mind so much if I eat my own cookies as long as I have something.

Let's face it. We will probably never get a really fine-textured cake suitable for a diabetic diet because the percentage of sugar in a cake is very important to the texture of the cake. However, we can get an acceptable cake if we use ingredients at room temperature and follow the directions for making the cake very carefully, using the recipes that follow.

A cake suitable for a low-cholesterol diet needs to avoid whole eggs, butter, cream, lard, and whole milk. Therefore, a cake suitable for a low-cholesterol diabetic diet needs to be made with margarine or oil, egg whites or liquid egg substitute, fat-free milk, and last but not least, very little sugar or other sweetener. I'm sorry to say that I haven't been able to make sponge cake, jelly roll, genoise, or those lovely Hungarian tortes with the liquid egg substitute. I've tried, but for me it remains an impossible dream.

I have managed to develop some cakes suitable for the low-cholesterol diabetic diet using approved ingredients which I think you will like. I found that cocoa used with buttermilk and baking soda gives a good texture. I also managed to develop several other good cakes, including some with syrup or molasses. I used the regular corn syrup, but you can use fructose syrup if you like sweeter cakes. I did use a little sugar or syrup, which I counted when I analyzed the recipes. You might discuss the use of either with your doctor before preparing these recipes, but since both are part of the carbohydrate allowance, most doctors feel that it is permissible to use them.

Instant nonfat dry milk and dry buttermilk are used in these recipes because I find them so convenient. They are generally lower in cost than the fresh skim milk or buttermilk made with skim milk and they can be kept unopened on the shelf or in the refrigerator after they are opened, if you like, for a fairly long period of time. It isn't all that easy in our area to get fresh buttermilk made with skim milk and for that reason also I like to keep the powdered buttermilk on hand. It is nationally available so if your store doesn't carry it, I'm sure they can get it for you.

Technique, or the way you mix the cake, is very important when you are making a cake, and even more so when you are working with very little sugar. Because of the high proportion of flour to sugar, it is easy to mix the flour too much, which develops the gluten in the flour. That is all to the good when you are making bread, but can be a disaster when you are making a cake. When the gluten in the cake has been developed too much, you get a very tough cake with large air holes. Therefore, it is important to cream the fat and the little bit of sugar very well—but to add the flour mixture very carefully and mix it only as much as is absolutely necessary.

I hope that you will use these recipes as a basis for your own needs. Add fruit to them for a shortcake, garnish them with a couple of tablespoons of Whipped Topping (see Index), layer them with diabetic jelly between the layers, and sprinkle them with Sugar Twin instead of powdered sugar—or add various flavorings to the cakes to vary their flavor. They can be the basis for lots of interesting desserts.

I have used a minimum of sugar substitute in these recipes because that is how we prefer them. If you want an increased amount, feel free to vary the amount according to your own tastes; it won't affect the final recipe if used within normal bounds. I have also shown the amount according to the sugar equivalents because that is how people tell me they prefer to have recipes written.

Of course, when you are making a low-cholesterol diabetic cake, you need to follow all of the suggestions for a good cake made with the ordinary amount of sugar:

1. Have all ingredients at room temperature unless the directions state otherwise. This is particularly important for the liquid egg substitute. Don't use it right from the refrigerator in a cake or cookie.
2. Use stick margarine unless the recipe specifies soft margarine.
3. Always read the recipe thoroughly before you start to prepare it to be sure that you understand it and that you have all of the ingredients on hand. I like to get out all of the ingredients and prepare the pans before I start mixing the cake. These recipes also presume that the oven will be preheated, so I generally start the oven also when I start to mix the cake.
4. Always use regulation-size measuring cups and spoons and bake cakes in the size pan specified in the recipe. An

otherwise good cake can be ruined if baked in the wrong size pan. If you want to bake a cake in a smaller pan, fill the pan ⅔ full of batter and bake any remaining batter as cupcakes.

5. Don't sift the flour unless the recipe directs you to do so. Sifting changes the amount of flour in a cup. I never sift flour. I always combine the ingredients and stir them together. This is much simpler and yields the same results.

6. Follow the recipe exactly the first time. Then you can change it if you like after you are sure that you want to make a change in it. Don't forget that if you add nuts or raisins or other goodies to a recipe, you need to count those added ingredients in your diet.

7. Use margarine, not oil, to grease your pans. I like to use the margarine wrapper with a little bit of the margarine left on it to grease the pan for a cake that includes margarine as an ingredient.

8. These cakes were all tested in metal pans. If you use a glass baking dish, decrease the baking temperature 25° F.

9. When you want to defrost a cake that has been frozen, it should be unwrapped and placed in a refrigerator until it is defrosted. If you try to defrost it at room temperature in the wrappings it will get sticky, and if you defrost it unwrapped at room temperature it will collect moisture and be soggy. I always had a rough time trying to get a cake defrosted without ruining it until Thelma Richburg of Columbia, South Carolina, told me how to do it successfully, and it really works this way. She is the mother of Olivia Sniffin, one of my favorite cousins-in-law. Mrs. Richburg bakes a lot of cakes and decorates them for special occasions and really knows how to bake good cakes—and how to take care of them after they are baked.

Chocolate Cake

¾ cup (1½ sticks) margarine at room
    temperature
¼ cup sugar
½ cup liquid egg substitute at room
    temperature
Dry sugar substitute equal to ⅓ cup
    sugar
2 teaspoons vanilla
2 cups cake flour
2 teaspoons baking powder
¼ cup instant nonfat dry milk
⅓ cup cocoa
1 cup water at room temperature

Cream together margarine and sugar at medium speed until light and fluffy. Add egg substitute, sweetener, and vanilla to creamed mixture and beat at medium speed for ½ minute.

Stir together flour, baking powder, dry milk, and cocoa to blend.

Add 1 cup water to creamed mixture along with flour mixture and mix at medium speed only until smooth. Spread evenly in a 9-inch square pan that has been greased with margarine. Bake at 350°F for 30–35 minutes, or until a cake tester comes out clean and the cake pulls away from the sides of the pan. Cool to room temperature and cut 4 × 4 to yield 16 equal servings.

Yields 1 cake—16 servings

Nutritive Values Per Serving

CAL	CHO (g)	PRO (g)	TOTAL FAT (g)	SAT. FAT (g)	CHOL (mg)	FIBER (g)	NA (mg)
154	16	3	9	1.6	trace	.5	183

Food exchanges per serving: 1 starch, 2 fat
Low-sodium diets: Use salt-free margarine and low-sodium baking powder.
Sugar content per serving: .8 teaspoon.

Cocoa Cake

This recipe is based on one from Lois Erickson, who lives in the country near Wadena. Lois has a way with roses and brought several wild roses for me to plant because I felt we should have some of Iowa's state flower in our backyard.

½ cup cocoa
½ cup boiling water
¾ cup (1½ sticks) margarine at room
   temperature
Dry sugar substitute equal to ½ cup
   sugar
2 teaspoons vanilla
3 large egg whites at room temperature
½ teaspoon cream of tartar
⅓ cup sugar
2½ cups cake flour
1 teaspoon baking soda
2 teaspoons baking powder
¼ teaspoon salt
½ teaspoon cinnamon
1 cup cool water

Mix together cocoa and boiling water to blend and set aside to cool to room temperature. Cream margarine at medium speed until light and fluffy. Add sweetener and vanilla to creamed mixture, along with cooled cocoa mixture. Mix at medium speed until well blended.

Beat egg whites at medium speed until foamy. Add cream of tartar and beat at high speed, gradually adding sugar, to form a meringue. Set aside for later use. Stir together flour, soda, baking powder, salt, and cinnamon to blend well.

Add 1 cup water to creamed mixture along with flour mixture. Beat at medium speed for 1–2 minutes or until well blended. Stir batter carefully into the meringue. Spread ½ of the batter evenly in each of 2 9-inch cake layer pans that have been greased with margarine and lined on the bottom with wax paper. Bake at 350°F for 30–35 minutes, or until a cake tester comes out clean from the center of the cake and the cake pulls away from the sides of the pan. Turn cake out onto a rack, remove the paper, and cool to room temperature.

Put diabetic jelly between the cake layers and frost at the last minute with Fluffy Frosting (see Index). Cut cake into 16 equal servings.

Yields 1 2-layer cake—16 servings

Nutritive Values Per Serving

CAL	CHO (g)	PRO (g)	TOTAL FAT (g)	SAT. FAT (g)	CHOL (mg)	FIBER (g)	NA (mg)
170	19	3	10	1.7	0	.8	291

Food exchanges per serving: 1 starch, 1 vegetable, 2 fat
Low-sodium diets: Omit salt. Use salt-free margarine and low-sodium baking powder.
Sugar content per serving: 1 teaspoon.

Banana Bran Cake

Please don't avoid this cake because there is bran in it. It is delicious, as well as good for you, and I think you'll like it.

> 1 cup All Bran, Bran Buds, or 100% Bran
> ⅓ cup vegetable oil
> ½ cup egg whites or liquid egg substitute
> ¾ cup water
> 1 teaspoon vanilla
> 1 teaspoon banana flavoring
> 1¼ cups all-purpose flour
> ¼ cup sugar
> 2 tablespoons dry buttermilk
> 1 teaspoon baking soda
> Dry sugar substitute equal to ½ cup
>   sugar
> 2 medium-size ripe bananas

Place bran, oil, egg whites or liquid egg substitute, water, and flavorings in mixer bowl and mix at low speed for 30 seconds.

Let the bran mixture stand for 30–45 minutes. (This timing is important.)

Stir flour, sugar, dry buttermilk, soda, and sugar substitute together to blend well and set aside.

At the end of 30–45 minutes, slice the bananas into the bran mixture and mix at medium speed until the bananas are dissolved and the mixture is creamy. Add the flour mixture and mix to blend. Spread the batter evenly in a 9-inch-square cake pan that has been greased with margarine or sprayed with pan spray and bake at 350°F for 25–30 minutes or until the cake pulls away from the sides of the pan and cake tester comes out clean from the center of the cake. Cool to room temperature and cut 3 ×4 to yield 12 servings.

Yields 1 cake—12 servings

Nutritive Values Per Serving

CAL	CHO (g)	PRO (g)	TOTAL FAT (g)	SAT. FAT (g)	CHOL (mg)	FIBER (g)	NA (mg)
166	24	4	7	.9	.9	2.3	208

Food exchanges per serving: 1½ starch, 1 fat
Low-sodium diets: May be used as written.
Sugar content per serving: 1 teaspoon.

Raisin Cake

This cake from Ruth Schoephoerster of Oelwein, Iowa, tastes like the fruitcake my mother used to make when I was a child.

> 1 cup raisins
> Boiling water as necessary
> Dry sugar substitute equal to ¾ cup
>   sugar
> 3 large egg whites
> ½ cup oil
> 1½ teaspoons vanilla
> 1 cup unsweetened applesauce
> 2 cups all-purpose flour
> 1 teaspoon baking soda
> 1 teaspoon baking powder
> 1¼ teaspoons cinnamon
> ½ teaspoon nutmeg
> ½ teaspoon salt

Cover raisins with water. Let stand 5 minutes. Drain well and place the raisins in a mixer bowl. Discard the liquid. Add sweetener, egg whites, oil, vanilla, and applesauce to raisins and mix at medium speed for a few seconds to blend.

Blend remaining dry ingredients well and add to raisin mixture. Mix at medium speed to blend. Spread evenly in a 9" × 13" cake pan that has been greased with margarine. Bake at 350°F for 35–40 minutes, or until well browned and the cake has drawn away from the sides of the pan. Cut 4 × 5 to yield 20 pieces. Serve 1 piece per serving.

Yields 1 cake—20 servings

Nutritive Values Per Serving

CAL	CHO (g)	PRO (g)	TOTAL FAT (g)	SAT. FAT (g)	CHOL (mg)	FIBER (g)	NA (mg)
127	17	2	6	.8	0	.9	154

Food exchanges per serving: 1 starch, 1 fat
Low-sodium diets: Omit salt. Use low-sodium baking powder.
Sugar content per serving: None.

Devil's Food Cake

½ cup cocoa
½ cup boiling water
2 cups cake flour
½ teaspoon baking soda
1½ teaspoons baking powder
⅛ teaspoon salt
⅓ cup sugar
¾ cup liquid egg substitute at room
    temperature
Dry sugar substitute equal to ¾ cup
    sugar
1 teaspoon vanilla
½ cup (1 stick) margarine at room
    temperature

Stir together cocoa and boiling water until smooth. Set aside to cool to room temperature.

Place flour, soda, baking powder, salt, and sugar in mixer bowl and mix at low speed about 1 minute to blend.

Add egg substitute, sweetener, and vanilla to cocoa mixture and mix well.

Add margarine to dry ingredients along with cocoa mixture and mix at medium speed about 1 minute or until well blended. Pour into a 9-inch square (for thicker cake) or 9″ × 13″ pan greased with margarine. Bake at 350°F for about 30 minutes, or until a cake tester comes out clean and the cake pulls away from the sides of the pan. Cool in the pan and cut 6 × 3 to yield 18 pieces. Serve cold with a tablespoon of Whipped Topping (see Index) or warm with some Chocolate Sauce (see Index). Allow 1 piece per serving.

Yields 1 cake—18 servings

Nutritive Values Per Serving

CAL	CHO (g)	PRO (g)	TOTAL FAT (g)	SAT. FAT (g)	CHOL (mg)	FIBER (g)	NA (mg)
117	15	3	6	1	0	.7	170

Food exchanges per serving: 1 starch, 1 fat

Low-sodium diets: Omit salt. Use low-sodium baking powder and salt-free margarine.

Sugar content per serving: .9 teaspoon.

Spice Cupcakes

2 cups cake flour
⅓ cup brown sugar
1 teaspoon cinnamon
1½ teaspoons baking powder
½ cup water at room temperature
Dry sugar substitute equal to ⅓ cup
    sugar
½ cup liquid egg substitute at room
    temperature
⅓ cup vegetable oil
2 teaspoons vanilla

Place flour, sugar, cinnamon, and baking powder in mixer bowl and mix at low speed to blend well.

Mix together ½ cup water, sweetener, egg substitute, oil, and vanilla with a fork. Add to flour mixture and mix with a spoon only until well blended. Grease 9 muffin tins with margarine or line with paper. Fill muffin tins about ½ full and bake at 375°F for 20–25 minutes, or until well browned. Serve 1 cupcake per serving.

Yields 9 cupcakes—9 servings

Nutritive Values Per Serving

CAL	CHO (g)	PRO (g)	TOTAL FAT (g)	SAT. FAT (g)	CHOL (mg)	FIBER (g)	NA (mg)
207	28	3	9	1.2	0	0	117

Food exchanges per serving: 1 starch, 1 other carbohydrate, 1 fat
Low-sodium diets: Use low-sodium baking powder.
Sugar content per serving: 1.8 teaspoon.

Wacky Cupcakes

My sister has been making this cake ever since she was a little girl. The original recipe said to put the dry ingredients in the pan and then add the rest and mix it in the pan you bake it in, but I like this way better.

1½ cups cake flour
¼ cup sugar
¼ cup cocoa
1 teaspoon baking soda
½ teaspoon salt
1 cup water at room temperature
Dry sugar substitute equal to ½ cup
    sugar
1 tablespoon vinegar
2 teaspoons vanilla
½ cup vegetable oil

Place flour, sugar, cocoa, soda, and salt in mixer bowl and mix at low speed to blend.

Beat together remaining ingredients with a fork to blend. Add all at once to dry ingredients and beat at medium speed until smooth. Paper-line 12 muffin tins or grease with margarine and flour. Fill muffin tins about ½ full and bake at 350°F for about 30 minutes, or until a cake tester comes out clean from the center of the cupcake. Serve 1 cupcake per serving.

Yields 12 cupcakes—12 servings

Nutritive Values Per Serving

CAL	CHO (g)	PRO (g)	TOTAL FAT (g)	SAT. FAT (g)	CHOL (mg)	FIBER (g)	NA (mg)
153	16	2	10	1.3	0	.5	197

Food exchanges per serving: 1 starch, 2 fat
Low-sodium diets: Omit salt.
Sugar content per serving: 1 teaspoon.

White Cake

This recipe is based on one from Margaret Foxwell of Elgin, Iowa. It has the texture of a firm European cake.

**½ cup (1 stick) margarine at room
    temperature**
¼ cup white corn syrup
**Dry sugar substitute equal to ⅓ cup
    sugar**
2 teaspoons vanilla
3 large egg whites at room temperature
2 cups cake flour
1 tablespoon baking powder
2 tablespoons instant nonfat dry milk
½ cup water at room temperature

Beat margarine, corn syrup, sweetener, vanilla, and egg whites at medium speed about 1 minute or until blended.

Stir together flour, baking powder, and dry milk until well blended.

Add flour mixture and ½ cup water to creamed mixture and stir with a large spoon until well mixed. Do not overbeat. Spread evenly in a 9-inch square pan that has been greased with margarine, and bake at 350°F for 30–35 minutes or until lightly browned and it pulls away from the sides of the pan. Cool and cut 4 × 4 into 16 equal servings.

Yields 1 cake—16 servings

Nutritive Values Per Serving

CAL	CHO (g)	PRO (g)	TOTAL FAT (g)	SAT. FAT (g)	CHOL (mg)	FIBER (g)	NA (mg)
124	15	2	6	1	trace	0	181

Food exchanges per serving: 1 starch, 1 fat
Low-sodium diets: Use salt-free margarine and low-sodium baking powder.
Sugar content per serving: .8 teaspoon.

Yellow Cake

---

2 cups cake flour
½ teaspoon baking soda
1½ teaspoons baking powder
⅓ cup sugar
3 tablespoons dry buttermilk
¾ cup water at room temperature
⅓ cup vegetable oil
Dry sugar substitute equal to ¼ cup
  sugar
2 teaspoons vanilla
½ cup liquid egg substitute at room
  temperature
¼ cup (½ stick) margarine at room
  temperature

Place dry ingredients in mixer bowl and mix at low speed to blend well.

Combine ¾ cup water, oil, sweetener, vanilla, and egg substitute and mix with a fork to blend. Add margarine to flour mixture along with liquid mixture and mix with a spoon only until well blended. Spread evenly in a 9-inch square pan which has been greased with margarine. Bake 30–35 minutes at 375°F, or until a cake tester comes out clean and the cake pulls away from the sides of the pan. Cool to room temperature and cut 4 × 4 to yield 16 equal servings.

Yields 1 cake—16 servings

Nutritive Values Per Serving

CAL	CHO (g)	PRO (g)	TOTAL FAT (g)	SAT. FAT (g)	CHOL (mg)	FIBER (g)	NA (mg)
144	16	2	8	1	1	0	141

Food exchanges per serving: 1 starch, 1½ fat
Low-sodium diets: Use low-sodium baking powder and salt-free margarine.
Sugar content per serving: 1 teaspoon.

Butter Cream Frosting

You'll be surprised how good this frosting tastes. The recipe was developed by my friend Patsy Spies, who wanted it as a special treat for her grandmother who was diabetic.

½ cup water
2 tablespoons instant nonfat dry milk
2½ tablespoons all-purpose flour
½ cup (1 stick) margarine at room
   temperature
10 1-gram packets Equal sugar substitute
½ teaspoon vanilla, lemon, almond, or
   other flavoring

Combine water, dry milk, and flour and stir until smooth. Cook, stirring constantly, over medium heat until thick and smooth, or cook in a microwave oven on high for 2 minutes, stirring every 30 seconds. Place container in cool water and stir until cool. Set aside. Cream margarine and sugar substitute together until light and fluffy. Add cooled sauce 1 tablespoon at a time while beating at medium speed. Add vanilla or other flavoring and beat at high speed until light and fluffy. Refrigerate until used. Use 1 tablespoon per portion (¾ cup for a 12-portion cake or 1 cup for a 16-portion cake). Return to room temperature before spreading the frosting on a cool cake.

Yields 1¼ cups—20 servings

Nutritive Values Per Serving

CAL	CHO (g)	PRO (g)	TOTAL FAT (g)	SAT. FAT (g)	CHOL (mg)	FIBER (g)	NA (mg)
48	1	1	5	.7	trace	trace	56

Food exchanges per serving: 1 fat
Low-sodium diets: Use salt-free margarine.
Sugar content per serving: None.

Fluffy Frosting

This recipe from the makers of Sweet'n Low reminds me of the seven-minute frosting my mother used to make. You can change the frosting easily by adding a couple of drops of food coloring and some flavoring, such as 2 drops of red coloring and some peppermint flavoring.

½ cup sugar
2 tablespoons water
2 packets Sweet'n Low
2 large egg whites
¼ teaspoon cream of tartar
½ teaspoon vanilla

Combine sugar, water, Sweet'n Low, egg whites, and cream of tartar in top of a double boiler and beat at high speed for 1 minute. Set over simmering water in the bottom of the double boiler. Continue to beat at high speed for 4–5 minutes or until soft peaks form. Remove from heat.

Add vanilla to frosting and continue beating at high speed 1–2 minutes or until thick enough to spread on a cooled cake. Use about 3 tablespoons per portion if frosting individually; or use this amount to frost a 2-layer cake or a 9-inch square cake, both of which would then be cut into 16 equal servings.

Yields about 3 cups frosting—16 servings

Nutritive Values Per Serving

CAL	CHO (g)	PRO (g)	TOTAL FAT (g)	SAT. FAT (g)	CHOL (mg)	FIBER (g)	NA (mg)
27	7	trace	0	0	0	0	7

Food exchanges per serving: 1 vegetable
Low-sodium diets: May be used as written.
Sugar content per serving: 1.5 teaspoon.

Lemon Sauce

This sauce adds a lot to a plain or spice cake—either warm or at room temperature.

> 2 cups water
> 2 tablespoons cornstarch
> ⅛ teaspoon salt
> 2 tablespoons margarine
> 2 tablespoons lemon juice
> Grated rind of 1 lemon
> 1 drop yellow food coloring
> 8 1-gram packets Equal (aspartame) sugar
> substitute

Combine water, cornstarch, and salt and stir until smooth in a small saucepan. Cook and stir over moderate heat until thickened and clear and then continue to simmer, stirring constantly, for another 2 minutes. Remove from heat.

Add remaining ingredients to sauce and stir lightly to mix well. Serve warm, if possible, over cake or pudding. Serve ¼ cup per serving.

Yields 2 cups—8 servings

Nutritive Values Per Serving

CAL	CHO (g)	PRO (g)	TOTAL FAT (g)	SAT. FAT (g)	CHOL (mg)	FIBER (g)	NA (mg)
38	3	1	3	.5	0	trace	69

Food exchanges per serving: ½ fat, ½ vegetable
Low-sodium diets: Omit salt.
Sugar content per serving: None.

Chocolate Sauce

This is good on ice milk or as a topping for cake or pudding.

> **3 tablespoons cocoa**
> **4 teaspoons cornstarch**
> **⅓ cup instant nonfat dry milk**
> **⅛ teaspoon salt**
> **1½ cups water**
> **1 tablespoon margarine**
> **2 teaspoons vanilla**
> **10 1-gram packets Equal (aspartame) sugar**
> **substitute**

Stir together cocoa, cornstarch, dry milk, and salt to blend in a small saucepan. Stir water into dry mixture until smooth. Add margarine and cook and stir over low heat. Bring to a boil and simmer for 2 minutes, stirring constantly. Remove from heat.

Add vanilla and sweetener to sauce. Stir lightly to mix. Pour into a glass jar and refrigerate until used. Return to room temperature before serving over ice cream, or it may be heated again to serve on cake or pudding. Serve 2 tablespoons per serving.

Yields 1½ cups—12 servings

Nutritive Values Per Serving

CAL	CHO (g)	PRO (g)	TOTAL FAT (g)	SAT. FAT (g)	CHOL (mg)	FIBER (g)	NA (mg)
28	3	1	1	trace	trace	trace	45

Food exchanges per serving: ½ vegetable
Low-sodium diets: Omit salt.
Sugar content per serving: None.

17

Cookies

A friend of mine commented when I started this book that she would like me to include some crisp cookies. She said that she was so tired of the soft cookies, which were all she knew how to make. I've never been too fond of those, either, so I tried to work on some rather crisp cookies. Sugar helps, but since we can't have much of that we need something else to give us that crisp texture. Egg whites also help, so I used those in several recipes; and believe it or not, just letting the cookies sit on a tray at room temperature for a couple of days helps. The buttermilk cookies in this chapter, which I'm very proud of, become much more crisp after you let them stay out for a couple of days.

I like to have cookies on hand for special occasions and therefore I generally try to keep some cookies in the freezer. All of the cookies in this chapter freeze well because I don't consider a cookie that can't be frozen very practical. If I'm having company and they don't need diabetic cookies, I always include some of my own cookies on the tray so I can have a cookie or two without comment—although it is amazing how many people tell me they would like to cut down on sugar and choose to eat my cookies instead of the ones with lots of sugar and fat in them.

Since our cookies need to be low cholesterol as well as low carbohydrate, we need to make them without butter, cream, whole milk, egg yolks, lard, chocolate, and coconut. I'm glad we can have cocoa, nuts, raisins, applesauce, and other fruits, even if we do have to count them, because we can use all of those to make our cookies more interesting. Cookies can't be frosted with powdered sugar frosting or rolled in powdered sugar, but they can be rolled in granular sugar substitute, which works rather well.

Of course, while we are making our diabetic low-cholesterol cookies, we still need to observe the fundamentals of good cookie-making. I have found that following these guidelines helps me to have better cookies:

1. Read the recipe to be sure you understand it before you start. Get out all of the ingredients and any equipment you will need to make the cookies before you start mixing any ingredients. I generally start preheating the oven after I am sure I have everything ready to go, since I need to preheat my oven for 10 minutes and that is about the length of time it takes me to mix up a batch of cookies.

2. Use good quality ingredients and don't substitute ingredients without regard to the proper substitution rates.

3. Don't sift flour unless the recipe tells you to do so because sifted and unsifted flours measure differently. I almost never sift flour. Flour is sifted to mix it with other ingredients and to make it lighter, and both of these are accomplished when it is stirred.

4. Always use regulation measuring cups and spoons. Cakes and cookies are delicately balanced formulas and won't respond well to irregular measurements.

5. It is important that ingredients be at room temperature if the recipe so indicates. This is especially important for liquid egg substitute and margarine.

6. All cookies on the same baking sheet should be the same size and thickness so they will bake evenly. If there is not enough dough for a full pan of cookies, bake them on a smaller pan or in the center of the larger pan you have been using.

7. Cookies should be placed on a cool pan before they are put in the oven. A hot pan will start them baking before they go in the oven and will generally result in imperfectly baked cookies. Cookies should also be loosened from hot pans and put on a wire rack to cool so they won't continue baking after they are removed from the oven.

8. Cookies should be defrosted in the container in which they were frozen or in another airtight container so they don't pick up moisture from the air, which softens them. If they are to be defrosted on a plate, the plate should be refrigerated so they can defrost at the temperature in the refrigerator and not at room temperature.

Chocolate Date Cookies

You can substitute raisins for the dates, if you like, without changing the exchange values, but we like dates for a change.

½ cup (1 stick) margarine at room
    temperature
⅓ cup sugar
⅓ cup brown sugar
½ cup egg whites or liquid egg substitute
2 teaspoons vanilla
2¼ cups all-purpose flour
⅓ cup cocoa
1 teaspoon baking powder
Sugar substitute equal to ½ cup sugar
¾ cup chopped pitted dates
⅓ cup water at room temperature

Cream together margarine and sugars at medium speed until light and fluffy. Add egg whites or liquid egg substitute and vanilla and mix until smooth. Stir flour, cocoa, baking powder, sugar substitute, and dates together to blend and add with the water to the creamed mixture. Mix only until blended and then drop by 1½ tablespoonfuls (level No. 40 dipper) onto cookie sheets that have been lined with aluminum foil or sprayed with pan spray. Press down lightly with your fingers or the back of a spoon dipped in water. Bake at 350°F for 12–15 minutes or until the cookie springs back when touched in the center. Remove from the hot cookie sheets onto a wire rack and cool to room temperature. Serve 1 cookie per serving.

Yields 2½ dozen cookies—30 servings

Nutritive Values Per Serving

CAL	CHO (g)	PRO (g)	TOTAL FAT (g)	SAT. FAT (g)	CHOL (mg)	FIBER (g)	NA (mg)
98	16	2	3	.6	0	.8	72

Food exchanges per serving: 1 starch, ½ fat
Low-sodium diets: Use salt-free margarine and low-sodium baking powder.
Sugar content per serving: 1.1 teaspoons.

Chocolate Bars

I'm a chocoholic so you know I tried very hard to develop a recipe for chocolate bars that I could eat. We like these best made with the black walnuts that grow so abundantly in this area, but they are also good with pecans or other types of nuts.

½ cup cocoa
⅓ cup boiling water
2 cups all-purpose flour
1 teaspoon baking soda
½ teaspoon salt
4 large egg whites at room temperature
2 teaspoons vanilla
Liquid sugar substitute equal to ½ cup
    sugar
½ cup white corn syrup
1 cup (2 sticks) margarine at room
    temperature
1 cup chopped nuts

Mix together cocoa and boiling water with a teaspoon until smooth and set aside to cool to room temperature. Place flour, soda, and salt in mixer bowl and mix at low speed about 1 minute to blend well. Add egg whites, vanilla, sugar substitute, and corn syrup to cocoa mixture and mix with a spoon to blend. Add margarine to flour mixture along with cocoa mixture and mix at medium speed about 1 minute or until well blended. Do not overmix.

Add nuts to dough. Spread dough evenly (this is very important) in an 11″ × 15″ jelly roll pan that has been greased with margarine or sprayed with pan spray. Bake at 350°F for about 20 minutes, or until the bars start to pull away from the sides of the pan. Cool to room temperature and cut 4″ × 6″ to yield 24 squares. Serve 1 square per serving.

Yields 2 dozen squares—24 servings

Nutritive Values Per Serving

CAL	CHO (g)	PRO (g)	TOTAL FAT (g)	SAT. FAT (g)	CHOL (mg)	FIBER (g)	NA (mg)
167	15	3	11	1.7	0	1	208

Food exchanges per serving: 1 starch, 2 fat
Low-sodium diets: Omit salt. Use salt-free margarine and unsalted nuts.
Sugar content per serving: 1 teaspoon.

Chocolate Balls

This cookie, based on a recipe from Frances Nielsen, is one of my sister Shirley's favorites. I hesitated to include it because it didn't seem to me that I got that much for my bread exchange, but she liked it so well that I decided to use it.

½ cup (1 stick) margarine at room
  temperature
2 tablespoons sugar
2 teaspoons vanilla
Liquid sugar substitute equal to ⅓ cup
  sugar
1¼ cups all-purpose flour
3 tablespoons cocoa
½ teaspoon salt
¼ cup chopped nuts
2 tablespoons raisins
Sprinkle Sweet granulated sugar substitute
  as necessary

Cream together margarine and sugar until light and fluffy. Add vanilla and sugar substitute to creamed mixture. Beat at medium speed for ½ minute. Stir together flour, cocoa, and salt to blend. Add to creamed mixture and mix at low speed about 1 minute or until blended.

Add nuts and raisins to dough. Mix lightly. Shape into balls using 1 tablespoonful (level No. 60 dipper) of dough per ball.

Place balls on a cookie sheet that has been lined with aluminum foil or sprayed with pan spray. Bake at 325°F for 20–25 minutes or until slightly firm. Remove from oven and cool slightly.

Roll lukewarm balls in Sprinkle Sweet. Cool to room temperature, and serve 2 balls per serving.

Variation:
CHOCOLATE MINT BALLS
Add ½ teaspoon peppermint flavoring along with 1 teaspoon vanilla instead of the 2 teaspoons vanilla.

Yields 20 cookies—10 servings

Nutritive Values Per Serving

CAL	CHO (g)	PRO (g)	TOTAL FAT (g)	SAT. FAT (g)	CHOL (mg)	FIBER (g)	NA (mg)
179	18	3	11	1.8	0	1.1	218

Food exchanges per serving: 1 starch, 2 fat
Low-sodium diets: Omit salt. Use salt-free margarine and unsalted nuts.
Sugar content per serving: .6 teaspoon.

Chocolate Raisin Nut Cookies

This cookie has a soft cakelike texture that many people enjoy.

2 cups all-purpose flour
½ cup sugar
½ cup brown sugar
⅓ cup cocoa
1 teaspoon baking soda
½ teaspoon salt
½ cup vegetable oil
½ cup egg whites or liquid egg substitute
2 tablespoons water
2 teaspoons vanilla
½ cup chopped walnuts
¼ cup raisins

Place flour, sugars, cocoa, soda, and salt in mixer bowl and mix at low speed to blend well. Add oil, egg whites or egg substitute, water, and vanilla and mix at medium speed until blended. Add nuts and raisins and drop by 1½ tablespoonfuls (level No. 40 dipper) onto cookie sheets that have been sprayed with vegetable pan spray or lined with aluminum foil. Bake at 350°F for 10–12 minutes or until firm. Remove to wire racks to cool to room temperature. These cookies should not be baked too long since they will get too hard if overbaked. Serve 1 cookie per serving.

Yields 2⅓ dozen cookies—28 servings

Nutritive Values Per Serving

CAL	CHO (g)	PRO (g)	TOTAL FAT (g)	SAT. FAT (g)	CHOL (mg)	FIBER (g)	NA (mg)
119	16	2	6	.7	0	.7	94

Food exchanges per serving: 1 starch, 1 fat
Low-sodium diets: Omit salt.
Sugar content per serving: 1.7 teaspoons.

Chocolate Chip Cookies

***

**1 cup (2 sticks) margarine at room
    temperature**
¼ cup sugar
¾ cup Brown Sugar Twin sugar substitute
3 large egg whites at room temperature
1 tablespoon vanilla
2 cups all-purpose flour
1 teaspoon baking soda
¼ teaspoon salt
¼ cup water at room temperature
½ cup mini semisweet chocolate chips

Cream margarine, sugar, and sugar substitute at medium speed until light and fluffy. Add egg whites and vanilla to creamed mixture and beat at medium speed for 1 minute.

Stir together flour, soda, and salt to blend well. Add ¼ cup water to creamed mixture along with the flour mixture and mix at medium speed for 1 minute or until smooth.

Add chocolate chips to dough and mix lightly. Drop by tablespoonfuls (level No. 60 dipper) onto cookie sheets that have been lined with aluminum foil or sprayed with pan spray. Press down lightly with fingers dipped in cold water to form a circle about 2 inches across. Bake at 375°F for about 12 minutes or until browned. (The cookies won't be crisp unless they are browned.) Remove cookies from hot cookie sheets to wire racks to cool to room temperature. Allow 2 cookies per serving.

Variation:
CHOCOLATE CHIP BARS
Instead of dropping dough onto cookie sheets, spread dough evenly in a jelly roll pan (11" × 15") that has been greased with margarine or sprayed with pan spray. Bake at 375°F for 20–25 minutes, or until lightly browned and the bars pull away from

the sides of the pan. Cool to room temperature and cut 9 × 4 to yield 36 bars. Serve 2 bars per serving.

Yields 3 dozen cookies—18 servings

Nutritive Values Per Serving

CAL	CHO (g)	PRO (g)	TOTAL FAT (g)	SAT. FAT (g)	CHOL (mg)	FIBER (g)	NA (mg)
182	18	2	12	2.4	trace	trace	229

Food exchanges per serving: 1 starch, 2 fat (Exchanges remain the same for the variation of the basic recipe.)

Low-sodium diets: Omit salt. Use salt-free margarine.

Sugar content per serving: .7 teaspoon.

Mocha Cookies

These cookies are a favorite of my friend Jan Franks.

> 1 tablespoon instant or freeze-dried coffee
> ¼ cup hot water
> 1 cup (2 sticks) margarine at room
>   temperature
> ⅔ cup sugar
> ½ cup egg whites or liquid egg substitute
> 2 teaspoons vanilla
> 2½ cups all-purpose flour
> ⅓ cup cocoa
> Sugar substitute equal to ½ cup sugar
> 1½ teaspoons baking powder
> ¾ cup raisins

Combine coffee and water. Stir to mix well and set aside.

Cream together margarine and sugar until light and fluffy. Add egg whites or egg substitute and vanilla and mix until smooth. Stir flour, cocoa, sugar substitute, baking powder, and raisins together to blend. Add to creamed mixture along with the coffee mixture and mix at medium speed only until blended. Drop by 1½ tablespoonfuls (level No. 40 dipper) onto a cookie sheet lined with aluminum foil or sprayed with pan spray. Press down lightly with your fingers or the back of a spoon dipped in cold water. Bake at 375°F about 12 minutes or until the cookies spring back when touched. Transfer from the hot cookie sheets onto a wire rack and cool to room temperature. Serve 1 cookie per serving.

Yields 2½ dozen cookies—30 servings

Nutritive Values Per Serving

CAL	CHO (g)	PRO (g)	TOTAL FAT (g)	SAT. FAT (g)	CHOL (mg)	FIBER (g)	NA (mg)
128	17	2	6	1	0	.8	115

Food exchanges per serving: 1 starch, 1 fat
Low-sodium diets: Use salt-free margarine and low-sodium baking powder.
Sugar content per serving: 1.1 teaspoons.

Date Graham Cookies

1 cup graham flour
½ cup all-purpose flour
3 tablespoons dry buttermilk
½ teaspoon baking soda
½ teaspoon salt
½ cup brown sugar
½ cup Brown Sugar Twin sugar substitute
2 large egg whites at room temperature
¼ cup dark molasses
½ cup (1 stick) margarine at room
    temperature
½ cup chopped dates

Place flours, dry buttermilk, soda, salt, brown sugar, and sugar substitute in mixer bowl and mix at low speed for about 1 minute to mix well. Add egg whites, molasses, and margarine to flour mixture and mix at medium speed for about 1 minute or until well blended.

Add dates to dough and mix lightly. Drop by tablespoonfuls (level No. 60 dipper) onto cookie sheets that have been lined with aluminum foil or sprayed with pan spray. Bake at 375°F for 10–12 minutes, or until lightly browned. Remove from hot cookie sheets onto wire rack to cool to room temperature. Serve 1 cookie per serving.

Yields 2 dozen cookies—24 servings

Nutritive Values Per Serving

CAL	CHO (g)	PRO (g)	TOTAL FAT (g)	SAT. FAT (g)	CHOL (mg)	FIBER (g)	NA (mg)
102	16	2	4	1	.7	.9	130

Food exchanges per serving: 1 starch, 1 fat
Low-sodium diets: Omit salt. Use salt-free margarine.
Sugar content per serving: .5 teaspoon.

Buttermilk Cookies

These cookies are based on a recipe for buttermilk cookies that Vera Wilson made for years. I have always loved them, and she used to save some of them for me whenever she or her daughter Mary made them. I hated to give them up when I became diabetic, but I feel better about it now that I have developed a cookie suitable for my diet that is almost like the original.

> ½ cup (1 stick) margarine at room
>   temperature
> ¼ cup sugar
> 2 teaspoons vanilla
> Dry sugar substitute equal to ⅓ cup
>   sugar
> ½ cup liquid egg substitute at room
>   temperature
> 2 cups all-purpose flour
> ½ teaspoon baking soda
> ½ teaspoon baking powder
> 2 tablespoons dry buttermilk
> 1 to 2 tablespoons water

Cream together margarine and sugar until light and fluffy. Add vanilla, sugar substitute, and egg substitute to creamed mixture and beat at medium speed for 1 minute. Stir together flour, soda, baking powder, and dry buttermilk to blend and add to creamed mixture.

Add to creamed and flour mixture as much of the water as necessary to make a soft dough. While adding, beat at low speed. Roll out on a lightly floured working surface to about ¼-inch thickness. Cut with a 3-inch cookie cutter and place on cookie sheets that have been lined with aluminum foil or sprayed with pan spray. Sprinkle with Cinnamon Shake (see Index) if desired and bake at 350°F for 12–15 minutes or until lightly browned. (The cookies need to be browned on the bottom to develop their best flavor.) Remove from hot cookie sheets to wire rack and cool to room temperature. Serve 2 cookies to a serving.

Variations:
SPICE COOKIES:
Add 1 teaspoon pumpkin pie spice, apple pie spice, or cinnamon along with the flour.

CHOCOLATE COOKIES:
Use ¼ cup cocoa and 1¾ cups all-purpose flour instead of the 2 cups all-purpose flour in the basic recipe.

PASTEL COOKIES:
Substitute ¼ cup fruit-flavored regular, non-diabetic gelatin for the ¼ cup sugar in the basic recipe.

Yields 30 cookies—15 servings

Nutritive Values Per Serving

CAL	CHO (g)	PRO (g)	TOTAL FAT (g)	SAT. FAT (g)	CHOL (mg)	FIBER (g)	NA (mg)
138	17	3	6	1	.7	.5	148

Food exchanges per serving: 1 starch, 1 fat (Exchanges remain the same for the variation of the basic recipe.)
Low-sodium diets: Use salt-free margarine and low-sodium baking powder.
Sugar content per serving: .8 teaspoon.

Oatmeal Cookies

Vera Wilson said that this cookie (with lots more sugar in it, of course) was one that she made ever since her oldest daughter Donna was just a baby. I like it especially well because it reminds me of the oatmeal cookies that my mother used to make when we were children. She also used to send them to me at college, and later to my sister and me when we were living in Chicago.

½ cup raisins
¾ cup boiling water
⅔ cup sugar
Dry sugar substitute equal to ½ cup sugar
1 cup (2 sticks) margarine at room
    temperature
½ cup liquid egg substitute at room
    temperature
1 teaspoon vanilla
2 cups all-purpose flour
1 teaspoon cinnamon
1 teaspoon baking powder
½ teaspoon baking soda
2 cups rolled oats or rolled wheat
½ cup chopped nuts

Combine raisins and boiling water and set aside to cool to room temperature.

Cream together sugar, sugar substitute, and margarine at medium speed until light and fluffy. Add egg substitute and vanilla to creamed mixture and mix at low speed for 1 minute.

Stir together flour, cinnamon, baking powder, and soda to blend well.

Add oats and nuts to creamed mixture along with flour mixture, raisins, and liquid in which raisins were soaked. Mix at medium speed until flour is moistened. Drop by 1½ tablespoon-fuls (level No. 40 dipper) onto cookie sheets that have been lined with aluminum foil or sprayed with pan spray. Press down lightly with fingers dipped in cold water to form circles about 2 inches across; bake at 375°F for 10–12 minutes. Remove from hot cookie sheet to wire rack to cool to room temperature. Serve 1 cookie per serving.

Yields 3 dozen cookies—36 servings

Nutritive Values Per Serving

CAL	CHO (g)	PRO (g)	TOTAL FAT (g)	SAT. FAT (g)	CHOL (mg)	FIBER (g)	NA (mg)
123	15	2	6	1	0	8	107

Food exchanges per serving: 1 starch, 1 fat
Low-sodium diets: Use salt-free margarine, low-sodium baking powder and unsalted nuts.
Sugar content per serving: .9 teaspoon.

Peanut Butter Cookies

This recipe from Frances Nielsen can be made with smooth peanut butter, but we prefer chunky.

½ cup chunky peanut butter at room
    temperature
⅓ cup (⅔ stick) margarine at room
    temperature
¼ cup dark molasses
2 teaspoons liquid sugar substitute
3 large egg whites at room temperature
1¼ cups all-purpose flour
½ teaspoon baking soda
⅛ teaspoon salt

Cream together peanut butter, margarine, molasses, and sugar substitute at medium speed until smooth. Add egg whites to creamed mixture and beat at medium speed until smooth.

Stir together flour, soda, and salt to blend and add to creamed mixture. Mix at medium speed until smooth. Drop by tablespoonfuls (level No. 60 dipper) onto a cookie sheet that has been lined with aluminum foil or sprayed with pan spray. Press down lightly with fingers dipped in cold water to form circles about 2 inches wide. Bake at 375°F for 10–12 minutes, or until lightly browned. Remove from hot cookie sheet to wire rack and cool to room temperature. Serve 2 cookies per serving.

Yields 30 cookies—15 servings

Nutritive Values Per Serving

CAL	CHO (g)	PRO (g)	TOTAL FAT (g)	SAT. FAT (g)	CHOL (mg)	FIBER (g)	NA (mg)
141	13	4	8	1.5	0	.8	163

Food exchanges per serving: 1 starch, 1½ fat
Low-sodium diets: Omit salt. Use salt-free peanut butter.
Sugar content per serving: .8 teaspoon.

Whole Wheat Spice Cookies

½ cup (1 stick) margarine at room
   temperature
½ cup brown sugar
2 teaspoons vanilla
Liquid sugar substitute equal to ⅓ cup sugar
3 large egg whites at room temperature
2 tablespoons water at room temperature
⅔ cup whole wheat flour
1⅓ cups all-purpose flour
½ teaspoon baking soda
½ teaspoon baking powder
¼ teaspoon salt
1 teaspoon cinnamon
½ teaspoon nutmeg
2 tablespoons dry buttermilk

Cream together margarine and sugar until light and fluffy. Add vanilla, sugar substitute, egg whites, and water to creamed mixture and mix 2 minutes at medium speed.

Stir together remaining dry ingredients to blend well. Add to creamed mixture and mix at low speed to blend. Roll on a lightly floured working surface to ¼-inch thickness. Cut with a 3-inch cookie cutter and place on cookie sheets that have been lined with aluminum foil or sprayed with pan spray. Bake at 350°F for 12–15 minutes, or until lightly browned. Remove from hot cookie sheet to wire rack and cool to room temperature. Serve 1 cookie per serving.

Yields 2 dozen cookies—24 servings

Nutritive Values Per Serving

CAL	CHO (g)	PRO (g)	TOTAL FAT (g)	SAT. FAT (g)	CHOL (mg)	FIBER (g)	NA (mg)
94	13	2	4	.7	trace	.6	116

Food exchanges per serving: 1 starch, 1 fat
Low-sodium diets: Omit salt. Use salt-free margarine and low-sodium baking
   powder.
Sugar content per serving: 1 teaspoon.

Hermits

These soft spice cookies are good with fruit for a snack or as dessert at a picnic.

1 teaspoon instant or freeze-dried coffee
½ cup very hot water
½ cup (1 stick) margarine at room
   temperature
½ cup brown sugar
Sugar substitute equal to ½ cup sugar
2 large egg whites at room temperature
2¼ cups all-purpose flour
2 tablespoons dry buttermilk
½ teaspoon baking powder
½ teaspoon baking soda
1 teaspoon cinnamon
½ teaspoon nutmeg
¼ teaspoon cloves
¼ cup raisins
¼ cup chopped walnuts

Combine coffee and water. Stir to mix well and set aside.

Combine margarine, brown sugar, and sugar substitute and cream at medium speed until light and fluffy. Add egg whites and mix well.

Stir flour, dry buttermilk, baking powder, soda, cinnamon, nutmeg, cloves, and raisins together to blend. Add to creamed mixture along with the nuts and the coffee mixture. Mix at medium speed to blend and then drop by 1½ tablespoonfuls (level No. 40 dipper) onto cookie sheets that have been sprayed with pan spray or lined with aluminum foil.

Bake at 375°F for 10–12 minutes or until firm. Remove from hot cookie sheets to wire rack to cool to room temperature. Serve 1 cookie per serving.

Yields 2 dozen cookies—24 servings

Nutritive Values Per Serving

CAL	CHO (g)	PRO (g)	TOTAL FAT (g)	SAT. FAT (g)	CHOL (mg)	FIBER (g)	NA (mg)
114	16	2	5	.7	trace	.5	106

Food exchanges per serving: 1 starch, 1 fat
Low-sodium diets: Use salt-free margarine and low-sodium baking powder.
Sugar content per serving: 1 teaspoon.

High-Fiber Cookies

These cookies, which provide 1.4 grams of dietary fiber each, aren't terribly sweet. We like them this way, but if you prefer them sweeter, you can add 1 tablespoon of Weight Watchers dry sugar substitute when you add the sugar without changing the nutritive values.

1 cup oat bran
1 cup rolled oats
1 cup Fiber One cereal
1 cup Kellogg's Bran Flakes
1 cup seedless raisins
1 cup chopped English walnuts
¾ cup sugar
¾ cup brown sugar
1 cup (2 sticks) margarine
2 large egg whites
2 teaspoons vanilla
2 cups all-purpose flour
1 teaspoon baking powder
1 teaspoon baking soda
½ teaspoon salt
½ cup water at room temperature

Place oat bran, rolled oats, Fiber One, Bran Flakes, raisins, and walnuts in a bowl. Mix lightly and set aside.

Place sugars and margarine in mixer bowl and mix at medium speed until light and fluffy. Add egg whites and vanilla and mix lightly, scraping down bowl before and after adding egg whites and vanilla.

In a separate bowl combine flour, baking powder, soda, and salt and mix at low speed about ½ minute to blend well. Add flour mixture and water to sugar mixture and mix at medium speed only until flour is moistened. Add bran mixture and mix at medium speed until well blended.

Drop by 1½ tablespoonfuls (level No. 40 dipper) onto a cookie sheet that has been sprayed with cooking spray or lined with aluminum foil. Bake at 375°F for 12–14 minutes or until lightly browned. Remove from oven and let sit for 1 minute. Remove cookies to a wire rack and cool to room temperature. Serve 1 cookie per serving.

Yields 4 dozen cookies—48 servings

Nutritive Values Per Serving

CAL	CHO (g)	PRO (g)	TOTAL FAT (g)	SAT. FAT (g)	CHOL (mg)	FIBER (g)	NA (mg)
121	17	2	6	.8	0	1.4	122

Food exchanges per serving: 1 starch, 1 fat
Low-sodium diets: Use salt-free margarine and low-sodium baking powder.
Sugar content per serving: 1.3 teaspoons.

Nut Slices

This recipe is based on one from Anita Kane of Shorewood, Wisconsin. We traded recipes frequently and hers were always good. I always felt safe giving away a copy of one of her recipes without testing it, because I knew she tested it thoroughly before giving it to me.

> ½ cup (1 stick) margarine at room
>   temperature
> 2 tablespoons sugar
> 4 large egg whites at room temperature
> Dry sugar substitute equal to ⅓ cup
>   sugar
> 1 teaspoon vanilla
> ½ teaspoon almond flavoring
> 2 cups all-purpose flour
> 1 teaspoon baking powder
> ½ teaspoon salt
> ½ cup chopped almonds

Cream together margarine and sugar until light and fluffy. Add egg whites, sugar substitute, vanilla, and almond flavoring to creamed mixture and mix at medium speed about 1 minute to blend. Add flour, baking powder, and salt to creamed mixture and mix at medium speed for 1 minute or until well blended.

Add almonds to dough. Turn out onto a lightly floured working surface and form into a roll about 2 inches wide and 12 inches long. Flatten the top of the roll, keeping it the same size, and place on a cookie sheet that has been lined with aluminum foil or sprayed with pan spray. Bake at 350°F for 25 minutes. Remove roll from hot cookie sheet onto a working surface. As soon as you can handle the roll, slice with a serrated knife into 24 slices about ½ inch thick. Place the slices flat on the cookie sheet and return to the 350°F oven. Bake 5 minutes on one side and then about the same on the other side. Remove from hot cookie sheet to a cooling rack and cool to room temperature. Serve 1 slice per serving.

Note: If another kind of nut is used other than almonds, use another flavoring instead of the almond flavoring. We use black walnuts in this area and I'm sure that everyone has their own favorites.

Yields 2 dozen cookies—24 servings

Nutritive Values Per Serving

CAL	CHO (g)	PRO (g)	TOTAL FAT (g)	SAT. FAT (g)	CHOL (mg)	FIBER (g)	NA (mg)
96	10	2	5	8	0	6	120

Food exchanges per serving: ⅔ starch, 1 fat
Low-sodium diets: Omit salt. Use salt-free margarine, low-sodium baking
   powder, and unsalted nuts.
Sugar content per serving: .3 teaspoon.

Mexican Wedding Cookies

These cookies are based on a recipe from Frances Nielsen. They freeze beautifully and look so nice when they are rolled in the Sprinkle Sweet.

1½ cups (3 sticks) margarine at room
    temperature
½ cup powdered sugar
2 teaspoons vanilla
Dry sugar substitute equal to ⅓ cup
    sugar
3 cups all-purpose flour
¾ cup chopped nuts
Sprinkle Sweet granulated sugar substitute
    as necessary

Cream together margarine and powdered sugar at medium speed until light and fluffy. Add vanilla, sugar substitute, and flour to creamed mixture and mix at medium speed about 2 minutes or until well blended.

Add nuts to dough and mix at low speed only until nuts are blended into the dough. Form dough into balls using 1½ table-spoons of dough for each ball. Bake on cookie sheets lined with aluminum foil or sprayed with pan spray at 350°F for about 20 minutes, or until lightly browned. Remove from heat.

Roll cookies in Sprinkle Sweet while they are warm but not hot.

Yields 3 dozen cookies—36 servings

Nutritive Values Per Serving

CAL	CHO (g)	PRO (g)	TOTAL FAT (g)	SAT. FAT (g)	CHOL (mg)	FIBER (g)	NA (mg)
129	10	2	9	1.4	0	trace	90

Food exchanges per serving: ⅔ starch, 2 fat
Low-sodium diets: Use salt-free margarine and unsalted nuts.
Sugar content per serving: .3 teaspoon.

Raisin Bars

This recipe is based on one from Vera Wilson. Her recipe is richer and is frosted, but I'm sure you will like this version, too.

⅓ cup raisins
1 cup water
¾ cup (1½ sticks) margarine at room
　temperature
¼ cup sugar
3 large egg whites at room temperature
Dry sugar substitute equal to ½ cup sugar
2¼ cups all-purpose flour
1 teaspoon baking soda
½ teaspoon salt
1 teaspoon cinnamon

Combine raisins and water in a small saucepan. Bring to a boil, cover, and remove from heat. Cool to room temperature.

Cream together margarine and sugar until light and fluffy. Add egg whites and sugar substitute to creamed mixture and mix at medium speed for 1 minute.

Stir together flour, soda, salt, and cinnamon to blend well. Add to creamed mixture along with the raisins and the liquid in which they were cooked. Mix at medium speed about 1 minute or until well blended. Spread evenly in a 9" × 13" cake pan that has been well greased with margarine. Bake at 350°F for 25–30 minutes or until browned and the bars pull away from the sides of the pan. Cut 4 × 5 to yield 20 squares. Serve 1 square per serving.

Yields 20 squares—20 servings

Nutritive Values Per Serving

CAL	CHO (g)	PRO (g)	TOTAL FAT (g)	SAT. FAT (g)	CHOL (mg)	FIBER (g)	NA (mg)
134	15	2	7	1.2	0	.5	209

Food exchanges per serving: 1 starch, 1 fat
Low-sodium diets: Omit salt and use salt-free margarine.
Sugar content per serving: .6 teaspoon.

Applesauce Bran Squares

This recipe is based on one from Betty Jane Walter of Jackson, Michigan. Betty Jane is a dietary consultant as well as a diabetic and we often discuss our work as well as our favorite recipes. She has been very active in the American Heart Association program in her area and is concerned about low-cholesterol diets as well as diabetic diets.

1 cup all-purpose flour
⅔ cup Bran Buds, All Bran, or 100% Bran
½ cup rolled oats
⅓ cup brown sugar
½ teaspoon salt
½ teaspoon baking soda
1 teaspoon baking powder
1 teaspoon cinnamon
¼ cup teaspoon ground cloves or nutmeg
½ cup (1 stick) margarine at room
   temperature
2 large egg whites at room temperature
1 teaspoon vanilla
Dry sugar substitute equal to ½ cup
   sugar
⅓ cup chopped nuts
1 cup unsweetened applesauce at room
   temperature

Place dry ingredients in mixer bowl and mix at low speed for 1 minute.

Add margarine, egg whites, vanilla, sugar substitute, nuts, and applesauce to flour mixture and mix at medium speed for ½ minute or until blended. Spread evenly in a 9″ × 13″ cake pan that has been greased with margarine or sprayed with pan spray. Bake at 375°F for 25–30 minutes or until browned and it starts to pull away from the sides of the pan. Cut 3 × 5 into 15 squares and serve warm or at room temperature. Serve 1 square per serving.

Yields 15 squares—15 servings

Nutritive Values Per Serving

CAL	CHO (g)	PRO (g)	TOTAL FAT (g)	SAT. FAT (g)	CHOL (mg)	FIBER (g)	NA (mg)
153	18	3	8	1.2	0	1.9	255

Food exchanges per serving: 1 starch, 1½ fat
Low-sodium diets: Omit salt. Use salt-free margarine, low-sodium baking powder, and unsalted nuts.
Sugar content per serving: 1.1 teaspoons.

18

Beverages

A good hot beverage or a well-chilled sugar-free soft drink can be a real lift when you are hot and tired—or cold and tired, too, for that matter. Beverages are such a part of our lives that we need to know what we can enjoy without going off our diet when we want something to drink. I used to hate those sugar-free soft drinks that were available, but now that they are sweetened with NutraSweet I find that I really enjoy them.

It is also nice to have beverages you can serve for parties or when friends drop in. I make my own low-calorie cocoa mix that I think is extra special. A friend of mine who was counting her calories asked for some of it the other day, and she told me she liked it even better than the regular commercial kind I had given our husbands. She took my recipe home with her and said she was going to make it up for herself to enjoy when she needed a pickup or had guests.

When you go to a party, and it seems like food and socializing always go together, you can always walk around with a cup of black coffee or a glass of iced tea or sugar-free soft drink and have just as much fun as anyone else.

If you are home alone and hungry or thirsty and don't want to spend any more of your exchanges, you can have a twist of lemon in ice water (which is one of my favorites), or a cup of hot bouillon or tomato juice with a twist of lemon in it. When I was visiting Bud and Frances Gunsallus in Miami, I discovered that half of a lime from the tree in their backyard put a lot of life into a glass of ice water or sugar-free 7-Up.

In other words, use what is available in the line of sugarless beverages and have just as much fun as everyone else at the party—or get a real lift when you are tired and just need a pickup.

Sparkling Punch

The first time I talked to Mary Agnes Jones and the other dietitians at Holy Cross Hospital in Chicago about this book, they told me that one thing that was high on the list of recipes they needed was a punch that would be free for diabetics. I think this answers that need very well. It's not only free, it's also delicious.

> **2 .14- or .20-ounce packets of Wyler's unsweetened flavored soft drink mix or Kool-Aid unsweetened soft drink mix (2-quart size)**
> **1 quart water**
> **3 quarts chilled sugar-free 7-Up or sugar-free ginger ale**

Dissolve drink mix in water and refrigerate until needed. Place in punch bowl along with a chunk of ice.

Add 7-Up or ginger ale to drink mix in bowl. Mix lightly and serve a 4-ounce cup per serving.

I like to freeze some of the drink mix (which has been prepared with water according to directions on the package) in a bowl or plastic container to be used instead of ice in the punch bowl. This keeps the punch from being diluted as the ice melts. To add a special touch, you can add a few grapes or strawberries in with the mix you are freezing.

Yields 1 gallon—32 4-ounce cups

Nutritive Values Per Serving

CAL	CHO (g)	PRO (g)	TOTAL FAT (g)	SAT. FAT (g)	CHOL (mg)	FIBER (g)	NA (mg)
1	0	0	0	0	0	0	25

Food exchanges per serving: None
Low-sodium diets: May be used as written.
Sugar content per serving: None.

Hot Spiced Tea

This recipe is from Edith Robinson, a dietitian from Decatur, Georgia. Edith and I worked together at the Army Food Service Center in Chicago. She told me that she got the recipe from our commanding officer Colonel Cozad's wife, who served it one cold day when she and Colonel Cozad entertained the members of the department at their home.

> **12 cups water**
> **1 teaspoon whole cloves**
> **4 sticks cinnamon**
> **6 tea bags**
> **¼ cup lemon juice**
> **1 cup unsweetened pineapple juice**
> **1½ cups unsweetened orange juice**
> **Sugar substitute equal to ¾ cup sugar**

Combine water, cloves, and cinnamon and simmer, covered, for 5 minutes. Remove from heat. Add tea bags to hot liquid and steep for 5 minutes. Remove tea bags and spices.

Add juices to tea and mix lightly. Tea may be cooled to room temperature and refrigerated overnight at this stage, if desired. If tea is refrigerated, it should be reheated before it is served.

Add sugar substitute just before tea is served. Taste for flavor and add a little more lemon juice or sugar substitute, if desired. Serve 1 4-ounce punch cup per serving.

Yields 15 cups—30 servings

Nutritive Values Per Serving

CAL	CHO (g)	PRO (g)	TOTAL FAT (g)	SAT. FAT (g)	CHOL (mg)	FIBER (g)	NA (mg)
14	4	trace	trace	0	0	trace	22

Food exchanges per serving: ¼ fruit
Low-sodium diets: May be used as written.
Sugar content per serving: None.

Hot Cocoa Mix

¾ cup cocoa
½ teaspoon salt
1 quart instant nonfat dry milk
Dry sugar substitute equal to 1–1½ cups
    sugar

Mix ingredients well and store in an airtight container in a moderately cool place. Use 2 tablespoons mix plus 6 ounces boiling water for 1 6-ounce serving of cocoa.

Variations:
MEXICAN COCOA:

Add 2–3 teaspoons ground cinnamon when mixing the total ingredients; or place a scant ⅛ teaspoon of cinnamon in a cup, 2 tablespoons of the mix, and 6 ounces boiling water for 1 serving.

MOCHA:

Add ⅓ cup instant coffee when mixing the total ingredients; or place ½ teaspoon instant coffee in a cup, 2 tablespoons of the mix, and 6 ounces boiling water for 1 serving.

Yields mix for 32 6-ounce cups of cocoa

Nutritive Values Per Serving

CAL	CHO (g)	PRO (g)	TOTAL FAT (g)	SAT. FAT (g)	CHOL (mg)	FIBER (g)	NA (mg)
39	6	3	trace	trace	2	.6	109

Food exchanges per serving: ½ skim milk (Exchanges remain the same for the variation of the basic recipe.)
Low-sodium diets: Omit salt.
Sugar content per serving: None.

Chocolate Milk Shake

This recipe from Patti Dillon, our Fayette County home economics extension agent, is cool and refreshing and costs a lot less in calories and exchanges than you would expect.

> **1 cup skim milk**
> **2 teaspoons cocoa**
> **1 1-gram packet Equal (aspartame) sugar**
> **substitute**
> **3 or 4 ice cubes**

Place ingredients in blender or food processor and beat at high speed until frothy and thickened. Serve immediately. Total amount is 1 serving.

Yields 1 milk shake

Nutritive Values Per Serving

CAL	CHO (g)	PRO (g)	TOTAL FAT (g)	SAT. FAT (g)	CHOL (mg)	FIBER (g)	NA (mg)
98	14	10	1	.6	5	1	128

Food exchanges per serving: 1 skim milk
Low-sodium diets: May be used as written.
Sugar content per serving: None.

Chocolate Liqueur

I like to sprinkle a couple of tablespoons of this over a chocolate cake before I cut it and put the topping on it. It adds a certain something to the cake without increasing the food value very much. In fact, 3 tablespoons on one cake doesn't need to be counted since the amount per portion is so small. Gail Olson of Volga City, Iowa, gave me this recipe and the one following. They are both good over ice milk or served with an after-dinner drink.

> 2 cups vodka
> 1½ cups water
> 1½ cups Brown Sugar Twin sugar
>   substitute
> 4 ounces chocolate extract
> 2 teaspoons vanilla
> ½ teaspoon peppermint extract (optional)

Combine ingredients and pour into a dark-colored glass bottle. Let stand for 2 weeks before it is used. Store as you would any liqueur. Consider 1 ounce (2 tablespoons) per serving when calculating nutritional values.

Yields 1 quart—32 1-ounce servings

Nutritive Values Per Serving

CAL	CHO (g)	PRO (g)	TOTAL FAT (g)	SAT. FAT (g)	CHOL (mg)	FIBER (g)	NA (mg)
48	2	0	0	0	0	0	trace

Food exchanges per serving: ¾ other carbohydrate
Low-sodium diets: May be used as written.
Sugar content per serving: None.

Orange Liqueur

Frances Nielsen taught me to appreciate the flavor of fruit and orange liqueur combined together, using about 1 tablespoon orange liqueur per serving of fruit. I had given that up because of the high carbohydrate content of liqueurs until Gail Olson of Volga City, Iowa, gave me this recipe. They are both good over ice milk or served as an after-dinner drink, and this one is marvelous with fruit.

> **2 cups water**
> **Thin peel from 2 large oranges**
> **2 teaspoons vanilla**
> **1 teaspoon lemon flavoring**
> **2 teaspoons orange flavoring**
> **1 drop yellow food color**
> **1 drop orange food color**
> **2 cups vodka**
> **Sugar substitute equal to ½ cup sugar**

Combine water and orange peel and simmer, covered, over low heat for 5 minutes. Cool to room temperature.

Add remaining ingredients to simmered mixture. Pour into a glass or stainless steel container. Cover and keep in a dark place for 2 weeks. Strain and discard any solids. Pour into a dark glass bottle and store as you would any liqueur. Consider 1 ounce (2 tablespoons) per serving when calculating nutritional values.

Yields 1 quart—32 1-ounce servings

Nutritive Values Per Serving

CAL	CHO (g)	PRO (g)	TOTAL FAT (g)	SAT. FAT (g)	CHOL (mg)	FIBER (g)	NA (mg)
38	1	trace	0	0	0	0	11

Food exchanges per serving: ⅔ other carbohydrate
Low-sodium diets: May be used as written.
Sugar content per serving: None.

19

Canning and Freezing Foods

If you have been canning and freezing fruits and vegetables, don't stop now. This is a good time to take advantage of your expertise to save yourself some money. Canning for the low-cholesterol, diabetic diet is no more complicated than any other kind of canning. You can can your fruits in a light or very light syrup as well as any commercial canner.

Sugar helps develop the flavor and color of canned fruits—so now that we can use small amounts of sugar in our diets (see Chapter 3), we can can fruits every bit as flavorful and tasty as any product on the market. I have always enjoyed seeing rows of canned fruits, vegetables, and pickles on my shelves and now I can continue to do so.

When we are canning fruits and vegetables for the low-cholesterol, diabetic diet, we need only worry about the diabetic part of the diet. The only canned item I can think of which includes cholesterol is mincemeat which is made with suet. You can manage that by canning mincemeat without suet and adding some margarine to the mincemeat when you are ready to use it. (You can add ¼ cup sugar per quart of mincemeat, providing 1½ teaspoons of sugar per ½ cup, when you are canning it and then add sugar substitute to taste when you use it.)

We can buy or can fruits in unsweetened fruit juice. (Count the fruit juice when you use it as a fruit exchange according to the kind and amount you use.) Fruit can also be canned using very light syrup, light syrup, medium and heavy syrup. I'm sure you know we should use very light syrup and add sugar substitute when we use it if we like it sweeter. To make the syrup, heat water and sugar together until the sugar is dissolved, skimming off any foam that rises to the top of the liquid. Processing time for fruit is the same whether heavy or light syrup or fruit juice is used. Canning fruit in a very light syrup will add about 1 teaspoon of sugar per ½ cup serving, which is acceptable. One half cup fruit and juice canned in very light syrup is 1 fruit exchange. Here are the proportions for preparing the syrup.

Very light syrup for 9 pints or 4 quarts of fruit
6½ cups water
¾ cup sugar

Organisms that cause food spoilage, molds, yeast, and bacteria, are present in the air, water, and soil. Enzymes that cause deterioration are always present in the fruit. Canning destroys the organisms that cause spoilage and inactivates the enzymes. Because fruits are high in acid they can be safely processed in a boiling-water canner or pressure cooker.

Choose fresh, firm, high-quality fruit. Wash all fruits thoroughly under running water or use several changes of water. Lift the food out of the water each time so dirt that has been washed off the fruit will not settle back on the fruit. Do not let fruits soak because they will lose flavor and nutritive value. Handle fruit gently to avoid bruising, and process fresh foods as soon as possible to avoid spoilage.

The amount of canned food from a given amount of fresh fruit will depend upon the quality, condition, variety, maturity, and size of the fruit, the size of the pieces packed, and whether the fruit is packed hot or raw. The amount of fresh fruit generally needed for 1 quart of canned fruit is as follows: 2 to 3 pounds apples, cherries, nectarines, peaches, or pears; 2 pounds apricots; 1 to 3 pounds berries; 2 pounds grapefruit or oranges; and 1 to 2 pounds plums.

Light-colored fruits, especially apples, apricots, peaches, and pears, darken when cut and exposed to air. This can be prevented by pretreating the fruit with an ascorbic acid solution. Keep the fruit in this solution until it is ready to be canned. The fruit should be drained well before it is placed in the jars. Ascorbic acid is available in several forms under various names. Look for it among the canning supplies in the grocery store or supermarket. (I also use it to keep fruit looking good when I'm making fruit salads.)

Use only jars and lids made especially for canning. Mayonnaise jars and others that may look as if they could be used for canning should not be used because they are not made of the same quality glass, may break during processing, and are not made for use with the two-piece canning lids. These guidelines also apply when you are making jellies and jams. Throw away all those odd-shaped jars and get some meant for canning to avoid risk of breakage or spoilage.

Most people prefer to use the hot-pack method for canning fruit. To hot pack fruit, preheat fruit in a small amount of hot syrup, juice, or water. Pack into hot jars and cover with hot liquid. Wipe the rims of the jars, tighten the lids, and process according to instructions. Cold packing is also approved and may be used if desired. To cold pack fruit, pack the raw fruit in jars, add boiling hot syrup, juice, or water to cover the fruit, wipe the rims, tighten the lids, and process according to instructions. Always make sure you have covered the fruit with liquid because any fruit not covered will darken. In either case, process in a hot-water bath according to the time required for that particular fruit. Plan on ½ to 1½ cups liquid per quart.

The space between the fruit and liquid and the jar lid is called headspace. Generally speaking, you should allow ½ inch headspace for fruits and ¼ inch headspace for fruit juices and purées. It's a good idea to run a spatula down the side of the jar to remove any air bubbles.

To use a boiling-water canner, fill the canner halfway with water and preheat to 140°F for cold pack or 180°F for hot pack. Put sealed jars in the water, making sure the water can circulate freely around the jars. Add boiling water so that the water is 1 to 2 inches above the tops of the jars. Bring the water in the canner to a vigorous boil, adjust the heat to maintain a gentle boil, and cover. Keep the water boiling during the entire processing time (never reduce the specified boiling time), keeping the water at least 1 inch above the tops of the jars (keep the lid on the canner). Remove the jars from the canner and place them upright on folded towels or a rack. Allow them to cool away from drafts for 12 to 24 hours. Do not tighten the lids. To test the seals, press the center of the lids. If the lid is down and doesn't move, the jar is sealed. Remove the screw bands carefully after the jars are cool. Wash the jars, if necessary, dry, label, and store them in a cool, dark place. If any of the jars haven't sealed, put them in the refrigerator and use them within a few days. Fruit can be placed in another jar and reprocessed but the flavor is never as good after the second processing. Canned fruit is safe as long as the jar remains sealed. Never use fruits that show mold or if the jar leaks liquid.

To use a pressure canner, partially fill the canner with 2 to 3 inches of water. Place a jar rack in the canner, put the jars on the rack, fasten the lid, and turn the heat on high. After the steam exhausts for 10 minutes, add weighted gauge or close the petcock. Allow the canner to reach the designated pressure. Start timing when the designated pressure is reached. Regulate heat to maintain a uniform pressure. Process for the recommended time. (Do not reduce the processing time.) When the processing time is ended, remove the pressure cooker from the heat. Let the canner cool at room temperature until the canner is fully depressurized, which will probably take from 30 to 60 minutes depending upon the type of canner. Do not try to reduce the time of cooling by setting the canner in cold water or by running cold water over the canner. Never attempt to hasten the pressure reduction by lifting the weight or opening the vent. When the pressure is reduced, carefully open the petcock or remove the weighted gauge. Wait 2 minutes and then slowly release and remove the canner lid. After the jars are removed from the canner, set them upright on a rack or folded cloth away from drafts. Do not tighten the screw bands. Allow jars to cool for 12 to 24 hours and then check to be sure that all of the jars are sealed correctly. If they aren't sealed correctly, refrigerate them and use the fruit within a few days. The fruit can be canned again but then it is not as good the second time. To test the seal, press the center of the lid. If the lid is down and doesn't move, the jar is sealed. It is best to keep your canned fruit in a cool, dark place. Canned fruit is safe as long as the jar is sealed, but never use canned fruit that is leaking or that shows any sign of mold.

There has been so much research in the last few years on the best methods to be used for canning that I thought I'd better consult some authorities regarding the correct procedures for successful canning. I started by calling Fran Passmore from the Iowa State University Extension Service. She is our local family specialist. She gave me quite a bit of information and suggested I consult the U.S. Department of Agriculture (USDA) Information Bulletin No. 539, *Complete Guide to Home Canning*. It is a wonderfully explicit and helpful bulletin. If you'd like to consult it, I'm sure you could get a copy of it from your local extension office or from the U.S. Department of Agriculture.

I want to stress to you that canning food safely at home is not difficult, but it does require you to follow specific directions exactly. Always use tested recipes and directions from a reliable source. Ignoring the recommended procedures can result in loss of your canned goods and sickness for your family. However you have a lot to gain if you do some canning and I urge you to try it. The rewards can be great.

Recommended Processing Time for Fruit in a Boiling-Water Canner

Fruit	Pack	Jar Size	Minutes of Processing at Altitudes (ft.)			
			0–1,000	1,001–3,000	3,001–6,000	Over 6,000
Apples	Hot	Pints or quarts	20	25	30	35
Apple juice	Hot	Pints or quarts	5*	10	10	15
		Half gallons	10	15	15	20
Applesauce	Hot	Pints	15	20	20	25
		Quarts	20	25	30	35
Berries	Hot	Pints or quarts	15	20	20	25
	Raw	Pints	15	20	20	25
		Quarts	20	25	30	35
Cherries	Hot	Pints	15	20	20	25
		Quarts	20	25	30	35
	Raw	Pints or quarts	25	30	35	40
Fruit cocktail	Raw	Half or full pints	20	25	30	35
Fruit purées	Hot	Pints or quarts	15	20	20	25
Grapefruit and orange sections	Raw	Pints or quarts	10	15	15	20
Grape juice	Hot	Pints or quarts	5*	10	10	15
		Half gallons	10	15	15	20

Peaches, apricots, or nectarines	Hot	Pints	20	25	30	35
		Quarts	25	30	35	40
	Raw	Pints	25	30	35	40
		Quarts	30	35	40	45
Pears	Hot	Pints	20	25	30	35
		Quarts	25	30	35	40
Plums	Hot or raw	Pints	20	25	30	35
		Quarts	25	30	35	40

*Foods processed under 10 minutes must be canned in sterile jars. Washing the jars is not sufficient. They should be washed well with hot soapy water, rinsed, and then immersed in boiling water for 11 minutes.

Processing Time for Some Acid Foods in a Dial-Gauge Pressure Canner

Type of Fruit	Pack	Jar Size	Process Time (Min.)	Canner Pressure (PSI) at Altitudes (ft.)			
				0–2,000 6 lb.	2,001–4,000 7 lb.	4,001–6,000 8 lb.	6,001–8,000 9 lb.
Applesauce	Hot	Pints	8	6	7	8	9
		Quarts	10	6	7	8	9
Apples, sliced	Hot	Pints or quarts	8	6	7	8	9
Berries, whole	Hot	Pints or quarts	8	6	7	8	9
	Hot	Pints	8	6	7	8	9
	Raw	Quarts	10	6	7	8	9
Cherries, sour or sweet	Hot	Pints	8	6	7	8	9
		Quarts	10	6	7	8	9
	Raw	Pints or quarts	10	6	7	8	9
Fruit purées	Hot	Pints or quarts	8	6	7	8	9
Grapefruit and orange sections	Hot	Pints or quarts	8	6	7	8	9
	Raw	Pints or quarts	10	6	7	8	9
Nectarines, apricots, or peaches	Hot or raw	Pints or quarts	10	6	7	8	9
Pears	Hot	Pints or quarts	10	6	7	8	9
Plums	Hot or raw	Pints or quarts	10	6	7	8	9
Rhubarb	Hot	Pints or quarts	8	6	7	8	9

Processing Time for Some Acid Foods in a Weighted-Gauge Pressure Cooker

Type of Fruit	Pack	Jar Size	Process Time (Min.)	Canner Pressure (PSI) at Altitudes (ft.)	
				0–1,000 5 lb.	Above 1,000 10 lb.
Applesauce	Hot	Pints	8	5	10
		Quarts	10	5	10
Apples, sliced	Hot	Pints or quarts	8	5	10
Berries, whole	Hot	Pints or quarts	8	5	10
	Raw	Pints	8	5	10
		Quarts	10	5	10
Cherries, sour or sweet	Hot	Pints	8	5	10
		Quarts	10	5	10
	Raw	Pints or quarts	10	5	10
Fruit purées	Hot	Pints or quarts	8	5	10
Grapefruit and orange sections	Hot	Pints or quarts	8	5	10
	Raw	Pints	8	5	10
		Quarts	10	5	10
Nectarines, peaches, or apricots	Hot or raw	Pints or quarts	10	5	10
Pears	Hot	Pints or quarts	10	5	10
Plums	Hot or raw	Pints or quarts	10	5	10
Rhubarb	Raw	Pints or quarts	8	5	10

There is little difference, nutritionally, between vegetables canned at home and vegetables purchased already canned. Several large packers are now offering low-sodium canned foods available to us so it is no longer as difficult to follow a low-sodium diet using canned vegetables. If you want to can low-sodium vegetables at home, prepare and process them according to directions, without adding any salt. They will keep as well as vegetables canned with salt.

It is important that you use the latest information when you are canning vegetables since research has shown that it is better to process foods for longer periods of time than we used to think was necessary. Vegetables, except for tomatoes, should always be canned in a pressure canner. Information on that process is available from the makers of pressure canners, your county extension agent, the library, the makers of canning jars, and numerous other publications.

The only food that needs salt when it is being prepared for canning is pickles. The pickles don't need salt for preservation but for drawing the liquid out of the vegetables to be pickled so it can be replaced by the vinegar-sugar solution that makes them crisp and flavorful. There are some recipes for making pickles without salt but they must be kept refrigerated or frozen and cannot be canned.

You can make pickles without sugar, if you like. In fact, there are some brands of pickles now available that are sugar-free, and they are very good. Dill pickles are made without sugar and are readily available, but I prefer a sweet pickle. Now that we can have some sugar in our diets, I worked on making sweet pickles and developed a couple of recipes I like well enough to include them at the end of this chapter.

Freezing fruits and vegetables is often faster and easier than canning. We generally think of fruits frozen with sugar but they can also be frozen without sugar. I like to IQF (Individually Quick Frozen) them. In order to do that, I clean the fruits, blot them dry with a paper towel, and spread them on a cookie sheet lined with aluminum foil or wax paper. I put them in the freezer, uncovered, until they are frozen and then put them in a freezer bag, label them, and return them to the freezer until I need them. I remember one time I was visiting Frances Lee, who was head of the Army's test kitchen at that time. We were talking about some fruit we had IQF'd (if there is such a word) and her husband Tom asked us what that meant and said dietitians had a language all their own. Strawberries, blueberries, gooseberries, currants, and rhubarb all respond well to being individually frozen. Of course all of these fruits except cranberries should be washed before they are frozen.

I also like to cook cranberries, rhubarb, and applesauce without sugar, freeze them in containers and then add sugar substitute when I'm ready to serve them. I love those frozen fruits during the winter when fresh fruit is not always all that good and available.

Squeeze as much air as possible out of the freezer bags before storage. Leave ½-inch headspace for expansion in rigid containers. Fruit should be stored at 0°F or colder and used within 8 to 12 months for best quality. Partially defrosted fruits taste best to me although they should generally be defrosted for use in salad or dessert. Fruit can be defrosted in the container in the refrigerator although it can also be defrosted by submerging the container in water. Once again, consult the authorities if you have questions about proper procedures.

Mrs. Riley's Pickles

This recipe is based on that old standby, 14-day pickles. We call them Mrs. Riley's pickles because my cousin Virginia Ballantine's grandmother, Mrs. Riley, used to make them every year.

Make only enough for one year because they are wonderful the first year—sweet, spicy, and crisp—they lose some of their quality the second year.

2½ quarts vinegar
2 cups sugar
2 tablespoons celery seed
1 ounce stick cinnamon
10 drops green or red vegetable coloring (optional)
2 gallons washed and sliced medium-size firm cucumbers with the ends removed
1 gallon boiling water
2 cups pickling salt
1 gallon boiling water (day 7)
1 gallon boiling water (day 9)
1 tablespoon alum
1 gallon boiling water (day 10)
Sugar substitute equal to 1½ cups sugar

Heat together vinegar, sugar, celery seed, cinnamon, and vegetable coloring. Cool to room temperature and return to the vinegar container. Cover tightly and let stand until needed. (I like to use some coloring because it enhances the color of the pickles and makes them look more like the commercial sweet pickle slices. I sometimes make a red batch for gifts and to use on relish trays on special occasions.)

Place cucumbers in empty glass gallon jars, stainless-steel pots, or crocks. Dissolve pickling salt in 1 gallon boiling water and then pour over cucumbers. Let stand, covered loosely, for 1 week. Remove any mold on top of the cucumbers at the end of 7 days.

On the seventh day, drain pickles well. Pour 1 gallon boiling water over them and let them stand, covered loosely, for 2 days.

On the ninth day, drain cucumbers well. Dissolve the alum in 1 gallon boiling water and pour over cucumbers.

On the tenth day, drain pickles well and cover with 1 gallon boiling water. On the eleventh day, drain cucumbers well and pack into 7 quart or 14 pint sterilized jars.

Strain the reserved vinegar mixture. Throw away the spices and heat the vinegar. Add sugar substitute and pour over the sliced cucumbers in the jars. (Do not use Equal [aspartame] since it is not stable to heat.) Cover and seal the jars.* Serve 2 tablespoons per serving.

Yields 7 quarts or 14 pints

Nutritive Values Per Serving

CAL	CHO (g)	PRO (g)	TOTAL FAT (g)	SAT. FAT (g)	CHOL (mg)	FIBER (g)	NA (mg)
10	3	trace	0	0	0	trace	292

Food exchanges per serving: 2 tablespoons are free, ¼ cup is 1 vegetable
Low-sodium diets: This recipe is not suitable.
Sugar content per serving: .4 teaspoon.

*Recommended Processing Time in a Boiling-Water Canner

Minutes of Processing at Altitudes (ft.)

Pack	Jar Size	0–1,000	1,001–6,000	Above 6,000
Raw	Pints	5	10	15
	Quarts	10	15	20

Zucchini Pickles

There are so many zucchini around that I thought I'd try to make some pickles from them. I used the recipe that I always use for bread-and-butter pickles and it really worked well. Everyone liked them very much.

> **1 gallon thinly sliced 6- to 8-inch-long zucchini**
> **4 cups sliced white onions**
> **½ cup salt**
> **2 quarts cracked ice**
> **5 cups cider vinegar**
> **3 cups water**
> **1½ teaspoons turmeric**
> **1 teaspoon celery seed**
> **1 tablespoon mustard seed**
> **Sugar substitute to taste**

Combine zucchini, onions, salt, and ice in a large bowl and mix well. Cover with a plate with a weight on top of it so that all of the zucchini slices are covered with the salted ice water formed as the ice melts. Let them stand for 3 hours and then drain them well. Place in a large saucepan.

Thoroughly mix vinegar, water, turmeric, celery seed, and mustard seed and add to zucchini. Bring almost to a boil but do not let mixture boil, stirring frequently with a wooden spoon. Pack the hot pickles in pint jars.

Add sugar substitute to taste to the hot liquid. I use about ¼ cup of liquid sugar substitute, but you may prefer them a little sweeter or even a little less sweet. (Do not use Equal [aspartame] to sweeten the pickles because it is not stable to heat and the pickles are processed in a hot water bath.) Pour the hot liquid over the pickles to about ½ inch from the top. Cover and seal.* Serve 2 tablespoons pickles per serving.

5 pints—80 servings

*See Recommended Processing Time chart on page opposite.

Nutritive Values Per Serving

CAL	CHO (g)	PRO (g)	TOTAL FAT (g)	SAT. FAT (g)	CHOL (mg)	FIBER (g)	NA (mg)
10	2	trace	trace	0	0	trace	84

Food exchanges per serving: 2 tablespoons are free, ¼ cup is 1 vegetable
Low-sodium diets: This recipe is not suitable.
Sugar content per serving: None.

Recommended Processing Time in a Boiling-Water Canner

		Minutes of Processing at Altitudes (ft.)		
Pack	**Jar Size**	**0–1,000**	**1,001–6,000**	**Above 6,000**
Raw	Pints or quarts	10	15	20

Frozen Sliced Sweet Dill Pickles

1 pound 3-inch unwaxed cucumbers
2 cups packed, sliced yellow onions
4 teaspoons salt
2 tablespoons water
¼ cup sugar
1 tablespoon Weight Watchers dry sugar
  substitute
½ cup white vinegar
¼ cup garlic wine vinegar
1 tablespoon dry dill weed

Wash cucumbers and slice them about ⅛ inch thick. Place cucumbers, onions, salt, and water in a 2-quart glass or stainless-steel bowl (don't use aluminum) and let stand for 2 hours at room temperature or overnight in the refrigerator. Drain cucumbers and onions, but do not rinse.

Combine sugar, sugar substitute, vinegars, and dill weed. Stir until sugar is dissolved and then add vegetables. The liquid should cover vegetables. Cover and refrigerate 2 hours.

Pack pickles lightly in jars or plastic containers, leaving 1 inch at top for expansion. Seal tightly and freeze. The pickles may be kept in the freezer for 6 months. Use within 3 or 4 days after defrosting. Two days of freezing is enough if you want to use them right away. Use ¼ cup per serving.

1 quart—16 servings

Nutritive Values Per Serving

CAL	CHO (g)	PRO (g)	TOTAL FAT (g)	SAT. FAT (g)	CHOL (mg)	FIBER (g)	NA (mg)
29	7	trace	0	0	0	trace	167

Food exchanges per serving: 1 vegetable
Low-sodium diets: Rinse pickles after they are drained before vinegar is
  added.
Sugar content per serving: .8 teaspoon.

20

Glossary

There are some words and phrases used in a discussion of diabetes that are important for you to understand when discussing your diabetes and its treatment with health professionals.

The new *Exchange Lists* for meal planning contain an excellent glossary so I decided to add the information in that publication to this revision. I hope they will help you to cope with your diabetes and its treatment.

Alcohol—An ingredient in a variety of beverages, including beer, wine, liqueurs, cordials, and mixed straight drinks. Pure alcohol itself yields about 7 calories per gram.

Calories—A unit used in expressing the heat or energy value of food. Calories come from carbohydrate, protein, fat, and alcohol.

Carbohydrate—One of the three major energy sources in foods. The most common carbohydrates are sugars and starches. Carbohydrates yield about 4 calories per gram. Carbohydrates are found in foods from the milk, vegetable, fruit, and starch exchange lists.

Certified Diabetes Educator (CDE)—Health educators who specialize in diabetes and have passed the Certification Examination for Diabetes Educators are certified by the American Association of Diabetes Educators. These educators stay up to date on diabetes care and can help you with your diabetes management.

Cholesterol—A fat-like substance normally found in blood. A high level of cholesterol in the blood has been shown to be a

major risk factor for developing heart disease. Dietary cholesterol is found in all animal products, but is especially high in
egg yolks and organ meats. Eating foods high in dietary cholesterol and saturated fat tends to raise the level of blood cholesterol. Foods of plant origin such as fruits, vegetables, grains,
and dried beans and peas contain no cholesterol. Cholesterol is
found in foods from the milk, meat, and fat exchange lists.

Dietitian—A registered dietitian (RD) is recognized by the
medical profession as the primary provider of nutritional care,
education, and counseling. The initials RD after a dietitian's
name ensure that he or she has met the standards of the American Dietetic Association. Look for those credentials when you
seek advice on nutrition.

Exchanges—Foods grouped together on a list according to
similarities in food. Measured amounts of foods within the
group may be exchanged or traded in planning meals.

Fat—One of the three major energy sources in food. A concentrated source of calories— about 9 calories per gram. Fat is
found in foods from the fat and meat lists. Some kinds of milk
also have fat; some foods from the starch list also contain fat.

Saturated fat—Type of fat that tends to raise blood cholesterol levels. It comes primarily from animals and is usually
hard at room temperature. Examples of saturated fat are butter, lard, meat fat, solid shortening, palm oil, and coconut oil.

Polyunsaturated fat—Type of fat that is usually liquid at
room temperature and is found in vegetable oils. Safflower, sunflower, corn, and soybean oils contain the highest amount of
polyunsaturated fats. Polyunsaturated fats such as corn oil can
help lower high blood cholesterol levels when they are part of a
healthful diet.

Monounsaturated fat—Type of fat that is liquid at room
temperature and is found in vegetable oils, such as canola and
olive oils. Monounsaturated fats can help lower high blood cholesterol levels when they are part of a lower-fat diet.

Fiber—An indigestible part of certain foods. Fiber is important in the diet as roughage or bulk. Fiber is found in foods from
the starch, vegetable, and fruit exchange lists.

Glucose—A simple sugar, the main source of energy in the
body. Insulin helps utilize glucose for energy, so if you lack

insulin, glucose remains in the bloodstream and you will have a high glucose count.

Glycosylated hemoglobin test—A test that shows your average blood sugar levels during the past 8 to 10 weeks. This test is done in the doctor's office or a laboratory.

Gram—A unit of mass and weight in the metric system. An ounce is about 30 grams.

Hyperglycemia—High glucose levels. Symptoms include fatigue, excessive thirst, and frequent urination. Mild to moderate hyperglycemia over a period of time may be the cause of many diabetic complications.

Hypoglycemia—Low blood sugar levels. Symptoms may include dizziness, irritability, and loss of consciousness. It may come on slowly or quickly and can be very serious if it is not treated.

Insulin—A hormone produced by the pancreas that helps the body use glucose for energy. Insulin, which is also manufactured commercially, is injected into the body to replace the insulin no longer manufactured by your pancreas.

Meal plan—A guide showing the number of food exchanges to use in each meal and snack to control distribution of carbohydrates, proteins, fats, and calories throughout the day.

Mineral—Substance essential in small amounts to build and repair body tissue and/or control functions of the body. Calcium, iron, magnesium, phosphorus, potassium, sodium, and zinc are minerals.

Nephropathy—A condition in which the kidneys can't filter wastes out of the bloodstream into the urine. Kidney failure may result from this complication.

Neuropathy—A complication of diabetes in which the nerves are damaged.

Nutrient—Substance in food necessary for life. Carbohydrates, proteins, fats, minerals, vitamins, and water are nutrients.

Oral agent—A medication that helps control blood glucose in some people with Type II diabetes.

Protein—One of the three major nutrients in food. Protein provides about 4 calories per gram. Protein is found in foods from the milk and meat exchange lists. Smaller amounts of protein are found in foods from the vegetable and starch lists.

Renal threshold—The glucose level at which excess glucose in the blood starts spilling out into the urine.

Retinopathy—A complication of diabetes in which blood vessels in the eye are damaged. This can result in blindness if it isn't treated, but it can be effectively slowed or stopped with laser beam treatment if it is discovered before permanent damage is done.

Sodium—A mineral needed to maintain life, found mainly as a component of salt. Many individuals need to cut down the amount of sodium (and salt) they eat to help control high blood pressure.

Starch—One of the two major types of carbohydrate foods. Foods consisting mainly of starch come from the starch list.

Sugars—One of the two main types of carbohydrate. Foods including naturally present sugars are those from the milk, vegetable, and fruit lists. Added sugars include common table sugar and the sugar alcohols (sorbitol, mannitol, etc.).

Triglycerides—Fats normally present in the blood that are made from food. Gaining too much weight or consuming too much fat, alcohol, or carbohydrates may increase the blood triglycerides.

Vitamins—Substances found in food, needed in small amounts to assist in body processes and functions. These include vitamins A, D, E, the B-complex, C, and K.

Index

Acidophilus milk, 14
Afternoon tea, 75, 76
Alcohol, 8, 83
Almonds, 23, 53
American cheese, 22
American Diabetes Association, Inc.
  contacting, 3
  sugar reduction guidelines of, xi–xii
American Heart Association (AHA) diet,
  77, 78
American Heart Association Diet, The,
  77
Angel food cake, 14, 100
Animal crackers, 10
Apples
  in fruit exchanges, 11, 12
  juice, 13, 45
  nutrient analysis of, 43
  pie, 319
  salad, 232
Applesauce
  bread, nuts and, 284–85
  cookies, bran and, 374–75
  in fruit exchanges, 11
  muffins, cinnamon and, 273
  muffins, oat bran and, 278
  nutrient analysis of, 43
Apricots
  in fruit exchanges, 12
  juice, 45
  nutrient analysis of, 43
  salad, molded spicy, 233
Artichokes
  baby brochette, Grecian shrimp with,
    140–41

nutrient analysis of, 38
  in vegetable exchanges, 17
Ascorbic acid solution, 386–87
Asparagus, 17, 38
Avocado, 23, 43

Bacon, 22, 24
Bagels, 9
Baking powder, 56
Baking soda, 57
Bamboo shoots, 38
Bananas
  bread, nuts and, 285–86
  cake, bran and, 335–336
  in fruit exchanges, 12
  nutrient analysis of, 43
Barley
  nutrient analysis of, 55
  soup, mushrooms and, 114–15
Bass, 50
Bean sprouts
  chicken and mushrooms with, 164–65
  nutrient analysis of, 38
  in vegetable exchanges, 17
Beans
  baked, 10, 219
  black, 42
  black-eyed, 11
  chili and, 26
  cranberry, 42
  exchanges, 10–11, 81
  great northern, 38, 42
  green. *See* Green beans
  green lima, 38
  kidney. *See* kidney beans

lima, 11, 38, 42
navy, 38, 42
nutrient analysis of, 38, 42
pink, 42
pinto, 11, 38, 42
red, rice and, 220
salad, three-bean, 257
soup, 27
in vegetable exchanges, 17
white, 11
Beef, 169
brisket, 46
Chicago chili, 186–87
chuck, 46
grades of, 172
green beans with, 177
ground, 46, 171
in meat exchanges, 20, 21
nutrient analysis of, 46
round. See Round steak
salad, 248
soup, broth, 110–11
soup, vegetables and, 27, 68, 128
spaghetti sauce, mushrooms and, 180
stew, vegetables and, 181
stir-fry, vegetables and, 182–83
tenderloin, 46
top sirloin, 46
Beets, 17, 38
Beverages, 376–83
chocolate liqueur, 382
chocolate milk shake, 381
on free foods list, 25–26
hot cocoa mix, 380
hot spiced tea, 379
orange liqueur, 383
sparkling punch, 378
Biscuits, 11
Blackberries, 12, 43
Blintzes, 224–25
Blood glucose monitoring, 6
Blueberries, 12, 43
Boiling-water canners, 387–88, 390–91
Bouillon, 25, 57
Bran
cake, banana and, 335–36
cereal, 9
cookies, applesauce and, 374–75
muffins, dark, 275
muffins, nuts and, 274
muffins, pineapple and, 281
muffins, raisin, 277

muffins, refrigerator, 276–77
nutrient analysis of, 55
Brazilnuts, 53
Bread makers, 89
Breads, 82, 269–313. See also Muffins;
Pancakes
applesauce nut, 284–85
banana nut, 285–86
challah, 290–91
chocolate nut, 288–89
cinnamon rolls, 306–307
corn. See Cornbread
country loaf, 296–97
crumbs, 55
dressing, 11, 168
exchanges, 9, 195
flour, 100
graham scones, 289–90
nutrient analysis of, 55
panettone, 300–301
raisin, 9, 294–95
recommended servings of, 79
sticks, 9
three-grain, 302–303
whole wheat, 304–305
whole wheat, Italian, 292–93
whole wheat, rich, 298–99
zucchini, 286–87
Breakfast menus, 66, 67, 73
Broccoli
casserole, rice and, 199
chicken and, 160–61
nutrient analysis of, 38
salad, 237
salad, mushrooms and marinated,
238–39
salad, special, 239
in vegetable exchanges, 17
Brownies, 14
Brussels sprouts, 17, 38
Buffalo, 20
Bulgur, 9, 55
Burritos, 27
Butter, 24
Buttermilk, 52, 95
cookies, 360–61
in milk exchanges, 13
pancakes, 309

Cabbage
nutrient analysis of, 38
salad, molded, 236

salad, traditional, 243
shredded, 201
soup, rice and, 115
in vegetable exchanges, 17
Cakes, 329–47. *See also* Cupcakes
angel food, 14, 100
banana bran, 335–36
in carbohydrate exchanges, 14, 15
chocolate, 333
cocoa, 334–35
devil's food, 338–39
raisin, 337
white, 342
yellow, 343
Calories, 6
from fat, 7, 103
food exchanges at different levels of,
60–61
on food labels, 103
Canadian bacon, 20, 48
Candy, sugar-free, 25
Canning, 385–94
methods, 387–89
processing times, 390–93
Canola oil, 23
Cantaloupe, 12, 44
Carbohydrates
composition of, 6, 30
on food labels, 105
foods containing, 7
list of other, 14–16
in sugar substitutes, 93
in vegetables, 195
Carob flour, 42
Carp, 50
Carrots
nutrient analysis of, 38, 39
salad, pineapple and, 241
in vegetable exchanges, 17
Casaba melon, 44
Cashews, 23, 53
Casseroles
broccoli rice, 199
chicken or turkey mushroom, 156
dishes for, 87
Fran's butternut squash, 211
green bean and mushroom, 197
Catfish, 50
Catsup, 26, 57
Cauliflower
nutrient analysis of, 39
Parmesan, 202

in vegetable exchanges, 17
Celeriac, 39
Celery
nutrient analysis of, 39
tuna fish and mushrooms with, 142
in vegetable exchanges, 17
Cereals, 82
exchanges, 9–10
nutrient analysis of, 55–56
puffed, 9
recommended servings of, 79
sugar-frosted, 10
Challah, 290–91
Chard, Swiss, 39
Cheddar cheese, 53
Cheese
American, 22
cheddar, 53
cottage. *See* Cottage cheese
food, 53
macaroni and, 26
in meat exchanges, 20, 21, 22
Monterey Jack, 22
mozzarella, 21, 53
nutrient analysis of, 53
Parmesan. *See* Parmesan cheese
Swiss, 22
Cherries
in fruit exchanges, 12
nutrient analysis of, 43
pie, 320
Chestnuts, 53
Chicken, 80–81
à la king, 159
bean sprouts with mushrooms and,
164–65
bouillon concentrate, 57
broccoli and, 160–61
casserole, mushrooms and, 156
chop suey, 163
emperor breasts, 154–55
in fast foods, 27
gravy, 167
jambalaya, 158
loaf, 166–67
in meat exchanges, 19, 20, 21
microwave, 157
nutrient analysis of, 49
oven-browned, 152–53
poached, 153
roast, 151
sandwich spread, 165

soup, broth, 112
spaghetti sauce, tomato and, 162
Chickpeas, 42
Chicory leaves, 39
Children, 6, 78
Chili
beans and, 26
Chicago, 186–87
Chitterlings, 24
Chives, 39
Chocolate, 83, 100
bread, nuts and, 288–89
cake, 333
cookies, balls, 353–54
cookies, bars, 352–53
cookies, chip, 99, 356–57
cookies, dates and, 351
cookies, raisin nut, 355
liqueur, 382
milk, 15
milk shake, 381
muffins, oat bran and, 280
sauce, 347
Chocolate chips
cookies, 99, 356–57
nutrient analysis of, 54
Cholesterol, xiii, 77–84, 90–93
American Heart Association
guidelines for intake, 78
in breads, 269
in cakes, 330
in dairy products, 91
in eggs, 91
in fats, 91
fiber and, 98
in fish, 92
on food labels, 105, 106
in giblets, 147
in meats, 92
in poultry, 92
in shellfish, 93
in soups, 108
Chop suey, chicken or turkey, 163
Chopping boards, 88
Chow mein, 11, 26
Christmas day menu, 65
Cinnamon
muffins, applesauce and, 273
rolls, 306–307
shake, 311
spread, 310
Clams, 19, 51

Club soda, 25
Cocoa, 83, 100
cake, 334–35
hot, 380
nutrient analysis of, 54
powder, 25
Coconut, 24, 80, 83
Coconut oil, 80, 83, 95
Codfish
in meat exchanges, 19
mushroom sauce with, 145
nutrient analysis of, 50
Coffee, 25
Cold-pack canning, 387
Coleslaw, 242
snappy, 244
sweet, 256
Collards, 39
Combination foods list, 26–28
Complete Guide to Home Canning, 389
Composition of Foods, Raw, Processed,
and Prepared, 31, 91
Condiments, 25–26, 56–57
Cookies, 348–75
applesauce bran squares, 374–75
buttermilk, 360–61
in carbohydrate exchanges, 15
chocolate balls, 353–54
chocolate bars, 352–53
chocolate chip, 99, 356–57
chocolate date, 351
chocolate raisin nut, 355
date graham, 359
hermits, 366–67
high-fiber, 368–69
Mexican wedding, 372
mocha, 358
nut slices, 370–71
oatmeal, 362–63
peanut butter, 364
raisin bars, 373
whole wheat spice, 365
Cooking spray, 25
Corn
nutrient analysis of, 39
Pandy's zucchini and, 216
in starchy vegetable exchanges, 10
Corn oil, 23, 54, 83
Cornbread
analysis of, 35
in starchy food exchanges, 11
Yankee, 283

Cornmeal, 9, 55
Cottage cheese
  garden salad, 247
  in meat exchanges, 20, 21
  nutrient analysis of, 53
Cottonseed oil, 83
Couscous, 9
Cowpeas, 39
Crab, 19, 51
Crackers and snack exchanges, 10
Cranberries
  gelatin, salad, 235
  juice, 13
  nutrient analysis of, 43
  sauce, 15
  stewed, 226
Crayfish, 51
Cream, 24
Cream cheese, 24
Cream of tartar, 57
Creamers, nondairy, 24, 95–96
Cress, 39
Croutons, 11
Cucumbers
  nutrient analysis of, 39
  salad, 245
  salad, lettuce and, 253
  in vegetable exchanges, 17
Cupcakes
  in carbohydrate exchanges, 15
  spice, 340
  wacky, 341
Currants, 43
Custard pie, 321

Daily values, on food labels, 106
Dairy products. *See also* specific types
  cholesterol content of, 81, 91
  nutrient analysis of, 52–53
Dates
  cookies, chocolate and, 351
  cookies, graham, 359
  in fruit exchanges, 12
  nutrient analysis of, 43
Devil's food cake, 338–39
Diabetes, 1–4
Dinner menu, 75
Dishwashers, 89
Doughnuts, 15
Dressings
  bread, 11, 168
  brown rice, 193

Drink mixes, 25
Drinks. *See* Beverages
Duck, 20

Eel, 50
Egg substitutes, 20, 97
  in breads, 272
  nutrient analysis of, 52
Eggplant
  nutrient analysis of, 39
  tomatoes and, 203
  in vegetable exchanges, 17
Eggs, 81, 97
  cholesterol content of, 91
  in meat exchanges, 21
  nutrient analysis of, 53
  whites, 20, 53
  yolks, 79, 81, 97
Elderberries, 43
Endive, 39
English muffins, 9
Entrées, 26–27

Fast foods, 27–28
Fat-free or reduced-fat foods, 24–25
Fats, 34, 82–83. *See also*
    Monounsaturated fat;
    Polyunsaturated fat; Saturated fat
  American Heart Association
      guidelines for intake, 78
  calories from, 7, 103
  cholesterol content of, 91
  exchanges, 23–24
  in fish, 133
  on food labels, 103–105, 106
  foods containing, 7
  list, 22–23
  nutrient analysis of, 54
  solid, 82–83
  starchy foods prepared with, 11
Feta cheese, 21
Fiber, xiii–xiv, 98–99, 100
  cookies with, 368–69
  on food labels, 105
  meat loaf with, 188
  water-insoluble, 98
  water-soluble, 98
Figs, 12, 43, 44
Filberts, 53
Fish. *See also* specific types
  baked, mustard sauce with, 136–37
  baked, steak, 137

characteristics of fresh, 131
characteristics of frozen, 132
cholesterol content of, 92
Creole, 143
in fast foods, 28
forms of, 130–31
in meat exchanges, 18, 19, 20–21
methods of preparation, 133–35
nutrient analysis of, 50–51
oven-fried fillets, 138
recommended servings of, 79
special menu including, 71
storage of, 132
Flavoring extracts, 26
Flounder, 19
Flour, 270–71
    bread, 56
    cake, 56
    carob, 42
    in cereal and grain exchanges, 9
    graham. *See* Graham flour
    nutrient analysis of, 55, 56
    rye, 56
    soybean, 56
    whole wheat, 56, 100
Food exchange lists, 8
Food exchanges, 5–28
    bread, 9, 195
    calculating, 29–57
    cereal and grain, 9–10
    crackers and snack, 10
    at different caloric levels, 60–61
    dried beans, peas, and lentils, 10–11,
        81
    fat, 23–24
    fruit, 11-13
    meat and meat substitutes, 18–22, 37
    milk, 13–14
    recipe adjustment in, 32–37
    recipe analysis in, 32, 33
    starchy vegetables, 10
    vegetables, 16–18
Food labels, 103–5
Food processors, 88
*Food Values of Portions Commonly
    Used*, 31
Free foods list, 24–26
Freezing, 394–95
Frosting
    butter cream, 344
    fluffy, 345
Frozen entrées, 27

Fruits, 81–82. *See also* specific types
    canning of. *See* Canning
    cocktail, 12
    composition of, 6, 30
    exchanges, 11–13
    fiber in, 98–99
    freezing, 394–95
    juice bars, 15
    list, 11
    nutrient analysis of, 43–45
    snacks, 15
    soup, 120
    spread, 15

Game, 19, 21
Garlic, 26
    nutrient analysis of, 39
    salad dressing, creamy, 261
Gazpacho, 117
Gelatin, 25
    basic salad, 230
    in carbohydrate exchanges, 15
    cranberry salad, 235
    fruit-flavored, 231
Gestational diabetes, 1–2
Giblets, 147
Ginger, summer squash with, 210
Gingerroot, 39
Gingersnaps, 15
Glucose, 6, 7
Gluten, 97–98, 271, 330–31
Goat's milk, 14
Goose, 20, 21
Gooseberries, 44
Graham crackers
    in cracker and snack exchanges,
        10
    nutrient analysis of, 56
    pie crust, 317
Graham flour, 100
    cookies, dates and, 359
    nutrient analysis of, 56
    scones, 289–90
Grains
    exchanges, 9–10
    recommended servings of, 79
Grams, ounces converted to, 29
Granola, 9, 11
    bars, 15
Grapefruit, 12, 44
    juice, 13, 45
Grapenuts, 9

Grapes, 12, 44
  juice, 13, 45
Gravy
  brown, 191
  chicken or turkey, 167
  pan, 192
Green beans
  beef with, 177
  casserole, mushrooms and, 197
  Creole, 198
  nutrient analysis of, 38
Green onions, 17
Greens
  southern-style, 205
  turnip, 42
  in vegetable exchanges, 17
Grits, 9
Ground beef, 46, 171
Groundcherries, 44
Guava, 44
Gum, sugar-free, 25

Haddock, 19, 50
Halibut, 19, 50
Ham, 20, 48, 173
Hamburgers, 28, 171–72
  buns, 9
Heart (meat), 21
Herbs, 26
Herring, 20
High-Carbohydrate High-Fiber (HCF)
  diet, 99
High-fat meats and substitutes, 18
  composition of, 6, 30
  exchanges, 22
Honey, 55
Honeydew melon, 12, 44
Horseradish, 26
Hot dogs, 20, 21, 22, 28
  buns, 9
Hot-pack canning, 387
Hummus, 15

Ice cream, 15
Ice cream dippers, 89–90
Ice milk, 52
Impaired glucose tolerance, 2
Insulin, 6, 7

Jam, 15, 25
Jambalaya, 158
Jelly, 15, 25

Juices
  bars, 15
  cranberry, 13
  grape, 13, 45
  grapefruit, 13, 45
  lemon, 26, 45
  lime, 26, 45
  nutrient analysis of, 45
  orange, 45
  pineapple, 13, 45
  prune, 13, 45
  tomato, 17, 45

Kale, 39
Kasha, 9
Kidney, 20
Kidney beans, 11
  nutrient analysis of, 42
  salad, 249
Kiwifruit, 12, 44
Knives, 85
Kohlrabi, 17, 40

Labor Day picnic menu, 63
Lamb, 20, 21, 46, 47, 169, 173–74
Lard, 24
Lasagna, 26
Lean, on food labels, 106
Lean meats and substitutes, 18
  composition of, 6, 30
  exchanges, 20–21
  recommended servings of, 79
Leeks, 17, 40
Legumes, 42–43
Lemons
  juice, 26, 45
  nutrient analysis of, 44
  pie, 324
  sauce, 346
Lentils, 11, 42, 43
  exchanges, 10–11, 81
Lettuce
  nutrient analysis of, 40
  salad, cucumbers and, 253
Light or lite, on food labels, 106
Limes
  juice, 26, 45
  nutrient analysis of, 44
  pie, 322–23
Liqueur
  chocolate, 382
  orange, 383

Liver, 21
Lobster, 19
Low-fat milk
    composition of, 6, 30
    exchanges, 14
Lunch menu, 75

Macadamia nuts, 53
Macaroni, 56
    cheese and, 26
Mackerel, 50
Mango, 12, 44
Margarine, 96–97
    in fat exchanges, 23
    fat-free, reduced-fat, 24
    nutrient analysis of, 54
Marinade, 170–71
Marshmallows, 55
Matzoh, 10
Mayonnaise, 23
    fat-free, reduced-fat, 24
Measuring cups and spoons, 86
Meat loaf, 171
    barbecue, 187
    fiber with, 188
Meatballs
    Mary's, 184–85
    Norwegian, 185
    spaghetti with, 26
Meats and meat substitutes, 169–93.
        See also High-fat meats and
        substitutes; Lean meats and
        substitutes; Medium-fat meats and
        substitutes; Very lean meats and
        substitutes; specific types
    cholesterol content of, 92
    composition of, 6, 30
    exchanges, 18–22, 37
    nutrient analysis of, 46–48
    organ, 79, 80
Medium-fat meats and substitutes,
    18
    composition of, 6, 30
    exchanges, 21–22
Melba toast, 10
Microwave ovens, 88
Milk, 94–96
    acidophilus, 14
    buttermilk. See Buttermilk
    chocolate, 15
    composition of, 6, 30
    exchanges, 13–14
    goat's, 14
    kefir, 14
    list, 13
    low-fat. See Low-fat milk
    nonfat dry. See Nonfat dry milk
    recommended servings of, 79
    rice, 10
    skim. See Skim milk
    soy, 22
    whole. See Whole milk
Milk shakes, chocolate, 381
Milk substitutes, 94–96
Millet, 9
Minerals, 8, 106
Minestrone soup, 72, 122–23
Miracle Whip, 23, 25
Miso, 11
Mixers, 87
Monkfish, 50
Monounsaturated fats, 7, 78
    exchanges, 23
Monterey Jack cheese, 22
Morning coffee with friends, 73
Mozzarella cheese, 21, 53
Muesli, 9
Muffins
    applesauce oat bran, 278
    bran nut, 274
    chocolate oat bran, 280
    cinnamon applesauce, 273
    dark bran, 275
    oat bran, 279
    pineapple bran, 281
    raisin bran, 277
    refrigerator bran, 276–77
    rye, 282
    in starchy food exchanges, 11
Mullet, 50
Mushrooms
    casserole, chicken or turkey, 156
    casserole, green beans and, 197
    chicken with bean sprouts and,
        164–65
    nutrient analysis of, 40
    salad, marinated broccoli and,
        238–39
    sauce, codfish with, 145
    soup, barley and, 114–15
    spaghetti sauce, beef and, 180
    tuna fish and celery with, 142
    in vegetable exchanges, 17
Mussels, 51

Mustard, 26
  greens, 40
  nutrient analysis of, 57
  sauce, baked fish with, 136–37

Nectarines
  in fruit exchanges, 12
  nutrient analysis of, 44
  salad, 234
Neufchatel, 53
New Year's day menu, 62
Nonfat dry milk, 94–95, 271
  in milk exchanges, 13
  nutrient analysis of, 52
Noodles, 312–13
  chow mein, 11
  nutrient analysis of, 56
Nutrition facts, on food labels, 103
*Nutritive Value of American Foods in
  Common Units*, 31
Nutritive Value of Foods, 31, 90
Nuts, 83. *See also* specific types
  bread, applesauce and, 284–85
  bread, banana and, 285–86
  bread, chocolate and, 288–89
  cookies, chocolate raisin, 355
  cookies, slices, 370–71
  in fat exchanges, 23
  muffins, bran and, 274
  nutrient analysis of, 53–54

Oat bran, 97–98, 100
  muffins, 279
  muffins, applesauce and, 278
  muffins, chocolate and, 280
  nutrient analysis of, 56
  pancakes, 308
Oatmeal
  cookies, 362–63
  nutrient analysis of, 56
Oats, 9
Oils, 83
  canola, 23
  coconut, 80, 83, 95
  corn, 23, 54, 83
  cottonseed, 83
  in fat exchanges, 23
  olive, 23
  palm, 80, 83, 95
  palm kernel, 83
  peanut, 23
  safflower, 23, 83

soybean, 23, 83
  sunflower, 83
  vegetable, 96–97
Okra, 17, 40
Olive oil, 23
Olives, 23, 57
Onions, 17, 40
Oranges
  in fruit exchanges, 12
  juice, 13, 45
  liqueur, 383
  Mandarin, 12
  nutrient analysis of, 44
Ostrich, 20
Other carbohydrates list, 14–16
Ounces, grams converted to, 29
Oyster crackers, 10
Oysters, 20, 51

Palm kernel oil, 83
Palm oil, 80, 83, 95
Pancakes
  buttermilk, 309
  oat bran, 308
  in starchy food exchanges, 11
Panettone, 300–301
Papaya, 12, 44
Parmesan cheese
  cauliflower and, 202
  in meat exchanges, 21
  nutrient analysis of, 53
Parsley, 40
Parsnips, 40
Pasta, 9, 82
Peaches, 12, 44
Peanut butter, 83
  cookies, 364
  in fat exchanges, 23
  in meat exchanges, 22
  nutrient analysis of, 53, 54
Peanut oil, 23
Peanuts
  creamed spinach with, 209
  in fat exchanges, 23
  nutrient analysis of, 53
Pears, 12, 44
Peas
  creamed, salmon patties with,
    144–45
  exchanges, 10–11, 81
  green, 10, 40
  nutrient analysis of, 40

pods, 17
split. *See* Split peas
Pecans, 23, 54
Peppers, 17, 40, 41
Percent daily value, on food labels, 103
Perch, 50
Persimmon, 44
Pheasant, 20
Pickles, 394
　dill, 26
　dill, frozen sliced sweet, 400
　Mrs. Riley's, 396–97
　nutrient analysis of, 41
　zucchini, 398–99
Pie crusts
　graham cracker, 317
　Mom's, 316–17
　southern, 318
Pies, 314–28. *See also* Pie crusts
　apple, 319
　in carbohydrate exchanges, 15
　cherry, 320
　custard, 321
　key lime, 322–23
　lemon, 324
　pumpkin, 15, 325
　pumpkin, scotch, 326
　strawberry chiffon, 327
Pike, 50
Pimiento, 26, 41
Pine nuts, 54
Pineapple
　in fruit exchanges, 12
　juice, 13, 45
　muffins, bran and, 281
　nutrient analysis of, 44
　salad, carrots and, 241
Pistachio nuts, 54
Pita, 9
Pizza, 27, 28
Plantain, 10, 44, 45
Plums, 12, 45
Pollock, 50
Polyunsaturated fats, 7, 78
　exchanges, 23–24
Pomegranate, 45
Pompano, 51
Popcorn, 10, 11
Pork, 169, 172–73
　baked, rice and, 189
　fatback or salt, 24
　in fat exchanges, 24

in meat exchanges, 20, 21, 22
　nutrient analysis of, 48
　sweet sour, 190–91
Pot pie, 27
Potatoes
　chips, 10, 15
　French-fried, 11, 28
　nutrient analysis of, 41
　salad, 254
　in starchy vegetable exchanges, 10
　sweet, 10, 41
Pots and pans, 86
Poultry, 147–68. *See also* specific types
　cholesterol content of, 92
　in meat exchanges, 19, 20, 21
　nutrient analysis of, 49–50
　precautions, 147–49
　recommended servings of, 79
Pressure canners, 388–89
　dial-gauge, 392
　weighted-gauge, 393
Pretzels, 10
Protein
　on food labels, 105–106
　foods containing, 7
Prunes, 12, 45
　juice, 13, 45
Pudding, 15
Pumpkin
　nutrient analysis of, 41
　pie, 15, 325
　pie, scotch, 326
　seeds, 24, 54
Punch, sparkling, 379

Quince, 45

Rabbit, 21, 47, 48
Radicchio, 41
Radishes, 17, 41
Raisins
　bread, 9, 294–95
　cake, 337
　cookies, bars, 373
　cookies, chocolate nut, 355
　in fruit exchanges, 12
　muffins, bran and, 277
　nutrient analysis of, 45
Raspberries, 45
Recipes
　adjustment, 32–27
　analysis, 32, 33

Rhubarb, 45
Rice
  baked pork and, 189
  brown, creamy, 221
  brown, dressing, 193
  brown, nutrient analysis of, 56
  cakes, 10
  casserole, broccoli and, 199
  in cereal and grain exchanges, 10
  milk, 10
  Monk's, 212
  nutrient analysis of, 56
  red beans and, 220
  soup, cabbage and, 115
  white, nutrient analysis of, 56
  wild, nutrient analysis of, 56
  wild, walnuts and, 258
Ricotta cheese, 21, 53
Rockfish, 51
Rolled oats, 56
Rolls, 9
Roughy, orange, 51
Round steak, 46
  broiled, 176
  Texas, 178–79
Rutabaga, 41
Rye
  flour, 56
  muffins, 282

Safflower oil, 23, 83
Salad dressings
  in carbohydrate exchanges, 16
  chef's French, 263
  creamy garlic, 261
  in fat exchanges, 23
  fat-free, 25
  French, 262
  Kay's cooked, 260
  spicy tomato, 264
  Thousand Island, 265
  vinaigrette, 266
  vinegar and oil, 267
  yogurt topping, 268
Salads, 227–68. *See also* Salad dressings
  apple, 232
  basic salad gelatin, 230
  broccoli, 237
  carrot and pineapple, 241
  chef's, 240–41
  coleslaw. *See* Coleslaw
  cranberry gelatin, 235

cucumber, 245
cucumber and lettuce, 253
farmer's, 246
frijole, 251
fruit-flavored gelatin, 231
garden cottage cheese, 247
individual beef, 248
kidney bean, 249
luncheon, 70
marinated broccoli and mushrooms,
    238–39
marinated vegetable, 252–53
molded cabbage, 236
molded spicy apricot, 233
nectarine, 234
potato, 254
sauerkraut, 255
special broccoli, 239
taco, 250–51
three-bean, 257
traditional cabbage, 243
walnut wild rice, 258
zucchini, 259
Salisbury steak, 27
Salmon
  in meat exchanges, 20
  nutrient analysis of, 51
  patties, creamed peas with,
      144–45
Salsa, 25
Salt (sodium), 8, 100–101
  American Heart Association
      guidelines for intake, 78
  in breads, 270
  in canned vegetables, 194–95
  on food labels, 105, 107
  nutrient analysis of, 57
  in pickles, 394
  in soups, 108–109
Saltines, 10
Sandwich crackers, 11
Sardines, 20
Saturated fats, 78
  exchanges, 24
  on food labels, 105, 106
Sauces
  chocolate, 347
  cranberry, 15
  lemon, 346
  medium white, 222
  mushroom, codfish with, 145
  spaghetti. *See* Spaghetti sauces

taco, 26
tomato, 17, 42
Sauerkraut
    salad, 255
    tomatoes with, 204
    in vegetable exchanges, 17
Sausage, 20, 21
Scales, 85
Scallops, 19, 51
Scones, graham, 289–90
Seasonings, 26
Secondary diabetes, 2
Seeds, 53–54, 83. *See also* Nuts; specific
    types
Serving size, on food labels, 103
Sesame butter, 57
Sesame seeds, 23, 54
Shallots, 41
Shellfish
    cholesterol content of, 93
    imitation, 20
    in meat exchanges, 19–20
    nutrient analysis of, 51
Sherbet, 16, 52
Shortening, 24
Shrimp
    etouffée, 139
    Grecian, baby artichoke brochette
        with, 140–41
    in meat exchanges, 19
    nutrient analysis of, 51
Skim milk
    composition of, 6, 30
    evaporated, 13
    exchanges, 13
    nutrient analysis of, 52
Sodium. *See* Salt (sodium)
Soft drinks, diet, 25
Soft-serve, 28
Soups, 108–29
    barley mushroom, 114–15
    bean, 27
    beef broth, 110–11
    cabbage and rice, 115
    chicken or turkey broth, 112
    in combination foods list, 27
    cream, 27
    cream, green and gold, 124
    cream, tomato, 116
    fruit, 120
    gazpacho, 117
    golden squash, 121

goulash, 118–19
minestrone, 72, 122–23
mulligatawny, 126–27
potage Pierre, 125
sandwich and, 69
split pea, 27, 113
Swiss, 127
tomato, 27
tomato, bouillon, 123
tomato, cream of, 116
vegetable beef, 27, 68, 128
vegetable chowder, 129
Sour cream, 24
    fat-free, reduced-fat, 25
    mock, 223
Soy milk, 21
Soy sauce, 26, 57
Soybean flour, 56
Soybean oil, 23, 83
Spaghetti, 26
Spaghetti sauces
    beef mushroom, 180
    in carbohydrate exchanges, 16
    tomato chicken, 162
Special menus, 59–76
    afternoon tea, 75, 76
    breakfast, 66, 67, 73
    Christmas day, 65
    fish for dinner or supper, 71
    Labor Day picnic, 63
    for lunch or dinner, 75
    morning coffee with friends, 73
    New Year's day, 62
    salad luncheon, 70
    soup and sandwich, 69
    Thanksgiving, 64
Spices, 26
Spinach
    creamed, with peanuts, 209
    frittata, 208
    nutrient analysis of, 41
    in vegetable exchanges, 17
Split peas, 11
    nutrient analysis of, 43
    soup, 27, 113
Squash
    casserole, Fran's butternut, 211
    golden, 121
    seeds, 54
    soup, 121
    summer, in vegetable exchanges, 17
    summer, nutrient analysis of, 41

summer, with ginger, 210
winter, 10
winter, nutrient analysis of, 41
Starches
composition of, 6, 30
exchanges, 60–61
list, 8–9
nutrient analysis of, 55–56
prepared with fat, 11
Starchy vegetables, 61, 82
exchanges, 10
Steamers, 89
Stews, vegetable beef, 181
Strawberries
in fruit exchanges, 12
nutrient analysis of, 45
pie, 327
Stuffing. *See* Dressings
Submarine sandwiches, 28
Sugar-free or low-sugar foods, 25
Sugar substitutes, 25, 34, 93–94
Sugars
adding to food, 34, 37
American Diabetes Association
guidelines for, xi–xii
in breads, 271
brown, 55
corn, 55
on food labels, 105
granulated, 55
maple, 55
molasses, 55
nutrient analysis of, 54–55
pickles and, 394
powdered, 55
sorghum, 55
Sunflower oil, 83
Sunflower seeds, 24, 54
Surimi, 51
Sweet potatoes, 10, 41
Sweet rolls, 16
Swiss cheese, 22
Syrup, 16, 25

Tabasco sauce, 26
Tacos, 28
salad, 250–51
sauce, 26
shells, 11
Tahini paste, 23
Tangerines, 12, 45
Tapioca, 56

Tartar sauce, 146
Tea, 25
hot spiced, 379
Tempeh, 22
Thanksgiving menu, 64
Thermometers, 87
Tofu, 22, 43
Tomatillos, 41
Tomatoes
baked halves, 213
eggplant and, 203
juice, 17, 45
nutrient analysis of, 41, 42
salad dressing, spicy, 264
sauce, 17, 42
sauerkraut with, 204
soup, 27
soup, bouillon, 123
soup, cream of, 116
spaghetti sauce, chicken and,
162
stir-fry, 214
in vegetable exchanges, 17
Tonic water, 25
Tortilla chips, 10, 16
Tortillas, 9
Trout, 19
Tuna fish
casserole, 26
in meat exchanges, 19, 21
mushrooms and celery with, 142
nutrient analysis of, 51
Turkey, 80–81
à la king, 159
casserole, mushrooms and, 156
chop suey, 163
in frozen entrées, 27
gravy, 167
loaf, 166–67
in meat exchanges, 19, 20, 21
nutrient analysis of, 49, 50
sandwich spread, 165
soup, broth, 112
Turnips, 17, 42
Type I (insulin-dependent) diabetes, 1,
2
Type II (non-insulin-dependent)
diabetes, 1, 2

Vanilla wafers, 16
Veal, 20, 21, 47, 169, 174
Vegetable oils, 96–97

Vegetables, 81–82, 194–226. *See also* specific types
canned, 194–95
canning of. *See* Canning
Chinese, 200
composition of, 6, 30
exchanges, 16–17
fiber in, 98–99
freezing, 394–95
list, 16
nutrient analysis of, 38–42
pickled, 206–207
purées, 217–18
salad, marinated, 252–53
sautéed, 207
soup, beef and, 27, 68, 128
soup, chowder, 129
starchy. *See* Starchy vegetables
stew, beef and, 181
stir-fry beef and, 182–83
Venison, 20
Very lean meats and substitutes, 18
composition of, 6, 30
exchanges, 19-20
Very low-fat milk exchanges, 13
Vinegar, 26, 57
Vitamins, 8, 106

Waffles, 9, 11
Walnuts
in fat exchanges, 23

nutrient analysis of, 54
wild rice and, 258
Water, carbonated or mineral, 25
Water chestnuts, 17, 42
Watercress, 17, 42
Watermelon, 13, 44
Wheat germ, 10
Whipped topping, 25, 328
Whole milk
composition of, 6, 30
evaporated, 14
exchanges, 14
Whole wheat crackers, 10, 11
Whole wheat flour, 56, 100
Wine, cooking, 26
Worcestershire sauce, 26, 57

Yams, 10
Yeast, 57
Yogurt
in carbohydrate exchanges, 16
in milk exchanges, 13
nutrient analysis of, 52
topping, 268

Zucchini
bread, 286–87
Pandy's, corn and, 216
pickles, 398–99
salad, 259
scramble, 215
in vegetable exchanges, 17